Hartmut Elsenhans

# Globalization Between a Convoy Model and an Underconsumptionist Threat

# POLITIK
Forschung und Wissenschaft

Band 25

LIT

Hartmut Elsenhans

# Globalization Between a Convoy Model and an Underconsumptionist Threat

LIT

Bibliographic information published by the Deutsche Nationalbibliothek
The Deutsche Nationalbibliothek lists this publication in the Deutsche
Nationalbibliografie; detailed bibliographic data are available in the Internet at
http://dnb.d-nb.de.

ISBN 3-8258-9219-0

A catalogue record for this book is available from the British Library

©LIT VERLAG Dr. W. Hopf Berlin 2006
Fresnostr. 2  D-48159 Münster
Tel. +49 (0) 2 51-620 32 22  Fax +49 (0) 2 51-922 60 99
e-Mail: lit@lit-verlag.de  http://www.lit-verlag.de

**Distribution:**
In Germany: LIT Verlag Fresnostr. 2, D-48159 Münster
Tel. +49 (0) 2 51-620 32 22, Fax +49 (0) 2 51-922 60 99, e-Mail: vertrieb@lit-verlag.de

In Austria: Medienlogistik Pichler-ÖBZ GmbH & Co KG
IZ-NÖ, Süd, Straße 1, Objekt 34, A-2355 Wiener Neudorf
Tel. +43 (0) 22 36-63 53 52 90, Fax +43 (0) 22 36-63 53 52 43, e-Mail: mlo@medien-logistik.at

In Switzerland: B + M Buch- und Medienvertriebs AG
Hochstr. 357, CH-8200 Schaffhausen
Tel. +41 (0) 52-643 54 85, Fax +41 (0) 52-643 54 35, e-Mail: order@buch-medien.ch

Distributed in the UK by: Global Book Marketing, 99B Wallis Rd, London, E9 5LN
Phone: +44 (0) 20 8533 5800 – Fax: +44 (0) 1600 775 663
http://www.centralbooks.co.uk/html

Distributed in North America by:

**Transaction Publishers**
New Brunswick (U.S.A.) and London (U.K.)

Transaction Publishers
Rutgers University
35 Berrue Circle
Piscataway, NJ 08854

Phone: +1 (732) 445 - 2280
Fax: + 1 (732) 445 - 3138
for orders (U. S. only):
toll free (888) 999 - 6778
e-mail: orders@transactionpub.com

# Content

Globalization and Historical Keynesianism: Some Introductory Remarks ................................................................................................7

Debunking the Spectre of Globalization: On the Limits of the Drive of the Internationalization of Capitalism for the Constitution of Transnational Social Structures (1996).......................................................28

Social Consequences of the NIEO: No Chance for Continued Reformist Strategies in the Center Without Structural Change in the Periphery (1981).......................................................................................68

Globalization in a Laborist Keynesian Approach....................................80

Productivity, Wages, Profits, and Exchange Rates in an Era of Globalization............................................................................................126

Intensifying Globalization to Make It Socially Acceptable ....................150

The Politico-Economic Basis of the Limits and Opportunities of Development Administration under Conditions of Globalization...............170

La mondialisation: mythes et véritables défis ........................................185

A Convoy Model vs. an Underconsumptionist Model of Globalization ....207

References................................................................................................262

# Chapter 1
Globalization and Historical Keynesianism:
Some Introductory Remarks

The book is a collection of articles which, with two exceptions, have already been published, for the most part in first-rate scholarly journals in Algeria, Bangladesh, Brazil, India and South Korea. The aim of this publication is to make available outside of these countries a point of view that is at variance with a mainstream position in the globalization debate and that has a certain following in the countries most affected by globalization. My main contention is that there are different types of globalization, and that a benign form of globalization is possible in combination with social reforms policies in favor of the poor.

## 1. Neoclassical assumptions and Keynesian critiques

The issue of globalization is not globalization itself. The tremendous increase in transborder economic interactions and worldwide communication is in itself not so exceptional. Comparable levels of worldwide economic integration led to labor solidarity at the end of the nineteenth century, at least within the developed world, whereas globalization nowadays extends to many territories where labor is said to be fighting for their jobs in order to avoid a race to the bottom. Thus, there are different types of globalization. The real concern is harnessing this process of increasing transborder interactions in the struggle between capital and labor over the orientation of capitalism globally.

Despite a large variety of positions, I would maintain that there are basically two camps. First, there are the forces close to business, united in the idea that a capitalist system produces equilibria automatically provided that the state intervenes as little as possible. I do not deny that there are a large variety of positions with respect to the social aspect of the market economy, even a social market economy, in the sense that some redistribution in favor of the poor and marginalized is deemed acceptable, especially in countries in the capitalist center with a welfare-state tradition, particularly in Continental Europe. But redistribution is not considered necessary for maintaining the economic equilibria of the system. It is accepted because it eases political tensions which might otherwise lead to disruptive events. It is acceptable because it will ultimately be abolished, as labor will be integrated into the dynamics of capitalist relations of production. The second camp represents the interests of labor. It denies that the automaticity of the market will lead to labor's empowerment by means of full employment.

Hence there is room for intervention. Two types of intervention may be distinguished. Intervention may aim at restoring the capitalist mechanism by driving the economy to full employment. This position is linked to a critique of the neoclassical interpretation of the propensity to invest. Investment and demand for the products manufactured with this (additional) investment occur at different points in time. Investment is therefore based on expectations. Expectations may be deceiving, however. Decision-making on the basis of expectations will make use of past experience about previous expectations. Labor might therefore not push its wages high enough to fully exploit the possibility of increasing consumption based on newly built productive capacity. Insufficient consumption demand leads, in turn, to the laying off of labor and ultimately to lower mass incomes and mass consumption, making the additional investment appear premature. New investment spending may be possible in terms of the available financial resources, but may nevertheless be discouraged due to expectations. Expectations are at the basis of the business cycle, because the herding of investment is unavoidable. Any policy of stabilizing the growth of investment is blocked by the simple fact that investment operates on the technical frontier. If an investment is made before it is deemed necessary, it may not only lead to additional interest costs, but may in fact be obsolete by the time it is really needed. As business will invest whenever a new technology appears on the market that allows new products to be produced competitively or market shares to be increased by means of cost-cutting, a reduction in the costs of financial capital for technology acquisition will only stabilize investment in branches where there is no longer any Schumpeterian progress.

Thus, Keynesian policy does not rule out the existence of global disequilibria, as businessmen can postpone investment despite having already earned profits or having the financial resources available for this investment.

Standard Keynesianism therefore comprises government spending, in order to directly influence global demand, and monetary policy, in order to influence global demand through the interest rate.

There is also a mercantilist-imperialist position, which justifies intervention in the market mechanism in order to improve the competitiveness of one's own economy. The analysis of international economies shows that economies earn more from exports if they sell sophisticated products than if they sell simple ones. Using the world market to reduce the sunk costs of introducing a new product by distributing these costs among a larger number of products and customers is a constant aim of industrial policy and trade strategy in order to remain a leader in the export of sophisticated products. It is reasonable to assume also that the technically more advanced economy generally needs less labor to manufacture less sophisticated products. The more advanced economy will therefore only be prepared to pay a low price for products it can produce cheaply at home anyway. Economies specializing on low-technology products will risk having their incomes aligned with those of economies with low productivity and low incomes. Thus, there is a race to "be first" and to improve skills. Any production process yields salable products and skills. The importance of skills varies from production process to production process. Government intervention in order to subsidize skill-creating branches by distorting comparative advantage is a government strategy that has long been advocated by business, from protectionism in the old days of the Industrial Revolution to today's strategic trade theory based on the promotion of high-technology industries through industrial policy and government contracts.

## 2. The specificity of underdeveloped economies

Underdeveloped economies share the general problem of market failure, albeit in specific ways. It is repeatedly argued in the essays of this volume that the capitalist growth mechanism is blocked in underdeveloped economies and that unemployment is no longer merely a problem of the business cycle. Rather, it has become a structural problem because of the existence of a large segment of the population that is unable to produce the amount it needs to survive.

The neoclassical mechanism of keeping the productive and consumptive capacity of an economy in balance entails automatic wage increases as a result of an increase in marginal product. It is, however, not higher marginal product that drives up the wage rate, but the scarcity of labor. Labor will be employed as long as it yields a marginal product higher than its wage rate. When all labor is employed, businessmen will compete for labor by offering wage rates higher than the going rates until the marginal wage rate rises to the level of marginal product.

In an underdeveloped economy there is overpopulation. A large share of labor cannot produce enough to survive on. This has been largely discussed in the so-called labor-surplus and overpopulation theories of underdevelopment, to which the essays here often refer. I do not know of any serious theory of development or underdevelopment which does not at least implicitly assume a poor population that, beyond being a Marxian labor surplus army, cannot produce a surplus for an employer, capitalist or "feudal."

There is therefore a fundamental difference between a capitalist and an underdeveloped economy. In a capitalist economy any labor produces a surplus, at least during an upswing and economic boom. In an underdeveloped economy there is always labor which cannot produce as much as it consumes. Surplus is available from more productive workers (who work on better plots of land) but mass demand cannot expand (because labor does not become scarce). Only particular demand elements can grow, e.g., the demand for luxuries, palaces, temples or cathedrals. Precapitalist society may have achieved levels of civilization far higher than the European-American capitalist world, but they have rarely instrumentalized technical progress for reducing the costs of everyday standardized mass-consumption goods.

Without spending on investment there is no appropriation of profit on perfectly competitive markets. Available surplus has to be appropriated by means other than the market, implying personal ties and power. The means are called political, and the income is qualified as rent, regardless of the large variety of forms this appropriation may take (slavery, captive labor, long-distance trade benefits, corvée, tithe or "rent" in the sense of a fee for something under the monopolistic control of its owners, such as – inevitably scarce – fertile land). Political power is always visible, whereas competition on the market in capitalism creates invisible power, the silent force of the conditions that be (Marx 1890/1972a: 755).

Due to the political character of the appropriation and allocation of surplus in noncapitalist societies, there is not by necessity a process of continuous investment of resources, resources through which labor could become scarce. Those in control of surplus may invest it, but they do not have to do so. They spend on the basis of their discretionary power, as even Adam Smith observed (Smith, 1976: 277). In a noncapitalist world labor becomes scarce due to the demand of the privileged for luxuries and military items. In a capitalist world labor becomes scarce because of the relatively privileged (relatively because permanently at the mercy of competition) claiming resources for investment, which in turn serves to supply a market comprised mostly of the demand of households with low or average incomes. In a non-capitalist structure a political deal is struck between the privileged and the underprivileged about the division of national income. In a capitalist society the deal between the privileged and the underprivileged leads to concessions on wages, achieved in part anonymously (wage drift) and partly in an openly political pattern (salary negotiations where both sides may win). These negotiations and deals are only superficially zero-sum games. If the result is commensurate to the rate of growth of productivity, increases in wages will render the process of accumulation more stable. If wage increases are in excess of productivity increases, the privileged, again, will only stand to gain, as prices will rise.

In capitalism there is no zero-sum game, but a sort of steady state, an evolving balance between the privileged and underprivileged which greatly contributes to the nonviolent character of conflict resolution. On the contrary, accommodation in an economy where the market does not produce full employment and rising mass incomes, and hence incentives for investment in average labor productivity for the greater production of mass consumption goods, has to be essentially political.

Rent, a politicized economy and state interventionism do not disappear following an opening to the world market. Any economy, whether capitalist, centrally planned, feudal or whatever, can reap the benefits of participating in world trade. International trade is in the interest of any economy that is able to purchase products from outside by paying with a quantity of own products less than the quantity of products it could have produced locally for consumption employing the same factors of production that are employed for export. The only condition for international trade is varied differences in factor productivity between economies, hence comparative advantage.

But being competitive does not mean that rent disappears. The entire discussion of deteriorating terms of trade teaches that producers have an interest in controlling supply if the price elasticity of their products is below unity. Raw-material cartels allow the appropriation of rents (differential rents as well as consumer rents). Specialization on manufactures does not remove the incentive to appropriate rents. Some of the contributions to the discussion on deteriorating terms of trade establish that the exporter of manufactures may have an interest in appropriating rents from manufactured exports too, using them to subsidize import-substituting products or even other manufacturing exports whose local costs are not yet low enough to make them competitive on the world market at the chosen exchange rate. Export orientation is therefore linked to rents, often – and not only in the case of raw material exports – rising rents.

Rents will disappear under the double effect of profit being reinvested in the local economy and employment expanding. A large body of literature agrees on the fact that despite surpluses earned in exports, reinvestment is low. H. W. Singer (1950: 482) and many others (e.g., Bagchi 1972: 20) warned early on that the availability of financial resources for investment leading to capital accumulation is an illusion. Where no opportunities for profitable investment exist, rentiers will export their monetary incomes. This is discussed under the label of capital transfers from underdeveloped to developed economies.

One of the items on the agenda of the rising anticolonial development state of the 1930s and 1940s was the drying up of channels of capital export from underdeveloped economies. One of the central arguments of the following contributions maintains that globalization allows the reinvestment of such rents into economic diversification of the initially rent-dominated underdeveloped economies provided that they not only devalue but also capture the rents, not through improving terms of trade but through intelligent means of basically state-interventionist rent channeling. The expansion of the international market as a major mechanism for keeping rents in the local economy in the form of investment depends, however, not only on the increase of employment but on reaching full employment. The devaluation-driven export of manufactures may lead to full employment and the subsequent empowerment of labor on the local labor markets, resulting in the effective transfer of the neoclassical mechanisms of capitalist growth via rising mass incomes.

Globalization as the internationalization of transborder economic interactions is linked to rents. It will lead to the globalization of capital only if its impact is sufficient to transform marginality-ridden underdeveloped economies into capitalist ones by means of full employment. The issue at stake today is the alternative between this benign form of globalization, which I call the convoy pattern, and the globalization of rent.

Can world capitalism be transformed into a world of welfare capitalist systems, or does the logic of business prevail, i.e., using the devaluation-driven competitiveness of technically backward production sites to outmaneuver labor even in the developed economies?

## 3. The mainstream as a challenge

I have decided to republish the various articles in this volume because I would like to promote the argument that there is a difference between the globalization of profit and the globalization of rent. Most of the articles have been published in prestigious reviews outside of Europe, primarily in major developing countries such as Algeria, Bangladesh, Brazil, India, and South Korea. I have also added two previously unpublished texts. The first of these is a paper that was read at a 1996 conference in Makuhari. Although well received at the conference, no one was willing to publish it. The major journals I sent it to were apparently so taken aback by my alternative mode of thinking that I failed to get even a single serious review. The second unpublished text was a paper read at the 2002 ISA conference in New Orleans. It was likewise well received by my audience, the convenor of the panel suggesting that I submit the paper to *International Studies Quarterly*. The article was later rejected there and I had a version of it published in Lucknow (Elsenhans 2004a). The reviewers of *International Studies Quarterly* made some valuable points, however, helping me to further elaborate my argument. I have therefore included an expanded version of the original paper in this volume, it having since become one of the most complete statements of my argument to date, with the exception perhaps of the paper presented at Taichung University (Elsenhans 2005a).

It is obvious that despite the great prestige of the journals in which my articles have been published, they are not easily accessible to readers in the Western industrialized world. The West often talks about the South, but rarely listens to it. It is my opinion, however, that scholarly writing on development economics should first stand the test of being published in the South. As the readership of reviews from the South is limited, I want to document for a First World public that the current alarmist discourse on globalization is devoid of theoretical foundations. I feel encouraged to do so since the recent publication of my argument in one of Germany's most respected journals of neoclassical economics, *Jahrbuch für Wirtschaftswissenschaften* (Elsenhans 2005b).

I feel obliged to do so, as my experience of participation in academic discussions in the First World has been largely unfortunate. To put it in the words of one of my most eminent German colleagues, who offered his solace in a letter to me: I have always been too early with my arguments, an argument which in this case has been explicitly advanced by one of the great heralds of the dangers of globalization.

Indeed, the crux of the problem had been laid bare in a paper presented in 1979 at the 8th International Peace Research Association Conference in Frankfurt (Elsenhans 1981c). Being enveloped by benign neglect is neither the result of having been published in so rare a language like German[1] nor of remote circumstances. The paper (chapter 3) was published in the conference minutes as well as in an extended form in the Annals of the American Academy of Political and Social Sciences (Elsenhans 1987a), places one would normally not qualify as remote.

This state of benign neglect is no accident. In 1971 the political science faculty of the Free University of Berlin, i.e., by the prevailing majority at that time, refused me any financial support for a project on European concerns about oil supplies. It was a time when the U.S., for global strategic reasons, favored the capture of rent by the producer states. In handing over the oil rent to the producer states, it was pivotal to the American strategy to assure that the main beneficiaries at the political level would be conservative regimes, especially the Gulf monarchies, which could then be credited with "imposing" the nationalization of oil concessions, and not the regimes which for years had led the campaign for a change of ownership structures and rent distribution in the international oil industry with the aim of using this oil rent for social reforms and industrialization. In May 1973, with the impending U.S. decision to leave the oil rent to the producer states, I was kicked out of a German-French conference comprising members of official think tanks, because I had argued that the more secular revolutionary governments, which were in a position to spend this rent on social reforms, would be more congenial to Western Europe's interests than governments accumulating balance-of-trade surpluses because their countries were small and their elites opposed to economic transformation. It was only the left-wing Gaullists who

---

[1] Three papers were published in Germany in the 1970s with close ties to the German labor movement in the 1970s: Elsenhans 1979b; Elsenhans1979c; 1980

spared me dishonor by asking the German delegation leader rather provocatively where the bright young assistant professor had disappeared to, for they were looking forward to having a discussion with him. They nicely evoked the incidents in their conference report (Levi 1973: 356).

One of the tragedies of the international system in the twenty-first century is the legacy of the West's interest in maintaining Arab disunity in the twentieth century by keeping oil resources away from their populations. This might have been reasonable if the rent did not go to the producer states. Now there are oil-rich states with little population and highly populated states with little oil (with some exceptions). Does anyone seriously maintain that the diversity between the four South Indian states, with their four Dravidian languages and populations around 100 million, and the Hindi belt in the North of India is less pronounced than the cultural differences between the Arab Mashreq and the Arab Maghreb, or even between Syria and Jordan? India was poor, so unity and poverty was the cheapest solution for the West. The Arab countries were rich, so disunity and a few rich countries to deal with was cheapest. In the 1970s even the oil companies accepted my argument that the second oil-price crisis of December 1973 served to create new sources of rent based on higher costs to Japan and Western Europe and additional investment resources for U.S.-based companies making rent incomes of subsequently cheaper American oil.

My argument about using the oil rent for subsidizing structural change in the Third World has gone unheard. When I submitted the first version of "Overcoming Underdevelopment: A Research Paradigm" (Elsenhans 1975b, Elsenhans 1974a, Elsenhans 1975a) in 1973 (at a political science congress in Hamburg and at a meeting of the Frankfurt Peace Research Institute) I was nearly stoned by my colleagues, although the necessity of using mass consumption for capital accumulation was widely accepted later on.

It was a short step from there to developing the concept of a state class. I appreciate that the concept has won a degree of recognition nowadays that most people do not even make reference to its origin anymore, whereas in 1975 I found myself confronted by so menacing a mainstream as to feel compelled to use the terms "state bourgeoisie" and "state class" interchangeably, despite a clear argument about the noncapitalist character of this class (Elsenhans 1976). The concept was born one night in the Taunus, and later won me the friendship of Alfred Schmidt from *Stiftung Volkswagenwerk*, which financed my project "Overcoming Underdevelopment through

Mass Production for Mass Consumption," later published in French (Elsenhans et al. 2000) and in German (Elsenhans et al. 2001).

An author is normally happy if a text is published in a pirate edition, as were my contributions on the debt problem (Elsenhans 1985b) and on globalization (Elsenhans 1999c), which I have included in this volume. Yet one would at least appreciate being mentioned when the author's arguments are used by competing authors, especially in the U.S., and not having one's ideas treated as public domain, free for the taking. Thus, one can read about the state class in Keller (Keller 1991: 138): The notion of a self-interested 'state class' that staffs the central bureaucratic and political apparatuses and autonomously pursues various goals and objectives has sparked lively scholarly debate." Even when one of my more famous colleagues in Germany sought to redress the matter by contacting the publisher, no reply was forthcoming.

Obviously, one could not bypass my *Frankreichs Algerienkrieg 1954–62*, since a prestigious publisher had taken it under it's wing. But even with the help of Alfred Grosser, the publisher was unable to obtain the (normally available) funding for a translation. It was said that the book constituted an encroachment on German-French relations, as it could provoke negative feelings in France. Grosser intervened on this point. Ultimately, I received the honor of being the only foreigner among fifty works presented by *Le Monde* in commemoration of the 50th anniversary of the outbreak of the Algerian War of Liberation in 2004 (LeMonde 28-10-2004: XXIV). The irony was that one of the leading historians of the French war in Algeria published his review in the London-based *Maghreb Review* (Pervillé 2003), whereas no major French historical, political science or sociological review (not so the newspapers) had produced a serious appreciation and discussion of the book until Gallissot (2005) and this despite the various presentations of the book by Gilbert Meynier. I felt vindicated at last in a statement made by a leading liberal French journalist during "les évènements d'Algérie," Jean Daniel, who in reviewing Mohammed Harbi and Benjamin Stora's book *La Guerre d'Algérie* compared my book in scope with a synthesis of more than a dozen top-notch French researchers. Guy Pervillé has rightly insisted on the role of constructed reality regarding decision-making processes in Algeria, to which virtually two chapters of my book were devoted (though some of the reviewers seemed to skip over these sections, presumably turned off or disconcerted by the economics, also a part of the book).

For the mainstream the problem seems not to be one of size alone, given that most of my publications have been relatively short articles in academic journals. The problem is interdisciplinarity and the impact of my dealing with the state of the art of international relations, the state of the art of international political economy, and the state of the art of international economics and development economics. The third of these matters is the most easy to deal with. International economics considers the world to be made up of principally capitalist economies, whose governments sometimes create market imperfections. These governments reduce the rate of growth, especially because they are ad-hocist and chaotic, i.e., organized with the aim of promoting rent-seeking. As a consequence, the discipline of the economics of underdevelopment no longer exists in the sense I have described it. The nonrational behavior of governments as well as social, political and even economic actors is considered a special chapter of institutional economics, where they are dealt with as problems of good governance. The point is rarely made that good governance is the outcome of a lean state, whereas the lean state, in turn, results from fulfilling the requirement of the neoclassical model of growth (marginal labor produces more than its inevitable costs of subsistence) (Elsenhans 2001b). In reality, the institutional, political and social elements of good governance are at best complementary, but usually the result of a well-functioning capitalist economy where labor can become scarce.

Political economy in the form it is practiced in North America or most of Western Europe can be qualified at best as a *contradictio in adiecto*, a contradiction in terms (Elsenhans 2000d). In its neoliberal version, political economy deals with the institutional framework that conditions a multitude of decentralized actors and the interest aggregation among these actors which determines the shape of institutions, organizations, rules and norms. In its Keynesian version, political economy is the essential complement to any theory of multiple equilibria. There is no longer one process, but several economic trajectories. The analysis of the degrees of freedom available is itself an eminent part of the political process; people rarely choose unrealistic issues. Political economy is certainly not what is currently being practiced: looking for an economic reason for a realist actor's strategies in the form of an economic interest. At present, the worst types of analysis of imperialism from the 1930s are being regurgitated and passed off as political economy.

Fifteen years ago, in at least ten nations that are today members of the United Nations, the Velvet Revolution was victorious in the name of a social market economy, which neoliberal economists presented as the ultimate stage of the civilizational development of humankind – though some of the same pamphleteers claim today that they had already proven back then that social market economies are impossible.

Keynesian global demand management has not disappeared as a political option in the industrial West because it has failed, but because – in an ideological offensive spearheaded by big business and comparable to the ideological offensive which led to the Great Depression of the 1930s – people have been taught since the fall of the Berlin Wall that Keynesian macroeconomics is doomed to fail, outmoded, and traditionalist. It worked very nicely, however, under Reagan, once again under Bush Jr., and not so badly during Kohl's first years of German reunification. The fact that British leaders did not manage to reach a consensus between labor and capital is not proof that the rest of the world cannot.

My contributions to the globalization debate are meant to reject the automaticity of a specific type of globalization, to open peoples' eyes to alternative patterns of globalization, and to show that such alternatives are neither too costly nor unfeasible because of a lack of constituencies. They are unfeasible because, in the ups and downs of social science, the return to idealism occurred in a political climate that promoted a turn to constructivism.

## 4. The favoring of economics and the constructive perspective

I admit that I have privileged economic issues in my political-science approach. To be sure, economic realities do not directly determine attitudes. I myself have dealt extensively with the issue of interests. And yet, in the field of society as formulated by Tönnies (1935) I assume that economic issues ultimately matter, as this field would otherwise belong to the sphere of community. We live in society because of the division of labor and our desire to limit labor to the amount necessary for acquiring the goods and incomes which in turn allow us to pursue other, more personal goals. With the exception of security, we are not forced into cooperation with unknown partners for the sake of non-social community-related goals. Political economy and security studies therefore share the insistence on "objective" facts. Whereas in economics this reality is largely determined by relatively unambiguous facts, security can be provided through conflictive as well as through cooperative patterns of behavior. Constructivism hence originated in the critique of simplistic, so-called realist interpretations of the security dilemma. The difficulty is in finding causalities for the choice of one approach to security over another.

Since time immemorial, there has been a consensus between nearly all sophisticated cultures that we ourselves construct the reality we live in. Nominalist is the name given to authors in mediaeval Scholasticism who considered that everything depends on the naming of objects. The mediated quality of any given reality is also a primary concern of Marx's theory of understanding: The politico-economic condition of a human being determines his consciousness. These "fetters" allow a political economy of the historical forces of science (and religion) to be written, such as, for example, *History and Class Consciousness* by Lukács (1923). Marx (1963: 258) himself posed the decisive question: If any understanding is linked to the fetters of our human condition, why did not only the Greeks find Greek epic poems beautiful, and why do we find them more beautiful today than contemporary epic poems, although our fetters differ from the fetters of the Greeks since we are conscious of ours, as Plato's allegory of the cave shows? The constructed character of the real world is a banal observation. The argument that constructed reality acquires importance because the construct itself acquires some semblance of autonomy and directs the actions of political leaders (but also political audiences) is likewise banal. How could Leopold von Ranke have written his histories of the main European nations if he had not assumed that the realities on which their leaders made decisions were constructed ones, which they and their counterparts constructed in their daily, in his type of approach mostly diplomatic, intercourse? Ranke's work can be summed up as a history of the construction of European political realities in the minds of elites of the ancien régime. Of course, I would not want to omit the parallel between Ranke and contemporary constructivists, namely, that both insist on identity as the link between constructed reality and the reality this construction refers to, i.e., the nations or – in Ranke's case – the elites which perceive themselves as nations. By accepting this identity, the constructed ones give legitimacy to the construct.

Moreover, the outbreak of the First World War was convincingly shown to be the result of widening gaps between reality and constructed reality on both sides of the conflict. Both sides overestimated their actual capabilities and the potential threats posed by their enemies, seeing only their last chance of safely winning an otherwise inevitable war (North 1963).

The relevant question is whether there can be isomorphisms in the process of construction enabling predictions to be made about the relations between realities and constructed realities. In the 1960s there were three basic answers to this question in West German international relations theory. E. O. Czempiel (1966) argued that bureaucratic structures are essential. Ziebura (1955) argued that conflicts are instrumentalized for maintaining power against internal foes, with internal interest accommodation and hence democracy the decisive factors for peaceful behavior. This largely echoed Kehr (1930), who had explained the aggressiveness and alliance strategies of Wilhelminian Germany as an outgrowth of the reciprocal blockage of the two privileged camps, big business and big landowners, especially in the last decades before World War I. Finally, Senghaas argued that conflictual behavior was the result of autistic perceptions of foes, a strain of argument that could be linked to any of the more structural approaches, but could also explain how the simple approach of major actors and their constructed realities became the basis for aggressive behavior.

The current German mainstream seems to follow the Senghaasian approach. As far as I understand his arguments, Senghaas asserts that if moral values and ethical standards are spread through verbal communication, a sort of virtuous circle can be established, mirroring the autistic and destructive mechanisms he described. If this is so, the resolution of conflicts becomes unnecessary, conflicts can be managed without really being solved – which is not to imply that the German mainstream is opposed to conflict resolution. If my understanding is incorrect, the current mainstream at least has to admit the legitimacy of a question posed in the late 1960s and early 1970s by a number of relatively well-known international relations scholars such as Franz Ansprenger, Lothar Brock, Klaus Busch, Christian Deubner, Hanns-Dieter Jacobsen, Gerd Junne, Salua Nour, Frieder Schlupp, Gilbert Ziebura and myself: Are there specifics in the formation of constructed realities to be observed in the post-World War II period and which can be deduced from strategic nuclear stalemate, the economic and social dynamics of European integration, globalization in the form of the rise of multinational enterprises, and the withdrawal of the West from the South through decolonization (Ziebura et al. 1974)?

## 5. Interdisciplinarity and the historical approach

Research funding for the Berlin project was later impossible, as most of the junior researchers had landed fine professorships by the time agreement on the major axis of research had been reached. They took with them the idea of analyzing how international social structures have determined external behavior in different periods of the unfolding of the capitalist world system and of the different power configurations within such a world system, notwithstanding the fact that dominant and dependent set-ups would influence each other.

The conclusion I drew myself from the Berlin endeavor can be summarized as follows. The problem can become the subject of systematic reflection only by intellectually reconstructing the development of the capitalist world system using a political economy that is in touch with modern economics and has dispensed with automatisms of accumulation, as was the case with what was later to become new endogenous growth theory. The approach therefore had to reject the Marxist automatic accumulation process and the Weberian unfolding of civilization, especially its historicist German school. This opened up the perspective that class struggles mattered at all levels of society, even at the level of orientation of the economy, and that the configuration of classes and disguising of classes by fabricating other conflicts were part of an overall conflictive behavior.

Capitalism was presented in my view as being dependent from its very inception on "rising mass incomes as a condition for capitalist growth" (Elsenhans 1983c). The history of the world system was the history of the emancipation of labor, as I had defined it in a research project (Elsenhans 1974b) of the international relations division of the German Association for Political Science (which, incidentally, won the support of nearly half of this division's members during the Hamburg political science congress of 1973, before the division split into two, one more specialized on the industrialized countries, the other on developing countries).

According to my findings, the emergence of the capitalist West was not an isolated development, but, rather, originated within the world system, which in the sixteenth century was not yet capitalist and not about to become so (Elsenhans 1992f; Elsenhans 2004b). The European expansion to the outer world was a most conventional process of empire-building, as any society in a tributary mode of production attempts to do. It was sea-bound, because all areas of land accessible to European conquest were well-guarded by the Muslim states. Despite the empire's sea-bound character the decisive form of surplus appropriation was rent, in sea-bound trade long-distance monopoly profits, as shown by the fierce naval battles fought over sea routes. The patterns of exploiting the peoples in the periphery created by naval expansion were based on political power, not on wage relations and profit.

The Industrial Revolution and the transition to capitalism in Europe were linked from the very start to rising mass incomes. The latter provided the markets making it reasonable to spend on machines as the major form of investment goods. It is clear that the periphery could contribute to this expansion of markets by the simple fact that it allowed additional sales of machine-produced products. It should be noted, however, that this became important only on the eve of the Industrial Revolution. The contradiction between monopoly and profit is demonstrated by the conflicts between English and French weavers and their East Indian Companies. The latter tried to earn monopoly profits from Indian textile sales worldwide and in Europe. At the beginning of the eighteenth century the weavers managed to impose the protection of their respective markets.

The transition to capitalism was followed by its expansion to not yet capitalist areas in the periphery. This coincides more or less with what some authors have called the imperialism of free trade. The struggle over peripheries was not justified by interests in expanding markets nor by the struggle over opportunities for capital exports. The low shares of peripheral economies in trade and total consumption, and more so in gross capital formation, show that the dynamics of the capitalist world system in the second half of the nineteenth century were basically triggered off by developments in the so-called center. The forces of the ancien régime were able to maintain their political clout despite these capitalist dynamics. They were able to turn nationalism into an exclusionary force, quite the opposite of its initial prospect as a vehicle for political partnership among the lower strata of society. The impact of the center was too weak to transform the noncapitalist peripheries into capitalist ones. Capital contributed to the disintegration of the noncapitalist systems and their modes of social integration, and therefore to the marginalization of their populations as well. The center imposed exploitation without transformation. The result was marginality.

The insufficient impact of world capitalism resulted in the formation of territorially confined systems in the center where the neoclassical mechanism could operate. The forces of the ancien régime got hold of these institutions and were able to turn back the cosmopolitan tendencies of early labor movements. The social democratic movements turned into nation-oriented ones, because the deal between labor and capital became more and more embedded in national cultures, as shown by the different forms of emerging welfare states in Western Europe and North America. Nationalism allowed the forces of the ancien régime to spread exclusionary ethnicist identities, not least because, for accidental reasons, the states inherited from the European past could be imagined (at least in many cases) as comprising one dominant ethnic group. The European aberration of the nation-state was born.

A world capitalist system made up of nation-states became unstable when all technically leading economies began pursuing policies of restrained mass consumption, as was the case after 1919. This instability spilled over into the interstate systems when some powers (Germany, Japan and Italy) opted for extremely nationalist strategies of aggrandizement under the leadership of ancien régime forces, which had learned how to mobilize the masses by creating external enemies (fascism).

The U.S.'s attempt to restore a free world economy in the mid-1930s was initially half-hearted, since the expansion of internal demand was too limited to have a sizable impact on the raw-material exports of the Third World. It also came too late to stop the interstate rivalry from transforming into World War II.

The simultaneous underconsumptionst crisis of the leading capitalist countries in the 1930s, the faltering of expansionary forces of demand in the leading industrialized countries for cheap products from the periphery, the discredit into which extreme nationalism had fallen in the 1940s, and the disintegration of precapitalist structures in the periphery accelerated by the world economic depression all combined to have two major results. In North-South relations, decolonization got underway. The incomplete capitalist restructuring of the periphery was attributed to imperialist exploitation. It was believed that imperialist exploitation could be overcome only by national independence. Nationalism was exported to the periphery, even where nations did not exist.

The well-documented failure of the secular anticolonialist nationalists in the Third World (Elsenhans 1981a, Elsenhans 1996e), who had at least paid lip service to the ideals of the bourgeois revolution in Western Europe and the United States, led to the rise of new cultural identitarian movements, new types of state classes, or externally dependent exclusionary regimes that benefit from the opportunities of export-led growth without laying the foundations of capitalist growth by eradicating mass poverty. It would be erroneous to expect them to abolish rents.

## 6. The opportunities of globalization

This admittedly very cursory overview of what world system theory has to deal with justifies concentrating on the problem of empowerment of labor (Elsenhans 2001a). If capitalism is transformed into a worldwide system of welfare "states" (here in the sense of territorially constrained systems embedding the neoclassical mechanisms of capitalist growth and providing a legal structure for them), the clout of the rent-based forces of the ancien régime will be diminished and democratic forces can develop without fear of falling behind economically.

The essays in this book show that in the benign pattern of globalization, the convoy pattern, falling behind is no serious threat for employment. It is a threat for terms of trade, but only to the extent that less income from the world market leads to rapid catch-up processes, provided that internal structures favor the transition to welfare capitalist systems with full employment.

If we succeed in creating a worldwide consensus about win-win situations between nationally delimited, territorially constrained units, these territorially constrained units will prefer cooperation to conflict.

The fact that military engagements in the state system cannot transform economic structures into world capitalist welfare ones does not exclude that, in the foreseeable future, a world safe for democracy would require a world of interstate relations marked by a balance of power that maintains peace and makes threats less effective.

A world safe for democracy would therefore have the following characteristics. The participation of major powers will be based on the principle of realism. Transaction costs will resemble the realist scenario of benign power politics, with a moderating agency like a reformed UN serving as the hub of changing coalitions for the business of world security. The overcoming of underdevelopment in more and more countries means a larger number of economies to share the burden of providing markets for catch-up economies and makes the competition for shares in markets less fierce. A greater distribution of innovative capacities in the world economy as well as between industrially leading countries makes economies less dependent on export earnings for engineering technical progress. The process of devaluation-revaluation will converge more smoothly. With a greater share of the world's population living in capitalist welfare countries, lean states operating according to the convoy pattern of globalization can become more generalized. Under these conditions, most regimes will develop some sort of moderate reform characteristics, moving the whole system towards a moderate reform process and giving extremist movements little chance to make their influence felt. With a sufficiently large area of the world organized along the principles of welfare capitalist systems – and I suppose that within a generation's time this will be the current OECD world plus China and India – those zones of the world system where the transition to capitalism has been blocked for internal reasons will be effectively absorbed by the capitalist center, in a manner similar to Switzerland or Liechtenstein in the nineteenth century.

The failure of secular nationalists to engineer this process themselves – probably due to a dogmatic reliance on the state as the main instrument of economic transformation and their relatively large opposition to small and medium-scale industry – presents the ancien régimes with an alternative, comparable to that in nineteenth century Europe. Some of them opt for the fascist alternative of mobilizing external enemies and spreading fear. Others will discover in their cultural heritages already existing models of social harmony and will compete with secular nationalist forces for better welfare states. If this process gets started, we will see a renewed globalization of democratic values.

I argue in some of the contributions in this volume that what the West calls fundamentalist movements is in many areas of today's Third World, in India, Turkey and Algeria already a conservative catch-all party of the European populist type from the end of the nineteenth century or the European Christian democratic parties of the twentieth century. The new cultural identitarian political movements are in any case open to different variants. The state of the world economy will partly – though not exclusively – influence their choice of orientation.

My divergence from constructivists and denying them originality in their approach can be reduced to two bones of contention. I do not expect a stabilization of cooperative behavior to emerge from an educative approach to values and norms. Instead, cooperation has to pay off for potential veto players. Thus, the realist game is important for inducing players to give up veto positions or for threatening them with violence in order to maintain cooperative behavior.

Moreover, I have great doubts whether rational players of the type found in top positions of national, transnational or whatever organizations can afford the luxury to follow patterns of behavior that are not interest-directed. The sponsors of these organizations do not normally convey to such organizations aims other than their interests in welfare and security. Some may pay for organizations which promise them salvation. All organizations concerned report a great reluctance of their constituencies to spend any considerable sum on them. I have also rarely observed, as some claim, that non-interest guides behavior and that ideas matter in the career patterns followed by individuals in such organizations. It seems that, at the microeconomic level, people are members of society who defend their interests in material welfare and security. It is difficult to imagine a civil society that does not reflect this priority.

Despite all the criticisms of the current pattern of globalization, I believe that it has opened up more chances for a variety of groups to achieve satisfactory results than is normally admitted. Globalization therefore has to be improved on, and not blocked. It can be improved by giving voice to the poor on their local labor markets. My contributions in this volume argue that peaceful reformist measures are available for governments and that the South and the West can achieve favorable results without incurring astronomic sums or encroaching on the sovereignty of reluctant Third World "elites."

The danger of the current constructivist approach is its tendency to push politico-economic matters into the background. It is no accident that in the German international relations debate it was not the constructivist guru Luckmann who served as a reference point. He was not even taken notice of (Börzel 2004: 347).

German constructivists in international relations preferred Habermas, the only prominent academic of the Frankfurt School, who replaced the materialist approach with a hermeneutic one structurally akin to the thinking of

Young Hegelians, the target of Marx's vitriolic sarcasm in "The Holy Family" (Marx and Engels 1969). In a practical perspective, the center of interest should be not so much the world of benevolence and Samaritan NGOs, but the politico-economic conditions for empowering previously marginal labor. I admit that this would require efforts in interdisciplinarity which do not pay off in the North American or British – and after the fall of the Berlin Wall the Western European – academic worlds, with their practices of financially rewarding academic careers.

The end of the East-West conflict freed the social sciences – from obligations, but of significance, too. Social sciences were no longer needed to develop sustainable political and social arrangements. They thus went on their flight of Icarus. New realities emerged once the commotion died down and the dust of collapsing old orders had settled, realities completely different from the one Icarus had expected to see.

The issue is whether polarization takes place in the world system due to the exclusion of marginal people in the not yet capitalist world or whether we are able to generalize capitalism on a world scale. The new cultural identitarian movements are potential partners in this task. One should beware of demonizing them. They are not demonic just because their religion is different than ours, or because they communicate in other languages, something which has always made other nations seem threatening to the Anglo-Saxon world.

# Chapter 2
# Debunking the Spectre of Globalization: On the Limits of the Drive of the Internationalization of Capitalism for the Constitution of Transnational Social Structures (1996)*

## 1. On the purpose of the argument

The focus of my contribution is that those who see in the globalization of the world economy the central feature of the new international system have the most promising approach for analyzing its perspectives and tendencies. In this respect, the papers draws very much on economic theory as I suppose that political structures are embedded into economic structures very much like psychological structures are embedded in biological structures. There may be degrees in autonomy, but I suppose that nobody suffering from a serious mental disease would consult a behavioral psychologist who has no knowledge about basics in medical science. I see a parallel to this in the Weberian "revolution" in social science, which consisted in opposing Marxism by insisting on the autonomy of social values and thus delinked social processes from economic ones. Against the mainstream globalization discourse I argue, however, that the underlying political economy has to be corrected especially by including exchange rates as a link between economic and political processes.

The difficulties which emerge in the dialogue between the supporters of economic globalization and those who detect processes of transnational coalition building and regime formation can be traced back to an inappropriate modeling of the mechanisms which govern the processes in the non-market sphere. Regime theories and similar approaches have dealt with increasing global dimensions in policy areas which cannot be governed by the market, the so-called commons or public goods. The contradictions in the process of economic globalization lead to further areas which seem to be out of control of the market and hence may be considered as areas where regime formation can provide appropriate solutions. So the connection between theories of globalization, theories of regime formation and the claimed emergence of a

---

* Paper presented at the ISA-JAIR Joint Convention, September 21st, 1996, Makuhari, Japan, Panel J-37: How Should International Exchanges Be Conducted in the Coming Asia-Pacific Century?" With the title: On the Limits of the Drive of the Internationalisation of Capitalism for the Constitution of Transnational Social Structures."

world civil society – which becomes rapidly also a civilized one – is the increasing global dimension of problems which arise due to economic globalization. Processes in the production system generate pressures which are said to work in the direction of the constitution of a transnational or world society through which a really new international system will be created.

This perspective can be plausible only, if shared interests and fears constitute already the basis of a society. However, society is based on much more fundamental processes of interaction, which I identify in the sphere of production and entitlement to exchange value and hence purchasing power. In this perspective, increasingly shared values with respect to the world commons will not yet lead to the emergence of a transnational civil society.

The redistribution of bargaining power in the wake of the globalization of markets requires therefore more careful consideration. According to my argument, national or regional strategies are available to a much larger extent at least for many territorially restricted, and hence by definition national societies. In some of these settings and regions internationalist strategies of simple integration into the world economy are nearly excluded because the drive of the capitalist motor of this world economy is too weak to absorb potentially available factors of production.

If models which insist on cultural segmentation or the return to state rivalries do not simply describe the opposition to internationalization by losers, they insist on non-economic factors such as cultural differences etc. Some cultures are considered as historically less open than others for coping with the challenges globalization issues. Such historical traditions are thought to keep these societies from developing a value system compatible with participation in the civilized transnational civil society. The argument of my contribution is that many of these contradictions can be considered as interrelated aspects of the globalization process, if the latter's economic structure is more appropriately analyzed with respect to its impact on the construction of societies of a capitalist type.

I start therefore with a criticism of the Marx-Weber perspective of a capitalist civil society by opposing to those authors a Tönnies-Keynesian one. At this level of my argument, I insist on the frailties of the autonomy of capitalist civil society, which in my analysis is the only historically existing autonomous civil society. I deduce from this argument that the tendency to global markets cannot be expected to (re)constitute autonomous civil society at a world or transnational level, but may simply destroy it at those national levels, where it happened to come into existence.

I combine my model of the constitution of civil society with a new analysis of the impacts of economic globalization on national production sites by combining two sub-models. It is argued that the only challenge issued by the process of economic globalization is the incomplete integration of those societies into the capitalist world system which do not show some features necessary for their own transition to capitalism. This unleashes tendencies among capitalist societies to take refuge from internationalization/globalization through mercantilist strategies on the basis of rent in order to gain comparative advantage in production lines where the underdeveloped world cannot achieve competitiveness. In order to pursue such strategies, non-internationalist mechanisms of creating support, hence cultural factors, are useful and used. As well, rent is important in societies which, due to the weakness of the capitalist drive to globalization, are characterized by large pockets of population which is excluded from the labor market. Both options for rent-seeking are not just a matter of choice of political strategy by elite groups, which may strive for support within the political framework of nation states which still exist or which they may try to assemble through the breaking-up of existing states or regional integration. It is the result of rents structuring these societies with important consequences for their internal dynamics.

The analysis presented here has therefore a clear conclusion: Economic conditions for an autonomous civil society, which may be civilized, have to be created. They don't come just from the globalization process itself. Interventions in order to promote their emergence are much less global than in the theoretical treatment of the globalization problem presented by other approaches, but cannot be dealt with extensively in this paper, which shows, however, the essential element, the overcoming of marginality in the South.

## 2. On the autonomy of civil society

### 2.1. Divergent definitions of civil society

The rediscovery of the notion of civil society in the demise of "really existing socialism" of Eastern Europe and the westernized state classes[1] in many countries of the South in the wake of the economic bankruptcy of these sys-

---

[1] Elsenhans 1981a. English translation: Elsenhans 1996e.

tems in the early 1980's focuses on an aspect which is totally different from the focus which was present at the birth of this notion in the 18th and 19th centuries. When this notion was rediscovered, initially and – as it was shown by the problems of transition in recent years – also subsequently small citizen groups, often single-purpose movements considered themselves as the most representative part of civil society and civil society as composed of social groups which were able to maintain themselves outside the organizational networks imposed on society in the form of the tentacles of a totalitarian or authoritarian state which did not tolerate any organizational nuclei out of its control. Such nuclei were suspected of becoming points of crystallization of opposition movements. When the term was coined in the 18th and 19th centuries, it meant the economically self-steering bourgeois society, based on a self-steering economy, the capitalist one. At the time of rediscovery, the notion meant freedom from state terror, ultimately a state of law which still had patrimonially defined economic tasks. This explains the high visibility of so-called "third patterns of development." At the time of its discovery, the term meant freedom of a society which for the first time in history was capable of resolving the problem of economic growth and social advancement without or with at least very little state intervention. The tutelage of the non-market economy, not only of the state but also of other monopolies, was rejected in order to allow profit to emerge under competitive conditions and as well as political freedom.

## 2.2. Autonomy of civil society as the result of profit

A civil society based on a self-steering economy is linked to capitalism and profit and, with its link to capitalism and profit, to economic structures which empower labor. There have been many forms of civil organization before capitalism. Feudalism can be considered as a political system where the degree of political centralization was extremely low. Centralized surplus-appropriating classes of precapitalist modes of production (of the tributary mode of production) were always threatened by privatization as state officials tried to transform their access to surplus through public office into private property, e.g., tax farms into estates. Whether such classes were centralized or decentralized, they depended on market barriers for appropriating surplus. This even applies to the craft (industrial) production and commerce as exemplified by guilds and trade monopolies and the close dependence of long-distance commercial capital on the favors of the rulers.

Capitalist profit is surplus which can be appropriated on perfectly competitive markets. In order that capitalist entrepreneurs can sell goods at higher prices than their costs of production, net investment has to take place. In the usual two-classes model of capitalism with capitalists not spending on consumption goods and workers not saving, the entrepreneurs of the consumption-goods sector can sell their total output at earnings higher than their costs for labor, inputs and amortization of investment goods only if there is labor which has earned incomes from employment, in which neither consumption goods, inputs nor investment goods replacing only worn out equipment have been produced. A positive rate of profit can emerge only if there is net investment (Kregel 1971: 145–147; Robinson 1951: 174).

As nobody would produce investment goods without a positive rate of profit in case of positive rates of profit in consumption goods production, the positive rate of profit in consumption goods production results in prices of investment goods which also yield a positive rate of profit. The positive rate of profit in both "departments" is the result of income creation and not capacity creation or productivity increases which result from market-oriented equipment production. Users of equipment order new investment goods on the basis of their expectations about future profits and hence about future outlets. Since Bortkiewicz[2] we know that any technology is efficient in capitalism only if it reduces the unit costs and, at constant wage rates, increases the resources available for profit. We can add that new products either substitute older ones, in which case the Bortkiewicz criterion applies, or satisfy new needs and in that case they can become mass consumption goods only in case of rising real wages. So the expectations of capitalists about future outlets can be fulfilled only in case of rising consumption demand. Rosa Luxemburg (1923: 107) was right in stressing that such a rise in demand cannot take issue from the capitalists and their social allies (middle classes) if competition is not reduced. Such additional (luxury) demand can take issue from noncapitalist privileged classes only if they are capable of restricting the capitalists' access to rent-generating assets or if they tax the capitalists, hence if the unfolding of capitalism is restricted. It has to be concluded that capitalist micro-economic rules of behavior, i.e., cost reduction, by itself does not create the expansion of demand which the system needs at

---

[2] Bortkiewicz 1907: 445–489. Cf. also Roemer 1979: 379–398. Further literature is quoted in: Elsenhans 1996a: 104, fn. 18 and infra chapter 7: 121, fn. 1.

its macro-level. This additional demand emerges from rising real incomes of the mass of the population (Elsenhans 1983c: 1–38. Elsenhans 1983a: 187–216; Elsenhans 1992f: 21–79).

I do not enter into the debate about whether rising real wages are the result of rising productivity of labor or political pressure of labor because for my argument it is sufficient to show that at the international level the economic bases of the autonomy of civil society may be not guaranteed, because the basis for a market-driven rise in mass incomes is absent, at least in important areas.

## 2.3. Preconditions for the existence of free labor

The argument about wage rates being pushed by productivity increases, the so-called marginal-product thesis of wage formation does not make the wage rate of a particular worker or group of workers dependent on his or their particular productivity. It maintains that as long as there are workers whose marginal product is positive, entrepreneurs will continue to hire at the going rate and finally raise this rate until no worker provides an additional product which can be sold at a higher price than his cost. It is obvious that in the marginal-product thesis of wage formation a tendency of the economy to full employment is already implied.

Marginal-product wage theory depends on scarcity of labor and hence on the level of technical development where in a closed economy every able-bodied worker produces at least as much as the cost of subsistence for himself and his nuclear family, which can be termed the cost of reproduction of labor. Because labor is scarce it can be freed from all other social links of dependency which may have existed in precapitalist types of society, even of the property in means or production. If this condition is fulfilled, the generalization of wage employment at high levels of economic activity is possible.[3]

## 2.4. Marginality as a restriction for capitalist growth, even for the transition to capitalism

Each able-bodied worker's capacity to produce more than his costs of reproduction may not be fulfilled at low levels of economic development in agri-

---

[3] This modelling allows to understand the basically economic orientation of the labour movement and the necessary deception of Marx's expectation of the proletariat's role in a general revolution which would free mankind from "all its chains."

culture. Suppose decreasing returns in agriculture as mentioned in the latifundio-minifundio paradox (Feder 1967: 507–511; Sternberg 1967: 12) and the labor-surplus models of the Indian debate of the 1960's (Dandekar 1962: 69–80; Sen 1966: 427–450). With agricultural production $Y_{agr} = f(L)$ and $1 > f' > 0$ and $f'' < 0$, and subsistence wages so that the costs of reproduction of agricultural labor $C_L = aL$, then demographic growth will lead to a level where $f'(Y_{agr}) = a$. Beyond that level, which I call threshold of marginality (Elsenhans 1994d: 393–428; Elsenhans 1995g: 193–221), any additional worker in agriculture produces less than his costs of reproduction. I call this excess labor marginal because it cannot be employed by any surplus maximizing landlord. As there is, however, a surplus, this labor can be fed if those in control of the surplus are willing to do so for non-economic reasons which I cannot deal with here. The form of the transfer will, however, imply that this labor does at least behave in a way that it does not constitute a threat to "society". It has to offer at least obedience as the basic element of a relation which is normally called patron-client, and which implies political mechanisms for the access of the patrons to the surplus and for the channeling of this surplus to the poor.[4]

The autonomy of civil society requires therefore a level of productivity where there is no marginal labor because only when this level is achieved the doubly free worker of Marx as well as surplus appropriation in the form of profit on competitive markets by independent capitalists is possible.

## 2.5. The capitalist mechanism of power diffusion

If the condition of absence of marginality is fulfilled, both classes of the stylized capitalist society empower each other by pursuing even ruthlessly their most selfish purposes, by the way without any serious necessity to coordination, as long as the economy can maintain its flexibility. The capitalists have to invest in order to maintain competitiveness and, if they increase investment in order to serve growing outlets, they call for additional labor in investment goods production. This investment has in the first time only income effects and creates scarcity of labor if already high levels of employment have been achieved. Labor is empowered because of its scarcity and therefore the boom phases in the capitalist cycle are characterized by the rise of labor's stand in the bargaining process. Often organizational innovation

---

[4] The argument is developed in Elsenhans 1995b: 141–145

occurs in such phases as the extension of unionization. By pressing for higher real wages either through scarcity or through unionization, labor increases the outlets for machine-produced mass consumption goods and hence the possibilities for profitable investment. Labor is not able to take from the capitalists the profit necessary for investment because any increase in consumption in excess of installed capacity evaporates through inflationary processes, the forced savings of Keynes.

## 2.6. Civil society is nationally constrained

This empowering process is essentially national in character and so is civil society. The mediation between productivity and average wage increases passes through the scarcity of labor. When productivity increases in some plant or production lines, profit rates will initially go up beyond average, thus remunerating the capitalist for his innovativeness. As profit rates in the rest of the economy are below this particular rate because at average levels, investment of profit outside the respective plant or production line yields lower profits. Higher production with – normally – higher employment in the more profitable plant or production line will bring wages up in case of scarcity of labor (in order to attract additional labor) and prices down. Production lines with productivity increases that are below average can maintain any volume of their production only if they increase wages in order to keep at least part of their labor force. Their prices increase in relation to the price level. Wages develop with average productivity and not with physical productivity in a particular production line. The link between all wages and average productivity constitutes the basis of the emergence of labor movements as one of the bases of the political systems of bourgeois pluralist societies.

In order to bring about this process, labor has to be mobile and scarce. A nation can be defined economically as that group of people where labor is mobile. Within a nation, labor migrates from branch to branch and from region to region so that regional wages can differ only in function of differences in the cost of living and transaction costs for migration. German unification amply demonstrates the model: In order to avoid the unification of the German nation on West Germany's territory, wages in East Germany had to rise even if productivity was too low to bear it. Germany was historically and emotionally perhaps a nation, economically it was a fragmented one. Scarcity of labor can only be maintained if transnational immigration is restricted. As long as, in the process of uneven development on a world scale, labor incomes in the technically leading countries do not largely exceed the level of comfort in the technically more backward countries so as not to compensate for the cost of migration, labor migration is limited. When incomes rise in the technically more advanced countries, migration may increase and be accepted, as at still low wages near the costs of reproduction, the immigrants cannot offer their labor power at substantially lower rates than the population already present. But when wage rates increase beyond this level due to rising average productivity, immigration will be restricted politically. The argument about an increase in transnational links and globalization has rarely taken account of the obstacles to transnational migration which are nowadays much stronger if compared to the 19th century. Civil society has an economic base linked to levels of productivity and is nationally restricted as long as there is no equalization of average labor conditions on a world scale.

In the full-employment situation with labor being scarce and wages increasing in line with average productivity, the two classes of a capitalist society, capital and labor, have no interest in piecemeal intervention of the state. For the first time in history since the emergence of surplus, the state becomes repressed because irrelevant for the appropriation and the circulation of the surplus, and has to limit itself to providing the framework for the unfolding of civil society. Max Weber's theory of bureaucracy is just a reflection of this process, the bureaucracy becoming now, in contrast to the state classes of ancient tributary modes of production, closely controlled by the two classes of the capitalist system. In such a Keynesian model where the investment decisions of private capitalists do not necessarily lead to full employment, the non-automaticity of capitalist growth and its dependence on a power relation favorable to labor makes the process of constitution of a civil society dependent on special traits in the economy[5] and not on values of the type of Max Weber. It is, however, possible, within this modelization, to come back to Tönnies (1935: 40) and consider a capitalist social structure, his "society" which is based on exchange, as the outgrowth of a "well-functioning" capitalist system.

---

[5] In more detail: Elsenhans 1991a: 23–52.

## 3. The limits of transnationalism

Against this view about the process of constitution of civil society, those in support of the argument that there is a tendency towards the emergence of a world civil society will object two arguments: They will hint at the much higher levels of transnational interaction and at the development of more and more problems which require international rule-setting. They will link these two aspects with the emergence of transnational coalitions.[6] I oppose to this argument that these new international issues will not trigger off the constitution of autonomous civil society but will create a rather uncontrollable set of politically and/or economically relatively independent organizations based on rent-type resources.

The increase in international interactions concerns less the economic sphere: trade dependence and investment flows in relation to GNP and national savings are lower in the technically leading countries of today than at the end of the 19th century, but this fact may be debatable at the level of the world economy. The increase in transnational communication and transborder tourism does not seem to create palpable transnational solidarity of the type to be found within nations. Workers in the more advanced countries who fear the loss of their jobs through low-cost imports from what they consider poor countries have not yet united for transferring funds in order to create full employment there. Putting the marginal population of the South above subsistence levels which would allow employed labor to enforce wages in line with productivity increases can be estimated as requiring about 50 bn of $ (1 bn of people below the poverty line which stands actually at about $ 100 per year, 50 per cent increase of the income of the lowest quintile), hence much less than is transferred annually in the only case where such an experiment is occurring, namely Germany (annually about 120 bn $ at the 1996 exchange rate).

The new issues on which international solidarity is said to be based are weak with respect to their capacity for producing societal interrelatedness. The wage bargain is such a powerful mechanism for "society-creation" because it can succeed only if every wage-earner participates and gets involved, by the way even in case of his possible inclination not to do so (then

---

[6] With a good overview of recent literature: Forschungsgruppe Weltgesellschaft 1996: 5–26. Cf. also: Olsen 1995: 253.

because of the picketers), and because it provides immediately privately appropriated benefits. The notion of international commons reveals already in the choice of words that the new transnational interests are based on public goods. Public goods require non-market structures for management as their consumption is not exclusive. This is even so at the national levels as shown by any anti-pollution law. Hence, transnational ties in the defense of public goods will not lead to large mass movements as large masses are not able to directly contribute to the defense of their interests in the respective policy areas. Just as at the national levels, at the transnational level it is difficult for any single group of people to directly threaten a polluter. The people who felt concerned with the floating of the Brent Spar in the ocean could not all participate in the occupation of this drilling platform.

The relevance of my argument about different capabilities of different interests in creating societal interrelatedness is felt by many actors in these transnational coalitions. Often they try to create a level of activity for the interests concerned which has similarities with the wage bargain especially in the form of boycott movements. Shell changed its plans with the Brent Spar when the environmentalists in Germany succeeded in persuading German automobilists to desert Shell petrol pumps.

As long as such movements are difficult to be institutionalized, the focus will be less on organizing permanent mass support, but on maintaining credibility in order to exercise political pressure by calling for support only in selected high-visibility cases. Inspecting the strategies of internationally operating environmentalist non-governmental organizations, an orientation to bureaucratic politics becomes visible. They have to maintain resources, but also prestige and influence. Standards which they consider to be essential and which scientifically cannot yet be proven (nobody knows whether the models about the causes of global warming are realistic) have to be made credible by careful parallel "tatonnement" processes where each institution or organization tries as well not to be behind others and not to be too much in advance of them in order not to be disavowed by the competitors' reaction. By apparently unjustifiably staying too much behind newly proposed standards by one organization, the competitors would lose credibility which they also cannot defend by simply adopting the new standards which may be very much in advance of their own ones previously proclaimed, so that the only solution available to them is to disavow the newly proposed standard (Obser 1997).

The new transnational coalitions are composed of relatively isolated elite groups. They operate at transnational levels in order to increase their resources, their prestige and their influence. Their resources are not the result of sales of products but of a careful creation of awareness which allows them to impress on governments in a negotiating process, hence on other non-market institutions with the means of non-market institutions.

Whether this should be called the beginning of an emerging world society is debatable. It depends on how the process of the creation of a society is modeled. The Weberian approach of criticizing Marx consisted in basically accepting Marx's economic model. His critique of Marx is limited to an interpretation of the moral value of the motives of the capitalist. For Marx, the capitalists are greedy because they accumulate. For Weber, they are thrifty, also because they accumulate automatically provided that they have this behavioral rule. But for both authors this behavior is capable of debunking all precapitalist forms of social control and hence to create modernity. Weber therefore only adds to Marx by putting importance to the non-economic realm of values and by providing a moral cloak to this behavior.

If, however, the process of society creation depends on the constitution of independent classes of civil society through certain features of the economic system, which may be there or not, the insistence on the importance of values for the creation of a capitalist civil society can only be maintained, if it can be shown that those who share the values Weber considers as important are capable of overcoming defects in the economic structures. The socio-political variants of the theory of modernization have been focusing on this very problem. This theory asked how to create political integration and investment in rent-based so-called underdeveloped systems through values instilled on modernizing elites. Although it would be foolish to completely subscribe the Washington consensus according to which the resulting over-extension of the non-market structures, especially the so-called "development" state, have definitely failed[7] – by the way despite centralization as decentralized oligarchies have been even less efficient – the tendencies to disintegration especially in their form of nativist movements (fundamentalism) draw their strength from the failure of such rent-based systems to pro-

---

[7] The World Bank (1997) seriously revises the anti-statist position without, however, addressing the problem of marginality which would allow to specify and limit the role of the state in enabling the overcoming of underdevelopment.

vide for economic as well as social integration. There is little hope that a rent-based increase in transnational interactions can reach far down enough into the up to now national societies and achieve truly transnational societal structures which as well may be civilized ones. This failure is the more probable as the capitalist mechanism seems to be too weak to transform the world economy into a capitalist one characterized by those processes of societal construction which were shown above.

## 4. The pitfalls of the globalization thesis

In the present debate on globalization it is argued that decreasing costs in international transactions will impose uniformization of labor conditions all over the world and require the old industrial nations to streamline their welfare states in order to maintain international competitiveness. The strong influence of social democracy especially in Western Europe is expected to vanish. The East Asian structures of labor management are considered to be superior.

However, the real problem is not constituted by labor costs but by the end of the hierarchies which the theory of the product cycle had considered as stable (Vernon 1966: 190–207) in a time where large parts of the noncapitalist world achieve the capability to benefit from long-term accumulated comparative advantages through devaluation. I will therefore first show that there is not a problem of international labor costs, but a problem of comparative advantage in the "wrong" branches of production for established technically leading economies, which becomes a political challenge due to new entrants' increasing capability of devaluing their currencies.

### 4.1. Competitiveness and surpluses in the balance-of-trade under conditions of unemployment

The massive reduction in transaction and transport costs in the transnational movement of goods, services, and capital does not establish the impossibility of pursuing national policies. Even less founded is the successfulness of a certain national policy of adjustment – adjustment to internationally lower labor costs of other countries by reducing the national wage rates. If labor costs in Germany were on the whole too high, it would necessarily mean that this country has enormous trade deficits and not trade surpluses despite unemployment, which is apparently the result of excessively high labor costs.

Despite labor costs which are internationally high, Germany sells more abroad than it buys on the foreign market.

To clearly retrace what the votaries of wage reductions actually maintain: Full employment could be achieved in Germany only if this country benefits to a larger extent than has hitherto been the case from the willingness of other countries to accept their own trade deficits, that is to say, to reduce their own level of employment. Indeed, it was on such behavior by leading capitalist economies, incidentally as an outcome of the assumed absence of real-wage increases for the workers that Rosa Luxemburg (1923: 79–106, 336–360) based her theory of imperialism.

The stimulation of employment through trade surpluses is not only dangerous given foreign policy and global-economy considerations – for ultimately the trading partners will resist further over-indebtedness through the restriction of free trade – but it is at the same time also ineffective. Sustained surpluses in the balance-of-trade lead to the revaluation of the currency concerned vis-à-vis other currencies, that is to say, to German factors of production being priced higher on the international market, this particularly applying to labor without wages in DM increasing along-side. It may be pointed out that since 1993 the "Handelsblatt,"[8] a newspaper which is not exactly pro-union in its affiliations, has been repeatedly drawing attention to the fact that wage settlements have not been too high in the past few years, but that the high international costs of German labor were the outcome of repeated upward revaluations of the DM. Recently, the conflict in business has become public.[9] The problem is not whether German international labor costs are too high but whether lower direct and/or indirect labor costs in German currency will allow to realize the 20 percent decrease in German international labor costs which business claims to be necessary for survival.[10] Even the ifo-institute joins business in the demand for wage restraint by an only vague perspective that the appreciation of the deutschmark following an

---

[8] Deutsches Institut für Wirtschaftsforschung 1992: 121–125; Flassbeck 1988: 255–267; Flassbeck 1995: 18–19; Mundorf 1995: 2; Mundorf 1994: 2; Neuthinger 1989: 138–148; Handelsblatt 29/30-12-95: 11; 3-8-1994: 3; 5-6-1993: 13. Cf. also: Elsenhans 1995c: 22–27; Elsenhans 1995a: 133–146.

[9] Mundorf 1996: 2; and subsequent issues with discussions.

[10] Cf. the Interview with Dieter Hundt (Leipziger Volkszeitung) 9-10-1996: p. 3.

improved competitiveness of the German economy would not occur immediately.[11]

These revaluations in turn are but the result of German export surplus: Certain as it is that the exchange rate mechanism will always create sufficient export avenues for payment of imports, there is just as little that can be said about the kind of export goods this will involve."[12] It goes without saying that this is also true of the trading partners of the Federal Republic of Germany who find themselves compelled to go in for devaluation due to Germany's trade surpluses. There is a decline in the international competitiveness of a section of the German enterprises because another section of German entrepreneurs remains so competitive (and this despite, high labor costs) that it reaps surpluses in its balance-of-trade even though the international costs of German labor rise as a result of devaluation by the trading partners. Thus, the international price of German labor rises with an increasing exchange rate, wholly regardless of wage settlements in Germany. It may be inferred therefrom that on the whole wages in Germany are not too high. Rather, in individual branches of the economy the Federal Republic is so competitive that other branches lose their competitiveness. It is the misfortune of the German worker that the highly competitive sectors do not generate sufficient growth dynamics to achieve full employment.

### 4.2. On the operation of the law of comparative costs

The grave misconception underlying the argument that through wage restraint international competitiveness could be regained to an extent where full employment would be created through a larger trade surplus is rooted in the assumption that external trade rests on absolute cost advantages. Rather, it rests on comparative cost advantages.

As per the law of comparative costs (Ricardo 1951: 134–153), an economy increases its welfare through specialization even if it produces all products with a lower factor deployment than its potential trading partners. If England produces 20 units of textiles or 15 units of wine with the same amount of labor and Portugal only 10 units of each product, then Portugal

---

[11] "In the medium term greater competitivity of exports will lead to a revaluation." Institut für Wirtschaftsforschung 1996: 5.
[12] Suntum 1986: 502. This was the only author business could get for contradicting the exchange rate driven character of German international labour costs, cf. Suntum 1996: 2.

would be better off exchanging 15 units of wine for 16 units of textiles. England in turn would stand to gain by receiving 15 units of wine for 16 units of textile where it would have otherwise produced just 12 units of wine instead of these textiles.

A specialization on the part of England is however not only desirable but also mandatory as long as Portugal engages in free trade. The English consumer can buy Portuguese wine only if it is cheaper than English wine. Taking labor as the factor of production deployed – as in Ricardo's example – as long as the costs of labor both in England and Portugal are equal, Portuguese wine cannot be cheaper than English wine. At this exchange rate Portuguese consumers would only buy English textiles and English wine, provided the quality of wine offered is to their taste. In order to purchase these products, Portuguese wine and cloth merchants would offer Portuguese escudos on the exchange markets in order to buy English pounds. Since English traders would not choose to buy any Portuguese goods when the factor costs are the same because these goods would be impossible to sell in England, the suppliers of escudos would take to devaluating their currency against the pound, at least until such time when, after a devaluation of 33 percent, the Portuguese wine costs exactly as much as the English wine. At this point English buyers of Portuguese wine offer English pounds. From now on, the Portuguese are only willing to buy English textiles until such time as the value of the escudo falls by at least half of what it was initially. If it is further devalued, both England and Portugal will buy nothing but Portuguese products. The price elasticity of demand for both commodities in the two economies as well as the evolution of marginal costs with rising production of English textiles and Portuguese wine (and decreasing levels of production for Portuguese textiles and English wine) determine the point at which the exchange rate stabilizes between the two possible rates of exchange – an aspect that will not be further elaborated here.

International labor-cost differentials do not depend on wage movements in the two countries even if the scope for real wage increases is enhanced in both countries as a result of trade. The change in exchange rate and, consequently, in international (and not national) labor costs is the mechanism by which the less productive country in the case of both products becomes competitive. If textiles and wine were the only tradable with textile being an item of mass consumption, but wine not in England, real wages would rise in Portugal despite a decline in the international costs of Portuguese labor, whereas English real wage rates would remain stationary despite the rise in international costs of English labor.

England could only stem the increase in the international price of its labor by levying export duties on its textiles, thereby rendering them more expensive and wiping out demand for them from Portugal. England could only prevent a decline in its wine production if its productivity lead in wine production is just as high as in textile production. In both cases this cannot be achieved through wage restraint but only through protection for the relatively less competitive sectors of production and through special duties for the relatively more competitive sectors. An overall wage restriction cannot save jobs in relatively less competitive sectors of production. To be sure, wage increases below the increase in productivity will make export products cheap in the national currency, so that initially an increase in exports may be expected. But thereafter, the trade surplus to be expected only results in a revaluation once more. This was happening in the early 1990's before our eyes. And as Ford (Germany) reported in early 1995, all savings achieved by wage restraint have been wiped out by revaluation.

The normal characteristics of oligopolistic competition suffice to explain why enterprises in the highly competitive sectors neither contribute to lower export surpluses via prices declining more rapidly than quantities of export increasing nor to increasing employment via higher levels of production.

Hence, wage restraint can only have an impact on the division of national income into profit and consumption income and not on international competitiveness. The greater the wage restraint the greater the revaluation and, consequently, the contraction of domestic demand.

Revaluation does not change the relationship between household income and the prices of indigenous products, leading to a (limited) revival in demand for indigenous products only in case of price inelasticity of demand for imports. Revaluation instead of productivity-oriented real-wage increases/ reduction in working hours gives rise to a combination of internationally higher labor costs and stagnant domestic demand, in other words to deflation and unemployment. With productivity-oriented real-wage increases, domestic demand can be maintained without external demand being jeopardized any more than in the event of revaluation. Thus the attempt to increase employment by abandoning the expansion of domestic demand is "self-defeating."

## 4.3. Comparative costs and specialization in backwardness

The challenge posed by globalization lies in the high degree of competitiveness of some German export sectors, which at the same time are not growth sectors of the future, and which by virtue of the high German exchange rate render other sectors non-competitive. Let us substitute textiles with high-quality automobiles and specialized machinery, wine with micro-electronics and standard automobiles, England with Germany and Portugal with the South East Asian and Far Eastern tigers. Germany must specialize in high-quality cars and special machinery, giving up the production of micro-electronics and standard cars although physical productivity in Germany may perhaps have been higher than in South East Asia and the Far East at least in the beginning. Due to Germany having to give up these branches of production, there will be an ever decreasing number of innovations made in these branches of German industry in future.

If world demand for micro-electronic products and for standard cars grows faster than world demand for luxury limousines and special machinery, then high productivity in the case of products with less future prospects leads to a specialization where the protection of a frontrunner position in technology on the expanding markets of the future is endangered in the long term.

This phenomenon is, however, not new. Not only is it at the basis of Britain overtaking France's high luxury industries during the industrial revolution (Crafts 1989: 427), but also at the basis of Germany's overtaking of Britain at the end of the 19th century until the 1960's. Until the 1960s the average productivity in England was higher than that of the German economy; however, by the end of the 19th century, England was lagging behind Germany in the export of some new products such as from the chemical and electrical sectors, although many of the discoveries and inventions crucial to these two industries were also made in England. Since standards in Germany were "miserable" in the old industries as a result of which its earnings on the world market were accordingly low, it enjoyed a comparative advantage in the new products, enabling it – despite an initially perhaps even lower productivity – to overtake England technically even here by specializing in these products (Fremdling 1991: 28–42; Howard 1907: 91ff). The Japanese overtaking of the US high technology competitiveness is just a case of repetition of the same. Even when Japan launched its export offensive with automobiles and micro-electronic products, its productivity was still far behind that of the USA, although this was less pronounced here than with older products (Watanabe 1991: 59; Audretsch/Yamawaki 1988: 446; Dollar/ Wolff 1988: 554). It was not because of its initial superiority that Japan overtook the USA but because in the case of these products the American economy had lesser advantages than with older goods.

Countries which lag behind in their technical development generally have little opportunity to catch up with the advanced countries when it comes to the older products. Consequently, their imports of such products are high. It is generally easier to catch up in the case of newer products whose production is just being developed even in the advanced countries. This is particularly true of new-generation technologies which are just emerging.

It has been assumed since the '60s that the "human capital" accumulated through technical development reduces the costs of developing and applying new expertise as against less advanced economies to such an extent that technical advantages could be maintained (Posner 1961: 329). Even if a leading economy enjoys advantages in new technologies vis-à-vis technologically backward countries by virtue of the training, discipline and management-friendly behavior of its employees, it can only avoid a specialization in old products if the advantages accruing from newer products were just as great as the productivity leads from older products which, at least theoretically, rest on the practice and routine handling of these older technologies.

The very notion of disembodied technical progress which is at the basis of capitalist growth as this would otherwise be blocked by a decline in capital productivity (Marx's law of tendential fall in the rate of profit on the basis of new products entering into demand and hence not subject to the Bortkiewicz criterion) makes most improbable the stability of the hierarchy in productivity advances. The superiority of the leading countries is based on elements which are no longer cost factors there and which are causing costs in the catching-up economy, analyzed in the theory of poles of development, especially by Perroux (1963: 151–196), such as an appropriate infrastructure, the lay-out of the education system, values of discipline etc. instilled on the population already by the families. There is little probability that these factors are equally important for the mastery of new technologies where both the advanced and the backward economies have to start to learn even if their endowment in skills is different. If a Japanese person learns Dutch as a foreign language after German, he is bound to make more rapid progress than a Japanese who is conversant with neither of the two languages. On the other hand, it is less probable that he will have the same head-start in Dutch over a Japanese attending Dutch classes with him as he would in German which the latter has not even learnt.

Such differences do normally not lead to devastating consequences for the lagging-behind economy. France was able to catch up in new industries and fell behind Britain in the long term not because of unequal specialization, but because of the lack of dynamics of its internal market (demography, income distribution). Britain's problems in competing with Germany did not cause its falling behind, but inappropriate internal policies. As well, the vision of the deindustrialization of the United States had been greatly exaggerated already at the time it was put forward and is now rejected by reality.

The reasons for this are to be found in the fact that the export surpluses which the catching-up country acquires due to specialization also lead to rises in the exchange rate, from which cost advantages of the gradually lagging-behind economy result. Even companies from leading countries may enjoy such comparative advantages and enlarge them through firm-specific cost advantages through foreign direct investment as shown by the international dissemination of affiliates of US companies since the beginning of the century. The considerable innovation through adaptation of local producers in lagging-behind economies has often been mentioned.

The new phenomenon is, however, that those countries which are falling behind and which are no longer specialized in the technically most demanding products are fearing to be definitely excluded from the leading group without being able to earn reasonable incomes by producing a higher share of the technically less demanding products. This is the result of production sites becoming competitive where international labor costs are much lower so that differences in international labor costs are now much higher than had been within the first group of the industrializers. The emergence of the new production sites demonstrates that capitalist methods of production can be transferred without totally transforming an economy as had been the case with the export-led examples of Denmark and Switzerland in the 19th century.

## 4.4. The integration of marginality-ridden economies into the global system

The uneven development of productivity according to production lines should have led since long to comparative advantage in industry for today's underdeveloped world, at least in some branches. The question should therefore not be why these economies become increasingly exporters of manufactured goods, but why it took so long for them to do so.

The fact that many of them enjoyed high earnings from raw material exports explains backwardness through Dutch disease (high exchange rates resulting from high prices for a limited set of export products with low technical spin offs) for those of them who effectively became raw material exporters. The decline in natural conditions of production at production sites close to centers of industrial growth explains why comparative advantage was acquired for underdeveloped economies here despite technical progress in mineral production also in the developed economies, which, by the way, led to massive technology transfer and foreign direct investment since the last quarter of the 19th century. New tastes in the wake of the rise of real wages explain new export opportunities for the tropical products of the South.

But many economies of the South did not become raw material exporters without, however, enjoying industrial specialization due to comparative advantage. The argument that a sluggish world demand precluded it, is probably valid to some extent for the 1920's and the 1930's, does not explain the massive character of Japan's textile export offensive in the same period due to comparative advantage, the restricted character of export specialization in the 1940's and 1950's were world demand was expanding, as well the success of new entrants during sluggish demand in the 1980's and the complete failure of Subsaharan Africa during the same period despite massive structural adjustment programs.

A key to an understanding of these differences is to be found in the following paradox, if it is explained in a Ricardoan way: Real wage rates in Southeast and East Asia are higher than in Subsaharan Africa, but international prices of labor are higher in Subsaharan Africa, even if adjusted to differences in labor productivity. Why then does Subsaharan Africa not specialize through higher rates of devaluation in order to benefit from comparative advantage in low-skill productions as the Asian countries are upgrading their technical capacities, i.e., experience shifting comparative advantage against their old export industries.

Devaluation has been shown as the mechanism through which comparative advantage is transformed into absolute cost advantage. The literature opposing devaluation insists on the compensatory effects of inflation triggered off through higher costs of imported goods in national currency.[13] Obviously, the more high income groups with propensities for imports are protected the more inevitable this result. But even if declines in such rent-based incomes[14] are neglected there may be limits to devaluation. They are linked to the agricultural sector which has already been shown as a potential obstacle to the transition to capitalism.

I will argue in the following that the already presented possibility of marginality can be eased by export-led growth but restricts the possibility of such growth and causes a benign and a malign situation which explain the attempt of industrial countries to avoid specialization on products where low-wage countries of the South are expected to become competitive in the near future.

Devaluation, i.e., the lowering of the international price of local labor for creating employment, can be pursued as long as this additional labor can be fed, either from the export earnings or from the surplus of local agriculture. Assume a low-income low-productivity economy of the type normally encountered in the Third World. Product wages of labor without specific skills are so low, that around 50–60 % of the incomes are spent on food and the rest on locally produced goods and services such as shelter, clothing, basic household equipment and furniture, as well as transport etc., where the import content, direct and indirect, is normally low. A country which has reached self-sufficiency in food production and basic non-food products, at least in principle can accept any rate of devaluation in order to increase employment in its export sector. International specialization can present two types of advantages: Static increases in welfare as described in the theory of comparative advantage and chances for long-term growth through structural transformation, as described by the infant-industry protection argument. Here specialization on future high growth branches is one element only

---

[13] Buffie 1986: 376; Hanson 1985: 407; Suh 1987: 111; Gulhati et al 1986: 399–423; Wilson 1976: 1–24; Porzecanski 1975: 364.

[14] Cf. on hidden rents: Elsenhans 1981b: 57–61.

among others. The impact of specialization on social structure and practices is important, especially if social structure and practices are considered as having an influence on the growth perspectives of an economy, as is now generally believed in the discussion about the "two types of capitalism" (Albert 1991: 119ff) or the East Asian "Confucian" model of development (Pye 1985: 59ff).

Devaluation may be therefore a vehicle of "modernization." Hence devaluation for intensified specialization may even be advantageous in case of negative marginal exports earnings if the increase in employment and the implied changes in social relations are important, e.g., by an orientation of the productive apparatus on mass consumption which may favor the development of a local investment goods production with potentially high multiplier and skill formation effects in case of the elimination of consumption out of rents in the wake of devaluation.

An economy which has not achieved self-sufficiency in wage goods production can devalue only to levels of the exchange rate where marginal export earnings are still positive and sufficient for covering, together with the surplus of local agriculture, the additional demand for wage goods which originates from additional export workers and from additional workers engaged in the additional wage goods production for the internal market.

An economy which does not produce a surplus in wage goods can devalue its currency only to levels where additional export workers can be paid at least subsistence wages out of the additional export earnings, these subsistence wages being determined not only by the basket of goods necessary for subsistence, but also by their price on the world market. The rate of devaluation which now is possible may not be sufficient for reaching full employment. Wages in this type of Third World economies may appear to be high in international prices although real wages will be much lower than in economies with higher levels of productivity in wage goods production and much lower international prices of their labor due to the higher levels of devaluation possible, as mentioned in the comparison between Subsaharan Africa and the second-tier generation of East Asian exporters.

It is now easy to understand that the Green Revolution in the industrial countries and in some Third World countries has been pivotal for the rapid increase in the competitiveness of Third World production sites. The Green Revolution in the Third World has increased the scope for devaluation and hence the possibilities of transforming comparative into absolute advantage.

Debunking the Spectre of Globalization 51

With an increasing surplus of agriculture, more workers in the export sector can be fed even if their wages in international currency are too low for buying the additional food necessary for their reproduction from international sources. The only requirement to this is that the local surplus cannot be sold to the world market. The subsidy of labor through the surplus of agriculture which this solution implies explains the central role of agrarian reforms in South Korea and in Taiwan for their export drive. Decreasing marginal product leads to cheap labor in the form of by-employment in rural industries (Elsenhans 1996a: 96) as farm families will opt for it already when they earn from it more than the marginal returns from their farm activities. The only condition for this is a higher marginal productivity of some of their fellow farmers and the absence of higher efficiency of these same farmers in non-agricultural activities. They achieve high earnings for a low amount of labor time employed on their family farms and prefer by-employment even for lower earnings than their average income from their farms as beyond a certain amount of time the additional toil in the farms will bring very little additional product. With some fertile plot which provides seventy-five per cent of its cost of reproduction by engaging half of its available labor time, a farm family may offer up to fifty per cent of its labor time in exchange for less than twenty-five per cent of its cost of reproduction; a rural proletarian has to earn with fifty per cent of his labor time fifty per cent of his cost of reproduction.

The Green Revolution in the industrial countries has raised the rate of productivity growth of agriculture above the rate of productivity growth in some industrial branches of production, even if average productivity growth in agriculture still may be lower than average productivity growth in industry.[15] Prices for the products of those industrial branches the productivity of which increases less rapidly[16] than agricultural productivity rise in relation to food prices. Hence, labor in the backward economy which is paid a subsistence wage will be capable to buy a same amount of food items with a smaller quantity of industrial products. Increases in labor productivity in agriculture in the industrial countries can bring Third World labor in industries with comparative advantage and lagging behind productivity into the

---

[15] For example: Luh/Stefanou 1991; Grigg 1984: 12–14.
[16] And, because of below-average industrial productivity growth, are by definition the ones where even technically stagnating economies acquire comparative advantage.

range of competitiveness without increasing the latter's productivity, by the simple fact that at the level of productivity it has already achieved, the now relatively lower food prices allow the transformation of comparative advantage into absolute cost advantage, whereas at relatively higher international food prices the same amount of exportables had not paid for the subsistence goods of these potential export workers. Subsidized food exports have the same result as increases in productivity in food production. The irrational character of the discussion about globalization is demonstrated by the demand for lower wages for industrial labor instead of a demand for an ending of farm subsidies, especially export subsidies, for farm products in the United States and Western Europe.

In addition, technology transfer by multinational enterprises and local governments, as well as multifaceted efforts for improving skills and infrastructures in the "backward" world have raised labor productivity in underdeveloped countries with the same effect: Labor which already had comparative advantage but which lagged in productivity to an extent that this comparative advantage could not be transformed into absolute cost advantage now is able to do so as the amount of exportables increases.

This should be expected to be the normal result of capitalist strategies of technology development. Since its inception capitalist enterprise has tried to banalize technologies in order to free itself from dependence on scarce skilled labor. The assembly line is just one example for this. The product cycle theory has described the process of banalization as an attempt to cut costs through capital-deepening equipment which is served by unskilled labor (Vernon 1966: 204). From this formulation of the process of diffusion of technology and from the assumption that any technological innovation is characterized by rapidly decreasing costs of duplication, it should be expected that industrial forerunners will have first cost advantages in the discovery and application of most modern technologies, the generalization of which will lead to decreasing superiority in the application of the technologies which undergo standardization. Forerunners will have comparative advantage in technology creation including the production of most sophisticated equipment and the production of high-technology products, the processing technology of which is not yet standardized.

The model implies a change in the international configuration of productivity and comparative advantage over the time of the development of a capitalist world system. Industrial forerunners were characterized in initial phases of the industrial revolution by a rather low advance in productivity in a multitude of industrial branches, not only in equipment production, but also in the use of machinery. Attempts to reduce costs of the capitalist entrepreneurs will lead to banalization of more and more technologies. If in an initial phase the forerunners of industrial production had low advances in a multitude of branches but heavy relative backlogs in some branches (initially raw materials) this banalization led to Third World countries enjoying now comparative advantage in a multitude of manufacturing activities with rather low productivity backlogs but heavy backlogs in high-technology products. The capitalist industrial countries retain comparative advantage in high-technology branches including the production of most modern equipment; these branches are productive enough to provide the technically leading countries with high foreign exchange earnings, but not employment-intensive enough for full employment. The high foreign exchange earnings lead to exchange rates which are too high for further production and employment in other branches.

The old pattern of comparative advantage provided the capitalist industrial countries with gains from improving terms-of-trade without threats to the level of employment. The rising consumptive capacity of the economy in the wake of improving terms-of-trade was absorbed by rising real wages in line not only with productivity increases but also in line with terms-of-trade improvements. The new pattern of distribution of comparative advantage provides the capitalist industrial countries also with gains from improving terms-of-trade but this time, due to less low income elasticity of demand for the products newly exported from the low-income countries, employment in the capitalist industrial countries suffers.

There are two conclusions to be drawn from this configuration. The first one is that the struggle of the leading industrial countries to seek shelter in specialization on high-technology products may be doomed to failure with very high probability:[17] The high-technology products have a limited share in total world demand. The consumption goods among them are accessible mostly only for the better-off of the world's consumers. The attempt of the leading industrial countries to achieve competitiveness through wage reduction makes this market shrink. The demand for investment goods in a capitalist economy depends on the outlets for consumption goods, as the Leninist

---

[17] A qualification of such attempts is found in: Albo 1994: 144–170.

solution (Lenin 1956: 54: 283, 556; Lenin 1951: 32) of an increasing organic composition of capital where, for the sake of accumulation, capitalists become their own costumers to an increasing degree is possible only for a "real socialist economy", but leads here as well as in capitalist ones to a declining capital productivity with the only difference of the socialist one being able to pursue that strategy over a quite long period of time – despite the reinforcement of these contradictions through exploitation by inefficiency (Elsenhans 1996e: 144, fn. 89) – and then collapsing politically, (Elsenhans 1993a: 16–33) whereas the capitalist one would face an underconsumptionist crisis to which there is in principle a reformist solution even if the free competition one of rising real wages due to stickiness of nominal wages and rapidly falling prices is precluded through oligopolistic structures since the 1930's.

The second conclusion is that there is a benign and a malign case. The benign one is constituted by those marginality-ridden economies which achieve full employment through exports. Obviously, the more marginality is also tackled by other measures, the more rapidly absorption of marginal labor is achieved and the more rapidly real incomes will rise, the more additional imports and international prices of local labor will rise. The malign cases are those economies which will not achieve full employment despite devaluation because the surplus of their agricultures is not sufficient to feed all additional export workers. They will have persisting low international costs of labor even if initially higher than in the benign cases. They reach a higher quantity of exports only in case of improvements of the terms-of-trade for their exports against food. Whether they can overcome marginality on the basis of more food imports is doubtful as the potential for future growth in food production lies in a probably high-cost intensification of food production in today's industrial countries with terms-of-trade moving in favor of agriculture.[18] In this case the industrially advanced countries would enjoy comparative advantage in food production where marginal costs increase and productivity declines in relation to some industrial productions. Industrially less advanced countries might enjoy comparative advantage in industrial production with absolute levels of productivity, however, being so low that world market prices for the food consumption of additional export

---

[18] This information is based on a modelization of my Leipzig colleague Prof. Dr. Albrecht Pfeiffer in his paper "Probleme der internationalen Nahrungssicherung" delivered in Leipzig on 18 June 1996.

workers cannot be paid for. It should be added that until now the bulk of the new competition comes from countries which represent the benign case. The real challenge lies still ahead.

From the new possibilities of transforming comparative advantage into cost-effective competitiveness and the new configuration of comparative advantage, the challenge for the leading industrial countries can be reformulated. The mechanism of the redistribution of gains in productivity which I argued to be at the basis of the constitution of labor as a political force is blocked. By making labor competitive whose opportunity earnings are determined by low productivity occupations especially in Third World agriculture, the rise of marginal cost of labor is no longer determined by the increase of marginal productivity in the First World but largely dependent on the increase of marginal physical productivity in the Third World, and the international cost of labor there, initially in the export branches but increasingly by marginal productivity in the Third World agricultures.[19] So the international cost of the First World labor is determined by the exchange rate which reflects the productivity differential not between the branches where both types of labor are forced to compete (which may be relatively low) but between the branches where both economies have comparative advantage (which most probably are high).[20] This may lead to lower real wages at which such labor can still be employed in the First World than the real wages in the Third World as non-tradables may be more expensive in the First World site of production (e.g., housing or services).

First World labor in the branches where competition is developing, loses its bargaining power because the reference income is no longer a relatively high marginal product in economic terms in its own society but the marginal product in economic terms in poor economies mediated through the devalued exchange rates. The mechanism by which globalization influences the macroeconomic equilibrium in the world economy is not simply the replacement of First World jobs by employment in the South, but the replacement of jobs in societies in which labor has bargaining power by jobs where due to low marginal productivity the emerging export-oriented sectors constitute high income islands. The workers employed here do not have the

---

[19] In case that the labour aristocracies in the export sectors are "replaced" by an increasing use of ordinary labour in export production.
[20] This implies, obviously, greater degrees of market imperfections for "leading" countries.

option of exit and therefore do not dispose of a bargaining power, which can avoid them easily being led into corporatist arrangements of the type described in the labor aristocracy literature, despite the fact that labor conditions may be objectively bad in comparison to capitalist industrial countries.

It is clear that this scenario implies the danger of a world-wide underconsumptionist crisis. In replacing high wage jobs by low wage jobs and in replacing high bargaining positions by low bargaining positions, the growth of consumptive capacity may lag behind the growth of productive capacity. It is not the replacement of workers in the West through workers in the South, but the replacement of world wide appropriate consumption capacity through world wide inappropriate consumption capacity through which the globalization process can hurt the maintenance of a capitalist world system (Elsenhans 1981c: 86–95; Elsenhans 1987a: 124–135).

## 5. Rent re-emerging and fragmentation

There are three options for today's leading industrial countries. A first solution which governments and business favor is reduction in the national costs of labor either general or selective for some types of labor. Wage restraint and increases in wage differentials are proposed. An increase in the spread according to skills would have the required results only if productivity depended on the particular skills of a particular worker. There are structural rigidities in any work process. Productivity does not increase if a particular workplace is served by a worker with better skills. The skill structure probably varies little as a function of relative prices. The overall labor cost in an enterprise matters. Lower wages in branches under import competition cannot be restricted to these branches. Exporting enterprises will avail themselves of these lower labor costs at least in the form of extended subcontracting. The resulting cheapening of exports in national currency will increase exports. Finally the exchange rate thwarts the attempt to maintain competitiveness in import-competing and export-oriented branches through lower real wages.

The second option are wage subsidies either for workers in branches under import competition or for the employment of labor in non-tradables such as social services where demand can be increased if costs decrease. This solution has been suggested by union leaders. It implies that the competitive sectors are taxed for the financing of the expansion of those sectors which only can expand production in case of prices which do not cover total costs. The competitive sectors can carry such additional costs only if they do not lose their competitiveness with respect to international competitors. A lowering of the exchange rate of the national currency can shelter them. Financial resources become available because the international price of local factors is lowered.

The third solution would be an industrial policy. Industrial policy aims at making profitable sectors of production with an expected high growth potential in the future and which are not yet profitable at the actual price and cost relations. The deepening of European integration is explicitly justified with the argument that the larger internal market will support the new industries (Cecchini 1988: 73–81). The rationale offered for industrial policy is that in such new industries cost reductions emerge already as the result of production, and are on the increase as the result of subsequent larger series of production which require that higher shares of the world market be captured (Krugman 1979: 469–479).

The difficulty faced by industrial policies is that no one can predict with any sufficient degree of certitude which new products and technologies hold promise for the future. The notion prevailing in America that a particularly discerning ministry for industry in Japan has picked out the "winner branches" of the future and subsidized them is exaggerated. For a laggard economy it would suffice to have those non-traditional branches of production subsidized where the country's level of backwardness is the least.

No particular investment project can be justified as being viable for the future by arguing that micro-electronics, new materials and bio-technologies will be the future growth branches, because such statements lack in precision on the effect of any such project to contribute to the spread of knowledge and skills in these branches.

It can, however, be assumed that indiscriminate protection of jobs is self-defeating as it tends to maintain high exchange rates. Especially the attempt to preserve jobs in less dynamic industries through export subsidies or import protection and also through diplomatic support as has become usual in the export business will increase the problems of the adaptation of the product mix via further revaluations of the currency. Protectionism which may be adopted for preserving jobs does not support exports, may limit employment and certainly keeps exchange rates high. An opening up of the own internal market may contribute to keeping exchange rates down, contribute to smooth transition (the pressure on import competing branches gets lower) and even support adjustment (employment growth in high technology branches through low international prices). Where high earnings on oligopolistic markets provide high rates of return on the basis of specialization on future low growth markets, timely adaptation is difficult to expect.

One way of staying competitive through structural change even in new products and technologies would be to dispense with subsidies to low productivity branches, larger low-technology imports (such as foodstuffs), and to favor expansion of the internal market through productivity and terms-of-trade-oriented real wage increases/reduction in working hours (which may lead to a particularly marked consumption of new products as a result of a greater amount of available leisure) while abandoning attempts to solve the employment problem through surpluses in the balance-of-trade particularly in the older products.

With smaller trade surpluses, perhaps even accompanied by devaluations, there is a greater likelihood of securing the highest possible share of new goods produced with future technologies – an objective which is far more important than the trade surplus – than by attempting to secure a surplus in the balance-of-trade.

From these examples it can be deduced that the means of adjusting consists in the appropriation of rents from sectors which are actually competitive and their channeling into uses which allow to increase employment and/or future growth potentials if they cannot be eliminated by declining terms-of-trade and rapid "diversification." Not all forms of the use of rents are equally suitable to achieve these aims. Those strategies which give priority to the growth of promising export sectors through lower exchange rates and a high international demand for new products are best. They imply changes in the structure of employment and the readiness of labor to accept flexibility, which is abusively called structural change and is probably more easily achieved in situations of high employment. Unemployment seems not to promote labor flexibility (Decressin 1994: 252).

Here the forms of management of labor which are often referred to as cultural factors become important. From the observation that some forms of state intervention for adjustment called industrial policies are superior to others it becomes clear, that the adjustment process has to be coherent. An additive strategy which aims at preserving any existing production line will be self-defeating although, at the level of political structures, it is best suited for the aim of maintaining coherence of the working class. Any selective strategy will consist in supporting small groups of business and labor against the immediate interests of others, but may allow coherence of the adjustment process. This applies to strategies realized within the framework of big companies as tried by Daimler-Benz, or within the framework of special state subsidies to new activities of old or new companies.

In the old model of comparative advantage with the leading countries in the leading branches of the future, political coherence of the working class, dominance of the market and coherence in the process of structural change were compatible with each other. Under the conditions of the threat of specialization in backward products for leading countries this compatibility is no longer existent. The coherent strategy implies differences in degrees of dependence of labor and business from a rent which is necessarily channeled through non-market institutions. These channeling processes are managed by the methods of bureaucratic politics. Labor loses its coherence. More and more segmented groups address themselves to the rent-managing authority for the preservation of their jobs whereas the rent-managing authorities can achieve coherence only by imposing at least on some of these groups flexibility, and hence costs, if they succeed at all.

There will be different degrees to which the segmented working class and its rent-connected groups will be able to engage in the deal proposed to them, which consists in smoothing hardship in exchange for flexibility. It is therefore not clear that only a break-up of the political power of the working class will allow successful adjustment. It is possible, that the traits of some East Asian models consist essentially in the successful combination of integrating the working class in the process of structural adjustment by getting acceptance for flexibility. There will be political set-ups which are more successful than others. Competitiveness will be influenced by the possibility of territorially restricted forms of social interaction to engage successfully in such strategies of flexible adaptation. This also is not quite new. The competitive position of Germany in the Post-World War II set-up was greatly enhanced by the centralization of its working class in comparison to France, by which labor was less inclined to go on strike in exchange for participation in decision making. The implied uniformity of working conditions and wages seems to be too less flexible in comparison to set-ups where labor is directly involved in the profitability of the particular company where it is employed.

Whatever the details of a particular solution, it is obvious they consist basically in the channeling of rents quite similar to an industrial strategy of an oil country which subsidizes economic diversification from the oil rent. Whether in an underdeveloped economy or in a developed one, the strategy risks to evaporate in waste because the whip of competition is eased and this easing allows small groups of business and labor to press for rent on account of their short term interests against the logic of coherence of the project of adjustment, to colonize part of the "administration," and to destroy any attempt to institute coherence at the level of the bureaucracy after it has broken down at the level of the market.

The strategies available for maintaining coherence depend on organizational set-ups and on the level of trust between social groups. Each of the small groups has particular short-term interests and benefits in different ways from the balance between short-term and long-term interests. The extent to which those who pay in the short-term accept the hopefully positive future perspective as sufficient compensation will decide about success in adjustment. In such a set-up, today's leading countries are far from the situation which had prevailed in the genesis and high days of capitalism, that is that each one of the two classes of a capitalist system contributes most to long-term growth by selfishly pursuing its most immediate interests. The autonomy of civil society, which is based on these simple structures, will be replaced by a continuous concertation between the non-market sectors and business, with various degrees of direct participation of labor. In such a system, market signals are simulated, and no longer develop spontaneously.

It was shown by Hilferding (1968: 406–452) that such a situation could be dealt with best within the framework of large economies as the new promising branches are characterized by high start-up costs and rapid cost degression. The leading industrial countries will hence benefit from regional integration, either voluntarily engaged or diplomatically "induced". The increase of the relevance of rent finds an extension in the field of international relations where the choice between strategies of global marketing of high technology products and regional preservation of protected markets has to be negotiated with players who pursue the same mix of goals. Any global strategy of one player aims at pulling down regional protection of the other and vice versa, with the result that international relations will become highly politicized despite the tendency to privilege economic issues as analyzed by most observers of the features of the international system of the post-cold world era.

The potentially disruptive increase of the importance of rent in the management of adjustment of the leading economies occurs historically in a phase were the political set-up for the management of rent in the underdeveloped world is changing. Both processes are not really interrelated, but they both lead to greater fragmentation.

The economic basis of the colonial system, i.e., integration into a world capitalistic system via specialization according to comparative advantage (in raw materials) had broken down in the World Economic Crisis in the 1930's. The class coalitions which emerged were rapidly dominated by state classes (Elsenhans 1991e: 273–278; Elsenhans 1994c: 98–101) which expected economic development from a partial delinking from the world economy. This delinking was partial in the sense that these state classes expected economic transformation through rent appropriation and rent channeling into industrialization. They combined the demand for the better terms-of-trade with import substituting industrialization and refrained from tackling the problem of marginality through economic empowerment of the poor, especially through a radical transformation of the agricultural sector which was neglected. The transformation of the Keynesian idea of empowering labor via the income effect of public investment into the idea of creating capacities of production via public investment (Elsenhans 1996d: 112–119; Elsenhans 1997e) is significant. Aiming at such industrialization through the import of most modern technology meant that the conditions for capitalist growth, expanding mass markets and local technology production were neglected.

The reasons for the bankruptcy of such strategies through foreign exchange gaps, savings gaps, technical dependency, distortion of markets etc. are well-documented in the criticisms of the state in the Third World and the import-substituting industrialization strategy. The economic decline of the westernized state classes who managed the rent-cum-import-substituting model leaves large middle income strata of their societies without the perspective of being any more incorporated into the "modern" sector. These strata have to orient themselves to new possibilities in order to avail themselves of the small resources they still might control, such as education and small amounts of financial capital. In order to impose the retreat of a failing state sector, which appears more and more as a rapacious fisk, they have to choose ideologies which can create a powerful link with those whom the rent-based model has kept marginalized. It is obvious that despite their economic orientation to market liberalism, this link not necessarily will be supplied by an adoption of a market-oriented ideology or a pluralist political doctrine. The ideology has to serve the aim of maintaining support from the poor and of protecting the position of the middle strata, especially their property rights. The discourse about the tendencies to fragmentation has paid too little attention to these internal conditions.

It is not necessary that support from the poor can only be achieved by an aggressive stand against the "alien," hence the global system. If marginality has been reduced and agriculture produces a sufficient surplus, the Washington consensus' "expectations" may be realized through an export-oriented strategy which may even go with political liberalism. This is the probable outcome of the successful exporters in East and Southeast Asia, after many political conflicts due to the fact that those in power are not challenged because of their economic success. The marginal may have lost any hope of improvement through the non-market structures. In that case a predominantly exclusionary model of economic liberalism with elite-dominated machine parties may work as it seems to be in Latin America. Where the middle strata do not see any chance for economic transformation on the basis of their local resources and the development of their internal markets, they may opt for a political discourse of the 1776 and 1789 tinge in order to reopen the flow of external resources as seems to be the case in Subsaharan Africa.

But even where good relations with the more advanced economies do not hold out perspectives which can be used in exchange of political support from the marginal ones, the then available alignment on traditional cultural values will not necessarily lead to an anti-Western stand. The revival of tradition in the form of nativist movements which many call fundamentalism provides three advantages for political organizations which draw their strength from the middle strata: most religions were "revealed" or reformulated during the process of state classes of tributary modes of production threatening the economic bases of the farming communities from which they drew their resources. Property rights were an important element of the resistance of these farming communities. Marginalized and other underprivileged groups which have to be drawn into an alliance are heterogeneous with respect to their position in the production process. Any clear cut economic project has divisive effects. Any shift in values for community building from economic ones to other spheres of social life eases the task of building political support. Western political values have been used by the westernized state classes and – by the way in varying degrees – tend to have lost therefrom in attractiveness. As the constitution of the free individual was in any case a complicated process also in the West, this understandable manipulation of traditional values reduces the cost of establishing political support.

The use of cultural values for building political solidarity needs the "alien," but this alien must not be necessarily the West. There are enough pre-Western contradictions in these regions of ancient empires which supply aliens. Some Muslim fundamentalism may define itself through its opposition to Western civilization and this allows Hindu revivalism to have a much more ambiguous stand on the West. As well, the degree of opposition against the alien will vary according to the internal structures in the societies concerned.

Rent tends to destroy social cohesion through vertical connections. Its action on the society resembles to the one exercised by a magnet on a heap of needles. They are all well-ordered with respect to the power field created by the magnet with very little horizontal relations among them. When the power field of the magnet collapses, there will be no structure among them. The multiple links by which precapitalist structures combine state and non-state elements in a decentralized manner in order to provide barriers to entry in favor of the more decentralized part which operates on imperfect markets, and tribute for the more centralized part which provides for the required values (among other goals) have always existed on the basis of rent. The amount of rents which became available through the economic intercourse with highly productive capitalist economies has destroyed these fragile structures. The whole process of colonization in the 19th century can be described as a disintegration of these old structures due to new economic opportunities which were not profit. As well, the state classes of the so-called development state which rose after the economic crisis of the 1930's and decolonization have finally failed because of the amount of rent. This can be shown by the consequences of the massive oil price rises 1973/74 on initially coherent industrialization strategies such as the Algerian one (Benissad 1979: 47). The stronger the rents had been in these state-dominated systems the more the crisis of the state will lead to anomia, as these precapitalist structures have been more deeply destroyed. Where these multiple links between notables, the state, trade etc. do no longer exist, political leaders which draw their inspiration predominantly from ideology will prevail over ones which are defending economic interests of the classes they represent. The differences between Algerian and Egyptian Islamic fundamentalism may be quoted, as well as the difficulties of the Hindu nationalists to get electoral support from the poor in the farming districts in North India (Krämer 1994: 58–77; Carlier 1994: 21–57; Jaffrelot 1996: 245).

Hence there will be various strategies at the political level for movements with very similar economic strategies. These economic strategies will aim at supporting the middle strata without important transfers in favor of the marginalized ones. Success will finally depend on the potentialities for overcoming marginality without massive redistribution. There are some possibilities, especially if the capitalist part of the world economy should grow rapidly. The less this capitalist part grows, the less these possibilities, as discussed in the literature about the chances of new Taiwan-Korea models. Hence one can expect a wide variety of strategies of combining rent and subsidy with controlled opening to the world market. Leading capitalist countries will also admit encroachments on capitalist orthodoxy more easily from some countries than from others.

Such a system will be operated neither on the basis of complete integration of the world economy nor on participants consistently opting for delinking or autarchy but on the permanent research of an optimum mix of both. Two types of actors will be prominent: globally operating enterprises will be most efficient in cost reductions and hence in the race for profit. States are the only actors entitled to territorially restricted rule setting which may be the major basis for their superiority in extracting surplus in non-profit forms. The rent-appropriating state can provide subsidies. The territorially not restricted global enterprise will earn profits at a global level. Both can complement each other, if intelligently managed. The state is efficiency-constrained. Its capacity of appropriating surplus is, however, limited only by the productive potential, not by effective demand which the state can create itself. The globally operating enterprise can appropriate profit in line with its efficiency, but it is demand-constrained. The total volume of profit depends on net profitable investment and hence on total demand, to some extent even on the expectations about the development of total and sectoral demand. On the basis of these two restrictions, productive potential and expectations about future demand, and the permanent threat of consumptive capacity being below productive capacity, states can pursue the aim of attracting investment and increasing employment through their capacity to extract surplus which they may transform into subsidy and/or final demand.

Even if we assume that spending out of non-profit sources is essentially consumptive, different types of such spending have different impacts on technical upgrading. Adam Smith had already distinguished between enriching spending on industrial products and impoverishing spending on domestic servants (Smith 1976: 351). Nef (1958: 131), Heckscher (1933: 719) and Brady (1964: 177) independently have presented models of spending on rapidly democratized luxuries in which luxury demand propels product innovation and democratization of such demand process propels in turn innovation. Since Sombart (1913) military spending especially on military hardware is quoted as a means of promoting technical innovation in industrial production.

The combination of types of consumption, rent-appropriation and competition provides for varieties of outcomes where the most competition-oriented system will not necessarily prevail. This is largely discussed in the interpretation of the East Asian cases which aimed at "getting their prices wrong" (Amsden 1989: 14; Page et al. 1993; Jomo 1996) in order to upgrade their technological competences. The frameworks in which such combinations will occur are territorially constrained by the powers of the rent-appropriating element. This is the basis for what some tend to call the competition of nations. Where the process of allocating rents to subsidy for productive investment, of promoting the consumption with the best spin-off for technology, and of manipulating exchange rates and comparative advantage for the specialization on technically advanced goods achieves the best results (specialization on high growth branches and favorable terms-of-trade), the capacity to appropriate rent will be highest. As long as rent channeling does not lead to losses in efficiency and the Dutch disease trap, leading economies may maintain technical superiority.

Such a system will be governed by ambiguous goals for actors. Actors will lose in efficiency with respect to the achievement of any particular goal as largely described in criticisms of feather-bedded development-oriented public enterprises. There is an other implication to this: actors will succeed on grounds which may not have been intentionally pursued. This will appear for organizations such as global enterprises or governments as a lack of precision in role definition, in the choice between short-term and long-term interests, and diverging interests to be pursued in both time terms. Thumb rules will prevail. Wherever there is uncertainty and degrees of freedom, the representation of the future reality is the result of negotiating processes which, if conducted within organizations – obey to the rules of rivaling segments of state classes who pursue the increase of resources, influence, and prestige and, by the way, manipulate information.[21]

Together with the interaction between territorially defined states, which may tend to be fragmented or agglomerate with others, and territorially unconstrained global actors, enterprises and also non-enterprises, the essentially political element in the process of surplus appropriation and surplus allocation will make the system look very much as a feudal one with a multitude of interactions, overlapping coalitions etc.[22]

It is quite possible that the disappearance of sovereignty which at least provided an addressee for demands of accountability will be regretted. Sovereignty may be considered in its historical genesis as a precondition for the rise of democracy through a simplification of relations.

So the predominant characteristic of the system will be rent, even if profit continues to be important. Profit will be however not strong enough as to simplify economic and social structures according to the lines described in the model of a self-steering economy and an autonomous civil society which support a restricted state. Rent travels North, because the North has not been able to export its social structures into the South, essentially by empowering labor through the eradication of marginality also in the South (Elsenhans 1992c: 244–268; Elsenhans 1992a: 41–78; Elsenhans 1992k: 4–48).

The socially disintegrating character of rent requires resources of cohesion which will not always go with a civilized society. Obviously collective solidarity can be created by a variety of values, among which also those values, which constitute the basis of the civilized civil society. But I doubt these territorially constrained political systems will be able to establish cohesion on the basis of identical values. Some will establish cohesion on the basis of creating scapegoats and with this on the basis of rejecting the values of the civilized civil society which may be considered as characterizing the alien.

This is all the more probable because such a global system will experience continuing security problems at various levels with attempts to create

---

[21] The argument is given in detail in Elsenhans 1987b: 83–86.
[22] Elsenhans 1993b: 35–39. Reprint in: 1994e: 561–563.

hierarchies between states and regional leaders in order to keep conflicts from spilling over to the global level (Elsenhans 1992g: 21–26).

There is little probability for a global capitalist system based on a restricted role of the non-market sphere in the economy. There is as well little probability for the lacunae in profit-based self-steering economy being reliably filled by civilized elements of the non-market sphere in a permanent perspective. This does not exclude that the economically leading countries may retain more elements of profit and civilized society than less advanced ones. As well, there will be no clear return to a Westphalian system, as also for the use of state power simple aims as the balance-of-power are not available, and some actors will deny the liberty of action implied for states in such a system to many of the other players, especially if there are stable hierarchies and regional leaders.

The most likely structure is slush, composed at the same time of more consistent and less consistent structures, as it occurs with snow melting and refreezing under different levels of pressure and to different degrees.

The attempt to structure such a system by the development of the new rules for prominent actors such as governments or companies is not very promising as such rules lead to very different behaviors according to the structures of the slush in which they are embedded.

The alternative to such an uneasy situation would be certainly the eradication of marginality in the South which, through empowering labor in the South, would also reempower labor in the North and thus create the basis for a global capitalist system. If such a system comes into being, labor will also be internationally mobile just as within a national system. Low productivity labor in an advanced economy would have no longer to be protected against productive labor from areas with low marginal products and levels of economic productivity will converge. This will be no longer an international system but a worldwide national system.

I suspect that some will argue that this neglects the persistence of cultural differences between nations. I submit that these differences are probably not very divisive if they do not impact on the economic and social situation of individuals. As well, they seem to be very much class-based. Poor people cannot afford to obey rules which are anti-economical.

# Chapter 3
# Social Consequences of the NIEO: No Chance for Continued Reformist Strategies in the Center Without Structural Change in the Periphery (1981)*

## 1. Introduction

This paper is concerned with only one aspect of the NIEO, the export-led growth of manufacturing industry in the Third World. I have examined other aspects, e.g., raw material prices, elsewhere (Elsenhans 1976d: 122–129; Elsenhans/Olschewski 1976: 1–2, 8–17). My question is a rather simple one: Does export-led manufacturing growth leave unchanged the fundamental social conditions of the growth of the capitalist world economy. The answer will be negative.

The successful transfer of manufacturing production to low-cost countries depends predominantly on the growth of markets in capitalist countries. The examination of the consequences of such a transfer for world economic growth requires therefore some brief remarks on the theory of accumulation. In fact, the expansion of multinational enterprise into the periphery of the world system has to be viewed in both Marxist and neoliberal economics as an engine for world economic growth. Any pre-Keynesian economic theory of the capitalist economy presupposes that long-term equilibrium is achieved if surplus is sufficient in relation to capital employed. This is true both if one believes in the actual operation of the law of the tendential fall of the rate of profit and if one considers that this tendency is counterbalanced by opposing tendencies. It follows that the reduction of production costs – the purpose for transferring export-oriented industries to the periphery – is necessarily beneficial for growth because it increases profits. However, my research on accumulation problems in the Federal Republic of Germany (Elsenhans 1976c: 78–134) and on the history of the process of accumulation seems to establish the dependency of accumulation on the growth of effective demand. This growth is dependent in a competitive economy and in the long term on the expansion of mass demand. The development of producer goods is necessar-

---

\* First published in: Jahn, Egbert; Sakamoto, Yoshikazu (eds.): Elements of World Instability: Armaments, Communication, Food, International Division of Labour. Proceedings of the Eighth International Peace Research Association Conference (Frankfort on the Main; New York: Campus, 1981): 86–95.

ily slower, given constant real wages, than the decrease of demand caused by the displacement of formerly employed workers. Capitalism in the center has been developing primarily in the rather egalitarian societies with rising real incomes in England and, later, the United States (Elsenhans 1976b). I refrain from discussing the implications for accumulation theory. But I would like to suggest in this context that the realization of profit and the automaticity of accumulation of surplus value become problematic.

The starting point – that capitalist accumulation is dependent on the expansion of mass incomes – has implications for the analysis of the social consequences of the NIEO. I am not much concerned with the penetration of capitalist relations of production into Third World societies. I accept that any decentralized system of production which is oriented on increasing productivity will necessarily have some form of wage-labor and of market steering. Only this will ensure efficiency and effective use of crystallized labor, i.e., capital. Workers' control in the units of production has to be balanced by market pressures. This pressure counterbalances differential rates of growth between plants and branches. It thus satisfies the requirement of an average wage rate or average rate of remuneration for "abstract" labor and an average rate of profit.

I also do not care much about the problem of the nationality of capital. Of course it might be of some importance for the growth process. Nevertheless, both so-called national and multinational capital in the Third World accumulate rather slowly. And this below-average rate of accumulation is the consequence of the unsatisfactory structure and growth of internal demand. The demand structure is lopsided from an economic point of view. Its transformation would require political intervention. This would limit free enterprise and would require the backing of mass movements. Both conditions are opposed politically by capital.

My concern with the social consequences of the NIEO is principally about the types of mechanisms which eventually allow the metropolitan working class to continue to appropriate productivity gains. This appropriation takes the form of real wage increases and other forms of consumption, e.g., the amelioration of working conditions or of the environment. The question is if there are social groups or classes in the Third World which could eventually supplant the metropolitan working class as a social force capable of increasing consumption proportionately to the growth of productive potential. This question is closely related to my accumulation hypothesis, that capitalist accumulation requires the intervention of the mass of population against the lowering of their living standard. A capitalist growth process collapses if this condition is not fulfilled. This in turn leads to the collapse of the capitalist system, because a capitalist mode of production is best described as a capitalist growth process.

In this context I would like to put forward the following five theses:
1. The transfer of manufacturing industries to the periphery causes, directly and indirectly, a decrease of effective world demand.
2. The decrease of world demand cannot be compensated by the metropolitan working class and its organizations.
3. The decrease of effective world demand does not primarily hit the core regions of the capitalist center. It affects the less developed periphery inside the center, which is already less acquainted with reformist strategies.
4. The periphery's working class is not capable of appropriating productivity gains to a sufficient degree. It will therefore not be capable of supplanting demand deficits originating in the center.
5. The continuation of reformist strategies maintaining the conditions of growth in the center depends on structural reform in the periphery. But the political possibility of reconciling working-class resistance in the center and movements aiming for structural changes in the periphery is nonexistent. The final outcome is therefore an underconsumptionist crisis of the capitalist world system.

## 2. Decreasing effective demand through the transfer of export-oriented industries to the periphery

A capitalist enterprise is looking for profit. Profit (P) is the difference between the market price and the cost of production, formalized by $c + v$ (where $c$ is constant capital, $v$ is variable capital, basically wages). The spending on constant capital is considered as a fix proportion of the value of fix capital ($C$) (plant, equipment). A new technology is introduced or a relocation of a plant is undertaken if $c + v$ of the first technology or plant location is higher than $c + v$ of the second per unit of quantity ($Q$) produced:

$$\frac{C_I + V_I}{Q_I} > \frac{C_{II} + V_{II}}{Q_{II}}$$

Putting aside profits, this means that the sum of incomes paid decreases.

Now, it could be argued that this effect is matched by an increase of profits. But as simple macroeconomic equations of the type $Y = C + S = C + I$ show that if $S = P$ (that is, if all wage earners spend their money on consumption and all capitalists save) $Y = C + S = C + I = W + P$; $W = C$; $P = I$.[1] That is, profits cannot be realized unless they are invested.[2] Investment takes place if effective demand increases or if new technologies are profitable. They are profitable only if they fulfill the above inequation, i.e., if they diminish effective demand, etc. Relocation suppresses well paid jobs and creates jobs for low-wage workers. The effect on final demand of more jobs for low-paid workers is necessarily smaller than the decrease of demand originating from the suppression of high-wage jobs in the center, capital requirements being equal. Relocation may be profitable even though the wage bill is higher in the periphery if the technology applied in the periphery is cheaper than the one used in the center. But the difference must be smaller than the difference in demand for capital goods. Effective demand is therefore smaller.[3]

The demand created by imports from periphery countries because industry relocates to the Third World cannot match the diminishing demand due to the destruction of jobs in the center. Three objections can be answered in the following way:

- Higher propensities to consume of low-wage workers in the periphery than of high wage workers in the center do result in an increased demand despite a lower payroll. This difference exists, but it seems improbable that it has a counteracting effect given its magnitude. In periods of constant or even slowly rising capital output ratios an increase in the propensity to save of wage earners inevitably compresses the mass of profits. If the identities $W = C$ and $P = I$ are no longer given, then $I = S = P + S_W$ ($S_W$ = savings of wage-earners). That is, profits are equal to investments minus wage earners' savings. A rising propensity to save out of wage earners incomes raises the part of investment financed by long-term debt.

---

[1] $Y$ = net product, $C$ = consumption, $I$ = investment, $S$ = savings, $W$ = total spending in wages.

[2] Lerner 1938: 297–309. Some interesting applications are found in Meade 1963: 673. Schmitt-Rink 1969–70: 361–377; Ozaga 1964: 363–371.

[3] There are a lot of arguments which pretend that the small extent of relocation of the induced purchasing power of LDC's would prevent global depression, for example: Lydall 1975: 226; Hsieh 1973: 9–28; Mukherjee 1978: 100; De Grauwe/Kennes/Peters/Straelen 1979: 112; Braun 1979: 62; Schumacher 1978: 11.

Private enterprises avoid financing, refraining from investment and creating unemployment. Crisis due to oversaving out of wage earners' incomes in the center in the case of unemployment in the center will probably occur earlier than an increase of global demand through lower propensities to save in Third World countries.
- Multipliers in the periphery do not seem to be considerably higher than in the center, and from an income point of view, and given the lower payroll, they must be lower than in the center.
- Acceleration effects may exist. A host of investments are necessary when production is transferred to the periphery given its low quality of infrastructure and the lack of appropriate facilities. This may counterbalance the decrease in demand, at least for some time. Nevertheless, this is nothing else than the general tendency for the cyclical concentration of fixed capital investments during boom periods, possibly even local booms during a period of general crisis. The requirement of lower unit costs implies that the sum of cost elements per unit produced in the long run in transferred affiliates has to be lower than in the case of production in the center.

## 3. The metropolitan labor movement is unable to appropriate sufficient purchasing power to match the decrease of effective demand in the case of general transfer of manufacturing industries to the periphery

Empirical research shows a variety of reasons for foreign direct investment. But export-oriented manufacturing firms are mainly transferred to Third World countries because of lower labor costs.[4] Lower costs of environmental protection and lower taxes are forms of lower consumption in the periphery and can be assimilated to lower wage costs.

In a conventional Marxist and neoliberal view, the gain of profit due to the difference between market value and cost of production in the periphery and the center can be used for metropolitan accumulation and higher wages for metropolitan workers. This view is evidently compatible with the hypothesis that accumulation in the center is dependent on the expansion of

---

[4] Fröbel/Heinrichs/Kreye 1977: 158–195; Diebold Institute 1973: 14; Agarwal 1978: 118; Halbach 1976: 17.

demand. The specialization of the periphery on raw-material exports did probably support such a mechanism.

Nevertheless, this mechanism only functions if the rise of real wages in the center does not accelerate the transfer of productive capacity to the periphery to a rate which threatens full employment during a boom in the center. This requires that unit costs in the periphery remain higher than in the center for a substantial part of production. The part of production which continues to be competitive with low-wage production in the periphery must be sufficiently large to assure full employment at least periodically. This maintains the bargaining power of wage-earner organizations in the center. This was probably the case in the period of classical imperialism. Competitive advantages then were due to the natural endowment of the periphery, and not primarily due to lower labor costs.

Today, multinational corporations often transfer to the periphery the most modern technology in use or recently used in the center. With a few exceptions, rather small increases in the actual wage-level differences between the center and the periphery would endanger the competitiveness of important new branches in the center, for example, automobiles.

If the hypothesis that accumulation is dependent on the expansion of mass markets to create the conditions for profitable investment is correct, the labor movement in the center is caught in the following trap:
- If it increases wages in proportion to labor productivity ± changes in capital productivity, further branches are transferred to the periphery. This creates unemployment in the center. The wage increase required for maintaining full employment and growth in the center has to be higher than the labor-productivity increase (plus or minus productivity change) through the improvement of terms of trade between the transferred and the remaining branches of the economy.
- If wage restraint policies are followed, internal demand does not increase with productive capacity. Expansion investments are limited or even stopped. Unemployment further compresses internal demand.

A wage policy oriented on productivity increase accelerates production transfers. A wage policy geared to maintaining competitiveness with low-wage countries creates an underconsumptionist situation. Both situations lead to economic crisis. The traditional instruments of intervention of the labor movement in the center lose their effectiveness.

## 4. The impact of the transfer of manufacturing hits different regions of the center in different ways

If wage differentials are the essential reason for the transfer of export-oriented manufacturing production into the periphery, the already less developed regions of the center are the first to be affected (Dicke et al. 1976: 112; Fralon et al. 1978: 183; Lettieri 1976: 97). The regions with the highest per-capita incomes in the center are characterized by significant agglomeration effects: external economic advantages, for example, certain expensive infrastructures, concentration of highly qualified labor, communications and complementarities of branches. They lower costs which can be distributed to workers through higher wages. These agglomeration effects have the same consequences as differential rents due to natural endowment; they are in fact man-made transformations of the "environment" of production which no longer need to be paid for. Increasing wages therefore only gradually endanger the international competitiveness of the core region in the center.

Less developed regions in the center are characterized by relatively labor-intensive production which does not require such agglomeration effects. It is this labor-intensive production which is most hit by Third World low-wage competition. Workers are paid there at the "average" wage rate of the center. In fact, wages are rather low, but nevertheless higher than in the periphery.

The industry mix of different countries in the center varies greatly. Italy and France, and to a lesser extent Belgium, participated considerably in these labor-intensive branches, with important consequences already observable in these countries:
- A high proportion of industries suffering from periphery competition does not permit rapid industrial reorganization for lack of investible funds. The Italian textile industry, for example, is unable to rapidly develop extremely capital-intensive technologies to cut costs as the West-German textile industry did, one of the branches with the highest capital-labor ratios. Nor is it able to avoid being undersold by cheap Third World products on its foreign and internal markets.[5]
- Weakening competitiveness creates for peripheral regions of the center balance-of-payment problems and particular efforts to cut costs. One

---

[5] The squeeze of the Italian textile industry between the capital-intensive (high-wage) production of the Federal Republic and labor-intensive low-wage exports from LDCs is analysed by Balliano/Bartone/Mosini 1975: 49.

form is increased subcontracting which widens wage/remuneration differentials between modern, large-scale industries and small-scale industry of artisanal production sectors (often with modern machinery, financed by banks). Statistics show rather high and growing wage differences between branches and according to firm size in the periphery of the center. The most important social and political consequences of this structure are the weakening of the social basis and the political effectiveness of reformist movements in the periphery of the center because rising labor costs create accumulation problems here. At any rate, the reformist tendency of the European labor movement has already been weak in these regions for historical reasons. The peripheral regions of the Western European center are predominantly formed by countries where capitalist penetration has been incapable of transforming rather inegalitarian and inflexible social structures. Lacking such a transformation, the labor movements have been rather isolated and weak. This explains their predominantly revolutionary ideological orientation. Although de facto reformist orientations can be observed since the 1930s as a consequence of antifascist coalition and subsequent extensions of audience, etatist traditions proclaimed as revolutionary ones still play an important role in attitudes. In such a context, the balance-of-payment problem limits the possibilities of increasing living standards. If small-scale production of the household or small-factory type increases under this condition, labor movement policy will be less inclined to trade union action, but will take the form of direct action oriented towards a complete change of the "market" system.

The degree, to which countries in the center are exposed to the consequences of export-oriented manufacturing in the Third World influences the extent to which the reformist "social-democratic" orientation of the labor movement in the peripheral regions of the center is decreased.

This reversal of the "eurocommunist" tendency to a more reformist outlook is to be seen in the light of an already higher level of social conflict and a rapid increase of wages at present in the periphery of the center. The higher level of social conflicts in the periphery of the center deters investment and growth (Busch 1978: 195; Kasper/Stahl 1971: 149). Wage increases by the so-called direct wage-wage-relationship and an increasing "demonstration effect" within the European Community are higher than productivity gains. They deprive the periphery of the center of potential comparative advantages vis-à-vis the core region of the center (Boeck 1974: 108; Caesar 1975: 196;

Stahl 1974: 223). Both developments limit the possibility of convergence within the center hoped for by neoclassical theory, and further increase political and social unrest in the periphery of the center by frustrating demand. The cost at which social-reformist strategies will become effective for social pacification rises above the level at which the periphery economies of the center are still competitive on the world market.

It should be observed that the idea of converging standards of living through the economic integration of Western Europe is disproven by industry-level indices of industrial production. For example, the growth of Italian chemical production takes place mainly in basic chemicals of low value added. By contrast, the German chemical industry specializes on "high-value" elaborated products for which Italy exports the first stage of intermediary products. The same tendency can be observed in electrical appliances and textiles. Aggregated branch indices no longer permit detecting unequal specialization within the center, nor probably between the center and "semi-industrialized" countries.[6]

## 5. The Third World will be unable to resolve the problem of managing consumption and supply

If continued capitalist growth depends on the possibility of transforming productivity gains into mass consumption, the periphery can contribute to the management of productive capacity and consumption in one way. The transfer of manufacturing production for exports into the capitalist center has to radically transform labor markets so that shortages of unskilled labor arise. This would increase the price of that category of labor. But this is definitely not going to happen. In order to reach the per-capita exports of Hongkong in 1977, India would have to export $ 900 billion of manufactured products. The transfer of all industrial tradables from the main industrial countries (the Common Market, United States, Canada and Scandinavia) would not absorb the jobless of the periphery. This is an unrealistic perspective anyway (Elsenhans 1979b: 116–118).

Multiplier effects are rather low in the Third World for two reasons. If highly skilled workers are used in capital-intensive plants, the import leak of the multiplier is high either directly (through imports for a diversified de-

---

[6] This point is elaborated in Elsenhans 1978: 208.

mand) or indirectly through imports of equipment for a small-scale, import-substituting consumer goods industry. If unskilled labor is used, worker incomes, and consequently accelerator and multiplier effects, are low for lack of subsequent consumer demand.

Wage or tax increases in order to promote state-owned accumulation can easily be matched by multinationals; they transfer production from a country with rising wages/taxes to a country where wages/taxes are still low. Consumption will rise inadequately as long as the transfer of export-oriented manufacturing production does not create shortages of unskilled labor in the periphery.

If the described mechanism is working, the transformation of labor markets in the periphery cannot be obtained before crisis in the center breaks out. Instead of developing the Third World, the build-up of export-oriented manufacturing in the periphery will "at best" lead to the peripheralization of the center instead of developing the periphery. It will probably lead first of all to protectionist measures on a very large scale in the center.

These protectionist measures will deprive the periphery of the potential stimulus of export-led growth for the LDC economies. If export-led growth does not lead to full employment in the periphery, it nevertheless helps to create larger markets for developing industries in LDCs. With larger markets, economies of scale become available and costs go down. Export possibilities still create some additional jobs. Protectionist measures of the center therefore intensify LDC difficulties in industrial development.

## 6. Reformist strategies in the center require structural reforms in the periphery

A protectionist strategy for the different capitalist systems in the center does not seem to be very workable. Tariff and non-tariff discrimination against the Third World would have to serve rather different interests in the industrial world. It would require a "superimperialist" decision-making center in the OECD region, or at least in the different subregions (such as the Common Market). Germany with its technical leadership in Europe would certainly accept Third World imports of low-cost shirts for its workers, but France and Italy would have to oppose such a decision in order to protect their textile industries. Even in the case of an agreement on protectionist measures, competitiveness outside this or these regions could not be guaranteed. I refrain from further investigating the protectionist scenario which might eventually lead to a situation like the one in 1930.

Nevertheless, it should be mentioned that the degree of interdependence achieved at least between the European countries would certainly lead to massive unemployment in the case of protectionism, since this would imply a rather substantial restructuring of the productive system for which "factor flexibility" (different qualifications of labor) is not sufficient in the short run.

It seems to be more interesting to inquire whether there are possibilities of using the transfer of export-oriented manufacturing production to the periphery for creating conditions of growth in the periphery and the center at the same time. This would require that structural reform in the periphery would increase the price of unskilled labor – even if only slowly – in order that demand for labor created by foreign direct investors will be transformed into an expansion of the market for mass consumption products in the periphery. This would then either attract inward-oriented new foreign investment or allow large-scale production by national private or public enterprises for home markets.

This condition can only be met if existing labor is transformed into value-creating labor power. Labor power is value-creating if it produces goods which find a solvable demand. The periphery is characterized by the fact that the prevailing skills of the factors of production (labor and infrastructure) prevents full employment given the existing internal or external demand. Demand has to be transformed in order to bring this "idle" labor power into production. The content of value creating labor changes with this transformation. If needs of the mass of the population in the periphery are translated into effective demand, unemployed agricultural labor with a low level of skills would become value-creating.[7]

In order to create higher and potentially full employment in the periphery, radical agrarian reforms and a price policy for agricultural products favorable to peasants are necessary. This would lead to increased agricultural production by mobilizing the labor force for production and investment purposes in agriculture. These activities very often require unskilled labor and simple industrial products. Rent spent largely on luxury consumption would

---

[7] For an interesting discussion of the relation between distribution and value-creating quality of labor, Georgescu-Roegen 1960; and Elsenhans 1979a: chapter 2–4.

also be suppressed, thus creating a market for simple industrial products in the countryside.

This is not the place to discuss the political economy of implementing agrarian reform. But the argument that the most varied types of agricultural reform/revolution, including state farms or the Chinese way of development, were ultimately capitalistic does not worry me. In effect, expansion of mass consumption and all forms of the development of productive forces in the periphery is helpful for the capitalist process of accumulation in the center, even though it is not capitalists promoting these developments.

This shows the problem. As long as the center had a quasi-monopoly in manufacturing, it was sufficient that the metropolitan working class, either by concerted or by parallel action, transformed higher productive capacities into higher consumption. The difference in real wages between the center and the periphery is now becoming larger than the respective difference in productivity. This was an inevitable development. Central capitalism with growth through increasing mass consumption coexists with periphery capitalism, which lacks this essential attribute of capitalism. If this turning point is reached, the metropolitan labor movement can only avoid its decline in power and a subsequent peripherization of capitalism in the center if resistance in the Third World is mobilized, focusing on agrarian reform, planned development to increase agricultural production, and the creation of industrial plants for mass-consumption goods. Such an admittedly vital extension of reformist strategy aimed at structural change does not seem likely, however. Historically, the metropolitan labor movement has been tied to the geographically based nation state, the lone means of "counterbalancing unequal forces in the interest of welfare" (Cox 1971: 584). A cross frontier alliance between different labor and peasant movements would have to create a completely new institutional framework, one barely existent in the European Community (Piehl 1974).

# Chapter 4
# Globalization in a Laborist Keynesian Approach*

## 1. Introductory Remarks

Globalization, or the intensification of transborder economic transactions, has been dramatized by its proponents and its critics. Their analysis is identical. The transaction costs of all kinds of transborder economic operations have dramatically decreased. The costs of surmounting the traditional barriers of space and time have fallen to such low levels as to become virtually negligible. The world has become a unified marketplace. The protective walls for implementing national economic policies no longer exist. Those who do not succeed in offering the lowest possible costs of production will be driven out of the world market. Similar processes are occurring on financial markets. National instruments of macro-economic demand management are no longer feasible, as financial capital is mobile. Measures which do not please international financial capital are doomed to fail because of the flight of capital. National economic policies are either harmful or simply ineffective if they are not designed to remove the obstacles to higher profit rates. Capital is foot-loose, whereas national governments and labor are territorially immobile so that they have to adapt to the needs and strategies of capital. A competition state (Cerny 1999: 16; Cerny 1997; Hirsch 1995) emerges which is supposed to support business by financing part of its costs (Schäfer 1999: 18). New labor claims to be more efficient, inducing business to invest in new jobs by improving complementary sources of technical progress such as human capital (Albo 1994).

It is argued in the following article that this identity of analysis has a common theoretical ground in the fundamentally identical economic paradigm of Marxist and neo-classical economic thinking, and shares with them a common political view in the enmity towards labor availing itself of the market economy by means of gradualist reform.

Against the backdrop of this age-old alliance between anti-reformist radicalism and roll-back neo-liberalism, the need arises to reformulate some basic requirements for capitalist growth in order to show that the scenario of

---

\* Paper presented at the 8th EADI General Conference on "Globalisation, Competitiveness and Human Security: Challenges for Development Policy and Institutional Change, Vienna 1996 and first published in: *Journal of Social Studies*, 89 (July-September 2000): 1–66.

mainstream globalization theories does not lead to a dynamic capitalist world economy, or even to a capitalist world at all. Indeed, the prospect is of an underconsumptionist crisis which will lead to political appropriation of surplus, hence rent seeking. In contrast, the laborist-welfarist approach of maintaining expanding consumption is the only realistic approach for maintaining a free world economy and, moreover, can be realized in a peaceful, gradualist and decentralized manner.

The results which radical and conservative mainstream theories depict – the disempowerment of labor and a race to the bottom – are not inevitably linked to globalization. It is possible to avoid these results, and this, without an unrealistic withdrawal from the world economy or a big-bang-type crisis which some may call revolution. Instead, realistic, decentralized and gradualist measures can provide immediate results, and promote world-wide coalition building in support of such an alternative.

The perspective of globalization ushering in a race for the lowest costs of production is based on the pre-Keynesian interpretation of the capitalist growth process. Capitalist growth is considered to be dependent on the availability of resources for investment, being unleashed when such resources are available and with final demand adjusting itself to the level of productive activity. The higher the profits of companies, the higher their tendency to invest, according to the holy trinity of Jean Baptiste Say (1803/1972: 139), Lenin (1956: 54, 69, 283, 556; 1951: 32), and, of course, the bankers.

In this paper an opposing view is presented based on the observation that capitalism is not characterized by capital accumulation but by demand expansion, especially expanding mass demand.[1] Capital accumulation cannot supply the amount of demand necessary for its continued expansion. It depends on the growth of incomes other than profit. There is a link between the growth of profit and the growth of other categories of income. Thus, there are limits to the globalization process if other incomes do not grow. If the disempowerment of labor in some areas of the world system is not compensated by the empowerment of other social categories which receive non-profit incomes, profit itself is endangered.

---

[1] The various implications of the argument that capitalist growth is led by mass demand cannot be intensively dealt with here. Cf. Elsenhans 1983c; Elsenhans 1983a.

In the case of perfect competition, the producers of consumption goods can sell their products at prices higher than their cost outlays provided that there is income generated outside the production of consumption goods which is used for purchasing consumption goods. The only sector which creates such incomes without claiming resources from the producers of consumption goods is the investment goods sector. In the case of net investment goods production, incomes used for consumption goods are higher than the incomes paid to labor in the consumption goods production. There is a positive profit rate in the consumption goods sector which leads to prices for investment goods which yield a comparable positive profit rate in investment goods production.

Enterprises do not distinguish at their levels of operation whether the financial surpluses they earn are profits or rents. They, likewise, have no direct interest in promoting competition, but, rather, are simply interested in the best selling conditions, which may include monopolies on their part.

From the alternative of either increasing profit or rent, two possibilities emerge for the use of increasing wealth in the wake of globalization. There may be a tendency to increase market imperfections, with more and more surplus being appropriated as rent in favor of the privileged members of the world society wherever they happen to be, geographically and socially. This is the economic basis for the government-business coalitions, which try to limit competition (Strange 1996). The same surpluses can also be allocated to consumption without directly jeopardizing profit, even strengthening profit by encouraging additional net investment. Yet capitalist enterprises will raise the wage rate to a level equaling the marginal product of labor only if labor is scarce. At this level and on perfect markets, enterprises will still earn the financial resources which are required for expansion of the productive apparatus, but they will not be able to increase surplus beyond this level, hence to earn rents.

This article explores the possibilities of avoiding the globalization of rent through the globalization of profit. It is based on a model of capitalist growth which is compatible with neo-classical new endogenous growth theory as well as with post-Keynesian growth theory. The model is formulated in such a way as to minimize assumptions which may be controversial between neo-classical and post-Keynesian growth theories.

The following assumptions are particularly important:

- The ex-post parity of savings and investment, and, in the case of workers not saving and capitalists consuming only their "labor" incomes, the parity of profit and spending on net investment. Neo-classical economics is at variance with this formulation from Keynes only in its explanation of why capitalists proceed to such net investment: neo-classical economics expects investment to take place if costs of labor are sufficiently low; Keynes expects this investment to take place only if future expected aggregate demand is sufficient.
- The marginal productivity theory of wage formation: capitalists increase wage rates as long as the additional product of an additional worker is higher than the going wage rate. Rising mass incomes are not dependent on a political structure which allows labor to impose a monopsony on some or the whole labor market. On the contrary, work contracts are freely negotiated. Slave labor does not exist. The bargaining power of labor depends on its marginal productivity.
- Wages increases are determined according to the rise in average productivity, not according to the rise in physical productivity in a particular branch of production. Marginal productivity equals the average productivity of labor after adjustments of relative prices in the economy have taken place. This assumes, once again, full employment and mobility of labor – which may not necessarily exist to the extent neo-classical economics assumes.
- Wages depending on average productivity is an essential element of the autonomy of a civil society (Elsenhans 1999a: 23–28) because it allows labor to be constituted as a collective actor. If average wages rise according to average productivity, there is no need for clientelistic networks to emerge between labor and the state. In addition, the profit rate is maintained without government subsidies for enterprises, namely, through the net investment spending of enterprises on the basis of their future expectations of expanding aggregate demand.
- There is no completely elastic supply of technical innovation. Financial resources available for investment spending may grow more rapidly than technical progress. In this scenario, either profitability declines or investment spending is lower than potential financial surpluses. This hypothesis – which is not controversial – has considerable implications: full employment depends on labor's capacity to limit financial surplus to an

amount of investment spending compatible with technical progress. I will begin my demonstration with this mechanism.

On the basis of these general hypotheses, it is argued that the empowerment of labor in the present context of globalization faces four principle obstacles:
- In the advanced economies, increasing labor insecurity implies increases in savings and a resultant tendency towards stagnation. This tendency is reinforced by the fragmentation of labor into competing fractions, who end up undermining their own collective interests for rent seeking activities.
- In less developed countries, the transition to capitalism is undermined by marginality, which simultaneously caps internal demand and the cross-sector spread of productivity growth. This, together with constant population growth, implies mass unemployment and poverty.
- Because of internal structures in the less developed countries, sectorally limited productivity increases do not limit devaluation races.
- These three tendencies are mutually reinforcing. Weak demand in the developed countries undermines their ability to absorb the excess productive capacity of developing countries, which, in turn, comes back to haunt the developed countries in the form of ultra-competitive imports.

In this context, statist solutions which aim to "roll back" globalization must be seen as misguided, and will therefore not be handled here in-depth. Firstly, they are unlikely to work, since domestic policies alone cannot deal with the competitive devaluation of less developed countries. Secondly – and more importantly – the problem is not globalization per se, but its particular form.

In fact, the best way to empower labor world-wide is to do so indirectly through the deepening of globalization. What is needed is (1) higher aggregate demand in the developed countries (coupled with measures to lower the savings rate), (2) anti-poverty policies in the less-developed world, and (3) an open world economy, so that the two processes augment each other to yield higher wages and employment levels.

According to the argument that capitalism is not constrained by the availability of financial resources for investment, as investment follows demand, there are resources which can be used in the political strategies of non-enterprise actors. The scope for policies and politics in the globalization process is much larger than assumed by mainstream globalization theory and the North American strand of mainstream IPE.

## 2. The impossibility of capitalist growth without rising mass consumption

There are links between the rise of consumption and the possibility of profitably exploiting invested capital which force us to consider the development of mass incomes. The three elements which I will draw from in order to demonstrate these links are:
- Marx's scenario of an inevitable fall in the rate of profit and the impossibility of this in the case of an appropriate expansion of mass demand; (1894/1972c: 222ff)
- Bortkiewicz's argument that at stagnant real wages capitalists can only introduce technologies which raise the rate of profit and which therefore reduce unit costs (1907: 455–465);
- the empirical observation of a relatively low and stable capital-output ratio in capitalism as opposed to Soviet-style really existing socialism and the "mixed economies" of the bureaucratic development societies of the underdeveloped world.[2]

This implies that the power relations between economic groups – even if their market power may be enhanced also by political means – depend on the overall state of the economy. Workers are disempowered when there is unemployment. Unemployment may not only be the result of wages being too high, but also of demand being too low.[3] Even in times of prosperity, workers cannot raise their consumption beyond the productive capacity for consumption goods. With full-employment of existing capacity, capitalists can respond to further increases in demand by increasing investment and selling at prices which cover the costs of this additional investment. Labor and capital can be substituted in the neo-classical production function, but not at the

---

[2] Bergson 1992: 26–30; Bergson 1971; Polanyi 1960; Easterly/Fischer 1995; Myant 1989: 223f; Obst 1983: 63; Feiwel 1971: 470. On the implied exploitation by inefficiency: Elsenhans 1981a: 118–192. English translation: Elsenhans 1996e: 144, fn. 89.

[3] "As the dramatic development of the present economic crisis proves abundantly there is no denying the fact that the depression may under certain circumstances grow to dimensions quite out of proportion with the preceding boom so that it loses more and more its function of readjustment and degenerates into a secondary depression void of any function whatsoever except to test the strength of the patience of the people in enduring a cumulative process of senseless and murderous economic destruction" (Röpke 1936: 119).

macro-economic level, since labor cannot eat the output of the investment goods industries.

The implication here is that consumption basically cannot limit profit, as unintentionally demonstrated by Baran and Sweezy's influential work on monopoly capitalism (1967: 62ff, 178ff). Their interpretation of capitalist growth is largely based on demand expansion through the wasteful state spending in response to insufficient mass consumption in order to support profit. But nowhere has it been proven that there are any obstacles, economic or political, to replacing this state consumption with mass consumption, if we disregard the general argument about the political weakness of labor.

The support of profit by means of waste implies that profit does not depend on low consumption and growth does not depend on high spending on capital. The basic dividing line between standard neo-classical and Marxist theories of growth on the one hand, and modern neo-classical and post-Keynesian theories of growth on the other is the limited importance of physical capital accumulation in the latter.

The empirical facts support this limited importance of capital accumulation. In all of today's developed countries, capitalist growth was characterized by a rather stable, for long periods even declining capital-output ratio.[4] The rise of the organic composition of capital, from which Marx deduced the inevitable decline in the rate of profit and the ultimate downfall of capitalism, has simply not taken place. This is the result of the absence of capital accumulation in a capitalist economy. In a simplified macroeconomic model, we may assume a constant supply of labor and a constant rate of amortization. If the capital-output ratio is constant, as empirically observed, capital per labor increases at constant prices. The full-employment wage level increases in line with average productivity growth. If we transform this model into a model expressed in labor units with all prices expressed in fractions of labor supplied, there is no growth of capital nor output in the system. Due to higher productivity, the labor value of all products declines despite their potentially higher use value. The share of capital goods in total output as well as the relation between the stock of fixed capital and total output remain

---

[4]   Clark 1965: 7; Kendrick/Sato 1963: 974; Kendrick 1961: 166; Bicanic 1962: 7–28; Helmstädter 1969: 48–91; Kuznets 1971: 67; Gordon 1969: 221; Mayor 1968: 498; Fellner 1961: 58–74; Domar 1961: 101–114; Sato 1971; Oshima 1961: 22; Phelps/Weber/Brown 1953: 270; Gillman 1969: 45ff; Abramovitz 1989: 163; Lorenzi/Pastré/Toledano 1980: 159; Arrow 1962: 155.

constant. The stock of capital does not increase in labor units. Capitalists replace worn-out equipment with newer, but in labor units not more expensive equipment in order to fight the devaluation of existing capital stock which results from technical progress. The fact that the economy is steered by prices and not by labor values allows this devaluation process to take on a socially more acceptable form for capitalists, as their struggle to avoid becoming relatively poorer appears as a struggle to become richer. For most of the history of capitalism, in contrast to Soviet-type socialism, capital accumulation does not really take place, but only the accumulation of skills and knowledge.

The standard explanation of the stability of the capital-output ratio is not a point of dispute between the various schools: it is due to technical progress, which Marx also mentioned as a countervailing tendency to the fall of the profit rate. But this technical progress compensating for the decline in the profit rate will be shown to be the direct result of the limits imposed on capital accumulation by rising mass consumption.

In the debate over Marx's tendential fall of the rate of profit, an incomplete yet important answer was given by Bortkiewicz (1907: 455–465), which was later reformulated by Okishio (1961: 85–90) and then discussed in the English-language literature on Marxism.[5] Bortkiewicz showed that, as long as real wages remain constant, no capitalist entrepreneur can competitively introduce a technology if it does not raise the rate of profit. In a capitalist system, there are no acceptable technologies which reduce the profit rate.

This argument about the microeconomic behavior of capitalists does not, however, exclude the possibility that the profit rate declines, since Bortkiewicz does not answer the question posed by Marx whether the amount of technical innovation available at any point in time allows capitalists to use their investible resources only for technologies which satisfy the Bortkiewicz

---

[5] Cf. also Roemer 1979: 379–398; Bowles 1981: 183–186; Hunt 1983; Parijs 1980. Critics insisted on the possibility of a falling profit rate in the case of joint-production of goods: Funke 1984; Salvadori 1981; Bidard 1988. Renten (1991: 87) neglects devalorization. Schutz (1987) insists on declining productivity due to natural resources, but then the process is not caused by capital accumulation. Armstrong/Glyn (1980: 67) and Scott (1992: 179–193) introduce imperfect competition and lack of correct technology assessment. Kliman (1997: 46) introduces false expectations without mentioning that this would lead to devalorization of capital.

criterion. There may be more funds than technologies which satisfy the Bortkiewicz criterion. This possibility can be explored by examining the behavior of entrepreneurs in a capitalist economy in light of Bortkiewicz's assumptions. The process of growth is accompanied by the introduction of new products which do not directly compete with existing ones. The new product satisfies new needs (and this implies that consumption increases). The Bortkiewicz criterion is satisfied if the price of the product allows a profit rate equal or superior to the profit rate in old products. This may be achieved even if capital intensity increases. There is no need for any measurable physical productivity increase in the production of the new product,[6] but only the readiness of the consumer to pay a high enough price. Bortkiewicz cannot rule out that such a product is produced with a very high amount of capital, which requires a high amount of profit in order that the profit rate equals the average profit rate. New products which are produced in capital intensive ways may allow for Marx's rise of the organic composition of capital to occur.

Let us assume a stylized macroeconomic growth process with a constant supply of labor. The rate of growth ($y$) of total net product (= $Y$ = total net income) is equal to the rate of growth of labor productivity.[7] The application of the Bortkiewicz criterion to the new product implies that the profit rate ($\pi$) remains at least constant and does not decrease. We assume first of all that the rate of growth of net income equals at least the rate of growth of the capital stock $\pi$, with $y_t = \pi_{t-1}$. If wages ($W$) stagnate, profits have to increase more rapidly than net income, so that $p_t > y_t > w_t$, with $p_t > \pi_{t-1}$, and $y_t = \pi_{t-1}$, so that $\pi_t > \pi_{t-1}$, etc. This results in explosive growth until $W/Y = 0$. Under the condition of stagnant wages, the full employment of available resources with constant capital productivity requires an unlimited supply of technical innovation – which for various reasons (which cannot be discussed here) seems to be unrealistic.

If, however, $\pi_{t-1} > y_t$, with $b_t < b_{t-1}$, is allowed for, the Bortkiewicz criterion requiring maintenance of the profit rate can be fulfilled only on the basis of the following mechanism. With $w = 0$, $p \geq y$, and $\pi > y$, $\pi_t \geq \pi_{t-1}$ is possi-

---

[6] Indeed, productivity in the production of different products can be compared only by means of prices.
[7] The model is presented in detail in: Elsenhans 1994d: 422–426; Elsenhans 1995g: 194–204; Elsenhans 1986: 269–271.

ble as long as $p_t/\pi_{t-1} \geq 1$. $p$ approximates $y < \pi$ the more the share of profit in net income increases. The profit rate therefore has to fall at some point.

This inevitable decline of the profit rate seems to be the result of the limited availability of technologies which satisfy the Bortkiewicz criterion. It is in fact, however, the dire consequence of wages not expanding in line with productivity growth. The "overaccumulation" crisis has its roots in an insufficient expansion of mass incomes, which is temporarily compensated by the acceleration of accumulation.[8] It leads, however, to the decline of the profit rate and unemployment. Overaccumulation is not radically different from underconsumptionism. A stoppage in the accumulation process due to under-consumption is nothing else than capitalists realizing in advance the futility of engaging in an acceleration of accumulation beyond the consumptive capacity of the society.

Declining capital productivity and a constant wage rate are contradictory in that new products can be introduced only if real wages rise. The more realistic assumption of $p \geq \pi > y > w > 0$ slightly modifies the above result, as it leads to a more rapid halt in the accumulation process.

In order to accommodate the post-Keynesian observation on the stability of the capital-output ratio, the theory of endogenous growth[9] has introduced technical progress into the production function. The neo-classical theoretical structure can be upheld by making technical progress the result of non-entrepreneurs (such as the state) spending on innovation systems and households spending on their skill improvement. Non-market actors may be considered to spend on even less measurable factors such as institutions. Assuming that, by the forces of competition, entrepreneurs are in the best position to discover new economic solutions, there is little probability that non-entrepreneurs will raise the rate of innovations with inputs comparable to

---

[8] Even a neo-classical author has shown that if the economy enters a crisis, the return to a full employment situation may not be realised despite low wages. He refers to this as a secondary crisis, cf. Röpke, op. cit. Fn. 3: 90: There exists in fact a close connection between the fundamental ideas of the underconsumption theory and the overcapitalization doctrine [...], even though this connection may be difficult to acknowledge in the face of the unscientific formulation of the popular variety of 'the underconsumption theory'." Cf. also Hayek 1966: 140ff; Hayek 1941: 34.

[9] Romer 1994; Romer 1987; Romer 1986; Romer 1990; Pack 1994; Segerstrom 1991; Paqué 1995; Klundert/Meijdam 1993; Caballé/Santos 1993; Amendola/Dosi/Papagni 1993; Homburg 1995; Grossman/Helpman 1990; Lucas 1988.

those of entrepreneurs. In this case, the only reasonable solution to the problem of how to balance $\pi$ (the profit rate and the rate of accumulation of the capital stock) and $y$ (the rate of growth of national income and the rate of growth of labor productivity) is reducing the rate of growth of profit and capital to the rate of growth of total output, hence to the rate of growth of the available technical progress. Such a solution is consistent with the literature on Kondratieff cycles, where basic innovation leads to a rise in $y$ and $\pi$, which afterwards decline until a new wave of innovations takes place.

The conclusion of this demonstration is that growth in capitalism depends on the availability of new products which can be produced without increasing capital intensity. This implies rising mass consumption from the demand side. The observation of a rise in capital productivity in the case of economies of scale can be integrated here into the macroeconomic model, supporting the argument of increasing mass consumption as a basis of capitalist growth from the supply side.[10] Expanding mass consumption contributes to an acceleration of capitalist growth, because it increases by process innovation the range of products for which the Bortkiewicz criterion holds. On the supply side, the capitalist accumulation process depends on labor's capacity to reduce available financial resources to the amount necessary for financing those investments which are compatible with the Bortkiewicz criterion of maintaining the rate of profit. The expanding mass incomes which result from this, support the capitalist growth process from the demand side. Expanding consumption is thus a condition for capitalist growth in order to keep financial resources for investment limited.

There is an alternative between rent and mass consumption. The expansion of consumption can be rent-led or wage-led. Rent-led consumption requires gates for rent-seeking. There is no doubt that consumption out of high incomes can replace mass consumption, although it may limit technical progress. Rosa Luxemburg[11] rejects this as a possible solution to her "realiza-

---

[10] This is not to mention other aspects of the equality of income distribution and their effects on technical progress which, to my view, was first formulated by Strassmann (1956) based on the deliberations of Young (1928) on economies of scale. Murphy/Shleifer/Vishny (1989) rediscovered this mechanism for endogenous growth theory. Cf. also Mommertz 1979: 121; Schlesinger 1925: 121; Freyberg 1989: 59; Brasch 1924; Hounshell 1984: 51ff; Barth 1973: 63; Young 1991.

[11] Luxemburg 1923: 90f. I should mention here that the argument of Rodbertus-Jagetzow is quite similar (1913: 27–30). Friedrich Engels, in a counter-argument to Rodbertus-

tion" problem by arguing that elite consumption cannot grow with perfect labor markets, because capitalists will not tolerate elite, i.e., more skilled, laborers monopolizing their skills. Increasing wage differentials in developed countries would have to be interpreted therefore as a result of imperfect labor markets and inefficient training systems. For a long time, the dominant trend in wage differences in all capitalist countries was towards more equality.[12] The reversal of this trend should not be attributed to globalization, but to an inappropriate training system with respect to the requirements of technical change. An increase in consumption on the basis of higher "luxury" spending thus requires an easing of competition on labor markets.

There is a basic difference between an increase in consumption through rising mass incomes and an increase in consumption on the basis of the rise of other incomes. According to neo-classical economy, mass incomes rise with average productivity increases on the basis of scarcity of labor. This implies that labor in branches with below-average productivity increases becomes scarce. After part of the labor in such branches has migrated to branches with above-average productivity increases, prices for the products of branches with below-average productivity increases rise because of scarcity, so that higher wages can be paid in non-dynamic branches as well. Rising consumption on the basis of rising mass incomes is compatible with perfect labor markets. Any other rise in consumptive spending requires either a higher share of government spending or a higher share of rent. The capitalist growth process requires scarcity of labor in order to impose competition on the rest of the economy. The limited possibilities of investment spending in a capitalist system means that the condition of full employment guaranteeing demand depends on rising mass incomes which keep the economy near full employment, at least in boom situations.

According to my model, Marx's argument that capitalism requires unemployment has to be rejected. The emergence of a surplus of workers which capitalism is said to create is deduced from the perspective of an unlimited rise in the labor value of constant capital employed in relation to variable capital (Marx 1894/1972c: 221ff). It has been shown in this article that this

---

Jagetzow, clarifies that Marx expects the profit rate to fall if there are rising real wages (Marx 1893/1972b: 24f; Marx 1894/1972c: 15f). Surprisingly, Engels' ironic comments on Jagetzow are sometimes quoted without really discussing his argument.

[12] Fogarty 1959; Franzmeyer/Seidel 1973; Oshima 1961: 23; Svennilson 1954: 39; Chiswick 1971: 38; Dobb 1960: 44; Borjas/Ramey 1994: 10–16.

is merely a theoretical construct. Critics of capitalism who do not refer to Marx's overaccumulation theory normally quote Kalecki (1971: 138–141). Kalecki, however, does not exclude the economic possibility of full employment, but argues that big business will put pressure on the government to limit employment levels by not incurring a budget deficit. Two specific developments – mild rates of unemployment in periods of growth following the World War II as well as full employment with low budget deficits until the late 1970s – invalidate the argument that governments under capitalism cannot create full employment. It is usually argued that capitalists will not allow governments to do so. Methodologically, the fact that capitalists are the privileged class in capitalism would never imply that their immediate interests are identical with the conditions for stability of the overall system.[13]

## 3. Household savings and the welfare state

The argument that globalization disempowers labor and therefore forces high-cost labor in technically leading countries (TLCs) to exercise wage restraint is a banal one. Marx was the first to mention such a scenario when he reported that English capitalists were threatening English labor with the transfer of jobs to Belgium (Marx 1890/1972a: 700). As Belgium became a high-labor-cost economy itself, this strategy of English capitalists was obviously thwarted – by the same mechanism through which capitalism grows, i.e., scarcity of labor on the European continent.

Neo-classical authors do not normally argue that wage restraint is necessary in order to maintain cost-competitiveness against foreign economies, since the operation of the exchange rate is admitted, which will be described below. Neo-classical theory argues instead that capital is too scarce and that therefore wage restraint is necessary (Boss/Döpke et al. 1994: 38).

I therefore introduce into my model of capitalist growth a rising propensity to save out of household incomes, which will still be considered as being constituted only by wages.

---

[13] This point cannot be elaborated here. Suffice it to say that the survival of a social system does not depend on the capacity of one or more elements of the respective system to clearly define these conditions of survival. Humankind has indeed developed without Plato's philosopher kings.

A higher savings rate corresponds to the requirements of mainstream globalization theory as well as to current developments in major West European economies:
- it allows the replacement of the welfare state: future needs are taken care of by private savings;
- it grants enterprises funds for which, according to my model, they have to pay less than the profit rate. Titles for future demand are bought by private households at very low rates of interest in a vent-for-surplus manner;
- a higher propensity to save corresponds to the theory of tendential saturation of present household needs.

There is no need to further elaborate on the reasons for an increased propensity to save in order to run the model. What is to be shown is that larger financial resources – even if supplied in the form of private household savings where earnings (designated by the interest rate $z$) are minimal, with $\pi > z > 0$ – will not provide the means to overcoming the dependency of capitalist growth on expanding mass consumption.

Households are assumed to be able to save because their wages rise. Consumption out of wages ($CH$) is therefore considered as a function of the level of wages:

(1) $CH = f_{CH}(W); \ 0 < f'_{CH} < 1; f''_{CH} < 0.$

Savings ($SH$) of households are by definition

(2) $SH = f_{SH}(W); \ 1 < f'_{SH} < \infty; f''_{SH} > 1.$

In order to create full-employment effective demand, enterprises have to be ready to increase their spending on investment out of borrowed funds. As enterprises are risk averse, their readiness to borrow ($B$) can be considered as a function of the difference between the profit rate to be earned on additional investment ($\pi$) and the interest rate ($z$), their readiness declining with an increasing debt-equity ratio. The growth rate ($k$) of the capital stock ($K$), which is composed of equity capital stock ($K_e$ with growth rate $k_e$) and debt-financed capital stock ($K_d$ with growth rate $k_d$) depends on the growth rates of these two elements and their respective share in total capital stock,

(3) $k = \dfrac{Ke}{I} ke + \dfrac{Kd}{I} kd$

The ratio $k_d/k_e$ is an indicator of the development of the debt-equity ratio. Borrowing is thus a function of $\pi - z$ and $k_d/k$

(4) $B = f(\pi - z, k_d/k)$.

The growth rate of national income ($y$) is determined by the growth rate of total fixed capital ($k$) and the development of capital productivity ($b$), with

(5) $y = (1 + b')k$

The sources of investment financing ($I$) are profits ($P$) which grow at $i$ and $p$, and savings of private households ($SH$), which grow at $sh > w$. National income is composed of wages ($W$), which grow at the rate $w$, and profits, and is spent on investment ($I$) and household consumption ($CH$), which grows at $ch$. This model can be run under different assumptions, two of which will be discussed. Both are assumed to be characterized by $k_e = p \geq y$. Indeed it would not be very realistic to consider that households would be able to replace equity capital accumulation in a globalization scenario where enterprises enjoy oligopolistic situations.[14]

In the first case, we assume that wages are increasing in line with productivity. As long as entrepreneurs transform household savings into investment in real plant and equipment, the following holds:

(6) $sh = k_d > k > k_e = p = y = w > c$.

Household savings grow more rapidly than national income. As long as capital productivity declines (because of $k > y$, $k_t > y_{t+1}$), the rate of accumulation $k$ can be maintained if the share of $SH + P$ in national income increases, which is possible if the propensity of households to save out of their incomes increases. The rate of profit ($\pi$) on capital declines, but the rate of accumulation is maintained due to the continual supply of new savings which grow more rapidly than national income. The model can continue depending on the possibilities of limiting the rate of growth of consumption ($c$).

Under the condition of declining capital productivity, with $b' < 0$, and $(1 + b') < 1$, the following holds:

(7) $(1+b')k = i\dfrac{I}{Y} + c\dfrac{C}{Y}$

In the case of $c = 0$, where consumption no longer expands but also cannot further decline,

---

[14] In the case of $k_e = p < y$, capitalists would have to accept that their incomes grow less rapidly than national income and wages.

(8) $(1+b')k = y = i(I/Y)$.

In the case of declining capital productivity, $(1 + b')$ is by definition lower than 1, whereas $i/y$ tends to 1 in the case of a rising share of investment in national spending, as implied in the model. If capital productivity is declining, the supply of finances required for full-employment growth will be blocked when the limit of the decline of $c$, the rate of growth of consumption, is reached ($c$ may become negative).[15]

A similar blockage will emerge when $sh$ is fixed at the rate of growth of national income, so that the supply of investible funds will not increase more rapidly than national income. This implies $w < y$ because of $w < sh$. Because of $w < y$, $p > y$, and hence $k_e > y$. The rate of return on equity capital ($k_e$) is maintained as long as the share of profit can increase. With $P/Y$ tending to 1, $p$ tends to $y < k_e$, so that the process of accumulation is blocked before $p = y$.

The results of the model replicate the standard Keynesian growth models as formulated by Hicks (1982: 36) and Harrod (1952: 264f): whenever the rate of growth of capital accumulation exceeds the rate of productivity growth, the share of finances for investment in national income has to grow – but there are limits to this growth.[16]

These limits appear in two different forms according to business expectations. If entrepreneurs are confident, and use available resources for spending on investment, the decline in capital productivity, together with the rise in the share of investment financing in total income, will lead to a decline of the "marginal efficiency" of capital and hence the profit rate. If entrepreneurs are more cautious, they will abandon investment spending early on. The difference between these two forms is to be found in the phase of accumulation where the underconsumptionist contradiction appears. In the case of early restraint, a demand gap appears, without large investments in inefficient plant and equipment. In this situation, Keynesian unemployment occurs. When accumulation is accelerated so that this demand gap is closed, a decline in capital productivity becomes inevitable. The amount of accumulated capital which must be devalued by new technical progress is much

---

[15] In this model, all profits go to entrepreneurs. As the share of $K_d$ in $K$ increases, the share of interest in profits also increases. Despite the fact that $k_e = y = p$, the rate of return on $K_e$ also decreases whenever borrowed capital is remunerated to any degree.
[16] Stürmer 1968: 26f; Helmstädter 1969: 51; Klaus/Stahmer 1970: 106; Oshima 1961: 25.

larger, and the crisis more painful.[17] Rising mass incomes[18] are not only necessary for avoiding Keynesian unemployment, but also for preventing the threat of Keynesian unemployment leading to a rise in the rate of capital accumulation which exceeds the rise in technical progress.

From this demonstration, I conclude that maintaining the welfare state – with its redistributive system, where future needs are not to be met by current savings, but where the gainfully employed are taxed in order to provide for the elderly and the needy – is necessary in order to avoid an oversupply of financial resources which private enterprise cannot invest without endangering the growth process.[19]

---

[17] The reasons for the breakdown of Keynesian state interventionism are more deep-rooted. The tendency of a politically emasculated Keynesianism to expect full employment from compensatory state spending instead of rising mass incomes seems to be linked to this crisis, indeed, the absence of any discussion about state failure. Keynes' work seems to indicate that he did not expect state spending to contribute to productivity growth, but to the empowerment of labor and increasing mass consumption which was expected to launch productivity increasing private investment.

The introduction of financial markets provides a temporary solution to the oversupply of financial resources. Such financial markets expand based on the supply of new savings from enterprises and private households, as well as from a monetary expansion in the wake of credit expansion for the purchasing of financial assets. The holders of financial assets perceive the increase of their assets as an indication of the rate of return, independent of the dividends and interests paid out to them. A booming financial market will also influence profit rates in the real economy. Any investment in real plant and equipment whose rate of return is estimated to be low will be crowded out. The current growth of financial markets in the industrialized world has been far beyond the growth of plant and equipment and of productivity, so that there is no real counterpart for the monetary "values" created on the financial markets.

[18] The integration of Keynesianism into mainstream economics in North America, which eliminated the political dimension implied in the original Keynesian analysis of the possibility of underemployment equilibrium, concentrates on state-financed investment for launching production. Keynes was aware of the inherent wastefulness. He did not introduce state spending in order to promote productivity and, consequently, production growth from the supply side. Rather, Keynes considered state spending to be the administratively cheapest way to bring the economy back to full employment, where the mainstream neo-classical mechanism of real wage following productivity growth can again be put to work. Keynes never assumed that the state is more efficient in promoting technical progress, but that the economy may face a situation where entrepreneurs hesitate to spend on investments in technical progress due to a lack of final demand. Elsenhans 1997e: 285.

[19] Two aspects should be added without being elaborated here. The provision of products in the future for those who save today will depend on the future productive capacity of the

## 4. Blockage of the transition to capitalism in underdeveloped economies

There has always been a considerable tension in capitalism between the representation of the accumulation process in popular minds and its macroeconomic requirements. This tension has had no social and political consequences as long as the drive for higher wages has proven resistant to political developments. The same applies to the ideological content of the opposing forces of capital. Labor had long argued on the basis of moral demands in line with the principles of moral economy, but this did not create obstacles as long as labor was only able to impose shorter hours or higher wages, and not growth-impeding employment arrangements. If the marginal product of labor is sufficiently high, any political conviction, even on the part of major political forces, about the necessity of keeping wages low is irrelevant. Entrepreneurs will employ labor as long as its marginal product is high enough to yield additional profit. The self-regulating forces of the economy allow capitalism to be characterized by a dominant social class which thoroughly misunderstands the macroeconomic framework of the economic system in which it operates.

The condition for the emergence of capitalism is the condition of its growth: a marginal product in wage-goods production which is high enough to induce capitalists to employ any available labor in order to make profit. In this sense, the political struggles of labor in capitalism have never aimed at establishing the conditions for the transition and the growth of socialism, but at counteracting the emerging tendencies which try to transform capitalism into a rentier system. Whatever the ideological orientations of labor, its struggle, if it is efficient at all, will invariably have to maintain capitalism.

The main impediment to the operation of the wage drift is cyclical unemployment. With sluggish demand, not physical productivity and the physically producible marginal product, but the price of this marginal product under conditions of cut-throat competition determine the employment decision. The great drives for political organization and institutional innovations in the political organization of labor – such as chartism or the rise of social

---

economy and the propensity of future generations to save, as the holders of financial assets cannot use the funds necessary for capital accumulation for their consumption. If they should withdraw these funds from the enterprises they own, these enterprises would lose their competitiveness in comparison to newly founded enterprises, which do not have to pay for such liabilities. Cf. Hankel 1999: 2.

democracy in Central Europe in the 1890s, as well as the new mass unionism in the United States in the 1930s – have therefore occurred during periods of economic downturn. Capitalism rose in Western Europe when marginal product was higher than the cost of subsistence or, as in the case of England, when the political power of labor was sufficient to establish social benefits for marginal labor so that marginality would not influence the operation of the labor market. The English Poor Laws are proof of this (Elsenhans 1980a: 283–318). In all major capitalist countries, the rise of capitalist industry was preceded and then accompanied by a rise in productivity in essential wage-goods production, i.e., the agricultural revolution.

The requirement of a marginal product higher than the costs of subsistence and reproduction of labor is by no means a banality. There were many precapitalist societies with marginal product lower than the costs of reproduction of labor which, nevertheless, survived on the basis of redistributive mechanisms (Chao 1986).

As long as the ever-present process of globalization in capitalism extended only to societies in which the conditions for capitalist progress had already been laid in the period of precapitalist development, with marginal product being higher than the costs of reproduction of labor, globalization went practically unnoticed. Levels of globalization in 1913 were just as high as today, but did not create comparable levels of anxiety.[20]

The new phenomenon which has brought the current globalization process to the fore and made it so threatening is its extension to societies where marginal product is so low that, with the destruction of precapitalist redistributive mechanisms, there is structural unemployment.

This structural unemployment is the defining characteristic of underdeveloped economies. Structural unemployment was a radically new concept for economics when it was discovered by labor-surplus theories.[21] Population growth had previously been considered a source of economic growth and a numerous population had been regarded as an asset for any state and society. Today, everyone is convinced that demographic growth in the South is a major obstacle to development.

---

[20] Verdier 1998: 43ff; Hensley/Schwartz 1968: 89; UNCTAD 1994: 120–121; Theurl 1999: 26; Bairoch 1996.
[21] Fei/Ranis 1964: 27ff; Lewis 1954; Berry 1970: 280ff. For an overview: Schäfer 1983: 5–42.

Although the existence of a population which is unable to earn what it needs for its survival constitutes a gold mine of exploitation for private capitalist enterprises, the structural unemployment in underdeveloped economies cannot be considered as the result of any capitalist accumulation process. It pre-exists the politicization of the economy in tributary modes of production (such as the existence of redistributive mechanisms) and the emergence of a privileged but noncapitalist, centralized ruling class which appropriates the surplus, provides some services, and engages in luxury consumption (for example, its vast achievements in the arts).

Suppose we have an economic structure where the wage drift cannot operate because average-skilled labor cannot become scarce under any scenario of demand increase. Such an economy may be characterized by technical progress. This technical progress, however, will be limited to areas of production which do not increase the marginal productivity of labor in wage-goods production. As this model has been presented at length elsewhere,[22] I will only summarize some of its characteristics here for further demonstration. Such an economy is characterized by a branch which is important for the supply of basic-needs goods and mass demand with decreasing returns and where marginal product is lower than the costs of reproduction (costs of subsistence of a worker and his nuclear family). If there are no decreasing returns and a low marginal product, there is by definition no available surplus; at such low levels of productivity, any labor is unproductive. Consequently, there are no resources to provide for the needs of the marginal laborers. Marginal workers cannot survive and, therefore, disappear. Very poor societies may be characterized by a low degree of marginality due to the absence of demographic growth (because of a high mortality rate).

As long as the environmental costs of output increases do not have to be borne by new entrants, manufacturing is characterized by the absence of diseconomies of scale of output, as there is no non-reproducible factor of production. Non-reproducible factors of production normally refer to land. If deep drilling for oil requires more petroleum than the well later yields due to the depth of the reserves, these reserves cannot be developed. The image of the limits to resources due to increasing entropy is based on such models.

---

[22] Elsenhans 1992b: 111–115; Elsenhans 1992i: 7–19; Elsenhans 1994d: 394–405; Elsenhans 1995g: 195–200.

Labor produces food on scarce fertile soils. At low levels of overall productivity, the share of income spent on food is extremely high (50 to 60 %). Non-food items consumed by labor consist of products manufactured by this same labor, with its comparably high share of food in total consumption.

Let us assume that average-skilled labor only receives incomes which cover the costs of reproduction. The remainder of returns on production accrues to the landlord. The cost of production ($Co$), assuming that this involves only labor and land, is $Co = wL$, where $w$ is the wage rate or tenant income per unit of labor ($L$) supplied.

With the expansion of agricultural production, fertile soils become scarce (Georgescu-Roegen 1960: 32–40). Thus, either less fertile land is brought into cultivation or more labor is employed on the available fertile soils. Marginal product of agriculture decreases. Total agricultural product can be described as $Y_{agr} = f(L)$ with $1 > f' > 0$ and $f'' < 0$ because of decreasing returns to scale of output.

Whenever demographic growth is high enough for more average-skilled labor to be available than simply labor which is able to produce at least a marginal product higher than the costs of reproduction, there is labor which cannot be employed by a surplus-maximizing landlord, regardless of whether the latter is a capitalist or not. The existence of marginal labor obviously disempowers average-skilled labor. Any labor which does not command special skills can be replaced at any time. Average-skilled labor will for this reason engage in networks of patronage (Elsenhans 1995b: 141–142). In such a situation, an autonomous civil society cannot exist.

Only certain types of technical progress can contribute to overcoming this situation. Technical progress in the manufacturing of industrial products consumed by the surplus-appropriating landlords will lead to the production of more (in physical quantities) or better luxuries. Technical progress in industrial mass consumption products will lower the cost of agricultural labor and hence raise the threshold of marginality, thus reducing marginality. This is, however, only possible up to the point where marginal product equals the amount of food in the cost of reproduction (this condition would be fulfilled either with industrial mass consumption goods becoming free for or being denied to agricultural labor). Technical progress in agriculture may be characterized by increasing the labor productivity of already productive labor, for example, through the use of new technologies or new inputs such as water or fertilizers on already fertile land. It is possible that these new technologies do not require additional average-skilled labor. In that case, the per capita output of this labor will rise, but not the level of employment on this land. After the costs of additional inputs are paid, the higher surplus which accrues to the landlord will be used for more or better luxuries, with employment effects in line with the landlord's propensity to spend on locally produced services and luxuries. Since this demand is characterized by diversification and high quality standards, there is no incentive to develop machinery which will reduce unit costs for standardized and average or low-quality products.[23] According to the theory that profit depends on net investment spending, profit appropriated on a competitive market is small, despite potentially high surpluses. Only technical progress which increases marginal product in agriculture can eliminate the existence of a marginal population which had previously produced less than its costs of reproduction.

The model of a marginality-ridden economy presented here conforms to the labor surplus models developed in the Indian discussion (Dandekar 1962: 69–80; Sen 1966: 427–450) and the micro-latifundio paradox developed in the Latin American discussion (Feder 1967: 507–511; Sternberg 1967: 1–26). The model allows us to understand why there is the simultaneous existence of production surplus and surplus of labor without capitalist growth taking place, and therefore the emergence of the rent-based bureaucratic development societies of the South which are dominated by state-classes.[24]

It shows the essential condition for the transition to capitalism, i.e., a sufficiently high marginal product in agriculture to allow for scarcity of labor. The doubly free proletarian of Marx's theory of previous accumulation cannot come into existence without marginal productivity in agriculture being higher than the costs of reproduction. If this condition is not met, ruthless landlords may shed excess labor, which will then starve. But they will tend to restrain from using this method of biological adjustment to eliminate marginality so as not to empower the remaining labor force by allowing it to become scarce. On the supply side, each laborer will try to increase the size of his kinship-based solidarity group in order to maximize this group's chances of being employed by the landlord. Both of the main social classes

---

[23] This observation had already been made by Adam Smith (1976: 351).
[24] Elsenhans 1981a: 118–192. English translation: Elsenhans 1996e: 173–254.

in this type of agricultural system will contribute to maintaining a surplus of labor.

On the basis of such a stylized description of an underdeveloped economy, it is not surprising that precapitalist modes of production are accorded a much higher degree of wealth and sophistication than the more meager reality of poor Europe would have it.[25] It is, in essence, a revision of history by authors who believe that accumulation depends on resources.[26]

A precapitalist, so-called tributary mode of production depends on the existence of a surplus. The transition to capitalism requires any able-bodied worker to produce a higher marginal product than his costs of reproduction (Elsenhans 1997c).

Depending on its endowment with natural resources, a society may be characterized by a low-average productivity and a marginal productivity still guaranteeing full employment in agriculture. Such a society will have a low surplus population, as the amount of rent out of which marginal labor can be subsidized will be low. Such a society will appear poor but will succeed in its transition to capitalism more easily than a "rich" one.[27] The rich society may also have a high marginal product in agriculture. However, as there is also a high surplus of agriculture, the surplus-appropriating landlord will encourage demographic growth – even breeding labor – in order to avoid labor scarcity. This surplus will allow the landlord to finance a political and military structure which enables him to check any potential for labor rebellions. Marginality has to emerge, provided that average and marginal productivity of labor diverge.

Before capitalism has effectively destroyed all other economic structures, the world economy will necessarily comprise marginality-ridden economies

---

[25] I have insisted on this for theoretical reasons (Elsenhans 1979d: 102–106; English translation: Elsenhans 1992f: 22–26) by distinguishing two different types of technical progress. The greater richness of Asia was well known for centuries in Europe. Cf.: Lewin 1974: 198.

[26] Frank has now abandoned his original theoretical design: Asia lost because of "polarized income distributions, [...] constrained effective demand for mass consumer goods" (Frank 1998: 301). He barely saves the old paradigm in claiming that, by his own model, Asia was superior, and explains the rising mass incomes in the West by slower demographic growth. Whether this is true is not examined in his book, because differences in demographic growth rates do not establish the scarcity of labour. Otherwise, sub-Saharan Africa would have been the winner.

[27] i.e., a society where the rich are rich, despite the non-rich being poor.

where there is a structural surplus of average-skilled labor so that full employment and capitalist structures cannot emerge, because no skilled labor can get entitlement to income other than its cost of reproduction, whatever the possible increases in productivity of its own labor.

In its own historical development, North America – the place where today's political science and economic theory and discourse most often originates – did not encounter the same obstacles to the transition to capitalism which are created by the current situation of marginality. Marginality implies land scarcity with respect to population. In today's world, there are no longer substantial tracts of land which, in the name of Manifest Destiny, can be cleared of their original occupants (Stannard 1992: 151). To put it mildly, the North American pattern of transition to capitalism cannot be followed by late-comers due to the absence of "empty" fertile lands.[28]

It is therefore unfair to offer land-scarce economies solutions which are politically or environmentally unfeasible, without at least being prepared to ease their problem of marginality by opening up one's own, larger territory for immigration of their marginals. Allowing the immigration of landless Indian peasants into the American Middle West would be a genuine free-world economy solution and a true process of globalization (Krishna 1985: 30).

## 5. The new dimension of globalization: possibilities of unlimited devaluation

The current process of globalization is not characterized by an unparalleled intensification of transborder economic activities. The openness of today's industrial countries for trade and long-term capital movements has not yet reached levels comparable to rates before 1913.[29] In no OECD economy do long term capital outflows come close to gross national investment, as was the case in Great Britain in the decade before World War I (Deane/Cole 1967: 308, 322ff; Kenwood/Lougheed 1971: 40). The share of foreign trade in the GNP of West European countries is just now beginning to reach the levels prior World War I (Bergeljik/Mensik 1997: 166). The only indicator

---

[28] The alternative is ecological devastation, as in Thailand (Cohen 1983; Trébouil 1993; Flaherty/Jengjalern 1995), or genocide as in Tibet (Kremb 1987: 49).
[29] Irwin 1996: 41–44; Bovenberg/Gordon 1996: 1057; Gosh 1995: 126; Feldstein 1994: 685.

revealing higher levels of transborder interactions (short-term capital movements) does not establish a higher degree of globalization today in relation to 1913. With the gold standard still in place, there is no incentive for speculating on foreign exchange markets. Hence there is also no incentive for financial markets to grow on the basis of speculations on foreign exchange rate developments. The current increase in transcurrency financial interactions is a sign of insufficient economic integration in relation to the volume of international trade and long-term capital movements.

The truly new character of globalization in relation to the situation before 1913 lies elsewhere. It can be described as the ability of economies nowadays to achieve high sectoral productivity without relatively high-average overall productivity and without those synergies which today's endogenous growth theory so greatly emphasizes. Economies with low-average productivity are no longer confined to competitiveness only in income-elastic raw materials exports, but are also competitive in income-inelastic products such as manufactures.

To some extent, this might be due to the higher mobility of knowledge and technologies. However, the Indian experience with textile manufactures and railway rolling stock[30] and the Japanese experience in the late 19th century[31] weaken this explanation of globalization. Multinational enterprises are capable of transferring technologies into Third World settings and achieving levels of productivity comparable to those in the industrialized countries of the West. But in the 19th century, it was often sufficient to attract craftsmen and engineers from TLCs in order to catch up, although this solution was only open to economies which had had a developed crafts industry in their precapitalist periods (which was the majority of them). The Cockerill's can be cited here as an example (Möckel 1987: 14ff). If a new level of international mobility of knowledge and technologies were the essential reason for the new competitiveness of hitherto economically and technically backward countries, the question would still remain unanswered as to why such transfers of technologies and knowledge do not lead to the improvement of productivity in all branches of these backward economies, but only in the export-oriented ones and, to a lesser degree, in more or less protected import-

---

[30] Furtwängler 1929: 9–11; Bandopadhyay 1987: 9f; Ellison 1886: 31; Bagchi 1972: 332.
[31] Among many others: Tuge 1961: 95–100; Mauer 1981: 158; Saito 1975: 176–180; Kiyosi 1965: 227; Sen 1979: 519; Harada 1980: 330; Honyden 1937: 37; Saxonhouse 1974: 163.

substituting branches whose products have a local market in the form of the local higher-income groups whenever export orientation is not accompanied by social reforms. Thus, the problem to be tackled consists not in the extent of globalization or its too rapid advance. On the contrary, the real challenge is the too limited spread of globalization and its lack of transformative capacity.[32]

From the sectorally limited growth of productivity in certain newly industrializing countries (NIC), we can deduce that globalization is demand-led. Its limits, therefore, are also demand-based (DN 1998: 1162). The spill-over of productivity growth to non-export sectors is greatly favored by the expansion of internal demand, as the successful NICs have demonstrated by equalizing their income distribution through agricultural reform. The successful NICs have been characterized either by political separation from the geographical areas of marginality (the city-states of Singapore and Hong Kong) or by the predominance of a small-holder agriculture in the wake of radical agrarian reforms (first wave: Taiwan, South Korea; at present: mainland China, Vietnam) or internal colonization (Thailand).

Mainstream approaches in academia and politics, however, deal with globalization from a supply-side perspective. These approaches concentrate on the TLCs and the central question of how to maintain competitiveness. It should be noted that there is rarely a discussion if there are balance-of-trade deficits, as the remedy is simple: with balance of trade deficits, such an TLC would devalue its currency, which occurs automatically.

Take a country with high international labor costs such as Germany or Switzerland (Elsenhans 1997b: 1–7). First of all, any country with such high international labor costs and balance-of-trade surpluses is characterized by short-term outflows of capital, as, otherwise, the statistical and commercial requirements of equilibrium in balance of payments would not be met. In other words, capital outflows do not indicate a lack of attractiveness for capitalist production. Furthermore, the observation that German labor costs are high lends itself to an altogether different interpretation than the conclusion that Germany has an employment problem because its labor costs are too high. Germany's export sectors are so productive that the country's balance-

---

[32] One might recall Marx's "Introduction" to the first edition of *Das Kapital*: As in most of the rest of Western Europe we not only suffer in all other spheres from the development of capitalist production, but also from the absence of its full development" (translation: H.E.): Marx 1890/1972a: 11–17.

of-trade surplus can be maintained at high exchange rate levels which assure that the owners of financial resources can export them profitably. At these exchange rate levels, a substantial part of German labor is too expensive internationally. But a lowering of its labor costs in international currency would only lead to further balance-of-trade surpluses and, ultimately, to a further appreciation of its currency.

Checking the rise in wages will not lead to more employment due to the resulting currency appreciation, whereas the demand for home products will rise in real terms only in the case of low price elasticity of imports.

In a world of floating exchange rates, no country can solve the problem of insufficient aggregate demand by cutting its internal consumption without at the same time harming other countries. This type of approach is referred to as a "beggar-thy-neighbor" policy. Keeping wage increases below average productivity growth contributes to deflationary tendencies, both world-wide and in the domestic economy, and disempowers labor, first at home, and then world-wide (due to insufficient possibilities for additional exports from the catching-up economies).

The supply-side perspective neglects the fact that trade is dependent on comparative advantage being transformed into cost competitiveness through exchange rate adjustments.[33] It assumes that international competitiveness depends on wages paid in national currencies. Even the more lucid parts of German business now admit that the exchange rate, and not wages paid in national currencies, determines the international costs of German labor.[34] The national wage bargain does not influence international competitiveness.[35] Moreover, there is no problem of international competitiveness as long as the level of exchange rate adjustments does not lead to an economy's incapacity to provide its own wage goods — not its inability to buy these wage goods on the world market. This is not the case for any of the TLCs. With the use of devaluation for employment creation in branches oriented on the internal market, high degrees of dependency on imported equipment may, however, create balance-of-trade problems when coupled with eco-

---

[33] On the relevance of exchange rate adjustments, cf. Golub 1994: 307; Nef/Dean 1984: 10; Klein/Rosengreen 1994: 379; Sparks/Greiner 1997.
[34] Most recently: Mundorf 1998: 2. For further references, cf. Elsenhans 1996c: 26, fn. 1.
[35] For agreement between different schools on this point cf. Hensley/Schwartz 1968: 89; Schumacher 1993: 124; Kantzenbach 1995: 20; Flassbeck 1992: 20; Fels 1988: 135.

nomic expansion of the internal market (Le Pors 1979: 41; Lombard 1995: 371).

Let us apply the argument that any economy is able to achieve equilibrium of its balance of trade not by low wages but by exchange rate movements to typically underdeveloped, hence marginality-ridden economies which are characterized by a labor surplus. Comparative advantage as formulated by Ricardo (1951: 135) (and quite contrary to its disfiguration in the factor proportion theory[36]) implies not only that the economy which is more productive in all tradables specializes in the goods where its productivity advance is highest, but also that this specialization can only be realized if the costs of the immobile factors of production differ between the more and the less advanced economy. Differences in real wages may contribute to differences in international labor costs. But for the differences in real wages to be essential for differences in international labor costs, they would have to be proportional to purchasing power parities. This is, however, not the case. Wage differences between more advanced and less advanced economies are but a fraction of the differences in labor costs as measured in international currency.

Purchasing power parities of exchange rates can be observed between economies with similar levels of development.[37] The purchasing power of local wages in the catching-up export-led industrial economies of the former COMECON and the NICs is typically a multiple of their international purchasing power.[38] The transformation of comparative advantage into cost competitiveness in an technically backward country (TBC) is based on the capacity of the catching-up economy to devalue. Any policy of wage repression in the TLCs is ineffective against devaluation-driven competition.

The capacity of TBCs to devalue and to become competitive in a limited sector makes labor in the TLCs, outside of their highly productive export

---

[36] Where productivity is explained by factor endowment hence by capital per worker. The theories of endogenous growth and the theory of strategic trade have completely abandoned the so-called Heckscher-Ohlin-Samuelson theory. Cf. Krugman 1987; Krugman 1991. For a critique: Bhagwati 1989.
[37] Frenkel 1986: 640; Deutsche Bundesbank 1993: 51–56; Fortune 1985; Hakkio 1984; Abuaf/Jorion 1990: 172; Wasserfallen/Kyburz 1985: 657; Siebert 1985; Junge 1985: 435.
[38] Cf. Mundorf 1998: 2, who quotes an OECD study. Mussler 1999: 2; Yotopoulos/Lin 1993: 11; Chen/Gordon/Zhiming 1994; Tzannatos 1997: 2–3; Guillaumont-Jeanneney/Hua 1996; Lafay 1996: 948, 963; Narrassiguin 1995: 325; Pilat 1995: 140.

sectors and their non-tradable-producing sectors, dependent on the marginal costs of competing labor in low-cost economies, whose price is not only lower because of lower real wages, but because of devaluation made possible by the existence of a local surplus of agriculture.

Comparative advantage in a variety of products may have emerged at the start of the Industrial Revolution only because of differences in productivity growth across the various branches of the TLCs. But an economy can increase its employment in export sectors only as long as it can provide wage goods to the additional export workers, i.e., as long as it can either supply these additional wage goods from a local surplus in wage goods production or buy them from the world market.

There are three reasons why technically backward countries nowadays are able to proceed to devaluation-driven catching-up strategies: the aforementioned mobility of knowledge and technology, the increase in productivity (real or "artificial" through subsidies) in agricultural exports of industrialized countries, and the Green Revolution in catching-up economies. All three mechanisms remove the basic limit to devaluation which had long hindered the TBCs from transforming comparative advantage into cost competitiveness.

The greater mobility of knowledge and technology allows export workers in the TBCs to produce certain exportables more productively than before, so that their increased earnings resulting from a greater quantity of exports per worker allow them to buy more (agricultural) goods than before from the world market for their reproduction.

The increase in agricultural productivity in the West leads to an improvement in the terms-of-trade for industrial goods from low productivity growth branches in which, by definition, TBCs have their comparative advantage. Better terms-of-trade for these products in relation to agricultural goods allow the workers who produce these low-productivity-growth industrial products to buy more food from the world market.

The Green Revolution has increased the agricultural surplus of many underdeveloped economies. An economy which produces a surplus of agriculture large enough to feed all its labor can accept any rate of devaluation and even negative marginal earnings from exports, as additional export workers are able to buy their wage goods locally:[39] food from the surplus of local

---

[39] For limits to devaluation because of imported inputs cf. Elsenhans 1999d: 41ff.

agriculture and industrial goods from the local informal sector – which is supplied, in turn, with wage goods from local agriculture. The only condition is that the surplus of agriculture cannot be sold more profitably on the world market. High transport costs and trade barriers against agricultural goods in the industrialized countries are a safeguard against the export of agricultural surpluses.

There is one condition for devaluation-driven exports not to be thwarted by exchange rate appreciation: competitiveness being limited to a few sectors. If productivity spilled over to the rest of the economy, exports would become more diversified and imports would start to be substituted by local production. With export surpluses rising, the exchange rate would also have to appreciate, as was the case with Japan, Singapore, Taiwan and South Korea.

Therefore, the strategy of devaluation-driven exports will only be blocked if devaluation leads to rapid full employment. Higher employment will be the result of growing employment in the already competitive sector, of the diversification of exports, or the growth of internal-market-oriented branches which produce substitutes for imports. The diversification of exports and the growth of internal-market-oriented branches will be the result of the spill-over of technical improvement into not yet dynamic sectors, either through subsidy and rent in the absence of rising mass demand or through income redistribution measures which contribute to an expansion of the internal market. Redistributive policies and a market-led broadening of productivity growth are simply two sides of the same coin.

I conclude from this observation that only a rapid deepening of globalization can ease the pressure on the world economy created by the new sectorally limited competitiveness of economies with low-average and marginal productivity. Dealing with globalization requires that industrialized countries follow expansionary and not deflationary policies. These expansionary policies, however, are difficult to implement in the absence of full employment and with an already weak bargaining power of labor, especially if opposing views prevail in the scientific and political discourse.

As long as labor is not empowered in the TBCs – not by a rise in average productivity, but through the elimination of marginality (as, otherwise, wages in the export branches will not rise, despite productivity increases) – labor in the TLCs will suffer from competition, whatever their levels of real wages, because of high productivity advances in certain sectors of their own economies which provide large enough export surpluses for high exchange rates but too few jobs for full employment. TLCs do not lose jobs because of their incapacity to innovate; they are, however, incapable of maintaining in all branches of production the same advance in productivity over TBCs that they have in those branches where their superiority in productivity is greatest.

## 6. The transfer of the underconsumptionist/rentier tendency to the TLCs

The ability of marginality-ridden economies to transform comparative advantage into cost competitiveness through devaluation has three major effects on the TLCs. First, there is a general underconsumptionist threat, which is rendered more threatening by the type of adjustment mainstream globalization theory suggests.[40] Secondly, fragmentation of labor in the TLCs disempowers this labor and contributes to the intensification of the underconsumptionist tendency. Finally, technical innovation cannot check this tendency under underconsumptionist conditions.

Through devaluation-led industrialization in the TBCs, costly TLC labor is displaced by less costly TBC labor. The cheaper TBC labor might be initially less productive than the labor in the TLCs which it displaces. Multinational companies have shown, however, that labor in off-shore plants can be rapidly trained. Physical productivity levels in TBC production sites often reach productivity levels in the TLCs on the basis of man-hours, and exceed productivity levels in TLCs on the basis of man-years of labor supplied because of more hours worked.

As long as labor productivity in the new exporting economies only rises in some export sectors, without marginality being overcome, the export-drive does not lead to scarcity of labor and wage increases according to productivity increases. Even if the new exporting economies increase their imports, this does not check the underconsumptionist tendency, as the prices of these new exports decline. The purchasing power of the branch which has delocalized to low-labor-cost economies tends to be lower than the purchas-

---

[40] This point was made long before the globalization hysteria emerged: Elsenhans 1976a: 23–24; Elsenhans 1980b: 484; Elsenhans 1981c infra chapter 2; Elsenhans 1987a: 124–135.

ing power of the same branch before delocalization. Therefore, balance-of-trade deficits of the new exporting countries are not proof of increases in world consumption, since they may be the result of lower unit prices of new exports in relation to the unit prices which prevailed in the delocalized branch before delocalization.

Increases in wage rates tend to be lower than the increases which are required for clearing the markets for consumer goods and services. The mechanism of delocalization is based on cost reduction; it is manifest as terms-of-trade improvement between the non-delocalized industries in the TLCs and the delocalized industries. The rule of equilibrium, requiring wage increases in line with productivity increases, is complemented in the case of foreign trade by wage increases not only having to follow productivity increases but also changes in terms-of-trade. As terms-of-trade improve, wage increases have to be higher than increases in the average productivity of the remaining branches. If increases in the average wage rate required to clear product markets have to be higher than increases in average productivity, the number of jobs threatened by imports from low-cost production sites tends to increase.

On the other hand, wage restraint in the TLCs cannot ward off devaluation-based cost competition, but contributes instead to mass and, ultimately, final demand expanding less rapidly than productivity, which is usually stated as follows: productivity grows more rapidly than production.

Only some segments of labor in the TLCs suffer from devaluation-based competition from the TBCs. The co-operative conflict between capital and labor in TLCs is modified. Highly productive labor and capital in the highly productive sectors will consider the problems faced by sectors which are more exposed to competition from low-cost labor as problems of structural change. The implied solution is restructuring the production mix, either with public sector support for new training and industrial restructuring or by simply leaving the economy to its own adjustment processes.

The difficulties involved in the implied industrial policies for economies operating on technical frontiers need only be mentioned. As with any oil country, an economy which engages in industrial policies to upgrade its productivity with the aim of raising average productivity does not escape the contradictions of rent. In contrast to an oil country or an NIC which diversifies its export mix by subsidizing not yet competitive exports, the TLCs cannot imitate more advanced economies, but have to discover new products and new technologies. But subsidizing innovations can be difficult to regulate, because the enterprise receiving subsidies can always argue that it is not responsible for the high costs involved in developing something completely new, and that the commercial viability of new products and technologies can only be gauged in the future.[41]

The typical case of an TLC exposed to competition with low labor-costs and characterized by threatened sectors consists in capital and labor demanding subsidies with the possible intent of engaging in adjustment processes. The success of such adjustment is difficult to predict, so that there are no objective criteria for making payment dependent on performance.

The implied tendency towards increasing protectionism is strengthened as the once stable hierarchies of specialization begin to break down. The theory of the product cycle (Vernon 1966: 190–207) argued that a leading economy is able to introduce innovation earlier than a follower economy because it has relatively lower costs for the introduction of the new technology and because it provides the most dynamic markets for new products. The dramatic decrease in costs for overcoming the barriers of space and time render the market argument less relevant. The stability of the product cycle, however, is endangered primarily from the supply side. The theory of the product cycle does not deal with the problem of specialization on older technologies which faces the leading country despite its higher productivity in new technologies, too. According to the theory of comparative advantage, not higher productivity but higher relative productivity determines the pattern of specialization. According to the theory of endogenous growth, the complementary factors of productivity increases may be immobile between economies as well as between branches, as assumed by the theory of the product cycle. The integration of East Germany into the West German economy has amply demonstrated that knowledge and skills are highly dependent on existing production processes, and may be completely devalued even in the same branch when jumps in technology occur, and more so, of course, when factors of production are shifted to new branches (Klodt 1991: 99f).

Thus, the TLC, by necessity, has to have comparative advantage in those branches where it has a history of efficient production, whereas TBCs will

---

[41] The relatively backward economy therefore has less problems engaging in industrial policy, cf. Leff 1985: 347ff; Paqué 1995: 250; Hofmann/Koop 1991: 93f; Elsenhans 1992h: 24.

benefit from comparative advantage in new products where the role of learning-by-doing in cost reduction is less significant. Economic theory hence argues that there is an end to the product cycle (Cantwell 1995: 155-179).

An TLC typically reacts to the threat of specialization on old products by making an effort to maintain comparative advantage in new products through subsidies. The amount of literature concerning innovation systems and industrial policies can be cited as proof of this.[42] Such adjustment policies lend support to austerity politics, which further compress internal demand in the TLCs.

When innovation occurs in an TLC with low expansion of internal demand – and especially with private households saving – it will not automatically transform the pattern of productivity through adjustments in relative prices, as assumed in textbook economies. The new products which restructuring can be based on will most likely not replace old products which satisfy old needs, but will open up new opportunities for consumption. Their outlets will be provided, above all, by consumers with relatively high incomes. A restriction of consumption in the TLCs therefore inhibits the expansion of innovative production lines.

If we grant the assumption that labor employed in innovative sectors is made up of high-wage labor which amasses relatively high savings, the process of transformation even in an innovative TLC is further blocked.

Let us assume that the new branch $j$ of production which is defined by high productivity growth will pay wages which correspond to its branch-specific physical productivity growth. In this case, the rates of growth of wages and productivity in the innovative branch are equal.

$$(9)\, w_j - y_j = 0.$$

Prices will not fall if there are no savings in other cost factors. As the branch's products are new, they can be assumed to face a growing demand despite stable or only moderately falling prices. Expansion, however, is slower than in the case of more rapidly falling prices if demand is price elastic.[43] By definition, physical productivity in branch $j$ grows more rapidly than average productivity. For simplicity, we will assume that physical pro-

---

[42] Cf., among many others, Freeman 1995; Nelson 1993.
[43] In addition, in the case of new products, there are barriers to entry (patent laws, technological monopolies, etc.).

ductivity growth in the rest of the economy ($y_R$) is 0. Because $f'_{SH} > 1$, the expansion of demand from $w_j$ is lower than $w_j$. Only part of the wages paid in branch $j$ are spent on goods and services supplied by the rest of the economy and contribute to the growth of net income in the rest of the economy, either through its expansion or through changes in relative prices. We may therefore assume the following:

$$(10) \quad w_j - y_R > \frac{w_j}{sh_j} - y_R \geq 0.$$

The savings of labor in branch $j$ limit the expansion of the rest of the economy, which is, however, also a customer of branch $j$. The innovative branch $j$ with initially high wages does not expand as rapidly as it would if incomes were to increase more rapidly in the rest of the economy. The lack of decline in prices for the booming branch is not perceived as a monopolistic exploitation of the rest of the economy. Prices will tend to fall as long as physical productivity growth in the booming branch is higher than wage increases, but, due to $w_j/sh_j < w_j$, the pull effect on the rest of the economy is low. Whether the innovative sector can exercise a large enough pull on the rest of the economy depends on its relative size. From $w_j > w_j/sh_j$ it appears, however, that with private households increasing their savings the pull effect on the rest of the economy is lower than with lower rates of savings, even if the newly engaged high-skilled labor receives wages above the average wage rate.

Consequently, it is probable that the process of labor becoming scarce for non-innovative branches also faces a serious obstacle in the form of sluggish growth in the innovative branches. Low-productivity growth branches with lower-skilled workers expand only slowly, not because low-skilled labor has a tendency to become too expensive, but because at limited levels of income elasticity of demand for traditional products prices for such products rise too slowly due to a lack of dynamism in the highly innovative branch.

The textbook model of the formation of an average wage rate, where skill-specific wage rates differ not according to physical productivity growth but according to the costs of skill acquisition, is blocked by an insufficient scarcity of labor. Hence the fundamental mechanism for the formation of a working class in a capitalist system is also blocked. The underconsumptionist tendency, and not globalization in itself, explains why those labor movements have declined which had drawn their strength from organizing labor nation-wide for the equal remuneration of work, i.e., by transforming the neo-classical theoretical construct of uniform labor into reality, despite market imperfections (Pontusson 1995: 497; Delattre 1997: 3; Olson 1995: 26). Moreover, according to the model, labor in the innovative branch will be characterized by an only limited flexibility.[44] Wherever it is capable of closing internal labor markets (i.e., within firms), it will do so. The model implies decreasing flexibility wherever this option is possible. In that case, both firm-based incorporation, as in East Asia, or the breaking of labor's collective bargaining power, as in Reaganomics or Thatcherism, allow for the successful management of labor.[45]

The TBC's capacity to devalue and hence to transform itself can be increased by diversifying into new activities, which is referred to as upgrading the export mix. Public decision-makers will analyze their exchange rate policies from the point of view of export earnings in foreign currency. They will consider devaluation unwise when there is declining price elasticity of demand for their exports.[46] As a result, they may combine devaluation with export taxes or other fees on already competitive exports.[47] The practice is wide-spread, as demonstrated by the auctioning of quota rights for exports from TBCs to TLCs or special taxes on quota-regulated exports (Morkre 1979: 110–118; Takacs 1988: 41; World Bank 1987: 148). It has even led to legal disputes being brought to the Indian Supreme Court (Khanna 1990: 93).

There are more sophisticated strategies: when South Korea faced declining price elasticity of its textile exports, the government blocked the import of textile machinery. Textile exporters had to address the local industrial sector, which produced more expensive, less efficient equipment. The cost of equipment led to higher local currency unit prices, which could be charged on the world market because of the low price elasticity of these exports (Mytelka 1986: 258).

Such strategies are linked to the politicization of economic transitions. An TBC can tax its export sectors in order to subsidize industrial diversification based on imitation (Holtgrave 1987: 59–81). An TLC may adopt an industrial policy which aims at achieving specialization in products where

---

[44] Unemployment is a cause of hysteresis, cf.: Franz 1987: 321; Pietsch 1978: 263. Cf. as well the excellent criticism of: Korpi 1996: 1742.
[45] For an overview: Lipietz 1997.
[46] The rational character of their option is argued by Jung/Lee 1986; Elsenhans 1983b: 145.
[47] Kaldor 1964: 220; World Bank 1987: 98; Balassa 1974: 178; Katseli 1983: 362.

catching-up economies cannot achieve competitiveness at any rate of devaluation.[48] Both strategies will achieve optimal results if they are supported by external demand, in other words, if they co-operate with the segment of business which has the best access to external markets.

Multinational corporations are thus gatekeepers which can charge a fee. They can even impose the costs of capital on the host country which engages in such strategies, as countries will compete to offer the best financial conditions in order to attract employment. Japanese trading houses, for instance, tend to avoid committing their own funds to the creation of productive plant and equipment.

### 7. Politicization of the global economy may vary in content, as rent allows for political options

Globalization is not the problem, but, rather, economies characterized by marginality and only sectorally limited competitiveness entering into the international division of labor.

Marginality and sectorally limited competitiveness result in economies with an abundance of labor, whose opportunity earnings are lower than their costs of reproduction, being integrated into the world labor market. With perfect labor markets, incomes for unskilled labor in the export branches of such an economy cannot rise as long as opportunity earnings outside the export sector do not rise. The restrictions on international migration prevent these marginality-ridden workers from offering their labor in countries where their opportunity earnings would be higher. We thus have an imper-

---

[48] It should be noted that the employment potential of these branches seems to be limited. The number of employees in the fields of "electronic and electric equipment" and "computers" in the US was listed as 2,778 thousand in 1983 and 1,922 in 1994, with a total employment outside of agriculture of 102,404 thousand in 1983 and 127,014 in 1994: U.S. Department of Commerce 1996: 411f. For Japan, employment in the production of electrical machinery was given at 2,381 thousand in 1990 (total employment in processing industries: 14,544 thousand, wholesale trade 13,822 thousand): Statistics Bureau 1994: 289f. According to IBM, in 1998 430,000 persons are working in information technology: Handelsblatt, 26 August 1998: 21. This is a high number, in relation to the number of employees in the "EDV-Geräte, Büromaschinen, Elektro-, Medien-, Mess-, und Regeltechnik" branches; the branch has had a decreasing employment level since 1980: (in thousands): 1980: 1084.9; 1990: 1143.5; 1995: 866.0. Cf.: Görzig/Schintke/Schmidt 1997: 21–22.

fect but global labor market – imperfect since the costs of labor are not equalized according to average world-wide productivity. The world labor market is global in the sense that the sectors with low-productivity lags in TBCs always have access to average-skilled labor at its opportunity earnings in national currency, which are equal to the costs of reproduction of labor until marginality is overcome. The mechanism of neo-classical wage formation is blocked at the global level by competition from substantial segments of labor in the TBCs. Under the conditions of globalization being characterized by the integration of marginality-ridden economies into the world market for manufactured products, rents inevitably emerge. Rent travels west from the marginality-ridden TBCs into the TLCs (Elsenhans 1991b: 11; Elsenhans 1994e: 562; Elsenhans 1992c: 261–263).

In fact, labor costs are determined on the basis of sectoral productivity in economies with different patterns of relative productivity and different levels of marginal productivity. In the textbook model, these differences are adjusted through perfect specialization and full employment. In this case, enterprises in non-innovative branches which cannot adjust through productivity increases disappear (in tradable-producing branches) or impose higher prices (in non-tradable-producing branches). But according to the model presented here, neither the innovation processes in the TLCs nor the catching-up processes in the TBCs are powerful enough to create world-wide full employment.

Thus, globalization does not represent the powerful expansion of capitalism to a not yet capitalist periphery which it transforms to capitalism, as Marx expected in his Communist Manifesto, but, rather, the impulse of a capitalist system which is too weak to accomplish such a task, because capital accumulation depends on expanding demand which it is unable to create itself. This weakness of the spontaneous tendencies to globalization leads to the emergence of rents, made possible by the weakness of labor.[49]

Globalization therefore has to be "deepened" for it to become manageable. The economic basis for this deepening is to be found in the very rents which are spontaneously produced by this process. Rents are a surplus which, under perfect competition, can be appropriated neither by enterprises in the form of higher profits nor by labor in the form of market-based rises in the wage rate. Any rent creates political options, since rent can be appropri-

---

[49] As a well argued example cf. Rhee 1994: 232–238.

ated by political means. Neither class, entrepreneurs or labor, can block rent appropriation on the basis of economic strategies.

Mainstream IPE tends to present globalization as a mechanism which pre-empts any such political strategy. It shares the view, with Marxism and very simplified views of neo-classical economics, that capitalism will only grant higher real wages when threatened by political upheavals. If it makes concessions, it has to find other, more exploited wage labor to pay for the "labor aristocracy" which it bribes (Lenin 1977: 286–288). But capitalists do not constitute a monolithic class which uniformly sets the wage rate. If the wage rate is below marginal product, there are always capitalists who will try to make a profit by employing such labor. Capitalists undoubtedly prefer cheap inputs; the decline in terms-of-trade of the Third World well suited their interests. Yet the volumes of studies which concluded from this that capitalism as a system depends on low raw material prices and cannot prosper with rising raw material prices suddenly proved worthless when OPEC raised its oil prices, prompting international oil companies to launch an unprecedented drive for capital accumulation for the development of hitherto non-profitable sources of energy. In addition, capitalists will never decide to maintain a reserve of unemployed labor beyond frictional unemployment, whose level may vary. According to the model of capitalist growth presented here, the interest of capital in easy gains, be they rents or profits earned on the marketplace, and the macroeconomic conditions for maintaining profit against rents are not identical. Capitalists do not defend capitalism as a system, but, rather, their possibilities to earn money.

A globalization process which is characterized by the emergence of rents can certainly end up destroying the basis of a countervailing power to rent, i.e., scarcity of labor through full employment, which had previously existed in the national economies.[50] Yet it is misleading to conclude from this disempowerment of labor that alternative forms of empowerment are impossible because of a scarcity of financial resources. Hence there is no basis for the argument that rent appropriation in favor of laborist strategies wrecks the financial equilibrium at the global level. Moreover, the observation that labor is disempowered by the current globalization process does not support

---

[50] The literature on the race to the Calcutta wage is summarized in: Langille 1997: 29f. Cf. also Tilly 1995: 16; Balassa 1984; Broad 1991; Broad 1995.

the conclusion that increased capacities of capitalist enterprises for rent appropriation are an indispensable element of further capitalist growth.

Globalization disempowers labor on the basis of two interrelated mechanisms: on the one hand, the integration of marginality-ridden TBC economies into the international division of labor and, on the other hand, adjustment processes in TLCs which intensify the already existing underconsumptionist tendencies in the world economy. Although different measures for coping with new challenges may exist in TLCs, overcoming marginality in the TBCs constitutes the decisive breakthrough for a laborist globalization strategy. If marginality is overcome in the TBCs, the adjustment strategies of TLCs can basically focus on keeping their markets open for further imports from TBCs by promoting full employment restructuring processes.

The realistic character of a strategy for making labor scarce in TBCs and hence cutting off the otherwise inexhaustible supply of very cheap labor can be deduced from the neo-classical rejection of the theory of imperialism and the exploitation-based wealth of TLCs. P.T. Bauer criticized Marxist theories of exploitation of the South as a condition for prosperity in the West, arguing that high factor-incomes in the West are based on productivity and not on improving terms-of-trade to the disadvantage of the South (Bauer 1965: 16). There are no signs of productivity decline in the TLCs. Instead, productivity in the TLCs is increasing more rapidly than production, while TBCs are also characterized by productivity increases. Reform strategies are not blocked by the problem of the availability of economic resources, but a problem of creating arrangements where the wealth created through innovation and competition can be put at the disposal of the world society.

Attempts to focus on the question of how to best direct globalization are discouraged by insisting that globalization is a threat which can only be dealt with by solutions which are either too costly to implement or which infringe upon large interest coalitions. Among them, one can cite the return to protectionism in the West or cost increasing, so-called "fair" labor standards in the export sectors of the South. Export-dependent TLCs cannot hide behind tariff walls. Artificially high labor costs in TBCs are not enforceable in an age of international sovereignty, nor do they tackle the problem of a low marginal product of labor. Moreover, the argument that the problem can only be solved if wage rates in the TBCs are comparable to the ones in the TLCs is not pertinent. As long as low wage rates increase in line with average productivity increases, low international costs of labor in the catching-up economies will be compatible with full employment in the TLCs.

The view that large-scale unemployment in the South precludes a strategy of overcoming marginality also has to be examined more closely. This argument is usually proposed together with predictions of the (very high) costs involved in creating the jobs required to overcome unemployment in the often protected and mostly inefficient modern sectors of the economies of the TBCs. Once more, the experience of growth processes in the TBCs demonstrates that the same mechanisms are at work here as in the model of capitalist growth of TLCs presented in this article. Investment is self-financing provided there is sufficient effective demand which creates incentives for local entrepreneurs to invest in their businesses. Even informal systems of financing such as the rotating credit association will lead to the creation of such investments in TBCs. Such local institutions for creating credit exist in extremely diverse cultural environments.[51]

The struggle over the use of rents is, of course, a political one. Political struggles are influenced by the perception of possible strategies; ideas matter. Therefore, the argument that strategies exist which allow dealing with marginality is an important one. Such strategies do not need to overcome low productivity through massive investments or to tackle marginality instantly in the whole of the underdeveloped world, nor are they necessarily incompatible with the interests of powerful lobbies which would render their implementation impossible.

The starting point is such that, with the present levels of marginality, the export drives of marginality-ridden economies will prove too weak for the short or medium-term elimination of marginality in the TBCs. The amount of marginal labor is simply too large to be absorbed by increasing import demand in the TLCs. Export drives therefore have to be combined with internal measures aimed at increasing employment through higher internal purchasing power.

If there are no possibilities of co-operation between TLCs and TBCs to implement social and economic reforms to ease the impact of marginality on

---

[51] For example: Geertz 1962; Alila 1998; Brink/Chavas 1997; Gentil 1996: 123; Levenson/Bastey 1996: 60; Anderson 1966; Bouman 1995; Schmidt 1986: 273; Shanmugan 1991: 210ff; Dijk 1983; Fei 1939: 279.

the labor markets of TBCs, TLCs would still be able to promote the absorption of marginal labor by creating an artificial export sector in the TBCs which would not disempower their own labor, because it would not produce goods which substitute TLC goods. This sector could engage in an economic activity which produces otherwise worthless goods. In discussing poverty eradication strategies for Bangladesh, I suggested that if the receptiveness of the local anti-poverty program administration is too low to expect any reasonable chance of success, donors might agree on a special kind of commodity money which, in the case of Bangladesh, would have the specific weight of water and could only be collected in a labor-intensive manner (Elsenhans 1991c: 281–284). The donors would announce that this money can be exchanged in Dhaka and other places at a rate which insures that the average collection meets the costs of satisfying the basic material needs of a poor worker and his family. This money would be dropped from helicopters in the remotest part of the country.

The poor would collect the money and exchange it under conditions of free competition in return for a basket of commodities, which would for the most part consist of foodstuffs and simple manufactured goods. As a result, labor incomes at the lower levels would become more or less stable. In order to increase their incomes, manufacturers and farmers would introduce innovations, and at a favorable exchange rate would order appropriate technology.

Through the controlled build-up of such a "gatherer economy," the poverty-ridden elements of the population would be elevated to an income level which is high enough to ensure the satisfaction of basic needs. The multiplier and accelerator effects of the newly created demand would be substantial due to the low propensity to import for direct consumption and for the indirect consumption in the form of equipment and inputs. Even though this type of aid is initially directed solely at increasing consumption, it generates investment in that producers holding assets demand new investment goods to increase their own incomes.

The one billion or so poor of the lowest income category – in this case, the lowest quintile – have an average per capita income of $100 per year, which is about two-thirds of the average income of the second lowest quintile. Uplifting the lowest quintile to the next higher level would require annual spending of about $50 billion for the artificial industry. This amount roughly corresponds to the annual concessional aid disbursements of DAC members, and is much less than the annual transfers from West Germany to East Germany. The latter example demonstrates that an inflationary danger for the TLCs can be dismissed.

Agricultural reforms are another mechanism for tackling marginality. A more egalitarian distribution of land in typical marginality-ridden economies will lead to a decline in marketable surplus. If efficient in easing marginality, land reform leads to "overcrowded" farms where marginal product is low. With an egalitarian agrarian reform, marginal labor is incorporated into the farm and is available as long as there are not better opportunities for earning incomes outside the farm. The farmers already achieve a high volume of output by combining only part of their available labor time with their scarce resource, fertile farm land. As long as this output is not sufficient for their survival, additional labor time with a low marginal product yet still higher than zero will be employed. The farmers will also offer their labor for industrial activities if the purchasing power of this off-farm labor allows them to buy more food than they can produce themselves with their own marginal labor on their farms (Dasgupta/Ray 1987: 177–188; Elsenhans 1979a: 559–562). Whenever there are more efficient farmers who produce food more cheaply than the average farmer, the less efficient farmers will engage in industrial activities, as their own food costs are higher, relative to non-food products, than for the more efficient farmer. Whereas any laborer has to earn a daily wage which covers his daily costs, off-farm labor has to earn only as much as the opportunity earnings of marginal labor on the farm, because part of the farm work is highly productive. The development of industry is subsidized and finds a market because rent from the already highly productive farm work is simultaneously channeled into mass consumption. This pattern of utilizing rent allows for this rent to support innovation through the promotion of appropriate technology, with profit emerging on the basis of spending on such investment goods. The mechanism put into effect here of supporting the poor from rent is the same mechanism at the basis of the English Poor Laws (Elsenhans 1992d).

NGOs merely constitute another form of channeling rents into consumption of the poor (Elsenhans 1995d: 156–158). They may certainly pursue other aims as well, such as transforming the worldviews of their target groups. Economically, they channel rents to the poor because, by nature of their size, they are much too small to devise or even implement large-scale industrial projects which aim at improving productivity in other economic sectors. NGOs are part of the rentier economy. As far as membership and even outlook are concerned, they do not greatly differ from the old state classes. The difference is that they are unable to directly proceed to wasteful investment, and can thus contribute to strengthening a demand-side-driven process of capitalist growth.

The three examples outlined above (an artificial industry, agricultural reforms and NGOs) show that tackling marginality can begin locally without having to arrive at a world-wide consensus. Such strategies can be managed decentrally. They are not incongruous with major political developments in the South. They are even compatible with the views of fundamentalist movements, which in terms of their promotion of small-scale industry and redistributive measures are not so different from Western-style NGOs. Coalitions for their implementation can initially be built up at the local level, and can spread elsewhere by imitation and co-optation, as their local success does not depend on support from elsewhere.

Presenting two scenarios of the increasing political dimension of the world economy – the briefly sketched intensification of business-government coalitions fuelled by rent, and the channeling of rent into overcoming marginality by political means – demonstrates the importance for IPE to choose an appropriate economic paradigm. IPE cannot avoid being descriptive or moralistic (and, thus, politically irrelevant) if it does not concede the embeddedness of capitalism in a power structure favorable to labor. The relevance of this power structure has rarely been discussed with respect to the TLCs' historical transition to capitalism, because this transition would simply not have taken place without labor which produced more than its costs of reproduction and hence was scarce. Marx's doubly free proletarian could not have existed without a marginal product above his costs of reproduction, as he would have otherwise had to engage in relations of clientelistic dependence, possibly even slavery (such as debt patronage). With the transfer of capitalism to economies which are not characterized by this condition, the possibility emerges that there are sectorally competitive economies which depend on absorptive external markets for their products until they are able to overcome marginality.

The condition of every worker being entitled at least to his costs of reproduction can be achieved by appropriate political strategies. Their main goal must be to tame the rent which emerges in the course of the transition process. Not addressing this issue at the global level will invariably induce labor in all walks of the global system to engage in nationalistic strategies, which in most cases will be self-defeating.

In the Keynesian paradigm, full employment is possible with the predominance of market relations provided that the empowerment of labor is guaranteed world-wide by the elimination of widespread marginal labor. It is therefore a reformulated Keynesian perspective like the one outlined here which will allow reaping the fruits of globalization.

Debunking the myth of globalization and a careful analysis of its specific, harmful features are more relevant for making the process manageable than focusing on its harmful, immediate results. IPE cannot achieve this goal by continuing to base itself on economic paradigms which fail to acknowledge the importance of politics. The situation has numerous parallels to the speculative debates on the chances of labor succeeding in nationally constrained reformist political activity in previous history. The same pre-Keynesian paradigms which, at present, mourn the process of globalization argued earlier that labor's activity is irrelevant: the Marxists claimed that reforms are ultimately impossible due to the necessity of maintaining the profit rate (Müller/Neusüß 1970: 33), whereas neo-classical economists argued that "reforms" (among others, rising wages) are the automatic result of accumulation and productivity growth, thus failing to consider that their own paradigm can only become operative if labor succeeds in making itself scarce.

By not following Marxism or neo-classical advice, the Western working classes have created the Western welfare state as the basis for capitalist growth. They were able to do so because their organization as a collective actor was based on their empowerment. They did not look for more complex strategies, because an important enabling mechanism had already been established through high levels of marginal productivity. In order to preserve its world-wide empowerment, this labor has to contribute to the empowerment of labor in marginality-ridden economies where a high level of marginal productivity has not yet been achieved. The task is much more manageable than more radical and more mainstream economics or the various approaches of IPE would suggest.

## List of Symbols

| | |
|---|---|
| $A, a$ | Labor and its growth rate |
| $f_B = (\Pi - z, k_d/k) L$ | Absorption of household savings by entrepreneurs as a function of the profit rate $\Pi$, the interest rate $z$, and the share of borrowed funds in investment spending |
| $CH, ch$ | Household consumption and its growth rate |
| $Co$ | Costs of production |
| $TBC$ | Technically backward country |
| $TLC$ | Technically leading country |
| $I, i$ | Investment and its growth rate |
| $K, k$ | Capital stock (net) and its growth rate |
| $K_d, k_d$ | Capital stock financed by the investment of private households in enterprises and its growth rate |
| $K_e, k_e$ | Capital stock financed and owned by capitalist enterprises and its growth rate |
| $L$ | Labor |
| $P, p$ | Profit and its growth rate |
| $SH, sh$ | Household savings and their growth rate |
| $W, w$ | Wages and salaries and their growth rate |
| $Y, y$ | Net product/net income and its growth rate |
| $Y_{agr}$ | Net output of agriculture |
| $Y_R$ | Net output of the rest of the economy |
| $Z, z$ | Interest and its growth rate |
| $\Pi$ | Profit rate $P/K$ |

# Chapter 5
# Productivity, Wages, Profits, and Exchange Rates in an Era of Globalization*

Globalization – the reduction of transaction costs for the flow of goods and services, investment and short-term capital across national borders – is said to deprive the "nation-state" of its capacity to engage in economic intervention except where this intervention increases the economy's competitiveness. The "competition state" is said to replace the welfare state (Cerny 1999: 16; Cerny 1997; Hirsch 1995).

The great majority of the population of the industrialized world feels uneasy about globalization or even fears it. In contrast, in the other great period of globalization, the worldwide expansion of capital under the banner of imperialism, a "revolutionary" labor movements not only submitted to the demands of capital, but even considered imperialism to be a civilizational process (Schorske 1965: 79), or viewed the "latest stage of imperialism" as preparing the way for the transition to socialism.[1] Thus, the reactions to globalization in two different historical periods have been different, notwithstanding the current globalization drive with respect to trade and long-term investment only in the 1980s regained a comparable level to the period before World War I.[2]

The much larger short-term capital movements on financial markets are not proof of a high degree of internationalization, but, rather, of a low one (Kregel 1994; Helleiner 1994; Epstein 1996). Most international financial transactions today are short-term and based on predictions of movements in foreign exchange rates. In a world economy where national currencies were linked to the international costs of production of a highly uniform commodity with nearly no transaction costs for its trade, such as gold, substantial exchange rate fluctuations would not occur; if the exchange rate of a currency was too low, the currency would be bought up and converted into gold

---

* Paper read at the 6th Post-Keynesian Workshop, Knoxville, Tennessee, June 26th, 2000, as: How Could the Politics of a World-ide Keynesianism be Organizes in an Era of Globalization". First published in: *Brazilian Journal of Political Economy*, 22, 1 (January-March 2002); pp. 53–78.
[1] Cf. the title of Lenin's analysis: Lenin 1964.
[2] Verdier 1998: 43ff; UNCTAD 1994: 120–121; Theurl 1999: 26; Bairoch 1996; Irwin 1996: 41–44; Bergeljik/Mensik 1997: 166; Bovenberg/Gordon 1996; Williamson 1996.

at its fixed rate. The growth of financial markets is therefore linked to the emergence of Keynesian interventionist monetary policies.

With the end of the gold standard, currencies are basically pegged to the overall productivity of their respective economies in tradables and non-tradables, the latter being an increasingly important category of mass consumption because of the rising consumption of services and, in some cases, of housing. The higher the share of non-tradables in the consumption of labor, which produces tradables, the greater the possibilities of indirectly subsidizing labor (making it cheaper) in the export sector through the exchange rate. A low exchange rate enables cheapening exports even to levels where export workers can no longer buy their wage goods from the world market (provided that the local non-tradable-producing sector supplies these goods). With the gold standard, this type of subsidization requires a fall in the nominal price of non-tradables – which is much more difficult to achieve, especially if the wage goods produced are only artificially non-tradable such as food. An exchange rate based on average productivity makes subsidizing the export sector relatively easy, whereas an exchange rate based on an internationally tradable commodity allows less such subsidies.

Globalization is also limited in the sphere of international communications. In the late 1940s and the 1950s, international communication was characterized by a globally shared vision of market failure, leading to the conclusion that state intervention into the economy was inevitable. With the defeat of fascism, it became clear that such interventionism required democratic legitimacy. The colonial powers were forced to withdraw, as they were neither elected nor were they able to present themselves as trustees in the interests of the populations in the territories they administered (Furedi 1993: 91; Elsenhans 2000c: 344–351). In those days, a local uprising not only rapidly caught worldwide attention, but often triggered off uprisings elsewhere. No colonial power was able to use its full capacity of repression against such movements because of the risk of facing worldwide condemnation, with consequences not only for its international reputation but also for the domestic political process. Only dictatorships in small countries, such as Portugal, which were not integrated in the world system, could continue to not pay attention to globally accepted values, and this only for a limited period of time. Yet even the colonial diehards here, at least the more intelligent factions, eventually had to admit the necessity of democratic principles, i.e., decolonization (Assunção 1987).

Despite the manifold encroachments on national sovereignty the injunctions of international financial institutions against debtor nations are rarely mandatory nowadays: no country, in the present framework of structural adjustment programs, faces punishment if it defaults on its debts, as was the case before 1914 (e.g., management of the Ottoman debt by a committee of representatives of the creditor nations, not to mention the military occupation of debtor countries for the sake of assuring good financial management, as was the case in Central America and the Caribbean). Fujimori's Peru has demonstrated that even a small country, which is not looking for fresh money and new loans, can relatively neglect financial markets, in contrast to "middle" powers in Asia, Africa and Latin America before 1914.

It is not globalization itself that constitutes the challenge, but its specific conditions and the patterns it has followed. This qualification implies that the problem of how to best manage the process is of greater importance than the necessity of resisting it.

There are two hypotheses with respect to these conditions and patterns. In a traditional, nation-state-orientated approach, focused on the relations between economics and politics, the territorial limitation of the "nation"-state is deplored, since no institutions have emerged – either at international, or regional level – which are capable of setting and enforcing binding rules and thus creating the framework for economic activity. This approach is largely adopted in the analysis of the protection of public goods at the global level, initially with regard to environmental issues, and increasingly with respect to human rights issues at the international level. It implies either resisting globalization, or, alternatively, extending it to the political sphere by creating international quasi-state institutions. Yet, the second alternative is not realistic in a global set-up where no one is really willing to risk the dangers of a world state.[3]

The Keynesian perspective is quite different. The state is only an actor in so far as the market fails. It is not primarily the institution of the state but the current state of the economy which largely influences outcomes. The economy may, however, be caught in a low-production trap, where low physical investment leads to low levels of employment and low effective demand, despite stagnating real wages. In this case, effective demand decreases even further in relation to productive potential, with further tendencies to low

---

[3] Cf. the discussion in Albert/Brock 1995: 95.

levels of economic activity. Keynes argued that monetary and fiscal policy would constitute instruments for overcoming short-term imbalances on the labor market, but that their usefulness would be otherwise limited. Planned savings may, however, rise because there is a long-term social problem of distribution linked to the unemployment/low-level-demand trap. The propensity to save being dependent on the level of household incomes and on expectations of future developments, the present long-term economic crisis and labor's loss of bargaining power contribute to a decline in effective demand, which further disempowers labor.

The improbability that the invisible hand leads to full employment increases as a result of the application of the Keynesian mechanism itself. Fiscal and monetary policy is possible because the creation of book money does not imply scarcity of resources in the future (as claimed by the theory of rational expectations), given the assumption that the factors of production employed would have otherwise been idle and that their employment through additional financial resources leads to productivity increases. The additional production which results from the upturn of the economy would in this case constitute the physical counterpart to these additional financial resources. On the other hand, book money may also appear on financial markets as savings without necessarily commanding additional factors of production. Thus the creation of book money implies the further necessity of intervening in the economic process. Hayek hinted at this problem early on by arguing that an upswing of the economy through the creation of additional financial resources already implies a future downswing (Hayek 1966: 140ff; Hayek 1941: 34).

## 1. Economic efficiency of capitalists makes full employment through capital accumulation not guaranteed

The process of economic growth is associated with rising mass incomes.[4] This empirical fact is not a point of controversy between Keynesian and neoclassical economics. Real wages have grown since the beginning of capitalism, with the exception of major political crises, such as the Napoleonic

---

[4] The various implications of the argument that capitalist growth is led by mass demand cannot be intensively dealt with here. Cf. Elsenhans 1983c: 1–38; Elsenhans 1983a.

Wars.[5] In the early stages of industrialization real wages normally grew at a slower pace than industrial productivity because of the slow growth of productivity in agriculture and the high share of agriculture in the supply of wage goods (food) at low levels of real wages.[6] But for neoclassical analysis, wages follow productivity. Rising real wages do not launch economic growth but, rather, limit it. At low wages and high profits, investment is high, so that the growth rate rises. Higher investment increases employment. Labor becomes scarce and enterprises raise wages in order to attract labor until the wage rate reaches the level of marginal earnings which can be realized on the market.

Keynesians doubt that financial resources are automatically transformed into investment, because these resources can also be kept as monetary reserves without contributing to real demand. The strategic character of various elements of final demand in raising investment (and employment) will be difficult to determine, however, and even controversial among Keynesians. Most Keynesians would insist on the possibility of returning to full employment via a short or medium-term increase in spending by enterprises and/or the state. Once the economy returns to full employment the neoclassical mechanism of bringing consumption and demand in line via scarcity-determined wage increases would be relaunched. Full employment with the implied rise of consumption demand may, however, not occur within a reasonable time period, so that investment does not trigger off the mechanism of demand expansion implied in the neoclassical theory of the wage drift.

In fact, additional investments are a limited solution to the dilemma because capitalism's microeconomic efficiency is so great that the system is unable to absorb unlimited shares of its total net product in the form of investment.

This problem was first dealt with by Bortkiewicz (1907: 455–465) in his analysis of Marx's law of the tendential fall of the rate of profit. It was reformulated on the basis of synchronized labor costs by Okishio (1961: 85–90) with the same results[7], and since then has only been refuted on the basis

---

[5] Crafts 1985: 144; Brown 1990: 591; Mokyr 1988: 77; Fisher 1992: 72; Shammas 1990: 228; Borsay 1989: 228.
[6] Clark/Huberman/Lindert 1995: 234; Shammas 1983: 91; Horrel/Humphries 1992: 872; Horrell 1996: 561; Tilly 1975: 405; Hobsbawm 1957: 59.
[7] Cf. Roemer 1979; Bowles 1981; Hunt 1983; Parijs 1980.

of very special conditions.⁸ Bortkiewicz showed that as long as real wages remain constant no capitalist entrepreneur can competitively introduce a technology if it does not raise the rate of profit. This argument about the microeconomic behavior of capitalists does not, however, exclude the possibility that the profit rate declines if real wages rise and lead to the introduction of new products which do not directly compete with existing ones. The new product satisfies new needs (and this implies that consumption increases in real terms). The implied Bortkiewicz criterion, that capitalists do not spend on technologies where the profit rate is lower than average, is satisfied if the price of new products allows a profit rate equal or superior to the profit rate in old products. This may be achieved even if capital intensity increases. There is no need for any measurable physical productivity increase in the production of the new product,⁹ but only the readiness of the consumer to pay a high enough price. New products, which are produced in capital-intensive ways, may allow for Marx's rise of the organic composition of capital to occur.¹⁰ The possibility of rising real wages implies the possibility of capital accumulation proceeding more rapidly than production. Capitalist growth on the basis of wage increases lower than productivity increases¹¹ and increases in investment higher than productivity increases ultimately has to lead to a decline in the profit rate.

This decline of the profit rate appears to be the result of a decline in the rate of technical innovation. Neoclassical thinking can be saved if, in addition to the old factors of production – capital and labor – new factors of

---

[8] Critics insisted on the possibility of a falling profit rate in the case of joint-production of goods: Funke 1984; Salvadori 1981; Bidard 1988. Renten (1991: 87) neglects devalorization of capital through technical progress. Schutz (1987) insists on declining productivity due to natural resources, but then the process is not caused by capital accumulation. Armstrong/Glyn (1980: 67) and Scott (1992) introduce imperfect competition and lack of correct technology assessment. Kliman (1997: 46) introduces false expectations without mentioning that this would lead to devalorization of capital.

[9] Indeed, productivity in the production of different products can be compared only by means of prices.

[10] Elsenhans 2000 infra Chapter 3.

[11] We assume only two types of income, wages and net profits, where all net profits are reinvested. If wages stagnate, profits have to increase more rapidly than net income. In the case of productivity increases in line with the increase of available resources for investment, growth is explosive. The model is presented in detail in: Elsenhans 1994d: 422–426; Elsenhans 1995g: 194–204.

production – technologies, skills, human capital, – are added.[12] New endogenous growth theory, in essence, explores these new factors of production. These additional factors usually have one characteristic in common: they are the unintentional outcome of activities financed by non-enterprise sources (such as households or the state) or the result of joint-production processes, so that their cost does not reduce profit. If the creation of these additional factors of production is financed at the cost of capital, their production is cost effective only if capitalists are less able to forecast future developments in the requirements of technical progress than the non-capitalist promoters of these additional factors. Capitalists would otherwise prefer to spend their own resources on a more efficiently organized technical innovation system, which is not necessarily owned by individual enterprises. Business associations, for instance, may be called to coordinate innovation.

A given capitalist set-up for promoting innovation may be less efficient than another. The consequence of this inefficiency is the decline of the less innovative set-up, and perhaps its future specialization on less dynamic branches.

The theory of endogenous growth[13] explains the stability of the capital-output ratio, which is incompatible with Marx and standard neoclassical thought, by adding factors to capital accumulation which are difficult to describe and even more difficult to explain. These factors are explained as the result of activities which can be pursued intentionally. There is no empirical proof to justify a rejection of the argument that these additional factors are simply the result of the old principle of capitalist growth, i.e., that large-scale production of identical items reduces the costs of technical discoveries and allows for their transformation into production processes based on better machinery (Elsenhans 1999e: 115–128). After a decade of research into the process of quasi-investment in these new factors, new endogenous growth theory has admitted the importance of learning-by-doing and, finally, the demand-dependent character of technical progress (Romer 1996). Innovation results from the discovery and generalized application of new production technologies. The experience gained at these new technical frontiers

---

[12] Becker 1964; Denison 1967; Faxen 1978: 131–134; Lall 1983: 527–535.
[13] Romer 1994; Romer 1987; Romer 1986; Romer 1990; Pack 1994; Segerstrom 1991; Paqué 1995; Klundert/Meijdam 1993; Caballé/Santos 1993; Amendola/Dosi/Papagni 1993; Homburg 1995; Grossman/Helpman 1990; Lucas 1988.

encourages new innovations, which can in turn be generalized. The diffusion process will be faster, the more the goods manufactured using these innovations are produced in large series (Schmookler 1966: 187ff; Allen 1983: 17; Dosi/Pavitt/Soete 1990: 90, 119ff). In this way more individuals will gain experience with new technologies. The widespread use of innovations can be considered the basis for further innovation. Among the two incentives for innovation – new goods and cheaper prices – the drive for new products, which is old as human history, has been a less powerful source of innovation than the drive for cheapening the manufacture of existing products, despite the artistic excellence of precapitalist societies such as Ancient Egypt, Ancient China, and Ancient India.

Learning-by-doing presupposes the time dependence on technical progress. At any point in time there is a multitude of technologies that contribute varyingly to cost-reduction, and therefore allow varying rises in the surplus value vis-à-vis the stock of capital. If the rate of capital accumulation is raised above the golden rule scenario (Nuti 1970; Phelps 1965) – i.e., a constant capital productivity, with identical growth rates for net income and the net stock of fixed capital, and, hence, above the rate of time-dependent technical progress –, additional spending on investment has to be for projects which are characterized by lower-than-average technical innovation. There is too much "money" available in relation to the potential for technical progress. The lag in wage increases creates financial resources for which there is not yet sufficient technical progress.

Hence the decline of the profit rate is in fact the dire consequence of wages not expanding in line with productivity growth. Without acceleration of time-dependent technical progress, spending all available financial resources involves spending on less productive projects, which forcibly reduce the profit rate. The "overaccumulation" crisis has its roots in an insufficient expansion of labor incomes, which is temporarily compensated by the acceleration of accumulation; yet, it eventually leads to the decline of the profit rate and to unemployment. Overaccumulation is not radically different from underconsumptionism. A stoppage in the accumulation process due to underconsumption is nothing else than capitalists realizing in advance the futility of engaging in an acceleration of accumulation beyond the consumptive capacity of the society.

Capitalism depends on the availability of new products that can be produced without increasing capital intensity. This implies rising mass consumption from the demand side.[14] Consumption is basically not able to limit profit, as Baran and Sweezy unintentionally demonstrated.[15] Even in times of prosperity, workers cannot raise their consumption beyond the productive capacity for consumption goods. With full-employment on the basis of existing capacity, capitalists can respond to further increases in demand only by increasing investment. Until new capacities can be put into operation, rising prices will help cover the costs of this additional investment. Labor and capital can be substituted in the neo-classical production function, but not at the macro-economic level, since labor cannot eat the output of investment goods industries, whereas productive capacity in consumption goods industries cannot increase without additional machinery.

There is an important implication for the rivalry between really existing socialism and capitalism in the twentieth century. In the planned economies, the share of investment in national income was able to increase far beyond the level of such shares in the capitalist West. But only during the crisis of the 1930s existing socialism was seriously considered capable of overtaking the capitalist West (Elsenhans 2000e). When the bargaining power of labor rose after the defeat of fascism and the end of Soviet military expansion to the center of Europe, the West returned to full employment and high growth rates, whereas the high shares of investment in national incomes in the Soviet bloc were linked to high and rising capital-output ratios, interpreted by the people of these countries as quasi exploitation by an inefficient nomenclatura (Elsenhans 1996e: 144, fn. 89).

This absence of a rise in the capital-output ratio under capitalist conditions and the absence of a decline in capital productivity are not the accidental result. On the contrary, they are the very expression of power relations between social classes in capitalism. Despite the manifold complaints about the power of money in capitalism, business has great difficulties engaging in the accumulation of wealth without developing productive forces – hence the scope for redistribution of income, and this not primarily via politically managed distributive measures but via the scarcity of labor whose marginal

---

[14] Strassmann 1956; Young 1928; Lafaiete Lopes 1972; Murphy/Shleifer/Vishny 1989 rediscovered this mechanism for endogenous growth theory. Cf. also Mommertz 1979: 121; Schlesinger 1925: 121; Freyberg 1989: 59; Brasch 1924; Hounshell 1984: 51ff; Barth 1973: 63; Young 1991.

[15] They assume that profit is maintained by unproductive spending. Baran/Sweezy 1967: 62ff, esp. 178ff.

product is high. By developing productive forces and, consequently, the marginal product of labor, which constitutes the basis of its scarcity, the "ruling" class in capitalism empowers labor. The result of this is that the stock of fixed capital cannot grow more rapidly than labor productivity beyond an initial upstart period.[16] Unintentionally and without the slightest insight into this process, the capitalist class is shielded from the decline of capital productivity because of the bargaining power of labor.

## 2. Globalization is compatible with full employment in developed economies

Globalization will not lead to the disempowerment of labor if there is not an already existing mass of labor with low bargaining power, which is integrated into a larger labor market. The empirical proof of this is the relative stability of purchasing-power parity of exchange rates between major industrial countries[17] as well as similar productivity lags in different branches between developed countries,[18] but not between developed and underdeveloped countries (Pilat 1995: 140).

In the present globalization debate two arguments are frequently advanced. It is maintained that wages in a given country – usually one's own, e.g., Germany – are too high. This is believed to explain high levels of unemployment, which are the result of a lack of competitiveness at the international level. It is therefore advised to follow a policy of wage restraint, so that labor costs per unit of output decrease with the increase in productivity. The second argument is the demand for fair labor standards, namely, the improvement of labor standards in the underdeveloped world, with the aim of protecting the standards of the developed industrialized countries (Langille 1997; Waer 1996; Feld 1996).

---

[16] The implications of this argument for so-called primitive accumulation cannot be discussed here. See Elsenhans 1997c. The argument also has implications for the catching-up process, as it implies that catching up should normally occur by means of market forces (imitation, technology transfer) as well as by state measures (rent-financed imitation), Elsenhans 1992l: 115–120.

[17] Frenkel 1986: 640; Deutsche Bundesbank 1993: 51–56; Fortune 1985; Hakkio 1984; Abuaf/Jorion 1990: 172; Wasserfallen/Kyburz 1985: 657; Siebert 1985; Junge 1985: 435.

[18] Yukizawa 1973: 40f; Rostas 1948: 47; Pilat/Rao 1996: 113–120; Ark 1993: 101f; Flux 1933: 33; Levine 1967: 20; Maddison 1964: 37.

In the system of flexible exchange rates, the observation that, for example, Germany's labor costs are too high does not lend support to any explanation other than the one that simply says that Germany's international competitiveness remains untouched as long as Germany does not have a balance-of-trade deficit (including services). German labor is internationally expensive via the exchange rate because it is productive. If Germany's labor were too expensive, German products would not sell on the world market, and, as a consequence, the German currency would depreciate. Currency fluctuations have been far more important in the case of Germany than changes in nominal wages.

If Germany resorts to further cuts in labor costs, its exports will further increase along with its export surplus. As long as capital flows supply purchasing power to the rest of the world, Germany can continue to ease its problem of unemployment by exporting surpluses, to the detriment of potential employment in its own consumer economy. Without such capital flows, German currency will become scarce and appreciate (Deutsches Institut für Wirtschaftsforschung 1992: 125). In early 1995, German managers appeared in a lavishly sponsored TV campaign where they appealed for wage restraints. The campaign was stopped when the DM rose against a massively devaluating US$ to 1 DM per 0.75 to compare to the about 1 DM per 0.66 US$ in ordinary times or 1 DM to less than 0.50 US$ actually.

Full employment in all participating economies also leads to equalization of productivity lags in various branches. Some economies may enjoy comparative advantage in a particular branch and specialize on this branch because of the good earnings for the factors of production engaged here. They compete for labor on the local labor market, and force businesses that are oriented towards the internal market to either charge higher prices or to modernize their production processes, if labor becomes scarce because of the export drive. Businesses which cannot maintain their competitive position, by either charging higher prices or by improving productivity, will not survive. The equalization of productivity differences across branches of production does not stem from parallelisms in technical development – which, of course, may exist as well – but from the simultaneous operation of competition and scarcity of labor.

If the globalization process only links economies tending to full employment, it takes the form of a convoy process (Elsenhans 1999b: 438–441). An innovation in tradables in a technically leading economy adds to its comparative advantage and opens up new export potential. Without capital flows to the rest of the world, the currency of the innovating economy appreciates. The non-innovative economy gains new possibilities for exports and import-substitution at low levels of devaluation if its productivity lag is low in non-innovative branches where it previously did not enjoy comparative advantage. As the costs of production in the innovative economy rise, the non-innovative economy may even benefit from improving terms-of-trade through specialization on backward products. The less the productivity lags of the non-innovative economy in hitherto internationally uncompetitive and non-innovative branches, the earlier this economy benefits from new export opportunities through the inevitable devaluation of its currency.

This possibility of specialization on non-innovative products has two implications. The non-innovative economy does not experience unemployment due to innovation in the innovative economy. It suffers only limited setbacks in its overall terms-of-trade, but cannot compensate its lag in leading technologies by devaluation of its currency. Its exports grow on the basis of old products even at low rates of devaluation.

It is still possible for the backward economy to overtake the advanced one on the basis of low lags in productivity in new products, at least relative to the high productivity lags in old products. This was the case in Britain's overtaking France in low quality but cheap industrial products in the late eighteenth century (Crafts 1989), and Germany's overtaking Britain in chemicals and electrical products at the end of the nineteenth century (Kindleberger 1975; Aukrust 1964; Fremdling 1991). But the number of cases is limited, because at that time not only the international monetary regime but also the relatively high productivity in backward branches of the lagging-behind economies limited devaluation.

In line with the observation of path dependency formulated in the theory of endogenous growth, a leading economy with considerable experience in old products may achieve higher productivity in new products than catching-up economies. But because technical progress stems from learning-by-doing – hence from production where the leader is more active than the follower –, it is highly improbable that the leader enjoys productivity advances in new products to the extent of those in old products.

## 3. Devaluation-based export drives characterize the strategy of successful developing countries

In contrast to the early twentieth century, the present globalization drive is characterized by the integration of marginality-ridden underdeveloped countries into the world economy on the basis of their capacity to supply cheap industrial products. This export drive, however, is not powerful enough to raise employment to levels where labor becomes scarce in the whole of the "overpopulated" area of the so-called Third World.

A benign and a malign case can be distinguished. In the benign case, the neoclassical mechanism can operate due to the scarcity of labor, which enables real wages to increase, as has been the case in South Korea or Taiwan (Fields 1994). In the malign case, the export drive is too weak to dynamize the rest of the economy. With low levels of employment, devaluation continues to be an important instrument for capturing shares of the world market, which is rendered possible by the existence of considerable agricultural surpluses, improving terms-of-trade between simple industrial products and food on the world markets, and the possibilities of technology transfers through foreign direct investment and government intervention (Elsenhans 1997e: 291–294).

Devaluation-based export drives constitute the essential aspect of the globalization process with respect to West-South relations.[19] Because the process is devaluation-driven, the attempts to check the new competitiveness of the underdeveloped countries by wage restraint cannot succeed. Devaluation is possible if wage goods are locally produced, since, in this case, the additional income paid out to export workers is primarily transformed into demand for the locally produced surplus of food and wage goods, mostly from the informal sector (Bhagwati 1984).

It is not the poor countries of sub-Saharan Africa, but the agriculturally successful rice-growing countries of East and Southeast Asia which have been most successful in launching devaluation-driven export drives, as they have been able to supply the wage goods for their export workers from locally existing productive capacities. Economies are more successful, the less import-dependent they are. Felix (1994: 14) has shown that East and South-

---

[19] Tzannatos 1997: 2–3; Guillaumont-Jeanneney/Hua 1996; Lafay 1996: 948, 963; Narrassiguin 1995: 325. Most recently: Mundorf 1998: 2.

east Asia are characterized by a low import propensity of their higher income strata, in contrast to Latin America.

Low international labor costs therefore do not mean low real wages. The domestic purchasing power of household incomes in the case of East Asia and Eastern Europe are a multiple of the purchasing power these incomes would yield if converted into dollars and used in a typical industrialized country of the West.[20]

The higher real purchasing power of an income on the local market in relation to its purchasing power on the world market implies a relatively high productivity in non-tradable sectors, including food production given the highly regulated world market in basic foods. Devaluation-driven export-led industrialization of the East and Southeast Asian type was made possible through early agrarian reforms which allowed mobilizing marginal labor, as predicted in theories on agrarian reform such as those based on the labor-surplus argument (Georgescu-Roegen 1960; Dandekar 1962; Sen 1966), or on the Latin American "macrofundio-microfundio" theoretical construct (Feder 1967; Sternberg 1967).

Labor has experienced productivity increases via real wage increases. The Washington institutions have referred to this as shared development (Page 1993: 157ff). Export-led industrialization in East and Southeast Asia has also been rent-based. Amsden (1989: 139) coined the phrase which was followed as a principle: get your prices wrong." Akyüz and Gore (Akyüz/Gore 1994) spoke of systematically created rents, and even free marketeers did not claim that the highly performing economies of East and Southeast Asia were characterized by free markets, but spoke of market-friendly or market-enhancing approaches (Aoki/Murdock/Okuno-Fujiwara 1995) where the market was used to discipline private enterprise without being allowed to guide major development decisions, especially concerning the launching of new activities.

The empirical evidence of states mobilizing rents which are subsequently allocated to politically determined strategies of economic growth and diversification within the framework of a controlled opening to the world market is not a coincidence, but a necessary consequence of the structure of capitalist growth. Any type of production has two results: a product which can be

---

[20] Cf. Mundorf 1998, 2, who quotes an OECD study. Mussler 1999: 2; Yotopoulos/Lin 1993: 11; Chen/Gordon/Zhiming 1994.

sold and a transformation of labor and infrastructures which improves productivity in the future. Technically backward economies in particular will often have comparative advantage in branches with low productivity-enhancing effects.

If the internal market is not sufficiently large – due to population levels, the extent of economies of scale, which are much higher today than in the period when European continental economies (and also the USA) were catching up with Britain, and high levels of poverty – the nineteenth-century solution (applied in Latin American import-substituting industrialization since the 1940s) will not work, so that export orientation is inevitable.

But also the implied solution of cheapening exports is based on rents. Levels of devaluation where purchasing-power parity is not respected are possible because of productivity levels in the production of non-tradables, which are relatively higher, compared to the world economy, than the productivity levels in the respective export sectors. This mechanism is especially important in the case of local food production, where non-tradability is induced artificially by keeping local farmers from exporting, for example, through monopolies on state-trading organizations or export taxes.

Export-sector employment is therefore a function of devaluation and of the capacity to subsidize the export sector, and thus, ultimately, a function of the agricultural surplus. The locally produced rent is channeled in its physical form to additional workers in the export sector who are hired in the case of devaluation. Part of the value of this rent goes to consumers in the industrialized world who enjoy rising incomes due to improved terms-of-trade between the branches which remain in their countries and those branches which migrate to the low-labor-cost economies. The implied exploitation of the catching-up economy can be limited by complementing devaluation with state-guided rent allocation to specific sectors of production or to factor-supply improvement.

The strategy of "remonter les filières"[21] – which was advocated quite strongly in the French discussion, especially for raw-material exporters (oil countries), where rents were used for developing forward and backward linkages of the oil industry – is certainly also possible with respect to industrial exports. In the 1970s, South Korea faced declining prices for its textile exports with low price elasticity of demand. The quantities exported could rise

---

[21] For example: Aoudia 1996: 35; Sid Ahmed 1990: 61.

only with a fall in price where the total earnings from these exports decreased. A government ban on the import of textile machinery forced local textile producers to turn to the local (small and medium) metal working sector for their machinery, which was initially quite expensive with respect to performance. The additional costs were passed on to the customer (and limited the possibilities of price cutting). In the end, Korean textile machinery producers benefited from learning-by-doing on the basis of close advice from their local customers, who knew perfectly well which machinery they needed.[22] Korean textile-machinery exporters rapidly acquired technical efficiency and became competitive on the world market. A similar strategy was followed by Singapore, where in the 1970s enterprises with low per capita wage bills (because of the employment of unskilled labor) had to pay special taxes which were used for financing efforts to upgrade the skills of labor (with less success than the South Korean strategy) (Holtgrave 1987: 59–81).

In the case of specialization on branches with low elasticity and low productivity-enhancing effects – not only in the raw-material sector, but also industrial branches – rent appropriation is possible by means of devaluation because there is the possibility of combining low exchange rates with taxation of those products where competitiveness would already be achieved at higher exchange rates.[23] Not yet competitive labor is subsidized from taxes on exports, which many countries have also levied on manufactured products (e.g., auctioning of textile import quotas[24]).

The more exports are import-dependent – e.g., because of the use of imported technology – the less the products can be cheapened by devaluation, as devaluation has an impact only on the local factors of production.

There are limits to devaluation if products which have to be exported are manufactured with high costs of physical capital, so-called capital-intensive products. At the same time, low skill levels in underdeveloped countries create comparative advantage in these products, much more than in high-skill labor-intensive products,[25] as already observed in the Leontief paradox (Leontief 1954; Leontief 1956).

---

[22] Mytelka 1986: 258. The rational character of their option is argued by Jung/Lee 1986; Elsenhans 1983b: 145.
[23] Kaldor 1964: 220; World Bank 1987: 98; Balassa 1974: 178; Katseli 1983: 362.
[24] Morkre 1979; Takacs 1988: 41; World Bank, 1987: 148. Khanna 1990: 93.
[25] Boatler 1975: 406; Boatler 1978; Clague 1967; Clague 1969; Clague 1991; Bruton 1968; Bitar/Moyano 1975: 237; Hardin/Strassmann 1968; Diaz-Alejandro 1965.

In order to overcome obstacles to market penetration, the underdeveloped economy has to diversify into the local production of technology and inputs in order to achieve further price cuts, despite the high local prices of these inputs. There is a fundamental difference between the cost of imported equipment and locally produced equipment. Locally produced equipment can be produced regardless of the price of local labor and other local factors of production without endangering the capacity to devalue, even if imported equipment is cheaper at the chosen exchange rate (Elsenhans 1999d: 41ff). Diversification into investment-goods production makes sense even if the cost of this equipment is higher than imported equipment, as long as the price-elasticity of current exports limits the earning capacity of the respective economy for foreign exchange at the prevailing exchange rate.

With respect to rent channeling with the aim of success in exports, a benign and a malign case can be distinguished. The malign case consists in not overcoming low marginal productivity in wage goods production. The consequence is persistent marginality. Wages will not follow productivity increases in the export sector because of continuing unemployment.

In the benign case, technical progress will raise marginal productivity either because of an ever growing export sector or because of the export sector's dynamic role in modernizing the rest of the economy. The internal market will also develop, and, ultimately, even imports will increase. Even if real wages were repressed, the tendency to full employment on the basis of the expansion of technical efficiency from export sectors to the whole of the economy would lead to exports in a large variety of branches of production, having as outcome considerable export surpluses. In the case of full employment, the consequences would be either "imported" inflation, as experienced by Germany at the end of the 1960s, or currency appreciation, as experienced by Japan in the 1990s.

The benign case is characterized by the spread of productivity growth to the entire economy, the malign case by sectorally limited productivity growth.

Growth therefore depends either on rent-financed subsidies to technology improvement in lines of production chosen by the state or an institution of the non-market economy, or on an equally state-dependent strategy which tries to imitate the growth mechanism of self-centered capitalism, i.e., the growth of the internal market, technical improvement and capital accumulation depending on rising mass incomes which triggers off innovation through small and medium-scale enterprises. Export-led growth has been most successful where a combination of these two strategies was used, with export drives being linked and supporting an improvement of income distribution. Yi (1988: 91–102; cf. also Fujita/James 1990) has shown that small-scale industry in Taiwan was launched most effectively in local investment-goods production, and that Korea was willing to accept much larger inequalities of income distribution than Taiwan, despite comparable levels at the start.

Export-oriented industrialization does not escape the contradictions of rent. The East Asian literature – in contrast to the North American – has always insisted on the rent-dependent inefficiencies of the political systems of these countries (Rhee 1994: 232–238). The East Asian countries have been quite successful in applying industrial policies, not because their bureaucracies are more efficient than the ones in industrialized countries, but because catching-up economies do not have to make sector choices, but can modify their industrial structures simply by imitating the examples of more advanced countries.[26]

Democratization only took root in these countries when labor became scarce, and hence powerful. Due to the expanding internal market, new business groups arose, whose memberships were too large to be able to benefit from privileged links to the state (Kim 1996; Lee 1993: 353). The development of the rule of law in Europe serves as a historical model for this process. The traditional pattern of transition from precapitalist to capitalist structures can be realized if labor becomes scarce (Elsenhans 1999a: 23–28). It is not the state which is essential for the catching-up process, as Gerschenkron (1962) suggests, but the state's incapacity to block the capitalist process if labor has become scarce.

The models of export-oriented industrialization presented here imply the existence of various underconsumption threats. Devaluation of the catching-up economies means improving terms-of-trade for the leading economies. Productivity-oriented wage development requires that wages rise not only on the basis of increasing average rates of productivity but also due to improving terms-of-trade, so that the process of delocalization of production tends to accelerate.

Furthermore, as the international prices of products whose production has been delocalized from the leading industrialized countries to the catching-up

---

[26] Leff 1985: 347ff; Paqué 1995: 250; Hofmann/Koop 1991: 93f; Elsenhans 1992h: 24.

economies may fall because of decreasing costs, the value of exports of the catching-up economy may be quite low. In this case, a country with a balance of trade deficit could present an underconsumption threat to the world economy.

Such immizering growth (Bhagwati 1958) has long been observed in the discussion about terms-of-trade for raw material exporters in the underdeveloped South. Despite growing productivity, their terms-of-trade and their incomes may decrease (Prebisch 1962: 1–2). The possibility of decreasing terms-of-trade also in the case of specialization on manufactured products was proven by the Asian crisis, where the local currency prices of exported manufactures did not increase despite massive devaluation. Devaluation was the consequence of decreasing dollar prices of exported manufactures.

## 4. Globalization also disempowers labor in advanced capitalist countries, but only in a specific manner

The sectoral competitiveness of the underdeveloped economies of the South destroys the economic and social cohesion of labor in the West and blocks the process of redistribution of incomes. Capitalist redistribution, however, constitutes the economic basis of the working classes. The possibility of redistribution is the condition for the existence of the working class as a political factor – a condition which is a constituent part of capitalist economies and their autonomous civil societies (Kim 1999: 57–70).

Capitalism involves the redistribution of financial resources among labor. As labor productivity increases differ from branch to branch, labor from branches with below-average productivity increases is hired by branches with above-average productivity increases by means of higher wages. The branches with below-average productivity increases reduce their output, can sell this reduced output at higher prices, and indeed have to do so in order to defend their earnings so that they themselves can pay higher wages to the labor they want to retain.

Specific activities cannot be associated with particular levels of productivity, nor can an inter-branch comparison of the productivity of various activities establish a link between levels of productivity and the development in physical productivity. Engel (1895: 3) was one of the first to show that utility is no measure. The teacher who helps create the productive capacity of a pupil is not able to capture the gain in productivity of this pupil. The physical productivity of a barber in Europe is not higher than that of a barber in India, but their incomes are not equal. The physical productivity of barbers has not increased in the last five centuries, but the incomes of barbers in the industrially advanced countries have followed average productivity increases.

Capitalism is based on redistribution. Unlike a feudal lord, the capitalist realizes profits on the basis of social relations, especially demand conditions based on net investment spending. Labor whose productivity does not increase benefits from the productivity increase of other labor – despite its own technical efficiency remaining the same – via changes in relative prices in favor of its own products. This mechanism requires tendential full employment. Without tendential full employment, labor in different branches will engage in a struggle over the relative importance of their respective specialization, that is, over the utility of labor. The now century-old discussion in Marxist theory about the reduction of concrete labor into abstract labor as a unit of value only shows that this issue cannot be resolved (Pietsch 1979; Morishima 1973: 4). What can be resolved, but only through the choice of professions and specialization, is equality with respect to the pains of labor – from the efforts of learning to the exertion of muscle power.

The mechanism of equalization of pay for equally "difficult" labor despite differences in productivity growth is the basis of the bargaining power of labor, as it allows organized labor to become a political factor despite its lack of property. This basis is threatened by the new competitiveness of labor from the low-labor-cost countries. Labor whose productivity growth is less than average is no longer able to impose wage increases in line with the average productivity increase of the technically advanced economies, because its unit costs rise on the world market, making labor with stagnant unit costs more competitive, because the rise in productivity in the technically most dynamic branches of the technically advanced countries is associated with exchange rate increases or other forms of terms-of-trade increases.

Because of high productivity in technically leading branches, the exchange rate of a technically leading country becomes so high that its labor in less productive branches is too expensive vis-à-vis labor in production sites whose international labor costs are not determined by such high technology branches.

Labor in the less dynamic branches of the technically advanced countries may lose competitiveness against the labor of low-cost production sites despite a very high productivity in relation to these competitors. At the same levels of income, labor in the West may not enjoy the – in international comparison – cheap non-tradables which its counterpart at the low-labor-cost production sites consume. It is not impossible that real wages in the West for this type of labor may become even lower than in the South, despite this labor being too expensive to be competitive. With the emergence of newly competitive production sites in the South through devaluation, labor in the West cannot assure that it maintains its competitiveness on the basis of wage restraint, although its disempowerment leads to wage compression, possibly together with currency appreciation.

The underconsumption threat presented by the South is therefore complemented by additional underconsumption tendencies in the West. The decreasing competitiveness of Western labor in branches with below-average productivity growth cannot be solved through market mechanisms if the still highly competitive high-productivity-growth sector in the West does not grow rapidly. The normal case of adjusting differences in average productivity growth and of the declining competitiveness of low-productivity-growth industries is characterized by structural change in the product mix of the leading country. The growth of markets for the sector with high productivity growth depends mostly on the industrially advanced countries (high-technology consumption goods) and their capacity to import from the catching-up economies, as the latter will not buy additional high-technology equipment without the perspective of expanding outlets in the industrially more advanced countries.

Wage restraint induces a vicious circle by limiting the growth of those sectors which could absorb labor from declining sectors. It is therefore not surprising that, statistically, the loss of jobs in the technically advanced countries does not stem from the employment balance of exports and imports between the West and the South but from productivity growing more rapidly than production in the West. The divergence between productivity growth and production is simply an indication of an underconsumption situation.[27]

Labor which is not successfully absorbed by a shift from sunset to sunrise branches will address itself to the state. State-led employment programs invariably involve increased state intervention on the basis of additional

---

[27] Thompson 1987: 13; Michie/Pitelis 1996: 4; Bell 1940: 83; Woytinsky 1935: 165.

financial resources being extracted from the highly competitive sectors, i.e., rents.

Protectionism is but one form. Although rejected by the international financial institutions it shares a common characteristic with the market-friendly approach so staunchly advocated by the Washington preachers of world-wide liberalism, as it discriminates only against foreign enterprises, but puts all local (national or regional) enterprises on an equal footing while maintaining (some) competition. It is the least harmful form of rent-channeling for the industrially advanced country as it limits rent-seeking in comparison to other strategies as state-financed employment in activities which do not earn market prices for their products. Protectionism adds, however, to the underconsumption threats in the South as the transformation of the internal surplus of wage goods into employment via the market becomes more difficult. It limits the foreign exchange earnings of catching-up economies as the rates of devaluation for becoming competitive increase.

The development of socially protected activities in the industrialized countries, which the market cannot bear because consumers will not buy them at their costs of production, creates a state-dependent sector. Those who depend on this employment become a political force which will not be willing to accept future cut-backs in state resources used to support of this sector. Even under less universalistic communication and participation, Malthus (1958: 57ff) did not succeed in demolishing the English Poor Laws (Elsenhans 1992d) before an alternative system of welfare was established. The proposals for a negative citizen tax, the least complicated mechanism of subsidizing labor with lower than subsistence earnings, are no different in their basic mode of operation than the English Poor Laws. Subsidies are used to complement low incomes due to market conditions and force the more productive sectors of the economy to pay the difference.

Industrial policy consists in the mobilization of resources in favor of branches which at the prevailing cost and price levels are not yet profitable, but where future profitability is expected due to the benefits of being first (Krugman 1979: 469–479). There are few means to distinguish whether "inefficiency" is due to the premature character of the investment or to less acceptable forms of waste.

## 5. Perspectives

Globalization leads to serious underconsumption pressures because marginality-ridden catching-up economies are able to proceed to massive devaluation with implicit export subsidies. They are able to do so if there is a sufficient agricultural surplus and hence an element of productivity increase without any mechanisms for redistribution other than employment growth on the basis of cheap exports of manufactured products, which does not, however, lead to full employment. It seems highly improbable that the bulk of marginality-ridden countries can achieve full employment and eliminate marginality only on the basis of exports and without complementary internal reforms.

More advanced economies cannot cope with this challenge merely by lowering their real wages, and not even by increasing the spread of their wages. An end to the self-sufficiency of catching-up economies in food production, or an end to the competitiveness of technically leading economies in high-technology branches (via taxes on such exports[28]) are theoretical possibilities but not very realistic options. The dilemma of the leading industrial countries can therefore only be solved if the catching-up economies not only increase their sectoral competitiveness but also their marginal productivity. This would lead to larger internal markets, to the trickling down of productivity increases to all branches, and, in the case of undervalued currencies, to a massive export expansion and currency appreciation, finally, to the end of the devaluation-driven growth process. Japan, Taiwan and South Korea are today no longer low-cost-labor countries, because export-drives in these countries led to the rapid expansion of internal mass markets and considerable currency appreciations in various phases.

These cases show that the main challenge is tackling the problem of marginality. Marginality, in reality, limits the effects of globalization; it is not the product of globalization, but existed long before. In order to increase the pull effects of demand that originate from the globalization process, the internal restrictions to the extension of multiplier and accelerator effects in

---

[28] The advanced countries could tax their high-technology exports, which would result in a lower exchange rate, so that labor in their low-technology branches is internationally competitive. This would probably prove to be a rather difficult measure, facing considerable political opposition since these export sectors are considered the engine of growth in the economies of the West.

these economies have to be removed. The implementation of such reforms, which I have described elsewhere (Elsenhans 1997e: 294–297), is assisted by further exports, as these allow managing agricultural surpluses without the burden of heavy administrative apparatuses. Export-led growth allows agricultural surpluses to be transformed into mass incomes without cumbersome planning agencies and a vast extension of the non-market economy. This aspect is important, as it seems that agricultural surpluses are more easily achieved than rises in the marginal productivity of agricultural labor due to the world demand structure for agricultural technology, which is dominated by the industrialized West.

It is not the globalization process which represents the challenge – apart from the fact that its intensity is too low – but the specific pattern it follows. As long as globalization is either indiscriminately welcomed or per se held responsible for the results which, in reality, it induces through its lack of intensity, the reforms necessary for making globalization to work more effectively cannot be expected to find substantial support in the international community.

What we are observing at present – just as in the nineteenth century – is various social policies in favor of the South. These measures invariably concentrate on increasing the productivity of labor, since it is assumed that labor is unemployed because it is not productive enough. Entitlement is thus neglected. Productivity, however, is not per se employment creating, as demonstrated by the criticisms of the neoclassical argument. The neoclassical model functions as long as labor is empowered; if labor is not empowered, wages cannot rise to the level of marginal product. All empirical studies agree that an increase in real wages took place in the nineteenth century, namely, during economic crisis via rapidly falling prices,[29] but, more importantly, that these conditions do not exist in the twentieth century. The challenge does therefore not consist in a massive restructuring of the world economy, which nobody is ready to engage in because of the sheer size of the task. The challenge is much more simple: to remove the fetters on large-scale productivity growth in poor countries by combating marginality for a transitional period, thus making the world safe for market regulation.

---

[29] Bernanke/Carey 1996: 881; Hanes 1993: 745; Tucker 1936: 83–84; Keynes 1939: 35–36; Richardson 1939: 431–441; Habakkuk 1972: 275; Rosenberg 1934: 185; Woytinsky 1936: 127–135; Montgomery 1938: 52; Rostow 1938; Mieczkowski 1972.

# Chapter 6
# Intensifying Globalization to Make It Socially Acceptable*

The social consequences of the current globalization drive do not result from the scale of this process but, rather, are due to the specific patterns of this globalization. The reglobalization of the world economy after fifty years of fragmentation in the wake of war and depression is characterized by the integration of economies with considerable degrees of marginal labor into the international division of labor. Because of marginality, labor does not become scarce following sectorally limited productivity increases. Labor loses its bargaining power if marginality, in other words structurally created unemployment, is not eliminated. The current reglobalization drive is too weak to abolish marginality in the periphery of the world system. Globalization has to be intensified by complementary measures in different areas of the politico-economic system if marginality is to be overcome. Such measures belong to the domain of development policy, and aim at transforming the prevailing pattern of globalization into a convoy model in which the both the South and the West can grow economically under conditions of a free-world economy.

The central argument of this contribution is that globalization itself, defined as the dramatic decrease of the cost of transborder economic activities, does not constitute the real threat, but certain conditions of this process do. This argument is particularly important, as a major obstacle to the management of reglobalization is the intellectual perception of this process. The level of today's globalization is not substantially higher than the level of globalization at the end of the nineteenth century. What is new is the participation of economies in an international division of labor where the preconditions for capitalist growth have not spontaneously emerged, i.e., a relatively high marginal product of labor which enables labor to secure bargaining power on the labor market despite its not having part in the ownership of the means of production. The result of persisting marginality is that labor risks being disempowered at a world-wide level. This disempowerment destroys the basis of capitalist growth.[1] Neo-classical economics, which may be considered to more or less coincide with the interests of business, accepts that

---

\* First published in: *India Quarterly*, 57, 1 (January-March 2001): 51–74.
[1] On the dependence of capitalism on rising mass incomes cf. Elsenhans 1983c; Elsenhans 1992f.

real wages will grow in line with economic growth, but deduces this tendency from the scarcity of labor. If labor can no longer become scarce at a global level because of marginality, the basis of neo-classical assumptions concerning the mechanisms of economic growth are destroyed.

## 1. Comparative costs advantages are decisive

A wide variety of globalization "theorists" have proposed the argument that wages are (too) high in the welfare states of Western Europe. Virtually all schools of economics, on the other hand, take this assertion quite differently. They conclude that an economy is always competitive, but perhaps in the "wrong" products or at only very low prices of its labor on the world market. The correct interpretation of the high dollar value of wages in export surplus economies is therefore that productivity in welfare-state economies is so high that their export competitiveness is not endangered despite relatively high exchange rates. They would otherwise incur balance-of-trade deficits. None of these welfare-state economies is massively indebted to foreign countries (as the United States and many of the "low"-wage economies of the Third World are). Only this indebtedness would prove that real-wage levels are too high.

The high dollar value of wages in parts of Western Europe is the result of a high level of international competitiveness, and is not an obstacle to competitiveness. To be sure, trade is guided by comparative advantage and not absolute price differences. Only with comparative advantage in a particular product can an economy profitably sell this product on the world market in exchange for imports of other products. Comparative advantage makes it profitable to import goods which the respective economy could only produce with higher costs. The economy sells a product on the world market not necessarily because it is more productive than other economies, but because it is more cost efficient for the economy to sell this product and to import another one, as opposed to not selling this product and not importing another one. Obviously, no economy can sell a product with comparative advantage if the same product is available from other economies at lower prices. Even if an economy has comparative advantage in a large variety of products, it will be able to sell none of these if the prices it charges on the world market are too high. If such an economy still continues to import instead of becoming autarkic, there will be an oversupply of its currency on the foreign exchange market and the price of its currency will decrease in relation to other currencies. It will be forced to devalue its currency. The prices of its own goods will decrease in international currency. The prices for goods with comparative advantage, which were previously too high, will fall and become internationally competitive before the prices of other goods produced by the economy. Comparative advantage will thus be transformed into price competitiveness. Conversely, any attempt of an economy to create export surpluses by keeping national costs of production – especially labor costs – down can only lead to currency appreciation (or to compensatory capital exports). The wage bargaining process does not determine the long-term costs of national labor at international currency.

The fluctuation of exchange rates in a system of flexible exchange rates and shifts in general price levels in a gold currency system are the mechanisms which transform comparative advantage into price competitiveness. The current globalization process is new in so far as technically backward countries (TBC) are not faced with structural barriers to devaluation in their drive to catch up with technically leading countries (TLC). There was a high level of globalization before 1913.[2] The share of foreign trade in gross national product of the TLCs attained in 1913 has only recently been reached by today's globalization process. The share of foreign investment in capital formation of the TLCs in the period from 1900 to 1913 has not yet been reached. The internationalization of financial markets, especially for short-term assets, is not an indication for a particularly high level of globalization. On the contrary, it shows that a globalized world currency system comparable to the gold currencies of the pre-war period does not exist today.

In the branches of income- and price-elastic goods, however, only those countries were integrated into the international division of labor before 1913 whose economic and social structures automatically transformed the growth incentives created by additional exports into expansion of the internal market and increasing bargaining power of labor. This transformation through export multipliers led to the emergence of a convoy model of globalization (Elsenhans 1999b: 438; Elsenhans 1998: 16–22).

---

[2] UNCTAD 1994: 119–121; Irwin 1996: 44; Bairoch 1996; Bovenberg/Gordon 1996; Ghosh 1995: 126; Verdier 1998; Feldstein 1994; Epstein 1996; Feldstein/Horioka 1980; Bergelijk/Mensink 1997: 166; Theurl 1999: 26.

This convoy model is characterized by two aspects: an economy which falls behind because of technical innovation in a more dynamic one has to accept devaluation and a deterioration of its terms-of-trade but not unemployment, and this because of low productivity backlogs in its non-innovative branches. Because of relatively low productivity differentials in non-innovative branches, relatively low rates of devaluation create new outlets for these non-innovative branches of the non-innovative economy, even in the external market. On the other hand, the non-innovative economy is not able to catch up with the TLCs by means of devaluation but, instead, has to make a much more serious effort to develop its own productivity based on its own internal market.

Suppose that there is a technical innovation in an innovative economy. Its comparative advantage shifts, along with the comparative advantage of all other economies, even the economies where no innovation has occurred at all. The exports of the innovative economy increase and its exchange rate appreciates. The non-innovative branches of the innovative economy will experience higher unit costs in international currency than their competitors in the non-innovative economies. In the non-innovative economies, suppliers which were previously uncompetitive in these branches become competitive, and replace imports from the innovative economies. They may even undercut suppliers from the innovative branches on the world market. At what point the improvement of terms-of-trade of the innovative economy has this compensatory effect for the non-innovative economy depends on the degree of backwardness in productivity of the non-innovative branches in the non-innovative economy (and not on the degree of backwardness in productivity in high productivity branches).

If the non-innovative economy is a capitalist free-market one, the extension of the internal market with tendential full employment leads to productivity levels in the non-innovative branches roughly comparable to the levels of productivity in the innovative branches of that economy, and this despite differences in the development of physical productivity within the non-innovative economy itself as well as between the non-innovative and the innovative one.

The reason for this convergence of sectoral productivity – the normal case for a capitalist world economy[3] – is not of a technical but, rather, of a

---

[3] Costello 1993; Wolff 1991; Alam 1992; Broadberry 1994a; Williamson 1996.

social nature. With a tendency to full employment due to a high level of marginal product, any innovation leads to increasing wages in the innovative branch (in order to attract new labor) as well as to the reduction of production and employment in non-innovative branches until the scarcity of their products drives up prices to such an extent that higher factor incomes can also be paid in the non-innovative branches. This mechanism operates in all capitalist economies if there is a tendency to full employment, and cannot operate in economies where there is structural unemployment, i.e., a labor surplus, as is the case of underdeveloped economies. The implication for the world economy is that sectoral innovation in a particularly dynamic economy leads to an appreciation of its exchange rate which renders backward capitalist economies competitive in non-innovative branches and even creates the possibility of price increases for the products of the non-innovative branches. Thus, non-innovative economies also benefit from productivity increases in the innovative economy.

At the same time a non-innovative economy is forced to specialize on non-innovative branches. It has comparative advantage in non-innovative branches, because its productivity backlog in relation to the innovative economy is lowest here. The non-innovative economy can balance its trade with low rates of devaluation, but this has consequences. These rates of devaluation are too low to enable a devaluation-driven catching-up process. They cannot provide low-cost inputs and low factor costs for branches which are innovative and where the backward economy is considerably more backward than in the innovative branches. Catching-up cannot be realized by devaluation-driven export drives, but only by means of imitation for supplying an at least mildly protected internal market. In the convoy model, the process of convergence is based on expanding internal markets and the bargaining power of labor, as well as mild protectionist measures and usually state-supported mechanisms for increasing innovation in the lagging-behind branches.

The decisive precondition for a convoy model of this type is the tendency to full employment in all economies which participate in the international division of labor in price and income elastic products. This tendency depends on sufficient levels of labor productivity in the essential branches of mass production (wage goods), allowing marginal workers to impose wages which are at least higher than the costs of reproduction for a worker and his family. Labor which produces less than its inevitable consumption requirements, i.e., its costs of reproduction, cannot be employed by owners of assets – whether capitalist or feudal – who maximize financial returns. The convoy model requires a minimum level of labor productivity, namely, marginal labor productivity. The marginal product of labor in wage goods production has to be higher than the costs of reproduction of labor. This is the condition which makes internal-market-based development possible, because only in this case will innovation lead to scarcity of labor, not only in the innovative branches but in all other branches as well, so that wages and hence mass demand can follow average productivity increases on the basis of market processes (i.e., scarcity of labor at labor costs which are too low). Today's globalization is new in that numerous production sites in the so-called low-wage countries have been capable of gaining competitiveness on the basis of devaluation without, however, creating the basis for self-sustained capitalist growth by means of subsequent devaluation-based export drives and the elimination of marginality.

## 2. The challenge: the integration of underdeveloped economies into the international division of labor

In the current globalization process there are economies which achieve relatively high levels of productivity in a limited number of sectors without this growth of productivity trickling down by means of the market mechanism to other economic sectors, especially wage-goods production. The absence of this automatism means that sectorally limited increases in productivity do not increase the marginal product of labor, because in economic activities with stagnant productivity labor does not become scarce and, therefore, the prices of the products of these sectors do not rise. Despite this structural defect, such economies are perfectly able to transform comparative advantage into price competitiveness by devaluing their currencies.

The defining characteristic of an underdeveloped economy is the low level of marginal product, as discussed, for example, in labor surplus theories (Georgescu-Roegen 1960: 35ff; Dandekar 1962: 71ff; Sen 1966: 432). In such an economy, the condition is therefore not fulfilled that every able-bodied laborer produces at least enough to cover his costs of reproduction, guaranteeing the survival of a laborer and his family. Average productivity is low, and so are mass incomes. The share of food in mass consumption is high (50–70 percent). Marginal product of labor is determined by the marginal product of agricultural labor, as agriculture produces the bulk of wage goods.

In contrast to industrial production, marginal product in agriculture does not only depend on the availability of technical innovation but also on the availability of fertile land. It is due to economic and social reasons (and less so cultural ones) that the rate of demographic growth in underdeveloped economies is very high until institutions other than the family emerge which can provide social security, especially old-age assistance. The relation between available fertile land and labor in search of employment deteriorates with demographic growth. The marginal product of labor may even fall below the level of the costs of reproduction – incidentally, even before the introduction of capitalist modes of productions (Chao 1986: 6ff). There is a labor surplus which produces less than its consumption requirements.

The simultaneous existence of a surplus of labor and a surplus of financial resources – which cannot be appropriated on the market under conditions of competition, where profit equals net investment spending – are decisive characteristics of underdeveloped economies and societies.[4] In a capitalist economy, the marginal product of labor has to be higher than the costs of reproduction, as otherwise the wage drift will not take effect and real wages will not increase, creating an outlet problem. In a precapitalist economy, the part of the population which produces less than its costs of reproduction can survive if there are "precapitalist" rules of redistribution. These may exist in order to uphold the power of the privileged class(es). No further explanations are necessary to understand why on the eve of the transition to capitalism in the West there were marginal populations which survived because the precapitalist society still produced a surplus, though not on the basis of their work. The marginality-*cum*-rent model explains the persistence of these mechanisms of redistribution which serve as the basis for clientelism and patronage, which in turn prop up the specific political structures of precapitalist societies, such as tributary modes of production under the leadership of traditional state classes.

If a considerable share of labor produces less than it consumes due to low average productivity and high dependence on agricultural production, there

---

[4] Cf. on this model Elsenhans 1994d; Elsenhans 1995g; Elsenhans 1992b: 111–115; Elsenhans 1995b: 141–142.

is structural unemployment or a surplus of labor. A tendency to full employment can therefore be ruled out. This implies that typical steering mechanisms of capitalist economies are blocked, e.g., real wage increases in line with productivity increases, the growth of mass demand in line with productive potential, incentives for process innovation and new investment goods with higher performance, and the production of local human capital.

Economies with a marginal product of labor below the costs of reproduction cannot achieve self-sustained capitalist growth.[5] "Free" private enterprises may exist, but will depend on state support and market imperfections, as internal demand is not large enough to provoke positive net investment under conditions of full competition. Under conditions of perfect competition, negative net investment spending would imply negative profit rates (Kalecki 1971: 71ff; Robinson 1951: 58; Kregel 1971: 145), since the latter discourage net investment. In this case, any attempt to promote private enterprise in branches with stagnant demand involves some sort of assistance to help maintain the profit rate, hence some violation of the principles of perfect competition, whereas the dynamism of the expanding branches is limited. Such economies, however, can become competitive on the world market. International competitiveness does not depend on technical superiority in the production of particular products. An economy can become competitive on the world market by simply being less than average inefficient in the production of one particular product, and by devaluing its currency. It is in the interest of the given economy to specialize on this product and to import other products, as long as the world market is able to absorb exports of this product.

An economy whose domestic industries can profitably produce the bulk of its wage goods is in principle able to accept any rate of devaluation. Devaluation is made easier if the share of imports in mass consumption goods – either directly or indirectly in the form of inputs and plant and equipment for the production of these goods – is low.

In a TBC still characterized by low mass consumption, food constitutes the bulk of demand out of low incomes. If the local economy can provide food for the entire population, even in the case of rising mass incomes (with rising food consumption), any exchange rate is compatible with full em-

---

[5] For a similar approach cf. Bai 1982; Minami 1966; Minami 1992; Manning 1995; Kaiwar 1994.

ployment. The Green Revolution has allowed major parts of the underdeveloped world to produce agricultural surpluses, enabling food self-sufficiency and hence virtually any rate of currency devaluation in order to become competitive.

Two additional mechanisms increase the scope for devaluation. The first is productivity increases in the agricultural sectors of the TLCs since the 1950s being as rapid as in their industrial sectors. Consequently, productivity increases in industrial branches with below-average productivity are lower than productivity increases in agriculture. It is in these industrial branches that the TBCs have comparative advantage. By exporting the products of these branches, TBCs can buy more food on the world market than before. Food subsidies reinforce this mechanism of TBCs becoming competitive in the non-dynamic industrial branches of TLCs. The second mechanism, technology transfers, reduce productivity differentials between TLCs and TBCs, even if comparative advantage remains unchanged. With the same amount of labor engaged in export production, higher export earnings can be achieved and more food can be imported. This in turn facilitates the transformation of comparative advantage into price competitiveness.

The new competitiveness of low-wage production sites in underdeveloped economies is therefore not necessarily the result of changes in comparative advantage. Comparative advantage even in industrial production has emerged in underdeveloped economies even where no particular developments have taken place in their industrial sectors, this due simply to developments in TLCs, where physical productivity has increased unevenly from branch to branch. The underdeveloped world may therefore dispose of a large variety of "dormant" comparative advantage. What makes the situation new are the increased possibilities for devaluation which allow transforming comparative advantages into price competitiveness.

The transformation of comparative advantage into price competitiveness does not depend on low real wages but on devaluation. The very poor regions of the underdeveloped world which have not yet reached self-sufficiency in food production, for example, sub-Saharan Africa, are not and will not be the forerunners of successful integration into the globalizing world economy on the basis of the low international costs of their labor, despite the fact that all indicators of poverty show that real mass incomes here are much lower than they were for today's tiger nations at the start of their export drives, and are also lower than in the new candidates for successful export-led growth in the rich, monsoon-agriculture countries of South and East Asia.

Furthermore, foreign exchange rates do not correspond to purchasing power parity in the export-led newly industrializing countries. The real purchasing power of poor and even some richer households with respect to the products such households consume is four to ten times higher at the prevailing prices on domestic markets in relation to the prices of the same commodities on the world market.[6]

Low international costs of labor are thus the result of this labor being supplied with mass consumption goods produced in large quantities in the local economy but which cannot be exported. Export-led growth which depends on devaluation and low exchange rates is based on a subsidy. Labor in wage-goods production produces wage goods for export workers whose share in the earnings from these export products on the world market can therefore be very low, even near zero. These export workers can survive because there is a locally produced rent which is channeled into a subsidy for otherwise uncompetitive labor producing otherwise uncompetitive products for the world market. There is a subsistence sector whose products are nearly valueless on the world market. Yet supplied to labor in the export sector of TBCs, these products allow the manufacturing of export products with almost zero value-added costs in international currency prices. Labor in the low-wage production sites of the Third World cannot be undercut by labor in the TLCs without state intervention into the market and price formation for its products. This is not because there are political, cultural or social obstacles which block a potential reduction of labor costs in the TLCs, but because labor in the TLCs is so productive that TBCs can impose an appreciation of the exchange rates of TLCs to render the labor of these TLCs more expensive. As long as there are no limits to devaluation, labor in TBCs can be cheapened almost indefinitely on the basis of subsidies to otherwise uncompetitive labor in non-export sectors of the TBCs.

The new competitiveness of low-wage production sites in the South is therefore the result of a too moderate level of globalization. The low labor costs of the South are the result of a subsidy. This subsidy results from the

---

[6] Yotopoulos/Lin 1993: 11; Guillaumont-Jeanneney/Hua 1996; Lafay 1996: 948, 963; Narrassiguin 1995: 325; Pilat 1995: 140; Chen/Gordon/Zhiming 1994; Tzannatos 1997: 2; Mundorf 1998: 2; Weliwita 1998.

low competitiveness of the wage goods production of TBCs on the world market. This problem would not exist if the integration of the underdeveloped world into the international division of labor were to create full employment in the South. According to a number of theoretical models, the export drive, or the pull effect of additional demand for exports produced with cheap labor, is not sufficient to create full employment with respect to the level of marginality.[7] The number of jobs in OECD countries in the production of tradables is less than 100 million, the number of poor in the South, at 1.2 billion, much larger. Moreover, this tendency is on the rise.

## 3. The import of rent-based structures through unsuccessful adjustments in the West

Adjustment strategies in the TLCs only worsen the problems outlined above, as they tend to slow down globalization with the aim of preserving jobs – at the price of increasing the role of political power and rent in the world economy, which suffers from intensified underconsumptionist tendencies.[8]

Industrial policy has been used by TLCs to restore the mechanism which prevailed earlier, according to which a TLC has the lowest costs for introducing innovations. TLCs are today, once more, aiming at a pattern of specialization which protects them against the devaluation-based competition of TBCs. They are trying to specialize in production lines where TBCs cannot become competitive at any given exchange rate. Thus, it is assumed that there are areas of economic activity where TLCs are unquestionably superior to TBCs and where they are always more competitive in the introduction of new products and new production processes. According to the theory of the product cycle, TLCs are endowed with skills and knowledge which enable them to engage in product and process innovation at much lower costs than TBCs. They also have outlets for such new products, as their mass incomes are high in comparison to the TBCs.

The economic basis for this type of leadership by the traditional TLCs is foundering today because of two mechanisms. The surmounting of barriers of time and space means that any market can be supplied from any given

---

[7] Cline 1982; Peet 1987; Ross/Trachte 1983; Elsenhans 1981c infra chapter 3; Elsenhans 1987a.

[8] This has been described by many authors, cf. Strange 1996: 196ff; Cerny 1999; Elsenhans 1992a: 37ff; Elsenhans 1994e: 560–562.

production site. The fact that the introduction of new products and new processes has become easier in TLCs does not necessarily guarantee price competitiveness, and this due to the very reasons for higher physical productivity in TLCs: the "disembodied" factors of technical progress such as knowledge, human capital, institutions, etc. In contrast to physical capital, these factors are very difficult to measure. They are created by "experience" and "routinization" in hitherto exploited lines of production, and contribute to increasing productivity – albeit predominantly in the old lines of production and less so in the new lines of production where production is just starting.

Suppose there are two economies, one which enjoys the productivity-increasing effects derived from technical leadership in old products, and another, a backward economy, which does not enjoy these productivity-increasing effects. Both economies are assumed to have similar problems launching new products. The TLC is probably more productive than the TBC also in the production of new products because of knowledge, experience and superior organizational and institutional arrangements in other production processes. Yet the advance in productivity of the TLC in new products is lower than its advance in productivity in old products. If there are no special factors favoring the production of new products in the old TLC, it is the newly industrializing TBC which has to specialize on new products, whereas the TLC has to specialize on old ones, even if it also produces new products more efficiently than the TBC.

TLCs can attempt to maintain leadership in the production of new products by massively subsidizing technical progress. But TLCs are blind in this effort, as they cannot imitate technologies as TBCs can.[9] The catching-up economy can employ industrial policy to imitate known production processes for the manufacturing of known products, even if this is not yet profitable due to the level of skill endowment of the economy or the availability of outlets. The available factors of production are then subsidized with the aim of either promoting consumption of the respective product on the internal or the international market or reducing the costs of production. The governments of TBCs know which products have been successful in other economies, as well as which standards apply in terms of the quality and cost of production. A TLC has to subsidize investment in unknown production

---

[9] Nunnenkamp/Gundlach/Agarwal 1994: 147–149; Keller 1992; Irwin/Klenow 1996; Lal 1993; Krugman 1993: 365.

processes for unknown products. It engages in state planning where competition for the discovery of unknown products and processes would be more appropriate. In a mixed economy, where the state only supports private enterprises in this endeavor, the state still provides guarantees for the loss of capital, which implies that the mechanism of the market imposing sanctions on less successful enterprises is removed. A reintroduction of these sanctions in the form of abandoning subsidized innovation processes also has to be negotiated. The anonymous character of the market is replaced by negotiations between a rent-collecting government and a business sector which is able to eliminate the disciplinary function of the market. Hence the industrial policy of a TLC is much more likely to result in waste and failure than the industrial policy of a TBC (Leff 1985: 347; Paqué 1995: 251; Elsenhans 1992l: 115–117).

A TLC cannot rely on an established scenario for increasing productivity, as a catching-up TBC can. Comparable to the negotiating process within state classes the definition of future realities and of the tendencies resulting from this future scenario are the subject of an uncertain political negotiation process.[10]

This increasing politicization of the economy is also promoted by the increasing co-operation between the state and business characteristic of all underconsumptionist situations. Governments and business strongly recommend wage restraint in order to maintain costs competitiveness. This proposal appears quite credible, as the high competitiveness of certain economic sectors of the TLCs leads to exchange rates which cause a growing share of tradables-producing labor in TLCs to lose its competitiveness vis-à-vis the labor of TBCs, even if labor in the former is more productive than the latter in physical terms. (To be sure, this loss of competitiveness is not so much due to higher real wages in the TLCs – which are possibly even lower than in the TBCs – but due to the exchange rate). All TLCs have experienced exchange rate appreciation following high export surpluses and increased cost competitiveness based on wage restraint, even if this appreciation occurred with some time lag.[11] Nevertheless, the illusion of being able to maintain growth and a high level of economic activity by economizing seems to be ineradicable. Bankers and orthodox Marxists are convinced that growth

---

[10] On these patterns of communication cf. Elsenhans 1987b: 81–85.
[11] Cf. Institut für Wirtschaftsforschung 1996: 5.

depends on growing capital intensity, more capital per worker, longer "detours" in the production process, and hence, ultimately, on a growing share of capital-goods production in total output (all of which is utterly false empirically). Successful industrialized countries are characterized by stable, often even falling capital-output ratios,[12] which are relatively low in comparison to Third World countries. This was the basic reason for the downfall of real socialism (Elsenhans 2000e), which postulated the rapid expansion of investment[13] and reaped high capital-output ratios.[14]

The process of globalization consists in the substitution of hitherto relatively expensive products with cheaper products produced in countries with low international labor costs due to devaluation. This means that productivity increases in relation to the costs of factors of production. Globalization therefore represents a world-wide increase in productivity. Assuming that TLCs enjoy improving terms-of-trade from the globalization process, wages in the TLCs have to rise more rapidly than the productivity of this labor. Outsourcing to low-labor-cost economies for the manufacturing of goods which had previously been produced in the TLCs is linked to a rapid increase in productivity in the TBCs' respective export sectors. The outsourcing process originates when enterprises perceive a reasonable chance of producing a given product cheaper in a TBC given the exchange rate situation, the infrastructure and the level of skills in this economy. As the investor normally transfers superior technology and succeeds in rapidly increasing productivity as well as in effecting an improvement of the infrastructure without the exchange rate appreciating, the prices of the goods produced in the TBC's new export sector should rapidly decline. The terms-of-trade between the branches of production which remain in the TLC and the branches of production have been outsourced to the TBC improve considerably. Out-

---

[12] Clark 1965: 7; Bicanic 1962; Helmstädter 1969: 48–60; Kuznets 1971: 67; Mayor 1968: 498; Kendrick 1961: 166; Kendrick/Sato 1963: 974; Fellner 1961; Domar 1961: 101–114; Sato 1971; Phelps Brown/Weber 1953: 270; Lorenzi/Pastré/Toledano 1980: 159; Abramovitz 1989: 163.

[13] On the so-called priority of Sector I in socialist accumulation, cf. Preobrazenskij 1971: 109ff. Cf. also Mahalanobis 1953 and Chandra 1968. There was an interesting discussion on this law in East Germany, cf. Bartl/Luck 1961: 1500; Reichenberg 1967: 1786; Barthel/Karbstein 1967: 221.

[14] Bergson 1992; Bergson 1971; Polanyi 1960; Easterly/Fischer 1995; Myant 1989: 223ff; Obst 1983: 63; Feiwel 1971: 470; Ark 1995: 89.

sourcing leads to a decrease in the total amount of incomes paid in relation to the total volume of goods produced, as is the case with any productivity increase not accompanied by real-wage increases.

Global demand can be maintained in such a situation only through demand in the TLCs, as real wages in the TBCs are kept low because of a surplus of labor. For global demand to keep pace with productivity increases, demand in the TLCs has to rise more rapidly than productivity in the TLCs, taking into account the additional effect of improving terms-of-trade. It is exactly this locomotive function that TLCs are not ready to assume, as they fear a loss of jobs in the case of wage increases beyond productivity increases. If the TBCs were specialized on price- and income-inelastic products, as at the end of the nineteenth century (raw materials), TLCs would not be threatened by a loss of jobs. They would then be able to enjoy improving terms-of-trade, as they did before World War I – with the political consequence of labor supporting globalization and the implicit drive for colonialism. As TBCs are specialized nowadays on price- and income-elastic products, TLCs would have to raise their rate of demand expansion far beyond productivity increases in order to assure their own structural change by specializing on new branches of production where they have comparative advantage and, in the case of expanding real wages, also demand. The shift to such a high growth rate of demand failed to take place at the end of the Keynesian age in the industrialized countries.[15]

Thus, globalization leads on the one hand to an underconsumptionist crisis, because it is too weak to create full employment and real-wage increases in line with productivity increases in the low-labor-cost countries. On the other hand, because of its incapacity to absorb this "pocket" of unemployment in the underdeveloped world, globalization disempowers labor in the TLCs. Both of these processes together with productivity increases and constant real wages create new financial resources which can no longer be appropriated by the market, but only by other, non-market means, so that they become the economic basis for rent-financed adjustment strategies which contribute to an increasing role of political power in the world economy and to the rise of new rentier classes on a global scale.

---

[15] It would be interesting to investigate why the turn to globalization has not coincided with a shift in the rate of demand growth in the industrialized countries.

The alternative is not between globalization and nation-states, but between the globalization of rent, with the implicit consequence of the disempowerment of labor in a strongly statist context, and the globalization of profit through the further intensification of globalization, which implies upholding the bargaining power of labor, and which is compatible with a cosmopolitan political environment and meaningful political mass participation in national, i.e., territorially limited, contexts.

## 4. The alternative of intensifying globalization

A xenophobic, resentful worldview threatens in the West, which echoes a similar xenophobic worldview in the South, where the perspective of economic development is lacking due to the discrediting of development policy and its instruments as well as the weakness of globalization, with the resulting weakness of the market and the state. There is, however, an alternative: an intensification of globalization with the explicit aim of abolishing marginality in today's underdeveloped world, at least in the long-run, and managing marginality in the short- and medium-term by means of appropriate compensatory measures to help keep labor markets from being structured by marginality, i.e., labor surpluses. In this perspective, export-led growth embedded in internal reforms in export-oriented economies produces scarcity of labor with rising real wages, an expanding internal demand, dynamized local small- and medium-scale industries, demand for appropriate technology which is locally produced such as local investment goods production, and the growth of human capital and skills. Experience, innovation, human capital and knowledge which emerge due to an expanding export sector can facilitate the transformation of internal-market-oriented branches as long as these branches face increasing demand.

This is an appropriate albeit rough description of the economic transformations of Taiwan and, with some qualifications, South Korea. The state has modified comparative advantage in order to favor specialization on branches with high learning-by-doing effects, but the trickling down of technical progress from the export sectors to the internal-market-oriented sectors was the result of an expanding internal demand with multiplier effects due to the increasing scarcity of labor and, subsequently, increasing mass incomes which followed average productivity growth. Because the state did not have to care for the details of such inter-industry linkages, since these were created by increasing internal demand, the state classes, with their tendency to waste rents,[16] were forced to accept their own political decline to the benefit of capitalist self-steering mechanisms, and this due to the increasing clout of small- and medium-scale industries and the greater bargaining power of labor. South Korea and Taiwan are no longer low-wage economies. They have caught up with the rest of the industrialized West. This is not because they had high real wages by international standards, but because they were successful in eliminating marginality.

Parallel growth in the center and the periphery of the world system does not require artificially high labor costs in the periphery to secure jobs in the center, but the overcoming of marginality. If marginality is overcome, the drive to modernization launched by the growth of exports will spill over to the rest of the economy, which will become dynamized by a growing internal demand. If productivity increases outside of the established export sectors, further devaluation will lead to rapid growth and diversification of exports, to the substitution of hitherto imported products, and, subsequently, to rapidly rising balance-of-trade surpluses. Currency appreciation can no longer be avoided.

In the case of export-led growth, the export sectors with comparative advantage are those which employ technology corresponding to local factor proportions and factor-cost relations. Innovations in the export sectors can trickle down relatively easily to the rest of the economies of the TBCs, if business is dynamized via markets, hence via demand. As the globalization drive triggered off by export-led growth is not strong enough to overcome marginality, this benign scenario can be realized only if export orientation is complemented by development policy measures which aim at overcoming marginality.

Agrarian reforms can be cited as one example. Egalitarian agrarian reforms eradicate marginality, contribute to a rise in food production, and increase the demand for simple industrial products via the homogeneity of final demand and lower costs of production for products which are produced labor-intensively. With an egalitarian distribution of land, marginal labor time is distributed equally among all owner-operator farmers. All families

---

[16] On the role of the rentier state in South Korea and Taiwan, cf. Rhee 1994: 232–238; Morkre 1981; Irwan 1989; Guha 1990; Moon 1997: 471; Kwon 1998; Zysman 1996: 158; Lehmann 1996: 47; Lall 1994.

have a deficit of land. Every family produces large quantities of food with only a limited share of its labor time, but these quantities are not sufficient for survival due to the limits on land. Additional labor has to be supplied, i.e., labor which, before the redistribution of land, could be furnished only by marginal laborers and, thus, was not employed under conditions of surplus-maximizing landowners. After redistribution, this labor is "employed", because farmer families – in contrast to landowners, who do not have to pay the subsistence costs of a non-productive worker they do not employ – cannot spare their own subsistence costs by choosing not to work.

Production increases, albeit slowly. Owner-operators will furnish this additional (marginal, not very productive) labor as long as opportunity earnings do not exist. They will try to improve the productivity of their plots. It can be assumed that long-term, labor-intensive measures for the improvement of land (erosion protection, terracing, irrigation systems) will contribute to future productive potential.

If the marketable surplus of some farmers increases, marginal labor will also be offered for employment in the rural and urban small- and medium-scale industries at wage rates which may be lower than the wage rates necessary for a landless laborer and his family to survive (Dasgupta/Ray 1987: 179f). The productivity of marginal labor in agriculture will vary from family to family. It can be assumed that this marginal labor is more or less equally efficient when employed in small- and medium-scale industries, as entrepreneurs (and not the laborers themselves) will set production targets. In this case, the exchange rates of individual farmer households for foodstuffs and the earnings from small- and medium-scale industry employment vary. The less efficient farmers will fare better offering their labor time to small- and medium-scale industries and buying with their earnings the surplus of more efficient small-scale farmers, as opposed to attempts to marginally increase output on their tiny plots. The result is an efficient division of labor.

Farmers who are less efficient in food production will offer their labor time to small- and medium-scale industries at a rate which only has to be higher than the earnings from their marginal labor time on their own agricultural plots. The wage earnings of these farmers engaged in by-employment in small- and medium-scale industry do not have to be proportional to the labor time spent in industry, as these farmers and part-time laborers draw significant incomes from the productive time spent on their plots. The family of a landless laborer will starve if this laborer does not earn at least one-tenth of his expenditures on basic needs with one-tenth of his labor time. A farmer needs to earn less in industrial by-employment than the proportionate share of his subsistence costs, as the farmer already earns a share of his subsistence needs higher than the share of labor time spent on his plot. With an agrarian reform, the rent a farmer receives from his highly productive labor time is channeled directly into industry in the form of a subsidy to labor costs, which ultimately benefits all consumers (also in the rich countries which import these industrial products) with the result that quantities sold also increase. Rural industry is dynamized, the demand for new technology emerges and there are new incentives for innovation and imitating the export sector.

An egalitarian agrarian reform involves the use of rent for subsidizing marginalized labor in order to increase mass consumption. Such a redistribution process may face political obstacles. I have therefore suggested the creation of artificial industries based on products for which there is no market at any time. The aim of such industries is to provide jobs for marginal labor (Elsenhans 1991d: 127–129). The amount of today's development assistance at $50 to $100 billion would allow increasing the per-capita incomes of about one billion marginal people, roughly 200 million families, from about $100 to $150 per year, so that these incomes reach the level of incomes in the fourth quintile.

This income could be channeled to the poor in the following manner. A certain, unmistakable kind of stone is dropped over remote areas. An exchange agency publishes its purchasing price, which will be fixed at a level where an average gatherer can earn his daily living by means of his daily gathering. The poor, but only the poor, will then start gathering these stones. They will offer their "yields" on local markets to traders who are not able to lower prices below the costs of reproduction, as the gathers have to survive, and would otherwise not bother collecting these stones. The newly active poor buy food and simple industrial products with their incomes. Farmers, but also landowners will proceed to capacity-increasing investment. Appropriate technology for increasing production at the lowest possible costs will be in demand and a self-sustained capitalist growth process can emerge.

## 5. Rethinking globalization theory

Globalization is manageable with limited means. However, new ways of thinking about globalization are necessary in order to exploit this opportunity. There are two obstacles to the introduction of a new mode of thought. The predominant, liberal-market theory of development is based on the experiences of the United States. Historically, there has never been marginality here, as this country has always had enough fertile land at its disposal to absorb potentially marginalized poor. And no society of today's underdeveloped world can increase its resources of fertile land by genocide. On the other end of the spectrum, the critics of market economies, such as orthodox Marxists of Soviet orientation but also the neo-Marxist (Western) approaches which emerged in the wake of the student movement of the late 1960s, consider the market to be an obstacle to development and exploitation as scandalous. The decisive aim of labor, however, should be the limitation of exploitation to the level of the requirements of financing physical investment for increasing productivity, and the orientation of this investment to the needs of labor through appropriate distribution of purchasing power for consumption goods. It is not the market itself which is the object of controversy, but its embeddedness into a power structure which, with the success of labor, should favor the orientation of the investment process to the needs of labor. Labor has to dispose of bargaining power if it hopes to achieve this aim. With marginality, marginal product is too low to enable average labor to hold its ground on the market.

The current process of reglobalization, following a period of statist fragmentation of the world economy due to the barriers imposed in the first half of the twentieth century, is too weak to overcome marginality in the underdeveloped world. This drive to reglobalization can, however, be intensified by complementary measures in the domain of development policy. If such an intensification is realized, the present pattern of globalization can transformed into a convoy model.

# Chapter 7
# The Politico-Economic Basis of the Limits and Opportunities of Development Administration under Conditions of Globalization*

My contention is that successful development administration cannot be construed in Weberian terms. The Weberian pattern considers "good" administration as being self-controlled because it follows rules and norms. In opposition to Weber's assumption that the acquisition of such rules results from an intellectual learning process, I propose a model which makes these desirable patterns of honest behavior dependent on the effectiveness of two mechanisms of non-bureaucratic control: the autonomy of civil society and the capacity of self-steering of the capitalist market economy. Neither the autonomy of civil society nor the autonomy of a capitalist market-regulated economy exists in the typical situation called underdevelopment.

Whereas the Weberian paradigm results in recommendations concerning the optimal organization and training of the civil service with the goal of enabling civil servants to execute tasks defined by other political or social forces, my model leads to recommendations with regard to overcoming underdevelopment with scarce administrative means and a minimum of rent-seeking, thus allowing an autonomous civil society and a self-steering market economy to emerge. The non-market organization called administration certainly has a role to play in this process.

## 1. My basic model

I base my argument on two interrelated models, which I shall outline here only briefly. The first model is the marginality-*cum*-rent model (Elsenhans 1994d: 393–402) of an underdeveloped economy. Let us suppose a low-productivity economy, the mass of the population having low real incomes of which up to about 50 per cent are spent on food; a production which is characterized by decreasing returns, and where the bulk of the population works in agriculture. The agricultural production ($Y$) is a function ($f$) of labor input ($L$), $Y = f(L)$, where $0 < f' < 1$, and $f'' < 0$. Labor cost is a function of

---

* Lecture at the Research Institute for Public Administration of Hanyang University, Seoul, August 19th, 1997. First published in: *The Annals of Public Administration Research*, No. 15 (1997): 69–90.

the quantity of labor employed ($C = aL$). A simple diagram can illustrate the point:

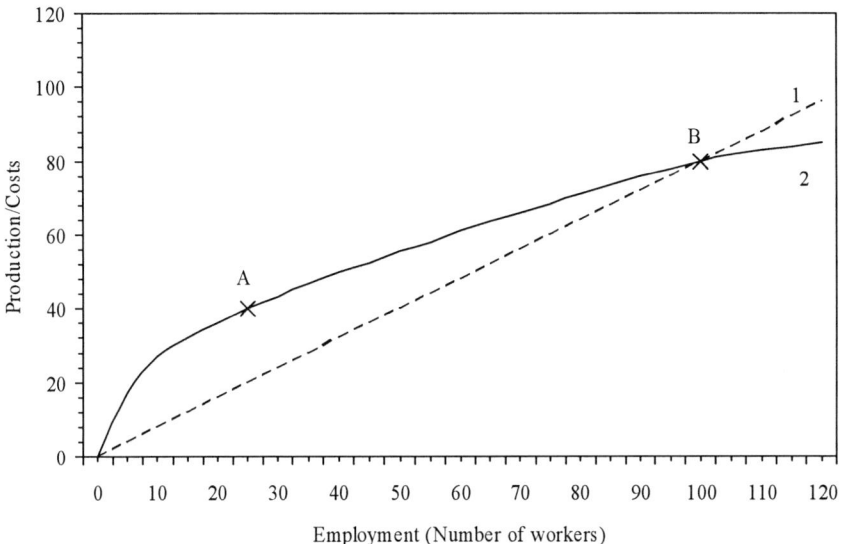

There is a maximum for profitable employment at a level of A, which I call level of marginality $f'(Y) = a$. In the typical underdeveloped economy this level is lower than the total supply of able-bodied laborers. Hence, there is a surplus of financial resources (the distance between the curve of production and the straight line of cost of labor at A) and a surplus of labor. The unlimited supply of labor at a mere subsistence level income disempowers all other average-skilled labor and precludes wages rising with productivity if technical progress should occur. As is shown later, mass incomes cannot rise without overcoming marginality.

Here, a second model intervenes (Elsenhans 1996b; Elsenhans 1997e). In a Keynesian world net investment depends not on available financial resources but on investors' expectations about future profitable outlets. The Bortkiewicz[1] criterion implies that at stagnant real wages any new investment reduces total incomes paid to labor employed in the production process

---

[1] Bortkiewicz 1907: 458ff. Cf. also Okishio 1961. For a discussion of the argument and the literature:cf.: Elsenhans 1996a: 59, 104, fn.18, 19. From this comparative advantage of developed countries in modern technology should follow, cf.: Elsenhans 1985b.

and in the construction of machinery so that only the available surplus increases, without final consumption demand increasing. Without expanding demand there is no net investment. Net investment determines at least ex-post net profit if the usual assumptions are made, i.e., workers consume their incomes and entrepreneurs save. I therefore skip over the questions whether there are other sources of increasing final demand, especially as more luxury or more state spending implies capital becoming either less subordinated to competition or more dependent on the state, with the increased resources of the state transforming it into a structure which frees itself from the controls of civil society. The model is consistent with the new growth theory where fixed capital does not increase more rapidly than total production. It implies the absence of a wage drift as long as there is marginality.

In such a marginality-ridden system there can be neither a self-steering market economy nor an autonomous civil society. The autonomy of civil society is based on an intensive organizational life which, in turn, cannot exist without its being supported by social classes which do not draw their incomes from the state and do not address themselves to the state in order to acquire their essential resources. In order that labor feels free to accept being liberated from old entitlements to subsistence on the basis of links of clientelism and patronage, labor has to be able to earn at least a subsistence income on the market. The doubly-free worker of Marx (free to sell his labor power, free from the property of means of production) can come into existence only if marginal product has risen to levels where there is no more marginal labor which would accept ties of clientelism in order to assure its mere subsistence. Such marginal labor is unable to offer better economic results in this model than the equally qualified employed workers, and therefore will offer other services which we can euphemistically describe as "veneration" for the powerful. As markets do not expand, owners of surplus cannot expect positive rates of return from net investment. They will try to care for the demand of those in control of the surplus, become suppliers to the court and ultimately transform their financial assets into land-holding or offices in the noncapitalist structure, as long-distance commercial capital has done for centuries.

We realize that there can be no autonomous social classes if capitalists do not face expanding markets which induce them to proceed to net investment above replacement. This in turn depends on rising mass incomes, which assume that marginal labor is able to produce more than its costs of subsistence so that it can become scarce and impose higher wage rates either because of increasing marginal product or its political bargaining power. If mass incomes are able to rise, both classes of a typical capitalist economic system empower each other in pursuing their most selfish objectives in a completely uncoordinated way (at least as long as transaction costs are low, which implies high rates of flexibility). By investing in technical progress and capacity extension, capitalists increase their demand for labor. Its scarcity allows labor to push up wages individually or collectively until the going rate equals the full employment marginal productivity level. By raising wages labor enlarges the outlets for capitalist production, which capitalist entrepreneurs react to by investing in capacity-creation as long as there are perfect markets.

In such a situation, both classes perceive the state as a resource-consuming entity and strive for the reduction of its scope of surplus appropriation and surplus allocation. The state is no longer allowed to fulfill any other tasks than those called public goods. The state becomes subject to the permanent scrutiny of both classes, which are eager to limit the costs of the privileged group which becomes labeled as civil servants.

The autonomous civil society and the self-steering capitalist market economy are dependent on the same condition: a level of marginal productivity where all able-bodied workers produce more than their costs of reproduction (i.e., the costs they inevitably have to incur in order to survive with their nuclear family). This condition varies from the condition for the survival of a noncapitalist/precapitalist system. Any society can survive if it produces more than it consumes. A capitalist society with an autonomous civil society and a self-steering economy also requires that marginal labor produces a surplus. Only if this condition is met, are both classes of a capitalist society interested in its maintenance, because labor does not appeal to noncapitalist patrons in order to protect itself, and because capitalists are earning net profits on the basis of their spending on net investment without having to create market imperfections.

## 2. The dominance of state classes in underdeveloped economies[2]

Suppose that this condition for a capitalist economy is not met because average productivity is so low that marginal product is less than the cost of reproduction of labor (Georgescu-Roegen 1960: 32–40). The model implies that there will be a surplus of resources and a surplus of labor. Obviously, there will be great social pressure to produce and appropriate the potentially available surplus. Capitalists can articulate a demand for the available surplus only by investing it. If they invest without afterwards achieving sales on competitive markets which do not compensate for their costs, they will go bankrupt. As long as there is no increasing mass demand, capitalists will not absorb the available surplus through their net investment. Other social groups will be there or even emerge, and will claim their right to the surplus on the basis of non-market mechanisms.

Their power to extract resources from the society cannot be challenged by capitalist entrepreneurs nor by labor if there is no important demand for machine-produced products which justify net investment and which takes its origin from increasing mass incomes.

The most recent form in which such a non-market-based ruling class has emerged was the state classes of the Third World which rose to power following the world depression of the 1930's and the process of decolonization (Elsenhans 1991e: 284–289; Elsenhans 1994c). This class was very strongly associated with development policy and development theory. The theory of modernization had taken Weber's ideas about values governing behavior and assumed that those in control of the state may use the surplus for productive investment, if appropriate patterns of behavior are learned. The westernized officers and civil servants who took over power from the old oligarchies and the colonial rulers were expected to be a new middle class, a sort of substitute to entrepreneurs, although their social origin had very often been the old, non-dynamic ruling classes or the petty bourgeoisie. Because of their westernized discourse about economic development, social reform or revolution etc., they were expected to give priority to investment, especially in light of their nationalist ambitions. There have certainly been such elements in these state classes, as has been shown by the success of some of them in

---

[2] Cf. on state class theory: Elsenhans 1981a. English translation: Elsenhans 1996e. Cf. also: Elsenhans 1992j; Elsenhans 1994b; Elsenhans 1997d; Elsenhans 1984: 19–28; Elsenhans 1995f; Elsenhans 1985a.

overcoming underdevelopment and by the obvious rise in the share of investment in national incomes in most of the countries where such political structures emerged.

The failure in many countries of the South is due to two other elements: the internal contradictions in any class which is based on rent and the western misunderstandings about technical progress in most of mainstream developmental thinking. The capitalist entrepreneur makes a profit because he is technically efficient in producing goods for which there is a solvable demand. If he fails, he is excluded from the surplus-appropriating class because he goes bankrupt. The members of state classes, however, will maintain their position; they have financial resources, power and prestige through political non-market instruments. Thus, they can win allies for defending their positions against challengers and rivals. Available resources have to be used for maintaining networks of social relations.

There are typical structures of organization, decision-making and communication in such state classes (Elsenhans 1987b: 83–85). In order to prevail, coalitions have to be formed. Coalition-building "from scratch" is a costly endeavor. The only members of state classes who have reasonable chances to survive in the power game are those who can initiate the enlargement of coalitions from already existing networks, which I call segments. Typically, segments are based either on ascribed (kin, regional origin, etc.) or achieved (common working experience in the same administration, shared convictions, etc.) roles. In the decision-making process, coalitions are formed around some projects which are not based on the intrinsic values of the projects themselves but on the capacity of the coalition-building around the project to increase the resources, the power and the prestige of the supporters and members of the coalition. The ministry of heavy industry will defend heavy industrial projects in order to increase the number of those who depend on this minister for their jobs and who can increase his political leverage because of their number. In order to push projects through, the projects are presented in an overly optimistic way with respect to returns and costs.

Plans are vitiated from the beginning because the data on which they are elaborated are manipulated to serve the interests of segments which, in contrast to capitalists, will not be sanctioned economically in case of losses, but which know how to renegotiate additional resources in further rounds of their power games. Unforeseen scarcities have to emerge and be solved according to the same rules, giving priority to the position of players in one's own coalition instead of economic rationality.

Prestige is the capacity to be believed to be powerful. Information, therefore, even the most innocent type of it, is systematically controlled for strategic reasons. The whole system is characterized by secret mongering and rumors, as the efforts to hide information provoke parallel efforts to disclosing.

Moreover, segments tend to be constituted more on the basis of achieved roles where economic alternatives are no more a criterion of membership. The more successfully segments grow – even the ones based on shared convictions and economic alternatives – the larger they become. The larger they are, the less they can add additional resources by eliminating rivaling segments, as opposed to falling apart with some new segments taking over the resources of other new segments which were members of the same coalition. As the previous coalition has most likely been characterized by a common economic outlook, the new rivalry can be organized only on the basis of ascribed roles, e.g., in extreme cases sections grouped around different members of the presidential family.

These brief remarks show that there is no politico-economic basis for the behavior the Weberians expected from the "new middle class" of officers and civil servants, and therefore that the American efforts at reform and administrative training in the underdeveloped world could have only limited success, even if these "new groups" were initially "idealistically-minded" (Sklar 1967: 8).

The main contrast to the state classes of the old tributary mode of production consists in economic development remaining an aim in order to preserve national independence against technically more advanced powers. This implies that some state classes may have been able to reach the goal of technical improvement and productivity increase because of commitment, discipline and healthy economic policies which made them follow pathdependent, successful models of overcoming underdevelopment.

## 3. The problem of development administration as distinct from other forms of administration

Two essential conclusions can be drawn from the analysis of the state classes. Firstly, there is no politically independent development administration. The realms of politics, administration and economics are deeply intermingled. The political game involves all groups. Decision-making is achieved on the basis of power games and not on the basis of an autonomous market. In these power games business and labor may be influential, but their access to their own resources, remunerative employment and profitable investment, is always mediated through the decisions of the state class. They tend therefore to enter into relations of clientship as largely described with regard to non-autonomous labor organizations in many countries of the South. Only if business grows in the process of transition, it can become more independent.[3]

Secondly, the patterns of behavior which are characteristic of the state classes are not the result of special cultural patterns of the societies concerned but the outcome of the rules of the rent game. Obviously, these rules are learned and shape behavior. In light of the economic and social environment where he has to operate, nobody will rewrite and reconsider his rules of behavior from scratch on a daily basis. Everybody will follow experience codified in some sort of rules. As long as these rules lead to success rather than frustration, they will not be changed.

From these two conclusions it is clear that any information campaign or education campaign will not be able to overcome these modes of behavior as long as profit remains weak and rent strong. Even the decision to launch such a campaign is normally realized on the basis of such a power game between segments of state classes, as many abortive attempts at liberalization in typical third world countries show, particularly in sub-Saharan Africa.[4]

---

[3] There is very interesting research presented in support of this argument by: Lew/Lee 1997: 15, and by Kim 1997.

[4] Taylor 1997: 149; Lewis 1996: 89; Bhagwati 1988: 546f. This had to be expected from a theoretical point of view which insists on capitalism being dependent on rising mass incomes: Elsenhans 1983c; Elsenhans 1983a; Elsenhans 1992e.

## 4. Modes of disappearance of rent

There are two basic patterns of overcoming the dominance of rent: its successful use for overcoming underdevelopment (through which it is replaced by profit) and its decline due to overconsumption of the state class or a changing international economic environment.

Rent is a source for the financing of investment which may lead to increasing marginal productivity of labor. In this case outlets for machine-produced goods will increase. Private entrepreneurs will make profits because of sufficient demand, partly created by their own growth and investment spending, partly by the inefficiency of the state class-directed public sector, which may decay.

The emerging bourgeoisie will realize that it does not need the state anymore for subsidies. It fights against the state and formulates two demands. Because it is inefficient the state should withdraw from direct intervention into the economy and leave more resources to private business. The internal and external controls over state spending, such as auditing and parliamentary participation in budgetary matters, have to be increased. The state has to rationalize its behavior and become more predictable. The rule of law is required. Business needs a legal framework on which it can operate.

Labor will become involved in these battles, as a more lean state will isolate its opponent in the conflict over working conditions and salaries. Where it had previously met with representatives of the state class, who argued about the superior interest of the nation and applied force on the grounds of defending this interest, labor will increasingly meet with private entrepreneurs with less powerful moral "persuasion."

Obviously, both classes will tend to avail themselves of continued state support in a transitional phase. This leads to the normal configuration of business giving priority to the rationalization of the state and the predictability of the legal framework, whereas labor insists on civil rights and democratic participation. The smaller the sizes of the different business undertakings, the more business will tend to accept political participation on the basis of enfranchisement, without by necessity being initially in favor of equal voting rights. The various phases of tax payment-based systems of representation can be quoted.

A process of disappearance of rent through profit will by necessity tend to a decline of the position of the state class. This will in turn increase the scope for participation and democracy, even if full democracy will ultimately have to be imposed by labor and ideologically committed elements of other social classes.

Let us now look into the second case of the decline of rent. This case is defined by the failure of the state classes to use rent for eliminating marginality by increasing marginal productivity of labor. Rent declines either because of overspending, as described by Ibu Khaldûn and the Chinese theories of the dynastic cycle,[5] or by changing conditions in the international environment. The contemporary situation is characterized by the drying up of many of these external resources: the project of the New International Economic Order with rising raw material prices (additional differential rents) has failed. The aid regime has been altered after the demise of the east-west conflict in the North. The debt regime limits the scope of state intervention for indebted countries.

With the decline of rent, the state classes in power lose their capacity to co-opt a social basis in other parts of the society. These middle strata can no longer expect remunerative employment in the public sector. They have to use the meager resources they dispose of, such as some productive skills and finance in small business. They turn away from the state which suddenly becomes a rapacious fisc (Elsenhans 1992g: 29–34).

There are three typical patterns of the reorientation of these middle strata to the non-state sectors. Engaging in small private business is limited by the extent of the market. The growth of a new non-market sector depends on transfers from the "rich" countries; these countries are prepared to do so in the case of so-called non-governmental organizations and voluntary agencies, the growth of which is impressive. Political entrepreneurialism is a third way, based on launching new social movements which challenge the powers in place. It takes the form of "fundamentalism," as it has to use traditional values, especially religion, which are the only ones available, as the state classes have discredited all other values such as revolution, reform, socialism, equality, capitalism, etc.

The use of traditional values and religion presents some advantages. The poor are heterogeneous with respect to their position in the production process (they are not generally wage workers). Any precise economic project

---

[5] On the so-called dynastic cycle cf.: Ibn Khaldûn 1967: 599–606, 570–571; Reischauer/Fairbank 1960: 117; Wakeman 1977: 204f; Skinner 1971: 273; Usher 1989: 1044.

will divide them, so that the economic program has to be vague and cannot be the basis for assembling powerful movements. In addition, most religions have been revealed or reformed in periods of intensive conflicts between the centralizing states of the old tributary modes of production and the not yet captured peasantries which opposed taxing with the argument of the sanctity of property rights. Thus, these religions normally support property rights with powerful sanctions. The leading elements of the new social movements are hence protected from encroachments by the poor and by the state on their property rights.

The three elements occur in the existing new social movements in different mixtures. As a rule, the more the previously available rent was important, the more precapitalist non-state structures have been weakened and the more the ideological component will prevail over the economic one. In impoverished India, the Hindu fundamentalists have difficulties in mobilizing the marginals. In impoverished Egypt, the Islamic movement is strongly influenced by small business and professionals. In oil-rich Algeria, the weight of low-class ideological leaders is so overwhelming that even small business has not joined the mainstream Islamic movement, but tries to preserve the existing structure by offering its co-operation as a moderate Islamic movement (Carlier 1994). The marginals are not a working class which fights for democratic rules and civil rights; they normally fight for the restoration of community (Bourdieu 1963: 312). They are oriented to the moral economy and may join a project of transition to an autonomous civil society and a market-regulated economy but not develop it on their own.

The weaker the asset-owning middle class is, the more such movements are radical. And the next generation of such movements, after the fundamentalists will also have failed in overcoming marginality, will by necessity be a secular, socialist-oriented one, ending in this manner the whole discussion about the clash of civilizations (Huntington 1993).

## 5. Remarks on the overcoming of underdevelopment through the elimination of marginality

The challenge a development administration has to deal with is the elimination of marginality. Technical progress and more competition will not in any case lead to the end of marginality. Rising productivity in luxuries production will lead to the consumption of more or better luxuries produced by the same amount of labor. An increase in productivity in non-agricultural wage goods production will lower the cost of labor and therefore slightly shift the level of marginality to the right (increasing the level of employment in agriculture). An increase in productivity in agriculture may be characterized by more surplus becoming available from the same amount of labor or by rising marginal product. Only in the latter case will mass consumption-oriented employment increase automatically. As long as technical progress only adds to surplus, even more deregulation will not lead to more competition, because private investors will not see opportunities for additional net investment and hence not contribute to enlarging mass demand through additional employment.

All efficient strategies of eliminating marginality therefore consist in shifting part of the surplus into mass consumption in order to strengthen profit. The most classical example is the redistribution of productive land (agrarian reform) (Elsenhans 1979a: 552–562). Productivity of labor on the newly organized small farms decreases: labor which otherwise would have yielded less than its proportionate share in costs of subsistence nevertheless has to be done, because total production of the farm does not match the needs of the farm family if only highly productive labor is realized. Without any further administrative measures the surplus of the highly productive hours is used for bolstering mass consumption among the poor, as long as there is no alternative employment which yields higher incomes than marginal labor on the small farmer's own plot. Obviously, surplus, and here marketable agricultural surplus, decreases but profit may increase as the demand for simple industrial items, which can be manufactured by means of locally produced machinery, grows. This is not different from the English poor laws, where the parishes taxed the rich and farmed out subsidized workers (the poor) to the same rich at wages low enough to match their low marginal product (Elsenhans 1980a). Non-governmental organizations in today's poor countries contribute to the reduction of surplus for increased mass consumption by channeling charitable offerings to the poor (Elsenhans 1995d). Obviously, state-led investment, especially in sectors where there are bottlenecks, may also contribute to such a process of rent-channeling, especially in the case of sectors where the economy has comparative disadvantage but high demand growth and high learning effects. I mention the promotion of equipment production (Westphal/Kim/Dahlman 1985: 201–213; Mytelka 1986: 258). Even the Washington Consensus of export orientation constitutes such a reduction of potential surplus in favor of mass consumption and profits. Its central element is devaluation in order to transform comparative advantage (e.g., lower than average lag in productivity in relation to industrially advanced countries) into cost effectiveness. Obviously, at wage rates lower than 1/50 of the wage rates practiced in the industrial countries, this labor would not be able to buy its means of subsistence on the world market. Devaluation to such levels is possible if there is a locally produced agricultural surplus from which additional export workers can be fed. Once more, the surplus of agriculture goes at least partly into additional consumption instead of going into investment (Elsenhans 1997b; Elsenhans 1996c).

In contrast to state-led investment under the economic theory of modernization, the redistribution of surplus in favor of mass consumption in the different forms mentioned above makes the investment process dependent on external or internal demand and reduces the role of the state in resource allocation in favor of market-oriented entrepreneurs, hence contributing to the efficiency and automaticness of rent channeling.

I assume that all the non-market instruments briefly discussed here are characterized by decreasing returns, so that a mixture will lead to the best results. Land redistribution may be considered by potential private investors as a threat to property rights; non-governmental organizations lose in efficiency and dedication with increasing size; income transfers to the poor inevitably create gates for rent-seeking, etc. The basic mechanism of eliminating marginality through redistribution for profit emerging in the wake of local equipment production until technical progress in mass consumption goods has raised marginal product to levels above the costs of reproduction (this being the eventual condition for self-sustained growth) will require the eclectic coherence of a variety of measures, whose exact combination will depend on local circumstances (Elsenhans 1996d: 122–134; Elsenhans 1997a).

## 6. Globalization and development administration

Eclectic coherence is opposed to the Weberian model. Patterns of behavior, rules and norms cannot be separated from aims. The threats of self-privileging, waste and corruption inherent in any rent-based decision-making process without market sanctions persist.

Obviously, cultural norms may be a factor. Favorable patterns of norms, however, will be upheld only if temptations are limited. Simplifying the tasks and programs, making transfers automatic, installing controls, etc. may be significant factors which could prevent development administration from derailing.

The importance of success in eliminating marginality in the "South" becomes greater for the industrially advanced countries the more globalization proceeds. The possibility of transferring many techniques into economic environments which otherwise are characterized by low productivity, means that the bargaining power of labor world-wide increasingly depends on the bargaining power of labor in poor economies, where it may be nil because of persistent marginality.

The availability of local agricultural surplus allows nearly unlimited devaluation and hence internationally cheap labor, whose real wage may be higher than the real wage at the prevailing foreign exchange wage rate in the rich country. Labor in the rich country cannot avoid such competition through wage restraint, as the cheapness of labor in the poor country is the result of exchange rate movements and low marginal productivity in the poor country. The more previously underdeveloped countries achieve the elimination of marginality through export orientation, the more their exchange rates appreciate. The international costs of labor of initially poor countries may rise in foreign exchange even if real wages in national currencies continue to be depressed. This is demonstrated by the fact that catching-up countries are also increasingly confronted by international competition in their previously well-earning export sectors, and experience the same phenomena they had been accustomed to detect only in the "decadent" West. Hence, the solution to the dilemma is an intensification of globalization, its deepening, with the aim of overcoming marginality through open markets in the West and complementary reforms in the South (Elsenhans 1997f: 147–158).

With globalization, everybody becomes dependent on the threat of marginality, so that efficient development administration becomes an overriding goal for everybody. It is often argued that there is no political force in the South capable of fighting marginality. Those countries which are economically advanced are, however, not without any possibility of creating mechanisms of eliminating marginality. Employment with an additional wage bill of fifty billion dollars seems to be sufficient in order to increase the per capita income of the one billion poor in the underdeveloped world, which can be considered as marginalized. I have suggested that if there is no other means of eliminating marginality, the industrially advanced countries may transform their development assistance into a demand for otherwise useless items with two essential characteristics: their collection must be labor intensive and they must be easy to identify and expensive to imitate (Elsenhans 1991c: 281–283). These items could be thrown from helicopters in remote areas and exchanged in one or several central offices against national currency at a rate where a marginal worker would get the means for his daily subsistence as a result of his average daily gathering, including the transaction costs of transporting the collected items to the exchange office. It is easy to see that only the marginals would engage in that business. The better-off farmers would face an additional demand for food. They would increase production, proceed to labor intensive investments and purchase simple tools, stimulate the local small-scale industry, etc.; hence, they would realize through the markets all those wonderful suggestions alternative development theory wants development administration to apply. Once more, we would create an intelligent mechanism of rent channeling for increasing mass consumption which would launch profit with a low exposure to rent-seeking.

# Chapter 8:
# La mondialisation: mythes et véritables défis*

## 1. Compétitivité et excédents de la balance commerciale dans une situation de chômage

Il est indéniable que la réduction massive des coûts de transport dans le cadre de la circulation transfrontière de biens, de services et de capitaux, induit un changement durable des choix à opérer pour une politique économique et sociale nationale. Toutefois, cela ne signifie pas qu'il soit impossible de mener une politique nationale. En effet, bien moins fondée est la réussite d'une certaine politique nationale d'ajustement – ajustement à des salaires plus bas dans d'autres pays en réduisant les coûts de la main d'œuvre à l'échelle nationale. Si les charges salariales étaient dans l'ensemble trop élevées en Allemagne, cela signifierait nécessairement que ce pays a d'énormes déficits commerciaux et non pas des excédents commerciaux malgré le chômage, ce qui est apparemment le résultat de charges salariales trop élevées. Malgré les coûts de main-d'œuvre élevés par rapport à la moyenne internationale, l'Allemagne vend plus à l'étranger qu'elle n'achète sur les marchés extérieurs.

Pour retracer clairement ce que déclarent effectivement les partisans des réductions de salaire: il ne serait possible d'atteindre le plein-emploi en Allemagne que si ce pays pouvait compter davantage – c'est-à-dire beaucoup plus que cela n'a été le cas à nos jours - sur la bonne volonté des autres pays à accepter leurs propres déficits commerciaux, c'est à dire à réduire leur propre niveau d'emploi. En fait, c'était sur la base d'une telle attitude des grandes économies capitalistes, laquelle fut d'ailleurs le résultat de la prétendue absence d'augmentation des salaires réels au profit des travailleurs, que Rosa Luxemburg (1923: 79–106, 336–360) a fondé sa théorie de l'impérialisme.

La promotion de l'emploi par le biais des excédents commerciaux est non seulement dangereuse, compte tenu des considérations de politique étrangère et d'économie mondiale – car les partenaires commerciaux vont en fin de compte s'opposer à un autre surendettement par le biais de la restriction du libre échange – mais aussi inefficace en même temps. Des excédents soute-

---

\* First published in: *Naqd – Revue d'études et de critique sociale*, No. 12 (spring/summer 1999): 105–123.

nus de la balance commerciale mènent à une réévaluation de la monnaie concernée par rapport aux autres monnaies, c'est-à-dire à des facteurs de production allemands dont le prix serait plus élevé sur le marché international, ceci s'appliquant en particulier à la main d'œuvre non salariée en DM puisqu'elle augmente parallèlement.

L'on peut faire remarquer que depuis 1993, le *Handelsblatt*[1] journal qui n'est pas exactement pro-syndicat dans ses affiliations, a attiré, à maintes reprises, l'attention sur le fait qu'il n'y a pas eu beaucoup d'accords salariaux au cours de ces dernières années mais que le niveau élevé des coûts de la main d'oeuvre allemande sur le marché international était la conséquence des réévaluations successives à la hausse du DM. Ces dernières sont dues, à leur tour, aux excédents de la balance commerciale allemande : « Tout comme il est certain que le mécanisme du taux de change va toujours créer des possibilités suffisantes d'exportation pour payer les importations, il n'y a rien à dire sur le type de produits à l'exportation que cela concernera »[2].

Il va sans dire que ceci est aussi valable pour les partenaires commerciaux de la République Fédérale d'Allemagne qui se trouvent obligés de dévaluer leur monnaie en raison des excédents de la balance commerciale allemande. L'on constate aussi qu'une partie des entreprises allemandes ont vu leur compétitivité baisser à l'échelle internationale parce qu'une autre partie des entrepreneurs allemands restent si compétitifs (et ce, malgré des coûts élevés de main d'œuvre) qu'ils enregistrent des excédents de balance commerciale même si le prix de la main d'œuvre allemande augmente du fait de la dévaluation à laquelle procèdent leurs partenaires commerciaux. Ainsi, le prix de la main d'œuvre allemande sur le marché international augmente de pair avec le taux de change croissant, tout ceci sans distinction des accords salariaux conclus en Allemagne. L'on peut en déduire que, dans l'ensemble, les salaires ne sont pas trop élevés en Allemagne. Au contraire, dans certains secteurs économiques, la République Fédérale est si compétitive que d'autres secteurs perdent leur compétitivité. Il est malheureux pour

---

[1] Mundorf 1995: 2. Handelsblatt, 29/30-12-1995: 11; 3-8-1994: 3; 11-8-1994: 2; 5-6-1993: 13. Cf. also Elsenhans 1994a; Elsenhans 1995c; Elsenhans 1995a; Flassbeck 1995; Flassbeck 1988; Neuthinger 1989; Deutsches Institut für Wirtschaftsforschung 1992.

[2] Suntum 1986: 502, cet auteur semble avoir changé d'avis dans un rapport écrit à la demande des hommes d'affaires allemands (Deutscher Industrie- und Handelstag, DHIT). cf. Suntum 1996 et Handelsblatt 27-8-1996: 1.

le travailleur allemand que les secteurs très compétitifs ne génèrent pas une dynamique de croissance suffisante pour réaliser le plein-emploi.

## 2. Du fonctionnement de la loi des coûts comparés

La grave idée fausse servant de base au raisonnement selon lequel une réduction des salaires permettrait de redevenir compétitif à l'échelle internationale au point de réaliser le plein-emploi grâce à un excédent commercial plus important, découle de l'hypothèse selon laquelle le commerce extérieur repose sur les coûts avantages absolus. Au contraire, il repose sur les coûts avantages comparés.

Selon la loi des coûts comparés, une économie améliore son bien-être par le biais de la spécialisation même si elle fabrique tous les produits en utilisant moins de facteurs de production que ses partenaires commerciaux. Si l'Angleterre produit 20 unités de textiles ou 15 unités de vin en utilisant le même taux de main d'œuvre et le Portugal seulement 10 unités de chaque produit, alors le Portugal gagnerait plus en échangeant 15 unités de vin contre 16 unités de textiles. L'Angleterre, à son tour, gagnerait en recevant 15 unités de vin échangées contre 16 unités de textiles alors qu'elle n'aurait autrement produit que 12 unités de vin au lieu de ces unités de textiles.

Que l'Angleterre se spécialise donc n'est pas seulement souhaitable mais aussi indispensable tant que le Portugal participe au libre échange.

Les consommateurs anglais ne peuvent acheter du vin portugais que s'il est moins cher que le vin anglais. Si l'on prend la main d'œuvre comme facteur de production utilisé – comme dans l'exemple de Ricardo et comme c'est en général le cas aujourd'hui puisque le facteur de production – le capital, à la différence de la main d'œuvre (ou du « travail ») – est mobile sur le plan international et tend par conséquent vers un prix uniforme à l'échelle mondiale – tant que les coûts de main d'œuvre en Angleterre et au Portugal sont égaux, le vin portugais ne peut pas être moins cher que le vin anglais. Si on appliquait ce taux de change, les consommateurs portugais n'achèteraient que des textiles anglais et du vin anglais, à condition que le vin soit d'une qualité qui corresponde à leurs goûts. Afin d'acheter ces produits, les marchands portugais de vin et de vêtements vendront des escudos portugais sur les marchés de change pour acquérir des livres sterling. Puisque les négociants anglais n'achèteront pas de produits portugais lorsque les coûts des facteurs de production sont identiques parce qu'il sera impossible d'écouler ces produits en Angleterre, les fournisseurs d'escudos seront amenés à dévaluer leur monnaie par rapport à la livre sterling et ce n'est qu'à ce moment là, soit après une dévaluation de 33 pour cent (33 %) que le vin portugais coûtera exactement le même prix que le vin anglais. A ce stade, les acheteurs anglais de vin portugais offriront des livres sterling. A partir de maintenant, les Portugais ne voudront acheter des textiles anglais qu'une fois que la valeur de l'escudo baissera d'au moins 50 % de sa valeur initiale. S'il y a une nouvelle dévaluation, les Anglais et les Portugais n'achèteront que des produits portugais. L'élasticité-prix de la demande en ce qui concerne deux produits au sein de deux économies détermine le moment où il y a stabilisation du taux de change entre les deux taux de change possibles – aspect qui ne sera pas approfondi ici.

Les différentiels de coûts salariaux sur le plan international ne dépendent pas des mouvements de salaires dans les deux pays même si, grâce au développement des échanges, il existe plus de possibilités d'augmentation des salaires réels. Le changement intervenu au niveau du taux de change et, par conséquent, des coûts salariaux au niveau international (non national) constitue le mécanisme par lequel le pays qui produit le moins compétitif ces deux produits devient compétitif.

Si les textiles et le vin étaient les seuls biens échangeables, le textile étant un bien de grande consommation mais non le vin en Angleterre, il y aurait augmentation des salaires réels au Portugal malgré une baisse des coûts salariaux portugais sur le marché international, alors que les taux de salaire réel anglais resteraient stationnaires en dépit de la hausse des coûts salariaux anglais à l'échelle internationale.

L'Angleterre ne pourra freiner la hausse du coût international de sa main d'oeuvre qu'en prélevant des droits de sortie sur ses textiles, les rendant ainsi plus chers et résorbant la demande relative à ces deux produits au Portugal. L'Angleterre ne pourra empêcher une baisse de sa production de vin que si l'avance qu'elle a en matière de production de vin est aussi grande qu'en matière de production de textiles. Dans les deux cas, ceci ne pourra être réalisé grâce à une réduction des salaires mais plutôt en protégeant les secteurs de production relativement moins développés et en prélevant des droits spéciaux sur les secteurs relativement plus développés. Un resserrement général des salaires ne peut pas sauver des emplois dans les secteurs de production relativement moins développés. Il est certain que des hausses de salaires inférieures à l'augmentation de la productivité donneront lieu à des produits exportables à bon marché en monnaie nationale et l'on peut donc s'attendre dès le début à une augmentation des exportations. Mais, par la suite, l'excédent commercial ainsi espéré ne conduira une fois de plus qu'à une réévaluation de la monnaie nationale. C'est ce qui se passe aujourd'hui sous vos yeux, et comme Ford l'a déclaré à Cologne, toute l'épargne a été absorbée par la réévaluation.

Il s'ensuit que le resserrement des salaires ne peut avoir d'impact que sur la répartition du revenu national en revenus destinés à la consommation et en profits et non sur la compétitivité à l'échelle internationale. Plus la réduction des salaires est importante, plus fortes seront la réévaluation et, en conséquence, la contraction de la demande interne.

La réévaluation ne modifie pas la relation existant entre le revenu familial et les prix des produits locaux, ce qui n'entraîne une (légère) remontée de la demande en produits locaux qu'en cas d'inélasticité-prix de la demande en produits importés. La réévaluation, au lieu d'une politique d'augmentation des prix réels orientée vers la productivité et la réduction des heures de travail, donne lieu à une combinaison de coûts salariaux élevés sur le marché international et à une demande interne stagnante, en d'autres termes à une déflation (baisse du niveau général des prix) et au chômage. Lorsque l'on procède à une augmentation des salaires réels dans le sens d'une meilleure productivité, il est possible de maintenir la demande interne à son niveau sans pour autant mettre plus en danger la demande externe que dans le cas d'une réévaluation. Ainsi, la tentative d'accroître le taux d'emploi en ignorant l'expansion de la demande interne est vouée à l'échec.

## 3. Coûts comparés et spécialisation en sous-développement

Le défi que constitue la mondialisation réside dans le degré élevé de compétitivité de certains secteurs allemands d'exportation, lesquels en même temps ne sont pas des secteurs qui connaîtront la croissance à l'avenir, et qui en vertu du taux de change élevé en Allemagne enlèvent leur compétitivité aux autres secteurs. Supposons que l'on remplace les textiles par des automobiles de haute qualité et par des machines spécialisées, le vin par la micro-électronique et des automobiles classiques, l'Angleterre par l'Allemagne et le Portugal par les Tigres de l'Asie du Sud-Est et de l'Extrême-Orient. L'Allemagne doit se spécialiser en automobiles de haute qualité et en machines sophistiquées, abandonner la production de biens micro-électroniques et d'automobiles classiques bien que la productivité matérielle en Allemagne ait pu être plus élevée qu'en Asie du Sud-Est et en Extrême-Orient, du moins au début. En raison de l'abandon de ces filières de production par l'Allemagne, il y aura à l'avenir un nombre sans cesse décroissant d'innovations dans ces secteurs industriels de l'Allemagne.

Lorsque la demande mondiale en produits micro-électroniques et en automobiles classiques augmente plus vite que la demande mondiale en limousines de luxe et en machines sophistiquées, la forte productivité dans le cas de produits offrant moins de perspectives d'avenir mène à une spécialisation où la protection de la place de « leader technologique » sur les marchés en expansion sera menacée à court terme.

Ce phénomène n'est toutefois pas nouveau. Non seulement, c'est ce qui explique que la Grande-Bretagne ait pris le pas sur les industries de luxe de la France durant la révolution industrielle (Crafts 1989: 427) et l'Allemagne sur la Grande-Bretagne du début du XIX$^e$ siècle jusqu'aux années soixante.

Avant les années 1960, la productivité moyenne de l'Angleterre était supérieure à celle de l'économie allemande; cependant, vers la fin du XIX$^e$ siècle, l'Angleterre était loin derrière l'Allemagne en ce qui concerne l'exportation de certains produits nouveaux tels les produits chimiques et électriques, bien que de nombreuses découvertes et inventions vitales pour ces deux industries aient aussi été faites en Angleterre.

Etant donné que les normes étaient « médiocres » pour des vieilles industries de l'Allemagne et que ceci a fait que ses recettes sur le marché mondial étaient en conséquence faibles, ce pays jouit d'un avantage comparatif au niveau des nouveaux produits – ce qui lui a permis, malgré une productivité peut être même inférieure au départ -de dépasser l'Angleterre sur le plan technique en se spécialisant dans ces produits (Fremdling 1991: 39, Howard 1907: 91ff). Même lorsque le Japon a lancé son offensive dans le domaine de l'exportation d'automobiles et de produits micro-électroniques, sa productivité était bien inférieure à celle des Etats-Unis d'Amérique, quoique dans des proportions moindres qu'avec de vieux produits (Watanabe 1991: 59, Audretsch/Yamawaki 1988: 446 ; Dollar/Wolf 1988: 554). Ce n'était pas grâce à sa supériorité initiale que le Japon a dépassé les USA mais plutôt, dans le cas de ces produits, parce que l'économie américaine avait moins d'avantages comparatifs que dans le cas des vieux produits. Les pays qui sont à la traîne en matière de développement technologique ont généralement peu de possibilités de rattraper les pays développés quand il s'agit de produits anciens. Par conséquent, ils importent ces produits en grandes quantités. Il est en général plus facile de combler son retard lorsqu'il s'agit de produits plus récents dont la fabrication vient juste de démarrer dans les pays développés. Ceci est surtout valable pour les technologies de la nouvelle génération qui viennent juste d'apparaître sur la scène.

L'on suppose depuis les années 60 que le « capital humain » accumulé grâce au progrès technologique réduit les coûts de la mise au point et de l'application de nouvelles compétences techniques par rapport aux économies moins avancées à un tel point que les avantages techniques peuvent être maintenus (Posner 1961: 329; Vernon 1966: 194). Même si une économie avancée a des avantages en matière de nouvelles technologies vis à vis de pays technologiquement arriérés en raison de la formation, de la discipline et du comportement responsable et amène des travailleurs vis à vis du patronat, elle ne pourra éviter une spécialisation dans les anciens produits que si les bénéfices découlant de produits plus récents sont aussi importants que la supériorité et l'avance qu'elle possède en matière de productivité des anciens produits, laquelle repose, du moins en théorie, sur la pratique et l'utilisation courante de ces anciennes technologies. Si quelqu'un apprend le hollandais en tant que langue étrangère après l'allemand, il est certain qu'il progressera plus rapidement qu'un Japonais qui ne connaît aucune de ces deux langues. D'autre part, il a moins de chances d'avoir la même avance en hollandais sur un Japonais prenant avec lui des cours de hollandais qu'en Allemand, langue que ce dernier n'a même pas apprise. La notion même de progrès technique désincarné, qui est à la base de la croissance capitaliste puisque ce progrès serait autrement freiné par une baisse de la productivité du capital, rend très improbable la stabilité de la hiérarchie au niveau des gains de productivité. La supériorité dont jouissent les grands pays est basée sur des éléments qui ne sont plus des facteurs de coût dans ces mêmes pays et qui occasionnent des coûts à l'économie en redressement, selon l'analyse de la théorie des pôles de développement, en particulier par Perroux (1963), comme par exemple une infrastructure insuffisante, la configuration du système éducatif, les valeurs de discipline etc., déjà inculquées à la population par les familles. Il y a peu de chances que ces facteurs aient la même importance pour la maîtrise des nouvelles technologies où les économies avancées et celles peu développées doivent commencer à apprendre même si elles sont dotées d'aptitudes et compétences différentes.

Ainsi, la mondialisation est devenue un problème car l'avance dont a joui l'économie allemande jusqu'à nos jours dans le domaine des anciennes technologies ne peut être maintenue au même niveau dans les nouvelles technologies. Ceci laisse espérer toutefois que les avantages compétitifs dont peut encore jouir l'Allemagne avec les nouvelles technologies pourrait être maintenus grâce à une réduction des charges salariales en gardant les coûts de main d'œuvre à un niveau aussi bas que celui des nouvelles économies industrielles en redressement. Ceci servira, c'est ce que l'on croit, à maintenir la compétitivité des prix des nouveaux produits dans l'industrie locale.

Cependant, cette tentative est vouée à l'échec tant que les secteurs les moins dynamiques technologiquement restent hautement compétitifs sur le marché mondial. L'Allemagne se retrouve dans la situation que vivent les pays producteurs de pétrole sous une forme extrême et que l'on connaît sous le nom de « maladie hollandaise » (Ansari 1989; Parvin 1988) après les répercussions des exportations gazières hollandaises sur le taux de change de la couronne (Braun 1989: 29). L'avance prise en matière de productivité est si considérable dans un secteur trop petit pour le plein-emploi que d'autres secteurs de l'économie (ex: le secteur agricole des pays producteurs de pétrole, Scherr (1989) sont inhibés.

Les grands pays industriels réagissent en essayant de poursuivre une politique industrielle, en ce sens qu'ils subventionnent des secteurs qui ne sont pas compétitifs de nos jours. Dans le Rapport Cecchini (1988: 73–81), l'approfondissement de l'intégration européenne est explicitement justifié par le fait que le marché extérieur élargi va soutenir les nouvelles industries. L'on justifie la politique industrielle par le fait qu'au sein de ces nouvelles industries, des réductions de coût commencent déjà à apparaître en raison de la forte production et que ces réductions sont de plus en plus importantes au fur et à mesure de l'augmentation des séries de production qui exigent de conquérir d'autres parts du marché mondial (Krugman 1979). En supposant que les nouveaux produits répondent aux nouvelles demandes, la politique industrielle des pays à haut revenu présuppose une augmentation des revenus collectifs de telle sorte à favoriser l'émergence de marchés/débouchés pour ces produits.

Le problème auquel sont confrontées les politiques industrielles réside dans le fait que personne ne peut prédire avec un degré suffisant de certitude quels nouveaux produits et technologies offrent des perspectives d'avenir.

L'idée répandue en Amérique selon laquelle un ministre de l'industrie japonais particulièrement clairvoyant a déjà choisi les « secteurs d'activité rentables/porteurs » de l'avenir et les a subventionnés est exagérée. Pour une économie retardataire, il suffirait de subventionner ces secteurs de production là où le niveau d'arriération/sous-développement du pays est le moins visible.

L'on ne peut justifier la viabilité future d'un projet d'investissement en prétendant que la micro-électronique, les nouveaux matériaux et les biotechnologies seront des secteurs porteurs de croissance à l'avenir.

Cependant, s'il ne fait aucun doute que la tentative d'accroître les exportations des anciennes industries grâce aux subventions et aux efforts diplomatiques causera – en passant par de nouvelles réévaluations – de plus grands problèmes au moment du passage vers les nouvel technologies sur le plan économique, il n'y a aucune raison de se prostituer aux dictateurs de Beijing.

L'une des manières de rester compétitif par le biais d'un changement structurel, même au niveau des nouveaux produits et technologies, serait de se passer des subventions aux secteurs à faible productivité, aux grandes importations à faible composante technologique (comme les denrées alimentaires), et de promouvoir le développement du marché intérieur par le biais de la productivité et des hausses de salaires réels orientées vers les termes de l'échange ou une réduction des heures de travail (ce qui entraîne une consommation particulièrement élevée de nouveaux produits découlant de l'existence de plus de loisirs) tout en renonçant à essayer de résoudre le problème de l'emploi par les excédents de la balance commerciale, en particulier au niveau des anciens produits. Avec moins d'excédents commerciaux, peut-être même avec des dévaluations du DM, il est fort probable que l'on puisse obtenir la plus grande part possible de nouveaux produits fabriqués avec des technologies du futur – objectif beaucoup plus important que l'excédent commercial – qu'en tentant d'obtenir un excédent de la balance commerciale.

### 4. Le problème de la concurrence des pays a bas revenu

Le problème de l'emploi ne peut être résolu par le mécanisme d'ajustement du taux de change si les économies participant à la division internationale du travail n'atteignent pas le plein-emploi (accompagné d'augmentations des salaires réels orientées vers la productivité) même si elles appliquent des taux de dévaluation[3] extrêmement élevés.

Telle est la nature du défi qui ressort de la compétitivité des coûts des économies sous-développées dans une large variété de produits avec un impact sur la situation de l'emploi dans tout le Tiers-Monde et, de ce fait, sur le pouvoir de négociation des travailleurs dans le monde et aussi dans le monde industrialisé (le Premier Monde).

Ce nouveau phénomène revêt au moins trois aspects : une nouvelle distribution des avantages comparatifs, de nouvelles possibilités de transformer l'avantage comparatif en compétitivité des coûts, et un chômage persistant malgré de forts taux de dévaluation dûs à une faible productivité des industries de biens de grande consommation.

Le développement technologique des pays industriels avancés d'aujourd'hui a été caractérisé par des niveaux différents d'augmentation de la productivité de la main d'œuvre pour les divers produits. Il va sans dire que les hausses des salaires réels sont allées également de pair avec le progrès technique, ces hausses ayant d'ailleurs considérablement contribué à de nouveaux pas en avant. Mais ceci est en fait dû à la forme sous laquelle les avantages comparatifs ont été transformés en avantages absolus bien que cette transformation ne peut être attribuée à des revenus réels croissants. Sans distinction de l'augmentation des salaires réels (qui a eu effectivement lieu), les différences enregistrées au niveau des taux de croissance de la productivité de la main d'œuvre devaient nécessairement entraîner de nouveaux avantages comparatifs pour les économies n'ayant connu aucun progrès technique (ni d'augmentation des revenus de la main d'œuvre).

Le développement inégal de la productivité selon les chaînes de production aurait dû, depuis longtemps, avoir conduit à un avantage comparatif dans l'industrie du monde sous-développé d'aujourd'hui, du moins dans certains secteurs. La question qu'il faudrait donc se poser n'est pas pourquoi

---

[3] J'ai déjà mis en garde contre cette attitude, bien avant le débat sur la mondialisation, comme par exemple dans Elsenhans 1981c et 1987a. Le risque d'une crise de la sous-consommation provoquée par le fait de remplacer des emplois bien rémunérés par d'autres mal payés – risque analysé dans les communications sus-citées – reste le même et n'est pas affecté par la position défendue ici. Une telle substitution ne peut être évitée par le biais d'un resserrement des salaires dans les pays industriels si le prix relatif de la main d'oeuvre est déterminé par les taux de change et par les prix internationaux des produits alimentaires.

ces économies sont devenues de plus en plus exportatrices de produits manufacturés mais plutôt pourquoi leur a-t-il fallu autant de temps pour ce faire ?

Au départ, le Sud avait des avantages comparatifs en matières premières (en raison de l'épuisement des gisements à faible coût dans les pays industriels occidentaux, du transfert de technologie à partir de 1880 à ce jour, d'une demande croissante en produits agricoles tropicaux découlant de l'augmentation des revenus réels dans les pays industriels de l'occident) accompagnés de l'appropriation des rentes économiques par les classes dirigeantes pré-capitalisme donnant lieu à des prix élevés et à de bonnes recettes d'exportation. De plus, leurs monnaies étant liées à celles des métropoles coloniales, l'option de la dévaluation n'était pas offerte aux colonies sous tutelle. La crise vécue par les économies coloniales exportatrices de produits primaires durant la récession économique mondiale des années 1930 a donné naissance aux mouvements nationalistes du Tiers-Monde qui ont abandonné la pratique des avantages comparatifs pour recourir à la substitution aux importations (Elsenhans 1994c: 98–101; Elsenhans 1991a: 276–278). La préoccupation essentielle était d'améliorer les termes de l'échange et l'appropriation ou le contrôle des rentes par les classes nationales qui rejetaient les pertes du pouvoir d'achat des « élites » découlant des dévaluations comme étant l'exploitation des pays pauvres.

Mais, pour les pays industriels développés se trouvant dans la même situation, c'était essentiellement aussi l'impact des termes de l'échange qui était important. Malgré la dévaluation des coûts de la main d'œuvre sur les sites de production à faible coût, la croissance et la diversification des exportations de ces derniers étaient suffisamment restreintes pour ne pas menacer les niveaux de l'emploi dans les pays les plus avancés. Dans de telles conditions de restriction, l'intégration de pays techniquement sous-développés a augmenté les possibilités d'accroissement des salaires réels dans les pays techniquement plus avancés au-delà de la croissance de la productivité de la main d'œuvre grâce à l'impact des termes de l'échange.

Une telle situation, où les pays plus avancés technologiquement jouissent d'avantages de coûts au niveau des termes de l'échange suite à la dévaluation dans les pays moins avancés mais avec peu de suppression d'emplois, ne peut se produire que si l'avantage comparatif des pays les plus avancés concerne une grande variété de secteurs de production et l'emploi ; de ce fait, si leur avance en productivité est plutôt faible dans un grand nombre d'activités pertinentes, celle qu'ils détiennent en productivité moyenne sera donc presque exclusivement déterminée par un désavantage comparatif important dans une petite gamme d'activités.

Au début de l'industrialisation, les principaux pays industriels jouissaient d'avantages comparatifs avec de petites avances en productivité pour une série de biens industriels, alors que les pays sous-développés avaient un avantage comparatif dans une petite gamme de produits avec de très faibles retards ou même des niveaux supérieurs de productivité, comme par exemple pour les matières premières.

L'investissement direct étranger et les efforts déployés par les gouvernements dans le cadre de la politique de développement ont accru les possibilités de transfert de technologie, à tel point que, dans certains secteurs du monde sous-développé, les retards ou écarts de productivité ont considérablement diminué ou même complètement disparu.

Les principaux pays industriels ont donc aujourd'hui un avantage comparatif dans un petit segment de la production industrielle mais ils possèdent néanmoins une large avance en productivité. Leur avance moyenne en productivité et, par conséquent, leurs salaires orientés vers la productivité moyenne sont beaucoup trop élevés dans de nombreux secteurs de production par comparaison à ceux de leurs concurrents du Tiers-Monde parce que la forte avance en productivité dans un petit segment entraîne un excédent à des taux de change élevés.

L'existence parallèle d'excédents de la balance commerciale et du chômage peut s'expliquer par le fait que les avantages de coûts des principaux pays industriels sont concentrés dans un petit segment de l'industrie ayant de larges avances en productivité, les avances en productivité dans les secteurs à composante technologique étant petites en même temps.

Cette tendance à une compétitivité accrue des sites de production à faible coût est renforcée par les nouvelles possibilités de transformer l'avantage comparatif en compétitivité (rentabilité). Une fois de plus, les taux de salaires en monnaie nationale importent beaucoup moins que les coûts internationaux de la main d'œuvre dans différents sites de production comme le met en relief le paradoxe suivant : les taux de salaires réels en Asie du Sud-Est et en Asie Orientale sont supérieurs à ceux de l'Afrique subsaharienne, mais les prix internationaux de la main d'œuvre sont plus élevés en Afrique subsaharienne, même s'ils sont adaptés aux différences en matière de productivité de la main d'œuvre là où ces dernières sont d'ailleurs en train de disparaître car les entreprises multinationales peuvent normalement gérer leur technologie dans des systèmes régionaux et culturels différents ayant des niveaux comparables de productivité.

Les différentes aptitudes à accepter une dévaluation sont à la base de ce paradoxe. Dans des économies ayant des salaires réels bas et, par conséquent, une part élevée des produits alimentaires dans la consommation des travailleurs non qualifiés, les possibilités de transformation des avantages comparatifs en avantages absolus par la dévaluation sont en principe illimitées tant qu'il y a une autosuffisance en produits alimentaires. Si l'agriculture peut produire un excédent en utilisant les technologies de la « Révolution Verte », alors une économie visant le plein-emploi pourra même se permettre des recettes d'exportations marginales négatives.

Foncièrement, la Révolution Verte élimine tous les obstacles se dressant devant les dévaluations jusqu'au moment où le plein-emploi aura été réalisé et il y aura en conséquence une hausse des salaires réels dans les pays où la part des importations dans la consommation de masse – essentiellement orientée vers les denrées alimentaires – est négligeable.

Là où l'on n'a pas atteint l'autosuffisance, les travailleurs supplémentaires employés dans la production destinée à l'exportation doivent recevoir un revenu qui leur permettra au moins d'acheter les produits de première nécessité disponibles sur le marché mondial.

La dévaluation dépendrait alors du rapport des prix des produits alimentaires et des produits industriels sur le marché mondial. Il est certain que, depuis les années 30, la productivité agricole des pays industriels a en moyenne augmenté moins rapidement que dans l'industrie mais plus rapidement que dans certains secteurs industriels à faible croissance de productivité. Les prix des produits alimentaires sur le marché mondial baissent par rapport aux prix des produits fabriqués par les secteurs à faible croissance de productivité. En outre, il y a de plus grandes possibilités de dévaluation même dans les pays sans autosuffisance alimentaire parce que ces derniers sont en mesure d'acheter une quantité constante de calories à des prix en baisse (par comparaison aux produits à l'exportation). Ils peuvent ainsi transformer leurs avantages comparatifs en avantages absolus avec des déficits plus importants en productivité alors que, plus haut, les taux requis de dévaluation n'auraient plus été en mesure de garantir la nourriture destinée aux travailleurs supplémentaires produisant pour l'exportation. A notre avis, cesser de subventionner les exportations alimentaires sera certainement bien plus efficace et utile qu'une réduction des salaires si l'on veut mettre un frein à la concurrence croissante du Sud. Tout en gardant à l'esprit le taux de change, il serait plus prudent d'autoriser l'importation de produits agricoles et d'accorder aux agriculteurs – qui se retrouvent ainsi au chômage – des pensions de retraite que de subventionner les exportations agricoles comme on le fait actuellement.

Aujourd'hui, en raison des prix inférieurs des produits alimentaires et de l'autosuffisance dans ce domaine ainsi que du coût moins élevé du transfert de technologie, les avantages comparatifs qui avaient déjà existé pourraient être transformés en avantages absolus parce qu'il est possible d'avoir des taux supérieurs de dévaluation ou alors – comme conséquence des retards de productivité absolus moindres – parce que des taux inférieurs de dévaluation sont nécessaires pour obtenir des avantages absolus.

Dans cette nouvelle concurrence, il y a un cas ordinaire et un autre qui l'est moins. La dévaluation comme moyen de baisser le prix de la main d'œuvre nationale sur le marché mondiale n'est qu'une forme sous laquelle les taux de change des pays techniquement peu développés se détériorent. Les limites de la dévaluation sont identiques à celles de la détérioration des termes de l'échange. Une économie ne doit accepter une détérioration des termes de l'échange que lorsque les coûts décroissants des biens produits à l'échelle nationale en fonction des produits importés ne déclenchent pas une substitution aux importations imposée et dirigée par le marché.

Lewis (1978: 16–19) a démontré que l'obstacle principal se dressant contre la nécessité d'une dévaluation illimitée est la productivité des biens de consommation courante (biens salariaux), en particulier l'agriculture à des niveaux bas de consommation réelle. Une économie au sein de laquelle la productivité est relativement élevée, même dans des secteurs toujours orientés vers le marché intérieur réagira rapidement à la dévaluation en procédant à de nouvelles exportations et à une production supplémentaire qui se substitue aux importations ainsi que par une croissance de l'emploi, limitant ainsi les effets du processus de dévaluation.

Les économies ayant une autosuffisance alimentaire peuvent en effet procéder à une dévaluation plus forte que celles dépendant des importations alimentaires, bien que le résultat fusse un plein-emploi entraînant une augmentation des revenus collectifs grâce à une croissance de la productivité là où les organisations syndicales sont encore faibles sur le plan politique. Par contraste, dans les grandes économies sans autosuffisance alimentaire, il existe le danger de voir les dévaluations éventuellement réduites ne pas mener au plein-emploi par le biais des exportations, la faible productivité agricole provoquant la perte de leur emploi pour une partie des travailleurs aptes à occuper un emploi rémunéré que ce soit dans le secteur agricole ou dans celui des exportations. Dans une telle économie, même si la productivité des secteurs individuels tels celui des exportations augmente, il n'y a pas augmentation des revenus des travailleurs non qualifiés. Aussi longtemps que le plein-emploi n'est pas atteint, la main d'oeuvre ne devient pas rare, les salaires n'augmentent jamais de pair avec la productivité moyenne. Ils augmentent non parce qu'un travailleur est plus productif mais plutôt parce que la main d'oeuvre se fait rare et seulement à condition que les entreprises soient disposées à rémunérer leurs travailleurs jusqu'au moment où les salaires soient au même niveau que le produit marginal de l'emploi supplémentaire.

Les normes sociales peuvent bien servir à améliorer et renforcer le pouvoir de négociation des travailleurs non qualifiés dans les pays à bas salaires. Mais, tant qu'il y aura du chômage à cause de marginalité (existence d'une main d'oeuvre robuste et forte qui produit moins que ce dont elle a besoin pour sa subsistance, Elsenhans 1994d: 393–401; Elsenhans 1995g: 193–200), il n'y aura pas d'augmentation du revenu collectif même en cas de croissance de la production industrielle de sorte que même l'emploi non agricole restera peu important pour le marché intérieur.

Plus le nombre de ceux recevant un revenu dans l'agriculture est élevé, moindre sera la pression exercée sur les travailleurs non qualifiés (ou manœuvres) pour qu'ils offrent leurs services contre un bas salaire en monnaie locale. Cette réduction de l'emploi dans l'agriculture peut augmenter par le biais d'une répartition égalitaire des terres [les heures de travail à faible croissance de productivité sont « subventionnées » (soutenues) par le résultat des heures de travail plus productives, (Elsenhans 1979a: 552–569)] et de l'investissement dans l'augmentation du produit marginal du travail qui est, d'ailleurs, encouragée par une répartition égalitaire des terres en raison de la rentabilité.

L'on peut démontrer que même une croissance provoquée par les exportations accompagnée d'une dévaluation théoriquement illimitée est le même type de mécanisme utilisé pour transférer une rente agricole à des travailleurs marginaux (qui ne gagnent pas de quoi assurer leur subsistance sur le marché mondial) que les lois anglaises sur les pauvres (Elsenhans 1992e: 130–162), les ONG d'aujourd'hui, sur le plan économique (Elsenhans 1995d: 156–159) et la création éventuelle à l'avenir d'une industrie de ressources artificielles pour créer des emplois financés par des organismes bailleurs d'aide (Elsenhans 1991c: 281-283).

Tant que l'on n'aura pas éliminé la marginalité dans les pays en voie de développement en faisant adopter par les gouvernements des mesures d'ordre économique et social, les échanges commerciaux comme résultat de la dévaluation ne pourront agir tel un moteur de croissance qui bat en brèche le chômage structurel que dans les petites économies, et ce n'est que lorsque l'on viendra à bout du chômage structurel qu'il sera possible de se passer – en principe – d'une dévaluation illimitée de la valeur internationale de la main d'œuvre nationale comme seul moyen d'augmenter le revenu national par le biais de l'économie de marché.

Il va sans dire que les instruments brièvement décrits de la lutte contre la marginalité, entre autres la réforme agraire, les exportations subventionnées par le biais d'une dévaluation sur la base d'un excédent agricole, la démarginalisation des pauvres à travers les ONG ou les programmes d'emploi, etc., visent tous à transférer la rente d'un secteur générateur d'excédents en revenus au profit des pauvres, ce qui nécessite donc un secteur non commercial efficace. Il est donc très douteux que le scénario associé à la mondialisation, à savoir celui de la domination du monde par les structures capitalistes, soit réaliste.

Ceci soulève la question de savoir si une croissance illimitée est possible, et quelles sont les dispositions éventuelles à prendre pour ce passage vers un système international capitaliste sans économies sous-développées, arriérées et marginalisées.

Prétexter une limitation/insuffisance des ressources ne veut pas dire que la croissance de l'emploi est impossible. Au contraire, ceci montre seulement que la disponibilité des produits peut diminuer dans l'avenir, peut-être aussi comme une des conséquences de la croissance à un stade où il n'est plus possible d'exploiter l'environnement. Ainsi, un volume de production obtenu aujourd'hui avec peu de travail et un effet négatif sur l'environnement peut être réalisé avec plus de travail et le plein-emploi à l'avenir. L'objectif consistant à permettre l'intégration économique des pays en voie de développement au sein de l'économie mondiale grâce au plein-emploi est facilité par le fait que l'environnement n'est plus librement disponible en raison d'une augmentation des intrants par unité supplémentaire de production.

Ceci se produirait même lorsqu'il y a une baisse temporaire de la productivité dans le monde entier tout en tenant compte du passage à la production écologique comme conséquence de l'apport additionnel à la production éco-efficace. Foncièrement, un tel modèle de croissance favorable à l'environnement est caractérisé par un coefficient de capital croissant qui entraîne une modification de la distribution du revenu utile en faveur du capital sans menacer le niveau de l'emploi, parce que, dans un tel cas, les importantes ressources financières des entreprises ne dépassent pas les débouchés qui se prêtent à un investissement rentable.

Il n'y a pas réellement de tentatives visant à surmonter les problèmes de la transition, si nous supposons que ces tentatives doivent surtout transformer les nouveaux concurrents en partenaires sur le marché mondial, contribuant à une capacité de consommation égale au potentiel de production grâce à l'élimination de la marginalité. de telle sorte qu'une hausse des exportations mènera à une augmentation des salaires réels, à une productivité croissante de la production de biens de grande consommation orientés vers le marché intérieur et donc enfin à limiter la dévaluation.

La stratégie à long terme des pays industriels avancés consiste à protéger l'emploi à travers une spécialisation en produits de haute technologie là où ils soutiennent que les pays à faibles coûts ne peuvent être compétitifs quel que soit le taux de la dévaluation. Il existe deux catégories de produits comme ceux mentionnés ci-dessus, en l'occurrence les biens d'équipement de haute technologie et les biens de consommation techniquement sophistiqués.

Etant donné que l'emploi dans la production de biens d'équipement des économies capitalistes ne peut être réalisé sans la croissance de la production des biens de consommation, il ne sera pas possible non plus de réaliser le plein-emploi par le biais de la seule augmentation de la production de biens d'équipement dans les pays industriels. De même, le fait que le Tiers-Monde soit pauvre ne lui permet pas d'acheter dans l'immédiat tous les biens d'équipement dont il a besoin. Les consommateurs de biens de consommation de haute technologie sophistiqués et de biens de consommation produits avec des biens d'équipement de haute technologie, se trouvent très certainement, dans leur écrasante majorité, dans les principaux pays industriels. D'où la tentative simultanée de ces derniers de s'assurer des parts importantes de ces marchés par le biais d'un blocage des salaires. Ceci a pourtant comme conséquence le ralentissement de la croissance de ces marchés de consommation à haute technologie.

## 5. La mondialisation et le processus de Maastricht

Grâce aux possibilités particulières de dévaluation offertes aux pays nouvellement industrialisés, les principaux pays industriels essaient d'éviter l'impact de la concurrence imposée par ce groupe en s'efforçant de conquérir les plus grands segments possibles des marchés où les économies qui se caractérisent par la marginalité ne figurent pas comme concurrents. Ceci accroît la concurrence entre les pays industriels occidentaux qui sont tous assez riches pour déployer de nouvelles technologies par le biais d'une politique industrielle. Certaines interventions sont moins problématiques : la décision de retirer de vieux produits du circuit de production entraîne un déficit de la balance commerciale et une baisse des coûts internationaux de la main-d'œuvre locale dans les secteurs à haute technologie. Une politique intelligente de l'emploi utilisant des bénéfices des termes de l'échange liés à la spécialisation (en se passant des produits locaux subventionnés et en les remplaçant par des importations moins coûteuses) pour subventionner des biens et services non échangeables peut encourager l'emploi et l'exportation de produits de haute technologie. En dernière analyse, des opérations telles que les réductions salariales et le subventionnement de secteurs de haute technologie financés par ces réductions ne peuvent que mener à une baisse des capacités de consommation à la suite de laquelle tous les pays industriels vont déclencher de commun accord une récession, tel que cela a été fait « avec succès » dans les années 30 avec la course à la dévaluation.

Avec l'introduction de l'union économique et monétaire, les dévaluations ne peuvent plus être utilisées comme instrument d'accroissement de l'emploi au sein de l'Union Européenne (U.E.). Les réductions des coûts internationaux ne pourront plus être réalisées que grâce à des réductions d'une égale importance des coûts de la main d'œuvre locale. C'est la migration qui devient le seul moyen d'ajustement. Cependant, il faut souligner qu'en dépit de la liberté de mouvement dans cette région, les barrières d'ordre culturel empêcheront les marchés de l'emploi dans les zones moins développées de se redresser grâce à l'émigration vers les régions prospères comme cela se produirait dans une nation culturellement homogène (Elsenhans 1995d: 143–150). Ici, la tentation serait forte de déplacer les sites de production vers les zones moins développées en raison de revenus très faibles des travailleurs.

Foncièrement, la concurrence sur les sites ne poserait pas problème si elle engendrait une capacité de consommation correspondant à la capacité de production. Cependant, rien ne garantit que cette concurrence n'engendre pas une capacité de consommation trop faible par rapport à la croissance potentielle de la production.

Dans ce contexte, le processus de Maastricht ne pourra réussir que si les partenaires, en particulier ceux économiquement plus puissants, veulent promouvoir la croissance économique en développant également leurs marchés intérieurs.

Les perspectives de voir ceci se réaliser sont plutôt pessimistes. L'approfondissement de l'intégration met en mauvaise posture les acteurs dont la capacité d'agir est ancrée dans les cultures nationales. Alors que les capitalistes qui essaient d'obtenir des coûts réduits peuvent facilement s'entendre sur une démarche commune transnationale, les travailleurs de leur côté, doivent rassembler des organisations aux structures très différentes, aux expériences et aux modes d'action différents dans le but d'avoir une influence certaine. L'on ne sait pas, cependant, si le lien (ainsi créé) plus fort entre les syndicalistes et les gouvernements nationaux va aboutir à un accord mutuel autour d'une politique économique, notamment une action concertée pour accroître la demande, tout en permettant en même temps aux zones moins développées de jouir d'avantages de coûts (au niveau des salaires, des normes sociales, etc.). Ceci est surtout valable pour les périodes de chômage, même dans des régions technologiquement avancées de la communauté.

Il serait donc bon de se demander si la recommandation faite après 1945 durant les négociations visant à la création d'une organisation commerciale internationale devrait être reprise et réexaminée par l'Union Européenne.

La proposition faite en ce temps-là consistait à utiliser les excédents de la balance commerciale pour financer les déficits des économies ayant des déficits commerciaux, sans distinction de l'intérêt à tirer de ce processus. Au sein d'une U.E. liée par une monnaie unique, les excédents réalisés grâce au commerce intra-communautaire pourraient être imposés en obligeant les pays excédentaires à apporter des contributions supplémentaires à l'Union Européenne.

## 6. Internationalisation des marchés financiers et développement du marché intérieur

La solution des problèmes relevant de la mondialisation dépend de la réalisation simultanée du plein-emploi au sein des diverses économies nationales.

Ceci est foncièrement possible si toutes les parties concernées se rendent compte qu'en essayant de régler le problème de l'emploi par le biais des excédents de la balance commerciale et des réductions de coût, elles vont inévitablement échouer sur les mécanismes des taux de change et elles renonceront à l'exercice beaucoup plus dangereux de monopoliser les marchés futurs grâce à des taux de change plus bas (découlant de l'abandon délibéré des balances commerciales positives). L'on s'oppose à une telle expansion de la demande sous prétexte que celle-ci échouera en raison de l'internationalisation des marchés de capitaux (Kregel 1994). Il y a ici deux positions distinctes: en premier lieu, la rentabilité des capitaux/investissements va baisser en raison de l'augmentation des revenus collectifs, entraînant de ce fait des sorties de capitaux vers des régions à faibles coûts de main d'œuvre (travail), et en deuxième lieu, le mécanisme de compensation/correction des déséquilibres commerciaux grâce à des modifications du taux de change cesse d'agir en raison des spéculations internationales sur les marchés fonciers.

L'on investit là où la productivité et les facteurs coûts sont annonciateurs de bénéfices. Le retrait des capitaux financiers augmente la compétitivité d'une économie parce qu'il a un effet de baisse sur le taux de change d'une monnaie. Cependant, les gouvernements devraient, à cette fin, se résoudre à ne plus protéger les capitalistes rentiers et à ne pas s'opposer aux dévaluations. Viser une valeur extérieure plus élevée de la monnaie nationale n'a aucun sens pour les producteurs d'une économie capitaliste ; pour ses rentiers, si. L'on peut supposer que ces rentiers ont une forte influence politique car, avec la capacité croissante des classes moyennes à épargner, ils représentent un immense potentiel d'électeurs indécis – potentiel qui a un impact certain sur les partis politiques. Toutefois, les Allemands ont une seule alternative: soit, ils veulent plus d'emploi, soit ils préfèrent se sentir tels des rois en vacances en vertu d'un DM fort. On est en droit de supposer que la réponse est claire pour la majorité des populations ouvrières.

La fuite des capitaux des pays à monnaie instable ou de ceux dont la monnaie est soupçonnée de dévaluation vers celles soupçonnées de réévaluation ne présente des risques que pour les économies sous-développées car ces dernières, en raison de leur faible productivité, ne sont pas en mesure de substituer leur production locale aux importations malgré des taux de dévaluation minimes.

De tels mouvements de capitaux n'ont aucune importance pour le financement des investissements dans des économies diversifiées. La Banque Centrale peut toujours garantir une offre suffisante de crédits par le biais des politiques monétaires. Le taux d'intérêt qu'elle applique a peu de chose à voir avec le prix des capitaux mais il sert plutôt à rationner les capitaux destinés à l'investissement de telle sorte à éviter une surchauffe ou un suremploi.

Tant que les marchés du travail flexibles sont accompagnés de sous-emploi, les taux d'intérêt qui sont « utilement » bas ne mènent pas à l'inflation. Le manque souvent déploré de flexibilité sur les marchés du travail est, en effet, dû aux espoirs perdus d'un retour rapide au plein-emploi. Il ne faut donc pas partir du principe que le fait de discipliner le travail (les travailleurs) par des bas niveaux de l'emploi soit le moyen le plus efficace d'obtenir un avantage comparatif dans les industries nouvelles à haute technologie grâce au transfert des travailleurs des activités déficitaires vers celles plus prometteuses.

Cependant, les transactions financières internationales sont citées comme freins aux possibilités d'une politique monétaire nationale. L'offre de crédit facilitée par la banque centrale pourrait aussi être utilisée pour l'arbitrage entre les taux de change sans qu'il n'y ait encouragement d'un investissement productif ce faisant. De tels mouvements transfrontaliers de capitaux ainsi que des flux de capitaux basés des spéculations sur les taux de change produisent les effets recherchés: ils font baisser la valeur externe de la monnaie; l'emploi augmente; une croissance est relancée grâce à la demande intérieure.

Même à court terme, ces mouvements de capitaux ne peuvent modifier les fluctuations des taux de change dues aux transactions de marchandises qu'à un degré minime. L'effondrement historique du dollar n'a pas été le résultat de mouvements de capitaux mais la conséquence de la baisse de la compétitivité de l'économie américaine.

Il existe toutefois des possibilités de combiner des faibles coûts d'investissements avec des taux d'intérêt compétitifs (donc élevés) à l'échelle internationale. Le coût du financement des investissements ne dépend pas seulement des taux d'intérêt mais également des crédits d'impôts liés aux investissements, comme les règles d'amortissement. De forts taux d'imposition et des crédits d'impôts généreux peuvent faire baisser considérablement le coût du financement des investissements par rapport aux spéculations internationales.

L'opinion selon laquelle la fixation des prix de cession érode l'assiette de l'impôt et ne permet pas des taux élevés d'imposition pour le secteur des compagnies (le secteur industriel) parce que les bénéfices apparaissant sur le bilan sont minimes, est pertinente, mais on peut la rejeter en disant que les compagnies peuvent aussi être imposées sur d'autres chapitres tels la production tant que celle-ci est rentable au taux de change correspondant. Ceux qui parlent de capitations (impôts levés par individu) devraient être prêts à discuter de la possibilité de demander à toute entreprise privée de verser un impôt minimal indépendamment du bénéfice figurant sur son bilan.

Tant que la production est rentable et rapporte des profits en fonction du processus global d'accumulation, la spéculation sur les avoirs financiers ne pourra pas retirer des ressources financières à l'investissement. Malgré les enjeux importants, les spéculations à court terme n'ont pu conduire qu'à des variations insignifiantes des taux de change, soit quelques points de pourcentage. Etant donné que les espérances à long terme des spéculateurs sont déterminées par l'évolution du commerce des produits de base, la spéculation fait aussi appel à des opérations de garantie de change qui représentent un pourcentage considérable des mouvements de capitaux à court terme.

La spéculation a lieu même sur les marchés boursiers mais les prix élevés des actions n'ont qu'un impact relativement limité sur les possibilités de financement à long terme ouvertes aux compagnies jouissant d'avantages à court terme. La spéculation financière internationale n'annule pas la base de l'échange de produits liée à la tendance du taux de change, mais au contraire, elle la partage avec celle-ci : ainsi, les économies qui misent sur une expansion de l'emploi sont renforcées par la dévaluation tandis que celles misant sur une contraction de la demande en faveur des profits (bénéfices) attirent des capitaux financiers et subissent une réévaluation. Toutefois, malgré les nouveaux instruments disponibles sur les marchés financiers internationaux, de tels mouvements de capitaux réduisent la confiance des entrepreneurs et ces derniers revoient leurs espoirs à la baisse à cause des effets du surajustement (de surréaction).

En raison, surtout, du fait que leur impact se limite à quelques points de pourcentage, un impôt levé sur chaque transaction serait un instrument utile pour les obliger à mieux suivre l'évolution du commerce des produits de base.

*Traduit de l'anglais par* KAMEL MUSTAPHA FERRANI

# Chapter 9
# A Convoy Model vs. an Underconsumptionist Model of Globalization*

## 1. Preliminary remarks

Globalization is defined in this article as an increase in the share of transborder transactions in trade, long-term capital and short-term capital. The cultural aspects, the constitution of transnational networks based on non-governmental organizations (often held to constitute a transnational civil society) and the international cooperation between governments with the aim of establishing international norms where national norms were once considered sufficient are not dealt with here. I will focus instead on the real economy.

Capital reacts by not investing in or withdrawing its assets from countries whose political "climate" it finds disagreeable. This reduces the international costs of these countries' currencies, hence the international price of local factors of production, a fundamental support mechanism for diversification and employment in already diversified economies, and poses problems only in the case of technical dependency and high levels of foreign indebtedness. Indeed, contemporary globalization will be shown to in reality be decisively promoted by devaluation, the central instrument for newly industrializing economies to increase competitiveness by transforming comparative advantage into cost competitiveness.

I will not deal with the specifics of inter-company trade. Even if it is true that inter-company trade is expanding more rapidly than trade itself (incidentally, less through greenfield investment than mergers and acquisitions, Nitzan 2003: 109), no multinational enterprise will produce for very long at production sites where unit costs are higher than elsewhere unless it has a monopoly on its products. It will shut down its affiliates and outsource production or invest in new plants elsewhere. The outsourcing of production from West Germany to its Eastern neighbors before the fall of the Berlin Wall shows that the costs of production matter more than close political ties

---

* Paper presented at the 43rd ISA Annual Convention, New Orleans, "Making Sense of Globalization". Submitted to International Studies Quarterly, rejected and published by Convergence Asia, here in an extended form taking into account some suggestions for more details made by one of the referees.

or ideological affinities as mainstream international relations theory of a constructivist type might be inclined to assume.

The current levels of globalization in production (trade) and finance (foreign direct investment) are not higher than before 1914.[1] They are considerably lower with respect to labor markets (Nayyar 1996; Strikwerda 1999: 385; Foreman-Peck 1992: 385). Long-term capital exports have not yet reached the shares of gross-capital formation many technically leading countries (TLCs) had before 1914[2] and investment in TLCs is still predominantly financed out of local resources,[3] because in a Keynesian world with active money, investment is financed to a large extent by banks.[4] A country with surplus capacity, especially in investment goods production, can always create investment by credit if there is demand. The only potential indicator of a higher degree of globalization today is short-term capital movements, mostly within computer networks. Their importance is, however, a sign of the absence of globalization. Before 1913 national currencies were fixed in gold parities. All money was at all times fully exchangeable into gold and there was no interest in hedging – preserving the future purchasing power of a claim labeled in foreign exchange.[5]

Thus, the central point of my argument is that the problem is not the extent of contemporary globalization but its specific pattern. The argument is put forth by contrasting a convoy model of globalization with an underconsumptionist one. In the convoy model the usual neoclassical assumptions about tendential full employment apply for all participating economies that are competitive beyond a small range of products with low price and income

---

[1] Bairoch 1996; Wade 1996; Verdier 1998: 1; Bovenberg/Gordon 1996; Williamson 1996: 302; Irwin 1996: 41–46; Theurl 1999: 26; Bergeijk/Mensink 1997: 166; Ghosh 1995: 128; Epstein 1996; Epstein 1995.

[2] Share of foreign investment in gross capital formation Britain last decade before World War I between 40 and 50 %: Dunning 1970: 18; MacMillan/Harris 1968: 9; Deane/Cole 1967: 266; Cairncross 1953: 169–180. France between 14 and 18 %: Michalet 1968: 138; White 1933: 101. Cf. also: Royal Institute of International Affairs 1937: 119–123; Feis 1930; Jenks 1927; Staley 1935; Woodruff 1966, 1975; Kenwood 1972; Feinstein/Pollard 1988.

[3] Feldstein/Horioka 1980; Feldstein 1994; Verdier 1998: 1; Bovenberg/Gordon 1996; Epstein 1996; Epstein 1995.

[4] Keynes 1973: 60–64; Sawyer 2001: 9; Hankel 1991: 50; Vickrey 2000: 4; Marglin 1984: 127.

[5] Welzmüller 1997: 24; Kregel 1994; Gosh 1995: 126; Helleiner 1995: 331f.; Epstein 1996.

elasticity of demand at the global level. All participating economies are diversified capitalist economies normally described as "developed" ones. In the underconsumptionist model economies become competitive in manufactured products with high price and income elasticity of demand without being able to reach full employment over a realistic period of time. They are underdeveloped with a labor surplus as described in the usual labor-surplus models of underdevelopment. It is assumed that this surplus labor cannot be absorbed through the effects of additional exports alone. The effects of these exports can be increased by complementing export-led industrialization with internal reforms. This article shows that the world can be made fit for globalization by accelerating the process of overcoming underdevelopment through internal economic reforms conceived in a Keynesian perspective, transforming underdeveloped economies into economies where the neoclassical assumptions apply.

## 2. The basic argument

Globalization is expected to lead to general welfare gains for all participating economies as long as mainstream assumptions about a tendency to full employment apply to all participating economies. According to Say's theorem (Say 1803/1972: 140–141), unemployment can only occur on a given market because prices are wrong or because factors of production are not flexible enough to react to price signals. In this contribution I will describe the possibility of an underconsumptionist scenario. It is based on the assumption that marginal productivity in significant regions of the world economy, technically backward economies (TBCs), is so low that the earnings of a worker there do not cover the costs of living for himself and his nuclear family, not even the physical minimum. There are large amounts of average-skilled labor, especially in agriculture, whose marginal product is lower than its costs of living. These workers are referred to as marginal, and will be shed off, i.e., marginalized, if the owners of assets, especially land, opt to maximize surplus by abolishing precapitalist bonds of solidarity. I consider a labor surplus of this type to be the main characteristic of underdeveloped economies. I therefore call them marginality-ridden.

Even if productivity rises in certain branches, e.g., in the export sector, labor can become scarce only if the impact of additional exports and their potential multiplier effects are strong enough to create full employment.

The model presented here resembles Georgescu-Roegen's (1960) critique of labor-shedding in the case of a premature introduction of capitalism.

A surplus of wage goods can be made available in such economies if there are other highly productive parts of the economy, e.g., rich agricultural lands, however limited these may be, or highly competitive export sectors. I argue that the success of the green revolution has greatly increased this possibility. Currency devaluation below purchasing-power-parity is an instrument for using the surplus of agriculture as a subsidy to additional export workers by allowing the earnings of these workers in international currency to be lower than their costs of reproduction measured in international prices for the wage goods they need to survive.

This does not exclude training and skill creation as an additional source of new competitiveness in the manufacturing sectors of such economies, which only bolsters the argument. By enabling marginality-ridden economies to engage in export-led industrialization, devaluation provides opportunities for skill creation even in initially low-technology branches (if only through greater labor discipline), mostly through learning by doing, which makes skill creation easier for state agencies and foreign investors.

Contemporary globalization is characterized by the integration of not yet capitalist, marginality-ridden economies into the world market. TBCs can achieve comparative advantage even if they are lagging behind in productivity, and can transform this comparative advantage into cost-effectiveness by means of devaluation. Under conditions of perfect competition a TBC has to specialize on high-technology industrial branches even if its productivity lags, provided that its productivity is lagging even more in all other branches of tradable products. This article maintains that the massive existence of poverty in Africa, Latin America as well as in most parts of Asia is sufficient proof that export drives – even when carried out with balance-of-trade deficits because terms of trade deteriorate following these export drives (Mayer 2003) – do not necessarily lead to full employment. Labor-surplus economies with a low marginal product of labor will be forced to massively devalue in order to increase employment, without necessarily achieving scarcity of labor. There is therefore neither a wage drift nor a strong tendency towards an equalization of factor productivities. Unemployment caused by a low marginal product of labor in the marginality-driven TBCs together with devaluation deprives labor in the TLCs of the benefits of productivity increases, because labor fails to become scarce if new production lines are not rapidly created whenever a massive displacement caused by imports from marginality-ridden economies occurs. The shift to new activities would require rising mass incomes in the TLCs in order to increase consumption. Given the devaluation-based character of export drives in marginality-ridden TBCs, the TLCs may very well not achieve this increase in consumption. It may even be thwarted politically in order to preserve competitiveness.

Since the new competitiveness of the marginality-driven TBCs is based on their capacity to devalue, wage restraint will not protect jobs in the TLCs. Productivity will outstrip production, the typical configuration in an underconsumptionist situation.

Both types of economies normally react to such a situation by their governments choosing the next-best solution. They opt for subsidies, protection, and other forms of state intervention that increase rent-seeking. A solution more likely to reap the benefits of globalization and maintain free markets at the global level would involve the deepening of globalization by transforming marginality-driven economies in such a way as to promote full employment there, too. The current globalization debate is in danger of fighting the wrong battle. The issue is not the question of globalization or no globalization, of capitalism or no capitalism, but which pattern of globalization and which orientation of capitalism. I see a danger in the globalization of rent, blocking the emergence of a worldwide civil society. Big business is hardly the best partner for defending capitalism. Big business is out to earn money, and does not object to its own earnings being based on market imperfections. Globalization has increased competition and therefore triggered off the current wave of mergers and acquisitions to restore a higher degree of monopoly at the global level (Lenel 2000; Wiesenthal 1998).

## 3. Capitalism and rising mass incomes.

In a manner similar to the 1920s and the post-World War II era, a period of social compromise is being followed by big business launching a new offensive against labor. When the revolutionary wave finally ebbed after 1924, big business had an interest in undoing the concessions that had been deemed necessary to block the spread of the October Revolution to Central and Western Europe.[6] The Western allies were also eager to combat the at-

---

[6] On the decline of the political clout of labor already before the world economic recession

tractiveness of the Soviet model after World War II by allowing Christian and Social Democrats to develop the market-regulated welfare state in Continental Western Europe. It seems that the psychological warfare of the West has succeeded in causing a whole political bloc in the East to collapse because it was successful in convincing millions of people that a solution like the one in Continental Western Europe could be implemented in the East, too, despite the fact that Western economists and business both claimed that the welfare state and social-market economy were never or no longer a viable solution. In Germany some even argue that a social-market economy is passé, and that the label "social" should be dropped. Since the fall of the Berlin Wall, business no longer fears labor as a political force. The catchwords have been globalization and international competitiveness.

The left bears its own responsibility for these developments, however. I will therefore start with a few brief remarks in order to draw the line between my own position and the blanket condemnation of capitalism, market economy and globalization. It is certainly true that profit-making is the rule of behavior for the class that determines the allocation of economic surplus in capitalism. The total profit of all enterprises, however, depends on spending on net-capacity-increasing investment and hence on rising mass demand (Kalecki 1971: 2–13), provided the usual assumptions are made, i.e., that workers consume their incomes, that capitalists consume only small parts of their incomes (the salaries of managers), and that, at least in the long run, governments cannot run up deficit spending indefinitely.

Capitalism originated in the successful struggle of the lower classes to increase their material well-being, and for that matter to reduce monopoly and rent in alliance with the middle strata (Elsenhans 1983a, 1983c). This began in Northwestern Europe in a process called "bourgeois revolution"[7] and has

---

cf.: Demarco/ Dhondt/ Fauvel-Rouif 1966: 5; Wolman 1936: 16; Peterson 1945: 10; Rayback 1966: 274–302; Latham 1966: 381; Mitchell 1962: 68; Petzina 1977: 33; Petzina/Abelshauser/Faust 1978: 111; Pirker 1980: 330; Winkler 1979: 69. Mommsen 1979: 349–375; Eliasberg 1974; Rosenberg 1961b 188.

[7] The observation that these revolutions were not led by the bourgeoisie and ultimately led to alliances between "bourgeoisies" and "aristocracies" is of little relevance. The decisive factor is the introduction of competitive markets against politically based privilege. Manning 1969: 156; Jacoby 1984: 113; Warren 1980: 28, against: Schilfert 1974: 66; Takahashi 1952: 342; Lefebvre 1973: 94. Cf. also Zagorin 1955: 908; Brenner 1973: 74; Chassinand-Nogaret 1975: 275; Taylor 1967: 489f; Guérin 1968: 35.

apparently been followed up by the successful democratization of the economically more advanced countries of the South, for example Korea (Kim 2005).

All new technologies decrease the unit costs of known products or of substitutes manufactured with these technologies (Bortkiewicz 1907: 459–89; Okishio 1961). Capital deepening therefore can exceed productivity growth only if new products are introduced. On perfect labor markets, where skill acquisition is not blocked by unequal access to training institutions, the introduction of new products requires rising mass incomes. Neoclassical economics, which is at the basis of the mainstream interpretation of globalization, does not exclude rising mass incomes. It considers rising mass incomes the inevitable result of sufficiently low wages. If wages are low enough for full employment in the opening phase of a new growth process, an innovation in any part of the economy will lead to part of business attracting labor by offering higher wages. Branches without innovation have to reduce their employment and their supplies decrease. If markets operate normally, prices for their goods increase, enabling them to retain labor by offering higher wages on the basis of higher prices. Innovative branches achieve above-average profit rates. They can only invest their profits in the expansion of their own plant and equipment, because profit rates are lower elsewhere. They will do so until prices decline due to the saturation of markets for their new products. Productivity measured in earnings converges between the innovative and the non-innovative branch. Real wages follow average productivity increases. If consumption out of wages exceeds the productive capacity of the economy, prices rise and entrepreneurs gain incentives for new investment, as well as the funds to finance them (so-called forced savings). Additional wages paid to labor in investment-goods production drive up the price of consumption goods if workers do not proceed to additional savings. There is never a problem of financing investment, only a problem of inflation, which can be managed by the central bank.

It is therefore obvious that neoclassical economics implicitly recognizes the reality of productivity-oriented wage increases. The divergence with post-Keynesians rests simply on the fact that neoclassical economics considers this development banal, being produced automatically and therefore not deserving of further inquiry. I would add, however, that the overall process of wages rising in line with productivity increases is dependent on the scarcity of labor and hence on full employment. I therefore argue against neoclassical economics by demonstrating that what it claims to be the standard scenario of a capitalist economy, scarcity of labor, is only a temporary state. In a cyclical downturn, labor is not scarce and, thus, its wage cannot rise, despite productivity increases. Even a famous neoclassical author, Wilhelm Röpke (1936: 119), has admitted that some downturns may be so substantial as to lead to an underconsumptionist – in his own analysis a "secondary" – crisis. It is quite true that unions cannot increase wages beyond productivity increases (which was true even for really existing socialism), but this does not at all justify the corresponding statement that unions are unnecessary, since the neoclassical mechanism of wage increases only works temporarily and has to be complemented during recessions by union activity. It is interesting to note that there was no controversy about that fact that real wages rose in periods of recession until the 1930s because of an unequal distribution of monopoly, with business under severe (price) competition and labor being able to impose "sticky" nominal wages (Richardson 1939: 431–41; Habakkuk 1972: 275; Hanes 1996).

There are more serious obstacles to the operation of the neoclassical mechanism of wage formation in underdeveloped economies. The defining criterion of underdevelopment is the existence of a surplus of labor (Lewis 1954; Fei/Ranis 1964). A large part of all able-bodied workers is unable to produce its consumption requirements, even at the lowest standards of living.[8] I call this a marginality-*cum*-rent model (Elsenhans 1994d), because the poverty of the poor in this case does not imply the absence of economic surplus. This surplus is, however, normally appropriated as rent for the luxury consumption or military spending of the rich, although it may also be made available for investment with the aim of overcoming underdevelopment. The important point is that labor can never become scarce if there is a permanent surplus of average-skilled able-bodied labor, and that the neoclassical mechanism of wage increase for average-skilled labor can never operate under these circumstances. This model has been dealt with extensively elsewhere (Elsenhans 1994e; Elsenhans 1995g), so I will not describe it here in detail. The model implies that marginality can only be overcome by certain types of technical progress. Marginality produces political structures that tend to block market regulation and horizontal political solidarity among the

---

[8] Georgescu-Roegen 1960; Dandekar 1962; Sen 1966; Minami 1966.

lower classes and make clientelism, political power games and the stickiness of information economically advantageous (Elsenhans 1995b: 141).

The idea that productivity increases empower labor because of the "human capital" it acquires are contradicted by empirical reality. Despite the tremendous advance of technology between 1890 and 1970, wage differentials narrowed in the industrially advanced countries.[9] If wage differences cause skilled labor to become temporarily scarce at some production sites, the labor with a lower level of skills can acquire scarce skills, making skilled labor abundant even with a surplus of unskilled labor. The American war effort from 1940 to 1945 showed that business can rapidly make unskilled labor productive (Faulkner 1949: 706f).

There is an abundance of skilled labor in many places of today's South which earns neither nominally (in international currency) nor in real terms (as measured in purchasing-power parity of its labor) as much as labor with comparable skills in the advanced industrial economies. It is not productivity or human capital but scarcity of labor that determines wages. The idea that low wage differentials in East Asia are proof for the absence of human capital (because low wage differentials indicate the absence of an income paid to human capital, Collins/Bosworth 1996: 138–140; Mankiw 1995: 281–283; Krugman 1994: 70) is a telling example of how divorced from empirical reality mainstream economics can be, because everybody admits the importance of education in Southern and East Asia.

Today's globalization is marked by the fact that many economies become competitive even in the production of high-technology manufactures when only a part of the labor force is employable in highly productive activities, with a large part producing less than its costs of subsistence. There are two possible reasons why these economies become competitive. On the one hand there is an undeniable improvement of skills. But the improvement of skills is not decisive, as it would easily spread to the entire labor force if these skills were in demand, with the result of incomes rising in line with average productivity.

Moreover, economies of this type become competitive despite their productivity still being lower than in the industrially advanced countries. The

---

[9] Keesing 1974: 25; Borjas 1994; Dobb 1960: 44; Svennilson 1954: 39; Chiswick 1971; Mulé 1998: 11; Fogarty 1959: 57; Caesar 1975: 199; Mouly 1967: 187; Reynolds/Taft 1958: 355.

reason for this is not the fact that this skilled but less productive labor also earns very low real wages. The often quoted difference in wages of about 1:50 reflects differences in the price of this labor in international currency. Measured in purchasing-power parity, wage differentials are much lower between TLCs and TBCs, somewhere in the range of 1:7 (Strack et al. 1997). The decisive characteristic of the contemporary globalization process is the low international costs of labor in catch-up economies that are able to transform comparative advantage into cost-competitiveness through devaluation.[10]

Devaluation below purchasing-power parity implies that additional labor in export industries uses its wages paid in local currency to buy goods supplied locally. There has to be a surplus of locally produced wage goods.

There are two ways to destroy the capacity of underdeveloped economies to devalue: demographic growth, which would exhaust the surplus allocated to workers in the export sector and result in a new genocide, or the alternative method of uplifting the productivity of marginal labor.

I will describe in this article some of the social-reformist policies I already advocated twenty-five years ago (Elsenhans 1975b: 299–306) in order to show that all of them involve the mobilization of rent in favor of marginal labor. The surplus theoretically available for investment but in practice most often used for luxury consumption decreases. Mass consumption increases and, at an appropriate exchange rate, internal-market-oriented industries grow, which may be accompanied by the launching of a local technology-producing industry.

Making the world safe for globalization requires implementing a growth mechanism for marginal labor, i.e., the poor in the South, and a distribution of world industry making local economies less exposed to external shocks. I will not discuss the environmental aspects of such a strategy, although it can be argued that raising environmental standards will raise employment levels (Köhler/Tausch 2002: 182). Given the current world population, environmental issues probably cannot be solved without growth. At any rate, capitalism provides the most effective means of integrating environmental costs into the cost-benefit calculation of enterprises, first because of competition, as shown by the much lower raw-material intensity of production in capital-

---

[10] Lafay 1995: 686; Yotopoulos 1996: XIV; Xu 2000: 267; Boltho 1996 13f; Basant 2000; Guillaumont/Guillaumont-Jeanneney/Brun 1999; Morimotu 1918: 144.

ism as compared to East European centrally planned economies,[11] second because of the decreasing raw-material intensity of production in capitalism noticeable over the last two centuries,[12] and third because of a certain degree of independence between the economy and the political system (Gonzalez-Vigil 1985; Wälde 1984; Tarr 1992).

I will conclude by presenting the alternatives available in the international system.

## 4. A Convoy Model of Globalization

I call a convoy model of globalization a pattern of globalization where economies falling behind do not suffer from unemployment but only experience deterioration in their terms of trade. This terms-of-trade deterioration is more limited the lower the productivity lag in the less innovative branches of production of the less innovative economy vis-à-vis to the same branches in the innovative economy. The salient point is not the difference in average levels of productivity but the difference in productivity in the branches the less innovative economy has to fall back on (either new exports or import substitution of hitherto imported products) when the more innovative economy discovers an innovation. In structural terms this argument resembles Lewis's refutation of the importance of terms of trade deterioration for explaining underdevelopment (Lewis 1978: 16–18). Lewis argued that agriculturally efficient countries can produce most industrial products themselves as long as their terms of trade deteriorate, because they can feed non-agricultural workers from their agricultural surplus. If import prices rise, they simply use their agricultural surplus to feed additional workers employed in the production of previously imported goods.

---

[11] Levcik/Skolka 1984: 13ff; Sik 1972: 6; Berend 1968: 84; Altmann 1987: 204; Obst 1979: 141; Zauberman 1964: 144; Selucky 1972: 110; Woroniak 1970: 92; Ufer 1975: 1135.

[12] Hughes 1964: 74; Ellison 1986: 58; Burns 1934: 131; Kravis 1970: 15; Neumeister 1910: 3; Rostow 1978: 616; Rosenberg 1973: 111; Brady 1933: 207; Kendrick: 1961: 95; Fabricant 1940: 268; Burckhardt 1963: 5; Furness/Leith/Lewis 1943: 20; Svennilson 1954: 106; Warren 1923: 181, 429; MacCloskey 1968: 287; Mommsen 1962: 736; Cameron 1991: 287; UNCTAD 1989: 3; Tarr 1992: 29; Schultz 1960: 381; UNCTAD 1984: V; UNCTAD 1985: 7; Maizels 1964: 39f; Clough/Marburg 1968: 20; Thoborn 1981: 33; Raffer 1983: 496; Gonzalez-Vigil 1985: 24; Bomsel 1987: 6; Wälde 1984: 28; Colm 1932: 36; Allen 1977: 608.

In a more general way, with deteriorating terms of trade, changing price relations trigger off new exports and higher production in import-competing branches if the levels of productivity in these branches are high in relation to the prices in local currency they fetch after devaluation, making the expansion of production rapidly profitable. The implied diversification is the result of a diversified local economy following the diversification of local demand which allows at least the import of technology from more innovative countries whenever there is a large enough local market to sell new products and new technologies in sufficient quantities to justify local production. The rapid internationalization of the production of sewing machines and bicycles in the late nineteenth century can be quoted as an example.[13]

Diversification and the capacity to imitate are accompanied by high productivity in most of the economy relative to its leading export branches. A loss of competitiveness in these export branches because of innovation in a more innovative economy leads to comparative advantage in the less innovative branches for the economy falling behind. A relatively high productivity in these branches in relation to the innovative economy's productivity in the same branches allows transforming this comparative advantage into price competitiveness, even at a low rate of devaluation.

I use the term convoy because high productivity in a non-innovative economy relative to an innovative and more dynamic one keeps the non-innovative economy from overtaking the more innovative economy due simply to the non-innovative economy's low exchange rate. Because the non-innovative economy becomes competitive at a low rate of devaluation based on new exports from non-innovative branches, further attempts to devalue will lead to excessive demand for local factors of production from the newly competitive export and import-substituting branches, and will ultimately result in imported inflation, as in the case of West Germany in the early 1960s (Ungerer 1997: 58; on Japan: Iwami 1992: 459ff). On the other hand, the diversified character and the possibility of maintaining high levels of employment in the less innovative economy will allow it to follow the leading economy at a variable distance, perhaps even catching up to it.

Let us assume that the international economy is only made up of economies that have achieved full employment. At the end of the long nineteenth century, only economies characterized by very high levels of employment

---

[13] Hounshell 1984: 145ff; Thomson 1984; Patel/Pavitt 1994: 534; Barth 1973: 63.

were internationally competitive in price and income-elastic products (manufacturing). The levels of technical development differed between different economies, but not their basic internal structure.

Let us assume that an innovation occurs in one of these economies, which I will call economy A. A increases its exports. The balance of trade will become excedentary. In contrast to the situation in 1913, I will further assume that exchange rates are floating. This difference is not essential. In a gold-currency system the balance-of-trade surplus of A will lead to price increases, because gold flows into the monetary system of A, whereas the less innovative economy, B, will experience deflation, as it suffers from gold outflows. In a world currency system with scriptural money, differences in price levels do not require changes in nominal prices within an economy, because the change in relative price levels between economies is brought about by fluctuations in the international value of currencies, i.e., the exchange rate. In order to continue to buy the products of A, importers from B compete for the currency of A. A's currency appreciates, i.e., becomes more expensive as more people want to buy it using the currency of B. Conversely, B's balance of trade deteriorates, because B imports the innovative products of A. B's currency becomes cheaper and depreciates.

Because A has had an innovation in a particular branch, the products of the non-innovative branches in A have become relatively more expensive than the same products in B. B will sell products from non-innovative branches where its cost competitiveness has improved. The degree to which B has to depreciate therefore depends on its relative backwardness in non-innovative branches. This backwardness is lower the more B resembles a developed economy, which does not necessarily have to be innovative, but has reasonable levels of productivity in all its economic activities and is a fairly diversified economy, say, Italy in comparison to Japan or the United States.

Through moderate devaluation, a diversified economy B becomes competitive in a whole range of less innovative products, and can therefore maintain full employment. It suffers, however, from a certain decline in its terms of trade.

The European convoy model of the nineteenth century was characterized empirically by low productivity differences in less innovative branches, many of which were still artisanal. Empirical evidence reveals similar differences in most manufacturing branches,[14] a fact that enabled newcomers such as Germany and the United States to achieve comparative advantage in most modern industries because they were relatively backward in textiles,[15] whereas Britain earned too well from its textiles.[16] Some experts even use the argument of overconsumption to explain the U.S. overtaking Britain in this period (Gilpin 1975: 91), despite much higher real wages in the U.S. Despite converging average productivities, differences in average productivity subsisted due to the size of the market, with America taking the lead ahead of Britain and Germany (Romer 1996). The important point, however, was that differences in productivity became more and more similar between different economies, so that even the lags in branches also tended to become uniform between these national economies, with the U.S. and Germany, however, leading in the most modern branches.[17]

This convergence in productivity lags is not the consequence of technical factors but of economic mechanisms fundamental to the convoy model as assumed in the flying geese model.[18] If an economy does not catch up in a branch technically, it simply focuses on its comparative advantage in other branches and reduces its share of production in the respective branch, which in the case of a non-innovative economy may be a technically innovative branch. It may be quite possible that the B economies do not experience any increase in productivity or diversification if they are able to specialize on a "traditional" product that continues to earn well by price increases on the world market in line with productivity increase in the innovative economy.

---

[14] Williamson 1996; Dormois/Bardini 1995; Rosenbloom 1993; Broadberry 1994a; O'Rourke/Williamson 1994.

[15] Howard 1907: 91ff; Brown, 1995; Matthews/Feinstein/Odling-Smee 1982: 525; Aukrust 1964: 32; Broadberry 1998; Wolff 1991; Kindleberger 1975: 482; Ranis 1978: 11ff; Singer 1953: 25; Barth 73: 8f; Anthony 1969: 25; Aldcroft 1964: 128; Rubinson: 1978: 43; Schmitt 1967: 100; Knowles 1926: 146.

[16] The British Departmental Committee on the Engineering Trade wrote: Our manufacturers do not turn out these cheaper articles, being content apparently to let cheaper trade go." (Platt 1972: 126).

[17] Siemens (1872) quoted in Ritter/Kocka 1974: 151; Frankel 1955: 105; Habakkuk 1962: 105; Saul 1970: 20; Musson 1975: 112; Schlesinger 1925: 48; Buxbaum 1921: 136; Rosenberg 1976: 161; Rosenbloom 1993; Broadberry 1994b; Clark 1929: 418; Broadberry 1997: 126; Fremdling 1991: 39; Aldcroft 1964: 128.

[18] Akamatsu 1961: 205; Akamatsu 1962: 12; Rowthorn 1996; Bernard/Ravenhill 1995.

At the same time, the more innovative economy loses its less innovative branches. Despite increased international trade between the more and the less innovative economies, productivity levels (measured in earnings relative to factor input) converge between branches nationally (and not internationally), making branchwise national productivities similar to average national productivities. Productivity differences between economies according to branches tend to equal average productivity differences. Any sectorally limited advance in a leading economy therefore rapidly creates new employment possibilities for non-innovative branches in the non-innovative economy, as it makes a large variety of non-innovative branches in the non-innovative economy internationally competitive.

The characteristic conditions for maintaining high levels of employment in economies lagging behind in the convoy model are much less comprehensive than generally thought. There does not have to be cultural homogeneity, nor are similar levels of technical development required. It is sufficient that all participating economies are characterized by full employment, enabling the neoclassical mechanism of price formation to operate.

In a national economy, enterprises in branches with above-average productivity increases will attract additional capital and additional labor by offering higher earnings. Branches with below-average productivity will lose factors of production. Depending on the price elasticity of demand for their products, they will enjoy rising prices which enable them to compete for factors of production even at higher prices. There are quantity and price adjustments of production in the non-innovative branch and the opposite in the innovative branch (saturation and declining prices).

At equilibrium in a capitalist economy, productivity measured as the ratio between earnings and costs of production is similar across all branches, irrespective of the rate of growth of physical productivity in different branches. The fact that a haircutter earns about as much as a low-skilled worker in an industrial enterprise despite the haircutter's productivity not having risen for the last 500 years and the productivity in assembly-line production having risen considerably in the last 80 years demonstrates that there is no such thing as branchwise productivity as an indicator for the level of wages, but that there is a process of redistribution within an economy based on the scarcity of labor and the preferences of laborers.

The same mechanism operates in a modified way between economies in a convoy model. Economy B in the convoy model is characterized by a low degree of backwardness in non-innovative branches, not because it experienced a growth process of productivity in backward branches but because, under conditions of full employment, the productivity of its backward branches measured in earnings had to correspond to productivity in its advanced branches. The innovation in A has three consequences for a competing branch in B. Part of the competing branch will die out, other segments will innovate, and some parts can survive because of devaluation, allowing them to charge the same prices in local currency as before without being outcompeted internationally. Because labor is shed off in the innovative branch, the less innovative branches of B can expand their production without rising costs. Productivity across all branches measured in earnings in local currency remain similar, and, in the case of unlimited flexibility of labor and capital, can even be identical. Vice-versa, the innovative economy A has to reduce production in branches that cannot keep up in productivity growth with innovative branches, limiting itself to the segments that can adapt by raising productivity themselves. Because of a rising exchange rate, at least part of the less innovative branches lose their price competitiveness vis-à-vis their competitors in B. Concentrating on the more adaptive segments of the non-innovative branches or the simple transfer of labor from non-innovative branches to the new growth branch allows maintaining productivity at similar levels in all branches of A.

The two economies are characterized by identical levels of productivity between branches of their own economy and greater differences in productivity between each other. Depending on elasticity of demand – A may sell internationally on a lower income market with more limited purchasing power for its products and B on a higher income market with higher purchasing power for its products (due to their being made cheaper because of devaluation) as during the Industrial Revolution – the rate of devaluation imposed on B may be lower than the rate of increase in productivity differences between the innovative branches of A and B. B will be specialized on relatively less innovative branches with good, even improving terms of trade. With barriers to migration, labor in B can only migrate to less innovative branches of B. These branches can expand only with declining prices in international currency. If A and B were one national economy, labor displaced in a less innovative branch would migrate to the highly productive branch, with this move reducing the supply of goods from the less innovative branch until the less innovative branch can either charge higher wages (up to the level of the national average wage) or disappears because of lack of competitiveness on factor markets. With barriers to migration, the demand of labor in highly innovative branches may be limited. Only massive deterioration of the terms of trade will increase employment. Emerging unemployment in the wake of productivity increases in the highly innovative branches can be absorbed only by non-innovative branches in the case of lower export prices. The innovative economy will experience declining terms of trade.

This seems to have happened between Britain and France in the early nineteenth century,[19] and might partly explain the deterioration of Britain's terms of trade (Imlah 1950; Imlah 1958: 103; Kindleberger 1956: 13).

These processes can be modified if there is a certain amount of capital flows. In this case, the sectoral convergence of national productivities between branches is complemented by a strong drive to international convergence of branchwise productivities between economies, as illustrated by the massive catch-up of Germany and Japan after World War II. Capital exports can be triggered off by both innovative and non-innovative branches of A, though only for two specific reasons: 1) Non-innovative branches in economy A fear competition from enterprises in B after the appreciation of A's currency; 2) Innovative branches in A fear imitation, and want to secure markets by combining new technologies with cheaper labor in A, thereby avoiding the emergence of competitors in the innovative branch of B. Both processes should favor convergence, although the degree of convergence will depend on the environment provided by the host country, B, for the trickling down of technical progress, the most important aspects being the expansion of the local market and improved competitiveness of investors on the world market.

In the convoy model neither innovative A economies nor non-innovative B economies require massive state intervention to subsidize investment in economic diversification and maintain competitiveness. The case of A is easily understandable – state intervention is useful only in a mild form, such as training and subsidized credit for enterprises. B wants to catch up with A and therefore orients itself towards branches that seem promising in A. As long as B does not achieve the same level of technical innovativeness as A, A earns technical monopoly rents which it may invest in newly innovative

---

[19] Nef 1958: 121; Crafts 1989: 427; O'Brien 1978: 21f. On the basis of the same mechanism the U.S. overtook later on: Payne 1967: 525.

branches (Posner 1961: 329). In the convoy model the leading economy normally has its highest productivity advances in the most promising future products, as described in the model of the product cycle (Vernon 1966).

The relatively high productivity of the non-innovative economy B in non-innovative branches implies a relatively high exchange rate which keeps B from overtaking A in branches on the technical frontier via currency devaluation.

This situation is not a given, however. Let us use Ricardo's (1951: 135–51) example, but replace England with Germany, Portugal with Singapore, textiles with luxury cars, and wine with microelectronics. Under these circumstances, Germany would have to specialize on luxury cars, even if the future markets are not promising, and leave microelectronics to Singapore, even if Germany is superior to Singapore in microelectronics, albeit not superior to the same degree as in the production of luxury cars. This situation appears more dangerous the more the insights of post-Keynesian and new endogenous growth theory are taken into account, i.e., that productivity does not only depend on the accumulation of physical capital but also – and essentially – on residual factors, some – but not all – of which may be extremely mobile. If, for instance, learning by doing is an important residual factor, the leading economy A should have a higher productivity advance relative to B in branches where B has never been active, whereas it seems unlikely that the disembodied factors of productivity created by production in old branches will lead to economy A having a comparable advance in the production of completely new products, when A and B are both only just beginning production and new learning is mobile. Immobility of the "disembodied" factors of technical innovation in old branches and mobility of the disembodied factors in new branches will favor B's overtaking of A. Mobility of the disembodied factors of technical innovation in old branches (e.g., through imitation) and immobility of disembodied factors in new branches will contribute to A maintaining its position of technical leadership. In models portraying the stability of hierarchies of technical innovativeness it is assumed that disembodied factors are less mobile between A and B the higher the average differences between A and B in average productivity, especially in branches with a promising future. If this assumption is dropped, a lower average productivity level of B (hence the more B is backward) and a higher potential to transfer certain disembodied factors of productivity growth, especially in innovative branches, increase the likelihood that leading countries will suffer because of their old leading industries, like an oil country from its oil industry: high productivity and therefore comparative advantage in old industries but low dynamics for employment and future growth. This has often been illustrated by Germany's specialization on the leading branches of the late nineteenth and the twentieth century, such as machine building, chemicals, and automobiles, resulting in its neglect of microelectronics.

Once the threat of being overtaken is realized, the leading economy A will certainly react with industrial policy, an effort economy B will of course try to counterbalance with its own industrial policy. The more the world economy moves away from a convoy model, the less plausible it becomes to further uphold an open world economy and the more likely there will be state intervention in transborder transactions as well as state intervention in the domestic economy via industrial policies – in end effect subsidies, hence rents distorting competition and the smooth operation of an autonomous market.

This option is, however, limited in a convoy model, for the following reason. A is a technically innovative and diversified economy. The mechanism underlying the transfer of technology described in the product cycle argument implies the capability to imitate even if A has fallen behind in the introduction of a new product. When A falls behind B in a new branch, A faces the following alternative: Either it uses state intervention to catch up to B in the new technology, where B has acquired comparative advantage and cost competitiveness, or A opts for specialization in an even newer technology where, because of having fallen behind B, it potentially has comparative advantage, since both A and B are newcomers in the newest technology.

All economies participating in a convoy model have the opportunity in the next round of technology introduction to overcome lock-ins in less promising products and technologies. The OECD world since the 1970s, when at least Germany and Japan had caught up with the USA, can be cited as an example. The USA's advance in microelectronics was checked by Japan, though the USA later regained its advance. The share of the US in environmental high-technology or biotechnology production is, however, much lower than in high-technology microelectronics. The spread of research centers – even ones controlled by multinational corporations – throughout the OECD world shows that it is possible for members of the OECD to periodically assume leadership positions previously held by others,[20] with catch-up economies like South Korea even becoming "laboratories" of innovation (e.g., in the diffusion of consumer microelectronics, Handelsblatt 12-12-2003: 12).

## 5. The marginality-*cum*-rent model

Underdeveloped economies lack full employment. All relevant theories of development have described them as being characterized by structural unemployment or as labor-surplus economies (Lewis 1954; Fei/Ranis 1964: 13–22). According to neoclassical theory, all labor is employed if it produces a surplus, i.e., if its wage is low enough to yield a surplus. If there are able-bodied workers who cannot produce enough to cover their subsistence needs, the neoclassical and, likewise, Marxist assumption (Marx 1890/1972a: 181) that any labor produces a surplus is no longer fulfilled.

Underdeveloped economies are characterized by the existence of a large pool of able-bodied workers who are unable, under any circumstances, to produce what they need for their own and their nuclear families' survival. As these societies ultimately survive, there have to be workers who are more productive. The labor-surplus model can exist only if there is a branch with diminishing returns when labor input increases. If environmental costs are not included in the cost-benefit calculation, any industrial innovation can be imitated and reproduced indefinitely. In manufacturing, diminishing returns are only possible temporarily, e.g., when enterprises operate near full-capacity utilization with special costs for overtime hours, etc. If in a growing economy with increasing labor productivity there is a branch characterized by diminishing returns (implying below-average productivity increases), the prices of its products rise in relation to the overall price level. The branch with below-average productivity increases – in the model presented here, even declining productivity – sees its prices rise relative to all other prices. This textbook solution of an economy adapting to branchwise differences in growth of physical productivity is excluded, however, if the bulk of inputs in the branch with declining productivity is composed of the branch's own products. If food is produced using labor-intensive methods with the major-

---

[20] Joly/de Looze 1996; Dolata 1999; Commandeur 1995: 3–4; Feddema 2003; Acharya 1999: 138; Swann/Prevezer 1998.

ity of the active population engaged in food production, and if food constitutes the usual 45 to 70 percent of the household spending of the poor (Khan 1963: 404; Ray 2000: 46–47), the threshold beyond which an increasingly expensive additional worker adds more additional earnings than his costs cannot be substantially raised by an increase in food prices.

I call all labor that produces less than its costs of subsistence marginal labor.[21] If this labor is shed off by surplus-maximizing landlords, it becomes marginalized, i.e., excluded from social integration via the labor market. This concept of marginality is narrower than the one proposed by Quijano Obregón and closer to Nun. Quijano Obregón (1977: 41) also includes social dimensions. Nun (1969: 183) insists on the differences between marginal labor and an industrial army reserve.[22] It is worth noting that Latin American authors, with their experience of capitalist actors penetrating their societies, insist on the social dimension of marginality. The marginal population here is already excluded from major elements of the political system and society. According to my own definition, marginalized workers may still have social ties, either to each other or to non-marginalized labor which – in the context of kinship solidarity – may even support them economically. They may even have links to institutionalized organizations. Indeed, non-governmental organizations often address marginalized labor of this sort.

I define marginality as the existence of marginal labor. Marginality-ridden economies are economies where there is marginal labor, regardless of whether or not it has already been shed off (the usual term is underemployed). The level of marginality is the production level a worker has to achieve in agriculture in order to earn an income sufficient to buy his basic necessities, comprising food as well as non-food products.

Diminishing returns in agriculture can coincide with a surplus of agriculture. The marginal worker still employed by a surplus-maximizing landlord has to add as much to production as his wage, which in the case of generalized poverty is equal to at least the cost of the minimum of commodities

---

[21] Elsenhans 1994d: 396; Elsenhans 1995g: 195. Similar approaches: Binswanger/Deininger/Feder 1993; Griffin/James 1979: 262; Furnivall 1937: 446–449; Minami 1966; Minami 1992; MacKinley/Alarcón González 1995: 1582; Chao 1986: 6–8; Rao/Sanyal 1978: 287; Brown 1994: 119; Bai 1982: 117–140.

[22] "respecto a la forma productiva dominante, tales mendigos resultaban superfluos pero, sin embargo, indiferentes, pues el sistema podía proporcionarlas medios de subsistencia sobrantes" (Nun 1969: 183)

necessary for his subsistence. If there is a surplus of labor, other agricultural laborers will not be offered higher wages as long as there are no special arrangements for social protection, e.g., treating employed workers as political clients. Yet those who are employed can produce more than this wage, as some of them cultivate more fertile land. In this case, the outmigration of labor from agriculture will lead to higher agricultural productivity, as observed by Rozelle, Taylor and DeBrauw (1999) in the case of mainland China. Labor surplus, i.e., a marginal population which produces less than its inevitable costs of subsistence, depends on three conditions: a low level of income, where the share of food in household consumption is high; a low level of development, where the share of agriculture in employment is high; and a low level of technical development in agriculture, where the technologies for compensating diminishing returns are not yet available.

This is the situation that is normally found in underdeveloped economies. These conditions explain how there can simultaneously be a surplus of labor and a surplus of resources. The surplus of labor creates political incentives for the powerful to "do something" for the poor. The surplus of resources has constituted the economic and financial basis for a variety of economic measures since the inception of development policies, ranging from poverty-alleviating distributionist measures to investment programs, implemented, at least officially, in order to raise productivity and overcome marginality.

Technical progress per se does not lead to overcoming marginality. Productivity increases in the manufacturing of luxuries will lead to more and more, and probably more sophisticated luxuries. Productivity increases in the manufacturing of industrial mass-consumption goods reduces the costs of agricultural labor, thus raising the level of marginality. This process comes to an end when non-agricultural mass-consumption goods become so cheap that their cost approaches zero, or if for climatic or cultural reasons the exploitation of the rural masses can be intensified to levels where they can no longer spend anything at all on clothing, shelter, and basic equipment (the three items which comprise about 70 to 80 percent of the non-food spending of poor households). Technical progress in agriculture can have two basic orientations, although these normally occur together in various mixtures. One form raises the productivity of labor already employed and contributes to an increase in the surplus of agriculture, the other raises the marginal product of labor (e.g., through the irrigation of hitherto barren land), and therefore contributes to an increase in employment. Thus, only one particular form of technical progress allows underdeveloped economies to break out of the marginality-*cum*-rent trap.

Two basic interests seem to converge at the political level and help maintain a surplus of labor: the interest of the powerful in having clients at the political level in order to increase their position in the struggle over the surplus, and the interest of marginal laborers in increasing the number of their offspring in order to improve the chances that one of them will get a job on the basically lottery-type labor market. Both result in patterns of behavior that allow a substantial part of marginal laborers not only to survive (because they receive a certain amount of food as clients) but also to reproduce (since parents prefer large families), thereby securing the supply of marginal labor. In any case, wages for average-skilled labor cannot rise on the basis of scarcity due to widespread marginality. Productivity may rise, however – and, along with it, surplus.

Without rising mass incomes there is no interest in expanding the production capacity for machine-produced mass-consumption goods. The transformation of surplus into investment spending is blocked, which contributes to the weakness of profit. Profit is a special category of surplus. It is earned on perfectly competitive markets, because workers' spending on consumption goods exceeds the spending of consumption-goods producers on wages. The additional demand for consumption goods arises out of wages paid in the production of goods other than consumption goods, i.e., investment goods. Profits are equal to spending on investment goods net of amortization (Kalecki 1971: 2–13; Robinson 1949: 48ff). Available surplus otherwise has to be appropriated by non-market mechanisms, as shown by Baran and Sweezy (1967: 117ff, 128ff) in their study on monopoly capitalism, and will be used for consumptive purposes – in Baran and Sweezy's modelization, for defense and publicity.

The important point is that, within the framework of the existing pattern of distribution of income entitlement in rent-based societies, the marginality-*cum*-surplus trap blocking the transition to capitalism cannot be overcome by an increase in financial surplus.

## 6. Marginality, surplus and the new possibilities of devaluation

TLCs characterized by marginality, hence structural unemployment, are being integrated nowadays in the international division of labor not primarily due to their low real wages (wages are low, though not as low as the international costs of this labor) but because of their capacity to devalue. Comparative advantage was said to be transformed into cost competitiveness by means of devaluation. This point is extremely important for the political issues being discussed nowadays. If the exchange rate is decisive for achieving cost competitiveness, wage restraint is useless for maintaining the high employment levels of leading economies. In 1995 numerous managers from the German business world appeared in TV advertisements with slogans promising future growth in exchange for austerity. This spectacle stopped when the exchange rate suddenly fell to 1.38 DM per dollar. The successful exporters of manufactures among the TBCs are not among the most poverty-stricken countries. Compare the levels of poverty in sub-Saharan Africa and the region's relative failure to export manufactures with the relatively high real incomes of the poor in successful export countries of Southeast and East Asia. The reason for the initial cheapness of labor in the successful export-oriented industrializing economies is their capacity to supply wage goods from their local production, especially food, which enables them to accept earnings from their exports which alone are not high enough to cover the supply of basic goods for labor employed in export sectors. The capacity of the local economy to supply wage goods at lower prices than available from the world market is the basis for these economies' capacity to devalue (Elsenhans 1997b: 3–8).

There is an empirical proof for this cheapness of labor being achieved through cheap wage goods. The exchange rates of most catch-up export-oriented industrializing countries do not correspond to their price levels. GNP per capita in mainland China in 1999 was $780, at purchasing-power parity $3,291; the corresponding figures for India were $450 and $2,149; for Vietnam, a country just beginning its export drive, $370 and $1,755 (World Bank 2000: 274). Even for the Republic of Korea, GNP per capita in 1999 was double when calculated at purchasing-power parity in comparison to its value at the exchange rate. It is surprising that so many economists are so far removed from empirical reality to mindlessly repeat that real wages in the catch-up TBCs are about 1/50th of real wages in the high-income TLCs. Who would be able to buy even the most basic necessities at one-fiftieth of the income of a German or an American worker in their respective countries? It would not even suffice for the caloric intake granted in the gulag. It has been estimated that if the income of a Beijing household were converted into Canadian dollars this household could afford only one-tenth of the goods it can buy in Beijing (Chen/Gordon/Zhiming 1994; Yotopoulos/Lin 1993; Yotopoulos 1996: 290). The reason for this is, first of all, low real incomes with high shares of income spent on food and housing. Housing is not a tradable good, and food, especially bulky grain, is difficult to trade because of high transport costs and different consumer preferences. Relatively high productivity in non-tradable goods allows devaluation to levels where additional export workers do not earn their subsistence incomes on the world market.

It is thus not increasing differences in real wages between the OECD economies and the newly industrializing economies (NICs) which are responsible for successful export-led growth, but the green revolution, which allows feeding an increasing number of export-sector workers who are only competitive on the world market at prices which are too low to provide them with high enough incomes to buy their subsistence goods from the world market. The real-wage differences between TLCs and TBCs seem not to have increased dramatically since the late nineteenth century (Lokanathan 1935: 358 ff; Morris 1965: 22ff), and seem to be declining between the OECD countries and the successful NICs (Lafay 1996: 948–63; Strack et al. 1997).

The green revolution of the OECD countries has also contributed to the competitiveness of the NICs. Agricultural productivity in the OECD countries grows as fast as average industrial productivity.[23] Industrial branches with below-average productivity growth in TLCs not only face the effects of comparative disadvantage vis-à-vis catch-up TBCs; branches located in TBCs with rising world market prices relative to food prices will become price competitive at lower levels of devaluation. As long as the remaining parts of these branches in the TLCs make TLC companies price takers, TBCs can buy more food on the world market in exchange for their new exports. These branches in the TLCs will disappear only if certain TBCs are able to undersell them, either because their own productivity increases or because of cheap food supplies. With the improving terms of trade of these branches vis-à-vis foodstuffs, catch-up TBCs can buy more food for the same quantity of exported goods. The transformation of comparative advantage into price competitiveness is facilitated once more.

---

[23] Luh/Stefanou, 1991; Grigg 1984: 12–14; Elliott 1955: 44; Kato 1965.

The transfer of technology naturally has the same effect, improving comparative advantage and creating favorable terms of trade between the products of new industrial export branches and internationally traded foodstuffs.

Subsidies from the European Union and the United States to agricultural exports obviously make the transformation of comparative advantage into cost competitiveness easier.

But as long as export-led growth in TBCs is based on devaluation below purchasing parity, the economic mechanism at the basis of export-led growth is a subsidy to the export sector from the rest of the economy. This subsidy is financed mainly from the rent of agriculture. The additional workers who find employment in the export sector when a country devalues are paid incomes in their national currencies. At low exchange rates, these incomes are sufficient only if the products they buy are supplied from the local economy. The two sectors that play a key role in this case are the informal sector, which produces low-quality mass-consumption industrial products, and food-producing agriculture. As the real-income situation of the informal sector also depends on the cost of food as long as incomes are still low, the basic resource allowing a high rate of devaluation is a surplus-producing food agriculture. Agriculturists who benefit from the ground rent of agriculture are prevented from selling basic foods cheaply on the world market, either due to regulations or because of high transport costs. Workers with local purchasing power can buy this surplus, which does not go to the world market. The rent of agriculture is transformed into cheap labor (measured in international prices). In its physical form, it is channeled to the additional export workers. In its value form, it is distributed partly as incomes to these workers, and partly in the form of cheaper prices for manufactured goods from low-income countries imported by the industrialized countries, which see their terms of trade improved.

## 7. Diversification through upgrading as a rent-based process

The technical upgrading of exports, first used by South Korea (Mytelka 1985: 12ff; Haggard 1983: 283), Taiwan (Shih 1968: 121–23) and Singapore (Holtgrave 1987: 58–81), allows enriching the model of devaluation-based export-oriented manufacturing by introducing a mechanism of rent allocation more nuanced than mere devaluation.

Upgrading through state support for technically more demanding products implies that rent is used for targeting subsidies to specific branches or enterprises. It is an alternative to a general lowering of costs through devaluation. As different branches of production have different learning effects, scarce resources are targeted to a branch where a maximum of complementary effects on skill creation, human capital formation, improvements in infrastructure and trust formation are achieved – in essence, a maximum of all the "things" described in new endogenous growth theory to explain why the neoclassical expectation of a decline in capital productivity does not occur. Rent can be used for export-led growth (Akyüz/Gore 1994: 8; Khan/Jomo 2000a: 8).

Let us start by describing a successful case, the start-up of Korea's textile-machinery industry (Westphal/Kim/Dahlmann 1985: 187–198). In the 1970s South Korea's export offensive proved so successful that it experienced declining prices with low price elasticity of demand for its textiles. Faced with the danger that earnings would decrease through the import of essential inputs, e.g., machinery, whose prices increased in relation to the prices of exported textiles, the government reacted by blocking all textile-machinery imports. To continue earning profits, local exporters had to turn to local metal-working shops, which produced small machine parts and spare parts according to specification. The shops had already existed (as they do in most other textile-producing countries north of the Sahara), and when called upon to do so were able to supply new machinery by copying existing machinery, albeit at higher costs than foreign suppliers at the existing exchange rate. The costs for textiles in local currency rose due to the blockage of machinery imports. If higher prices could only be achieved by selling lesser quantities, the low price elasticity of demand meant higher overall earnings with a loss of employment in textile production but an increase in employment in textile machinery production. Further devaluation was possible as long as the aim was to maintain the quantities produced; it had no additional impact, neither on the foreign-exchange element of the costs of production nor on the local element. The major input, hitherto imported textile machinery, did not increase in price through devaluation (but due to initially low efficiency of local production).

The strategy was an intelligent appropriation of a rent and its channeling into investment in physical capital with high learning-by-doing effects. A machine is an assembly of metal parts worked at $1/100^{th}$ of a millimeter in order to transform force into the regular and precise movement of tools. Anyone who masters the building of one type of machinery can easily copy other machines from a blueprint or from a single model, as demonstrated by any small child with a toy construction set. The challenge lies not in understanding the mechanisms of transforming force into movement, but in precisely working and fitting the parts needed to support the transport of energy involved in this transformation.

A local textile-machinery industry could have likewise been established by taxing textile exporters and subsidizing local machine-builders on an application basis through local promotional agencies. In the South Korean case, local exporters used their own money and turned to companies they trusted. They used their own knowledge of performance criteria to specify requirements and evaluate the machinery they ordered. They rapidly exchanged information about the reliability and performance of different producers. The selection process was truly decentralized. Competition between producers was upheld, as in the case of the many car-repair shops in most cities of the underdeveloped world. There was no bureaucratic selection process to decide who should receive subsidies, and thus neither corruption nor distorted information, as is often the case with the application for subsidies at promotional agencies (as well as in the West when applying for loans at private banks). Moreover, copying and improvement were possible, because companies ordering machinery have enough expertise to make suggestions regarding innovation.

Economically, the South Korean solution involved the allocation of a rent. From the viewpoint of administrative efficiency and effectiveness, the rent was channeled into the desired project by the cheapest available method: arms-length sales between competing machine-builders and competing textile exporters.

Upgrading usually involves a similar challenge to increase the local content of exports by import-substituting strategies if devaluation is to remain a viable instrument of export promotion. There are few branches where unskilled labor significantly contributes to value creation. Those commonly mentioned – textiles, footwear, bag and toy production – do not face a very dynamic demand on the markets of TLCs. Successful upgrading requires entering the production of standard machinery, consumer electronics, microelectronics, basic chemicals and even automobile production. The foreign content of the products in these branches is high in catch-up TBCs.

If the foreign content of a product to be exported is high, the effect of devaluation on its international prices is limited. Devaluation only reduces the international price of local factors of production. It does not reduce the price of the overall product in a comparable manner if the product has a foreign content. Protecting the production of not yet price-competitive inputs will allow the emergence of the unidentified factors of technical progress alluded to in new endogenous growth theory, together with increasing employment and perhaps even identical export earnings, as shown by the following example. If all inputs apart from machinery are produced by local labor, with a capital-output ratio in textiles of 2 and a turnover rate for machinery of four years, a value added of 100 without interest payment is attributed 50 % to capital and up to 50 % to local labor. At a rate of devaluation of 50 %, the international price of the products of this branch falls to 75. Suppose that locally produced equipment costs are twice as much, making the local cost of production of the same quantity of goods 150. After 50 % devaluation, the international price is reduced to 75,[24] but with additional employment in the learning-intensive industry of machine production, where a favorable learning curve may even allow cost reductions and form the basis for launching other machine-building. The success of certain underdeveloped countries in upgrading is ample evidence of the fact that the greatest obstacle is not formal knowledge but the skills to be acquired through learning by doing, which can take place only if the necessary or similar products are locally produced.

A broadening of devaluation-driven industrialization of this sort is largely dependent on property rights and state intervention, as shown by Ireland (Fink 2004). Ireland was extremely successful in attracting foreign investors through the almost free use of import facilities and possibilities of profit remittance. But there was no incentive for these investors to accept higher prices from less efficient local suppliers, so they continued to rely on intercompany trade. The high competitiveness of the export sector led to a high exchange rate, which discouraged investment in the local-market-oriented economy and further diversification. The export sector grew, but remained isolated.

---

[24] Before devaluation without local technology: 50 labor + ¼ · 200 capital = 100 cost; with local technology: 50 labor + ¼ · 400 capital = 150 cost; with local technology and devaluation: ½ · 100 labor + (¼ · ½) · 400 capital = 75 cost.

This result should not be surprising from the perspective of new endogenous growth theory[25] and given the Keynesian observation of a tendency towards declining capital-output ratios in the technically most advanced economies (Elsenhans 2003: 176; cf. also chapter 4, fn 4). If the profit rate tends to rise during the process of industrial growth, the economy lagging behind should be characterized by a lower profit rate in the rest of the economy vis-à-vis its export sector and the TLCs. Its high competitiveness in certain activities may lead to full employment, but not necessarily to local technological capacities, especially if the respective economy is well located with respect to markets with high purchasing power. Moreover, its flexibility to react to crisis on the world market by launching internal demand remains quite limited, because the profit rate for alternative export and import substituting activities remains rather low. Its manufacturing sector causes Dutch disease in protecting against further diversification, just like Irish cattle production did in the nineteenth century.

The success of export-led growth may therefore take different forms. Export orientation may lead to diversification, as in the case of the leading East Asian economies which survived the 1997 currency crisis unscathed, or to dependency. Where successful adaptation to new conditions on the world market has been observed, as in South Korea, Taiwan and mainland China, export orientation was accompanied by the intelligent combination of devaluation and a channeling of rents into economic diversification through state intervention.

This has been repeated in other forms by second-tier export-led manufacturing nations, where raw-material rents are openly used to subsidize industrial diversification, promoting the processing of raw materials and taxing exports in their crude form (Jomo 1996: 3).

The simultaneous use of devaluation and targeted rent allocation for diversification underlies the theoretical paradoxes the World Bank has tried to account for through a discourse on good governance.[26] Alice Amsden (1989: 139) proposed the maxim of "getting your prices wrong," whereas the contributions in Jomo and Khan (2000b) outlined the potentially beneficial effect of rent.

---

[25] Young 1928; Kaldor 1981; Romer 1986; Krugman 1979; Krugman 1991.
[26] Adam 2000; Waller 1993; Mürle 1997: 50; Taylor 2003: 93; Masujima 2003: 121; Oman 2000: 11; Weiss 2000: 805.

Upgrading through an intelligent use of rent and devaluation implies two conclusions. First, upgrading is a rent-based strategy. As long as it provides full employment it increases the scope for devaluation. Second, the argument that it is based on the targeted utilization of rent implies that it may not be linked to the expected results of globalization at the political level: a lean state, an autonomous civil society, and a largely state-free market economy capable of self-sustained growth by absorbing marginal labor. Even with high levels of diversification through upgrading, the possibility of solving employment problems by means of devaluation may still exist, perhaps even enhanced by diversification, as the instruments for combining taxes on export sectors and subsidizing new entrants on the world market will be well-established.

## 8. The limits to devaluation

There are two limits to devaluation-driven export-oriented industrialization: the amount of rent available for subsidizing labor in the export sector, and scarcity of labor due to a rising marginal product of labor. An economy which is able to supply its entire workforce with food and simple industrial goods can accept any rate of devaluation (Mathur 1991 WHY: 23). If its goal is social and economic transformation through full employment and rising mass demand, it can even have declining export earnings due to declining export prices. This can be a costly process, however, as it implies a potentially rapid decline in terms of trade due to low price elasticity for products where productivity lags are low in relation to the leading industrial economies.

The West cannot morally enforce a reduction in the capacity to devalue by reducing agricultural surplus, either by withholding necessary imports, such as seed or fertilizers, or by promoting demographic growth. Such unrealistic solutions can be dismissed out of hand.

The other solution, scarcity of labor, is the result of a rising marginal product of labor. Scarcity of labor will be achieved more easily the more employment creation in the export sector is complemented by employment creation through the expansion of internal demand. The internal market grows on the basis of higher employment in the export sector, higher incomes for the poor, who consume food and simple industrial products, often produced by small-scale industry, and, with rising mass incomes, on the basis of standard consumer durables with only the most rudimentary quality requirements, making local production possible more rapidly than for very sophisticated products.

There is a benign and a less benign case of this mechanism. In the benign case, the economy reaches full employment and is transformed into a standard capitalist economy. It will experience a pressure towards democratization from two social classes: labor, which becomes reformist and claims a bigger piece of the cake, and small-scale business, which wants to abolish the special relationship between big business and the state (Kim 1996: 84; Lee 1993: 353; Kim 1999). A similar configuration of social forces was found in late Imperial Germany (small-scale manufacturing eventually agreeing to co-operate with reformist labor in democratizing the political system) and can be witnessed today in Korea, where small industries need the support of labor to pass laws against the exploitation of monopolistic Chaebols (Kim 2005).

In the malignant case, full employment is not achieved. Sectoral productivity increases lead neither to scarcity of labor nor to general wage increases. There will be a strong tendency to appropriate rents, especially in the case of price inelastic exports, not least of all because this rent appropriation can be presented to the public as an element of economic development involving subsidized diversification. The Asian crisis revealed what Korean analysts[27] had described long before: the ambivalence of rents in East Asia (Baer/Miles/Moran: 1999: 1743; Wade 1998).

The present pattern of globalization is characterized by economies that have become sectorally competitive by means of technology transfer, foreign direct investment, and government-sponsored imitation, but which due to the internal social structures of these societies, especially the economic and political weakness of labor in the wake of marginality, only succeed in the transition to full employment in exceptional cases, a transition which would allow the neoclassical mechanisms of wage drift to be established. Most often, and probably to an increasing degree, the expansion of the internal market is limited. The growth of the export sector alone cannot create a great enough impact on the labor market to create full employment, except, perhaps, in small city-states.

---

[27] Rhee 1994; Shin 1993; Heo 2000: 44–54; Bello/Rosenfeld 1990; Morkre 1979; Han 2000; Moon/Mo 2000; Rhee 2000; Kwak 2000; Yoon 2000.

## 9. The transfer of rent and underconsumption as structuring elements of the capitalist West

The possibility of, in principle, nearly unlimited devaluation has implications for TLCs. Labor loses its position of scarcity on the labor market and its power to negotiate wage increases, which implies that wages no longer automatically rise with productivity increases. The high exchange rates of TLCs result from the advance in productivity in certain branches. But not all labor is able to be employed in these high-technology branches, as its impact on the labor market is limited. Labor in underdeveloped economies is competitive in many, if not most manufacturing branches. A labor-cost spread within the TLCs to the degree existing between TBCs and TLCs is unrealistic. No realistic lowering of wages in branches of the TLCs under import competition can lead to wages in international currency lower than the labor costs in devaluation-driven export-oriented TBCs. Lowering wages too much in the TLCs would destroy social cohesion, even if decreasing wages were to be complemented by decreasing prices for wage goods following a general decrease in wages for labor with average skills, making the nominal fall in wages higher than the reduction in real wages.

Even if a spread like this existed, there would most likely still be unemployment, as the majority of labor in branches under import competition can acquire the skills it needs to work in high-technology branches, resulting in an oversupply of this labor until demand for high-technology products dramatically increases. If the state does not provide adequate training opportunities, the private sector will step in.

Improvement in the terms of trade of the TLCs in the wake of increasing devaluation-driven imports from TBCs means that full-employment demand requires wage increases in the TLCs, not merely in line with the increase in productivity in branches not transferred to the TBCs, but higher than these productivity increases, in line with both productivity growth and the rate of improvement of the terms of trade. With a general increase in wages, the range of branches under import competition from TBCs increases. The employment situation further deteriorates. A sectorally limited increase in wages in high-technology branches worsens the social consequences of the wage spread mentioned above.

A general increase in wages would facilitate the implementation of a second option, a more rapid specialization on high-technology products. The markets for these are mainly made up of high-income consumers (in the more developed countries, especially the TLCs). It is unlikely, however, that such a rapid shift in the structure of production can be implemented, since it would imply that entrepreneurs in the high-technology sector greatly accelerate investment. They would have to be very confident that their future markets expand fast enough, and this on the basis of their own employment growth and general wage increases in their own enterprises. Moreover, they would have to assume that technical progress is dependent on hard-to-transfer agglomeration effects – infrastructure, skills, the industrial fabric – that make these disembodied factors immobile and technical progress path dependent. As long as the shift to a new pattern of specialization is slow due to narrow markets and entrepreneurs being skeptical in their expectations, branches under import competition will opt for rationalization. The often proposed argument that job losses in the manufacturing of TLCs is less the consequence of TBC competition than of rationalization would correspond to this explanation (Alderson 1997). In the attempt to maintain production in the TLCs, enterprises opt to improve productivity without a corresponding expansion of production, resulting in a loss of jobs.

The third solution would involve increasing the rate of accumulation. A new investment in better technology for the production of known products is economically viable only if it reduces unit costs (Bortkiewicz 1907: 455–460; Okishio 1961). The total sum of incomes of capital and labor per unit decreases, so that the capacity-creating effect of the investment is higher than the income effect, at least in the long term. Any investment in new products requires, on the one hand, new demand and hence rising consumer incomes, on the other hand, an acceptable profit rate, which has to be as high as the profit rate in older branches. An acceleration of investment therefore has to be accompanied by minimum productivity increases. Growth with stagnant real wages has been modeled by Elsenhans (1986, 1994d, 1995g), and can be summarized as follows. The growth rate of the stock of capital has to increase beyond the growth rate of income during the previous period if capital productivity has to remain stable. With constant capital productivity, the economy must engage in an explosive growth process, with growth rates of income and labor productivity far beyond any levels hitherto observed, even in catch-up economies (also Lucas 1988). The economy stabilizes at high rates of growth when the share of labor tends to zero. Growth rates of this scale ultimately depend on the availability of technical innovation, since technical innovation is the factor that keeps capital productivity from declining. It is measured against the growth rate of labor productivity, which with a constant capital productivity follows the growth rate of capital stock, the latter increasing from period to period. Thus, such a model is unrealistic. If capital productivity falls because national income does not grow at the rate of growth of capital stock from the previous period, the profit rate necessarily declines after a certain period of time, the share of profit in national income initially increasing with constant wages, and ultimately with decreasing wages.

These results can be formulated in a politically more relevant manner. In capitalism, an increase in real wages limits the surplus available for accumulation, with the result that finance for investment limits investment to levels where technical progress can keep up with net capital formation, so that the capital-output ratio remains constant within a limited corridor. The expansion of demand due to the rise of mass incomes creates new possibilities for profitable investment, and therefore allows further capital formation in monetary terms. If prices in such a system are transformed into synchronized labor time (Wolfstetter 1973; Weizsäcker/Samuelson 1971) – which can be done approximately by dividing the annual level of capital stock in constant prices by the index of real wages (or the capital stock in actual prices by the index of nominal wages) – no capital deepening will be observable. This means that capitalists do not accumulate, but, instead, combat the obsolescence of their technology by investing in better machinery and equipment. It was Sinn (1975: 653) who first showed the importance of technical progress as a source of capital depreciation (the worth of capital decreases when it becomes technically obsolescent) keeping capitalist economies from succumbing to the tendential fall in the rate of profit, which Marx expected to bring about the ultimate demise of capitalism.

The rising capital-output ratio and the overall high levels attained in the centrally planned economies of Eastern Europe just before the fall of the Berlin Wall[28] as well as the high capital-output ratios "achieved" under

---

[28] Ark 1995: 89; Baar 1995: 31; Ritschl 1995; Ritschl 1996. Cf. For previous observation: Selucky 1972: 3–6; Bergson 1973: 7; Feiwel 1971: 62; Feiwel 1978: 15; Bettelheim 1985: 47; Tatur 1983: 14; Kosta 1978: 100; Obst 1979: 142; Amacher/Conger 1977: 320; Krol 1972: 52; Kaplan 1968; Zielinski 1973: 4; Bajt 1971: 61; Brubaker 1968: 309; Barry 1976: 38; Allais 1958: 85; Goldman 1971: 4; Powell 1979: 71; Leptin 1968: 75;

state-led import-substituting industrialization in Third World countries[29] both demonstrate that a rate of accumulation higher than the rate of increase of national income is economically viable yet inferior to capitalism. The rise and fall of real socialism between the 1930s and the 1980s has been explained elsewhere (Elsenhans 2000e) as the result of centrally planned economies, despite their inefficiency in the use of scarce factors of production, becoming attractive against the backdrop of serious unemployment in the capitalist world and eventually losing their attractiveness in the contest with full-employment welfare capitalism. Despite higher shares of investment, the growth rates of centrally planned economies fell behind the growth rates of capitalism at a time when capitalism could not risk high levels of unemployment due to the inherent political dangers of the "competition between politico-economic systems."

The devaluation-driven export-led growth of TBCs renders the neoclassical "automatism" of wage drift economically inoperative in the TLCs and makes the Keynesian voluntarism of injecting demand into the economy politically unfeasible.

The TLCs seek new solutions with two basic characteristics: Business and labor disintegrate as cohesive actors, and policies are based on rent-seeking. There are some factions of labor and business which remain competitive despite devaluation-driven imports from TBCs. They oppose taking on financial burdens in the interest of the rest of the economy. In the rest of the economy, business and labor call for protection, which ultimately involves the mobilization of resources from highly productive branches in order to pay for subsidized or protected employment or for the expansion of new activities in social services not subject to import competition. It is obvious that the already existing level of protection has created institutional mechanisms capable of administering such programs of redistribution and protectionism, whereas intensified international competition limits the resources the internationally competitive sector is willing to contribute to rent-seeking.

---

Woroniak 1970: 94; Chambre 1967: 269; Liberman 1977: 117; Nove 1979: 39; Lorenz 1976: 130; Szelenyi 1978: 72; Weitzman 1970: 677.

[29] Among many: Ikonicoff 1974 : 337 : 77 ; Pickett/Robson 1977: 881; Chakravarty 1984: 845; Baer/Figueroa 1982: 82; Fry 1971: 307; Fajnzylber/Martínez Tarragó 1976: 270; Patel 1964: 349; Zimmermann 1971: 17; Bhagwati 1988. 546; Oshima 1984; Bardhan 1984: 69.

The West imports rent-dominated structures because its own mechanism of eliminating rent, rising mass incomes in line with productivity increases (and improvements in terms of trade) and accumulation on the basis of expanding mass markets, is undermined by the following mechanism: Devaluation and productivity increases in the South lead to an increase in the worldwide supply of goods without the South participating in a parallel increase in demand for such goods. There is a greater increase in worldwide productive capacity than in worldwide consumptive capacity.

There is a parallel here with the argument of Cline (1982), proposed earlier by Elsenhans (1981c infra chapter 3, 1979b). The generalization of the East Asian model of social and economic transition to capitalism with full employment based on export-led manufacturing implies levels of imports in the West that are incompatible with the maintenance of certain fundamental social structures in the West. Havrylyshyn's (1982) criticism of Cline's "export pessimism" does not apply in this case, because the problem is not the level of import penetration but the impact of these exports on the expansion of demand and the social fabric of the TLCs. The destruction of the bargaining power of labor in the TLCs blocks rapid structural change towards a new pattern of specialization in the TLCs. The lack of bargaining power of average-skilled labor in the TBCs – which will continue to be the case as long as marginality persists there – triggers off a similar disempowerment of labor in the TLCs. Given the disempowerment of labor, the TLCs can hardly avoid the emergence of an underconsumptionist situation with an increase in rent-seeking.

The underconsumptionist tendencies originating from the devaluation-driven export of manufactures from the TLCs exist despite the potential balance-of-trade deficits of TBCs. Deteriorating terms of trade can lead to balance-of-trade deficits despite rising quantities being supplied to the world market. Terms of trade for manufactured exports from the TBCs can deteriorate (Sarkar/Singer 1991; 1993), as demonstrated by the massive devaluation of East Asian countries after the Asian crisis. The West's recent demand for appreciation of the Chinese yuan shows that even massively rising quantities of exports do not automatically lead to rising currency parities.

Although the theory of devaluation-based export-led growth implies that the underdeveloped world is forced to engage in unequal exchange in the sense of Emmanuel (1969: 109 ff), and is therefore exploited in the sense of Lenin's (1817/1977: 245) theory of imperialism, it is radically opposed to theories of unequal exchange or international exploitation. "Exploitation" through devaluation leads to development (Suh 1987: 111), because companies producing in low labor-cost areas will always earn the money they need for expansion. Exploitation in the classical theory of imperialism of Rosa Luxemburg (1923) also led to capitalist development. Lenin likewise did not deny the possibility of development through exploitation. Lenin, followed up in the dependencia debate by Ramos (1974), Palma (1978), O'Brien (1975) and Warren (1973; 1980), argued that this kind of exploitation prolongs capitalism, because it supplies additional profit to TLCs, allowing the tendential fall in the rate of profit to be counteracted. His argument loses validity, however, if capitalism is not characterized by a fall in capital productivity (which Marx, 1894/1972c: 221–240, terms, the consequence of a rising organic composition of capital). The observation at the core of dependencia theory that the drive for raw-material exports in the late nineteenth century did not lead to development has nothing to do with exploitation but, rather, with Dutch disease.[30] Comparatively high prices for raw materials led to internationally high costs for local labor which, in turn, blocked diversification, as productivity was much lower in manufacturing than in raw-material production in comparison to TLCs. Such economies may have been too rich to prosper (Mahon 1992). Raw-material production, especially in minerals, was characterized by technical breakthroughs in the late nineteenth century which did not allow diversifying into equipment for raw-material production in the new raw-material-exporting countries – Latin America (copper and tin), Asia (tin)[31] and, later on, Africa – as well as for the globalizing oil industry.

Export-led growth in manufacturing allows a country to engage in investment-goods production because technology is simple, at least in the branches it starts in.

---

[30] Enders/Herberg 1983: 473–495; Wijnbergen 1984: 41–55; Ansari 1989: 804–813; Allub 1983: 169–190; Parvin/Dezhbakhsh 1988: 469–477; Corden/Neary 1982: 825–848; MacCoy/Smith 1995: 123f.; Poirine 1993: 1181; Auty 1994: 11–26; Kamas 1986: 1177–1198; Davis 1995: 1001; Younger 1992: 1587–1597; Seers 1964: 235; Scherr 1989: 557; Braun 1989: 46; Edwards 1984: 1113; Barchiesi 1996: 351; Rimmer 1987: 435–446; Looney 1990: 119–133; Ezeala-Harrison 1993: 193–198; Hutchison 1994: 311–329.

[31] Ruffert 1996: 59; Hillman 1984: 420; Blainey 1970; Harvey/Press 1989: 83; Schmitz 1986; Yamada 1971: 237; Valenzuela 1990: 686; Levin 1960: 8f.; Harvey/Press 1990: 103f.

My argument does therefore not claim that the TLCs need export-led manufacturing in order to get surplus from the TBCs, or that exploitation of the South through devaluation and declining terms of trade in manufacturing keeps the TBCs from getting transformed into capitalist economies capable of self-sustained growth. The crux of my argument is that the impact of globalization is too weak. Because TBCs do not achieve their transition to the benign case by the impact of globalization alone if they are unable to establish entitlements – to use Sen's (1981: 162) argument – for the marginalized, their becoming competitive in manufacturing on the basis of improved agricultural productivity destroys in the TLCs the very mechanism capitalism was built on: the empowerment of labor.

The challenge is not creating a more just world, which may indeed be a desirable goal, but in globalizing the conditions for capitalism. The current pattern of globalization, i.e., export-led growth, is too weak to absorb marginal labor in the South and to establish worldwide conditions for the operation of the neoclassical model.

Labor-surplus models of the Fei/Ranis (1964: 13ff) or Lewis (1954) type assume that a benign, development-oriented government might use state intervention to achieve this goal. The crisis of the state engaging in import-substituting industrialization contradicts the expectation of modernization theory. Historically based models in the tradition of Sombart (1921a; 1921b; 1921c), as well as Akamatsu's (1961: 197) referring to the earlier work of Sombart, are based on pre-Keynesian economics, as is the whole historical school of German economics referred to by Akamatsu, where any available surplus is used for the purchase of goods and services ultimately produced by labor. In this case, according to Say's theorem (Say 1803/1972: 140), all labor is employed productively provided it is cheap enough.

The argument of the simultaneous existence of surplus labor and a surplus of resources is opposed to this perspective. Its central organizing concept is that the identity between resources available and resources in demand is not necessarily achieved under capitalist conditions. The argument is expanded by showing that, under the conditions of marginality-ridden economies becoming competitive in price and income-elastic products on the world market, there is a structural tendency to labor surplus. This tendency also affects the TLCs in the form of the new, devaluation-based competitiveness of marginality-ridden TBCs.

## 10. Some of the model's implications concerning the danger of a globalization of rent

The conclusion to be drawn from this analysis is that where marginality-ridden TBCs are integrated into the world market, globalization as the intensification of transborder flows of goods, services, and capital has to be complemented by appropriate policies for absorbing the labor surplus in marginality-ridden TBCs. It is these internal structures in marginality-ridden TBCs that block the tendencies to equilibrium described in neoclassical economics, and not the intensification of transborder economic flows of goods and capital itself. The offensive of business against labor in the OECD countries has been successful precisely because of the availability in marginality-ridden TBCs of a cheap labor force subsidized from internal wage-goods production. Hopes that TLCs will always maintain some comparative advantage and that Porter's (1990: 72) diamond will be accessible only to more virtuous countries displaying bourgeois thriftiness and a dedication to learning are irrelevant if specialization depends on the transformation of comparative advantage through devaluation in countries with reasonably large supplies of wage goods from the local production of food agriculture. Obviously, the fact that all TBCs have some comparative advantage, even if they are unable to transform it into price competitiveness due to the limits of devaluation, also implies that all TLCs have some comparative advantage at a given point in time, since at least one of these economies initiated technical progress. The decisive point is not new comparative advantage but the capacity to transform comparative advantage into price competitiveness through devaluation.

In the convoy model, high levels of employment in all participating economies allow an economy that is falling behind, economy B, to specialize on backward products at low rates of devaluation and to achieve high levels of employment through this specialization. If, however, there are marginality-ridden economies, C, with comparative advantage in backward or even in innovative products, the capacity of C to proceed to further devaluation implies that B can maintain its competitiveness only if it itself further devalues. The emergence of marginality-driven economies of the C type with large capabilities for devaluation and still large surpluses of labor destroys the possibility of B to remain backward but still part of the convoy.

Upgrading in TBCs and falling behind in TLCs create an intermediate category of economies. Wallerstein's (1974: 84) notion of a semi-periphery is perhaps an appropriate concept for describing them. They are not yet or no longer competitive in all high-technology branches, but only in some or many intermediate technologies, and have diversified economies. They lag behind the leading TLCs and are under competitive pressure from technically less advanced TBCs capable of devaluation.

The economies of this semi-periphery show the greatest tendency towards statism in international economic relations, as long demonstrated by France.[32] Their level of productivity is high enough to skim off rents for subsidizing investment and skill promotion in their high-technology branches. Their statist policies are more efficient than the statist policies of the leading TLCs. Catch-up economies can follow the leader; they do not have to discover which products, technologies or branches will be the future leaders. Statist policies are much more efficient in promoting imitation and selecting the most efficient among different technologies than in selecting new branches and products for which new technologies still have to be developed (Leff 1985: 343–347).

At the same time, in contrast to technically more backward economies, the more advanced among technologically backward economies are rich enough in financial resources, skilled labor, infrastructure and technical experience to succeed in implementing statist policies of technical promotion. Bastian (2001) shows the capacity of the more advanced among the former centrally planned economies of Eastern Europe to benefit from statist policies, as does Schömmel (2005) in his analysis of Brazilian foreign economic policies.

The leading TLCs can react to these challenges by accepting catching up and falling behind as the normal outcomes of a ping-pong-like process of shifting competitive advantage. They are advised, however, by strategic trade theory[33] not to rely on this mechanism, but to constantly strive to be first and reap technological monopoly rents. Still, Krugman (1987: 143) has admitted that picking winners can be problematic, and that free trade and renouncing sectoral industrial policies might still be advisable.

The contemporary pattern of globalization is causing the coalition for free trade to shrink. The leading branches in the leading TLCs are for it, but in a

---

[32] Pollard 1981: 162; Viallatte 1937: 23; Caron 1979: 79; Kemp 1971: 109; Schmidt 1996; Cole 1939: 363; Nye 1991.
[33] Krugman 1979; 1981; 1987; Bhagwati 1989; Grossman/Richardson 1985; Grossman 1992; Grossman/Helpman 1990; Helpman 1981.

set-up where they defend technical monopolies, using economies of scale to enable themselves to capture the entire world market for new products. The less performing advanced branches in both the leading and lagging-behind TLCs opt for industrial policies that are sometimes accompanied by government-business cooperation with business in the driver's seat. The more competitiveness can be sectorally achieved on the basis of devaluation, the more intensive the following choice: Should one try to become an Ireland, with high foreign-sector employment and blockages to the rest of the economy (Fink 2004), or skim off export rents in order to finance diversification? It is obvious that the second option will be chosen by the less favorably placed among the catch-up economies. They will be joined by backward TBCs, which enter the world market through the classical primers of export-led growth – textiles, toys and shoes – whenever their possibilities of employment growth in these branches have been exhausted.

The parallel tendencies to intensified state intervention – and the enabling state is indeed state interventionist – will prevail as long as falling behind becomes definitive under free competition and can be overcome only by state interventionism, as the launching of alternative branches with lower technological requirements does not allow for full employment with acceptable terms of trade. This alternative solution of export-led growth leading to full employment in the TBCs, too, was shown to be based on TBCs being diversified, hence able to shift from exports to internal-market-oriented production in the case of declining terms of trade. The convoy solution ultimately depends on all convoy members being able to remain in the convoy without getting stuck in a marginality-*cum*-rent trap.

With today's new capacities for transforming comparative advantage into cost competitiveness by means of devaluation, maintaining a free world economy therefore depends on transforming the marginality-ridden economies into truly capitalist ones, perhaps at a relatively low level of productivity for a long time to come, but with tendential full employment. There are development policies that can contribute to this transition of TBCs from marginality-ridden economies to (welfare) capitalist ones where the mechanisms of neoclassical economics function.

It is highly improbable that under conditions of high-productivity growth the expansion of capitalism, currently called globalization, will lead to worldwide capitalism. Imperialism will not be the pioneer of capitalism (Warren 1980) but an obstacle to worldwide capitalism, encouraging mechanisms on the "supply-side" that allow temporarily disregarding the precondition of capitalism on the "demand-side," rising mass incomes. Imperialism would then have to be considered as a truncated form of globalization, the globalization of rent.

From this point of view, Lenin's theory of imperialism and the neoclassical theory of the worldwide spread of capitalism and convergence between different economies can be integrated into my theory of globalization with an open outcome. According to Lenin (1917/1977: 245) imperialism is a form of reaction among capitalists in the TLCs to the falling rate of profit. According to the neoclassical theories of convergence, the marginal efficiency of factors of production decrease if the employment of a particular factor of production in relation to other factors of production increases (Sachs/Larrain 1993: 49). In international economics, this modeling is associated to the Heckscher-Ohlin-Samuelson theory of international specialization (Ohlin 1927; Heckscher 1949, Samuelson 1948).

According to new endogenous growth theory, the increase of physical capital in relation to labor does not provoke a drop in the efficiency of capital or the rate of profit because there is technical progress that is not embodied in physical capital, i.e., human skills, efficient innovation systems or other elements of technical progress that cannot be easily identified.[34] These are produced by the production process without directly incurring outlays. Training workers within the firm is an outlay for the firm as long as no other competitor can compete without incurring the same outlays. To some extent, these "disembodied" elements of technical progress[35] can be understood as the unintended result of joint production processes, where a saleable product is the primary goal, one that cannot be achieved without the production of skills. According to Bortkiewicz (1907: 455f) and Okishio (1961), a minimum of this kind of technical progress is involved in introducing any new technology.

Generalizing the empirical observations of new endogenous growth theory for all capitalist systems and basing growth theory on the Okishio-

---

[34] "The engine of growth in the models (...) is human capital (...) human capital is simply an unobservable magnitude or force, with certain assumed properties, that I have postulated in order to account for some observed features of aggregative behavior." (Lucas 1988: 35).

[35] Denison 1967: 298; Barro/Sala-i-Martin 1991; 1992; 1995; Barro 1992; Fagerberg 2000; Grossmann/Helpman 1994; Hemmer 1999; Lucas 1988: 35.

Borthkiewicz criterion for technical innovation can have serious implications on hierarchies in the international division of labor and the strategies capitalist enterprises can use.

TLCs have high profit rates in all sectors of production and keep high-technology sectors only if international competition in high-technology tradables production does not drive the profit rate down in these high-technology sectors. The fact that profit rates are equal in the different sectors of a national economy results from the equalization of sector productivity through the adjustment of relative prices, a basic mechanism of any capitalist system. This does not exclude that technical progress is linked to the emergence of high-technology sectors and spread to other branches in line with the ICT revolution (Gordon 1999a; 1999b). It is also possible that the high factor productivity in non-high-technology sectors is simply the result of adjusting relative prices.

Let us assume that the high profit rate in the TLCs depends on all sorts of disembodied technical progress. Let us assume further that technical innovation is triggered off by the interaction between this environment and innovation in the technically leading branches which, partly due to wage pressure, leads to the modernization of all other branches in the TLCs, including their non-tradable products. Let us assume that the TLCs are not able to drive down the profit rate in their non-tradables production and in their less innovative branches. TBCs are able to modernize their technically backward branches only by launching mass consumption, hence with full employment locally. If this condition is not fulfilled, the catch-up economies have low average profit rates. Their integration into the world economy via high-technology branches may lead to full specialization and full employment. If it does not, high profits in these branches have to be plowed back into the rest of the TBCs by means other than the market. Until full specialization is achieved, however, these TBCs are neither capable of catching up on the basis of their local markets through high productivity increases in backward branches, nor through launching their internal mass consumption, as they will not be able to rapidly satisfy mass consumption with local production. With higher profit rates in the backward branches of the TLCs and low average profit rates in the TBCs, only labor in the TLCs is able to combat the rising rate of profit through rising mass consumption. It will, however, accept wage cuts if international competitiveness appears to be in danger.

## A Convoy Model vs. an Underconsumptionist Model 251

The development of physical productivity in the technically leading branches and the spread of this productivity to backward branches in the TLCs, as well as the rise of productivity in the dynamic branches of TBCs, lead to an overall increase in the availability of products worldwide that is not matched by an increase in worldwide consumption. The position of the TLCs can only be defended if industrial policy is successful. Strategic trade theory gives indications of how to behave (Krugman 1992: 441). The TLCs will constantly look for technical monopolies in order to maintain high levels of employment. As technical progress is transferable, this advance is only temporary, and has to be permanently recreated. The instrument for this support for innovation is a form of rent allocation. It will be associated with permanent attempts to create market imperfections. The TBCs also try to use high profit rates in their technically leading export branches to transform their economy.

We should therefore expect the TLCs to opt for political instruments to protect their position on the world market and in the international division of labor, and this because of an overall lack of global demand. The combination of political instruments to defend one's position corresponds exactly to the configuration of state and market in imperialist policies. Imperialist policies are possible as long as the leading industrialized countries can opt for some sort of rent appropriation, allowing global production growth to match the lag in global consumption.

If rising mass incomes are an impossibility in the TBCs, only three scenarios are left: a world of rent seeking triggered off, in particular, by the TLCs attempt to defend their leading position through rent appropriation; a world underconsumptionist scenario, where nobody is able to appropriate increasing global production capacities; or removing the factor that allows TBCs to catch up, namely, the agricultural surplus. The latter would imply a Third World holocaust. All three scenarios are untenable. Thus, maintaining a free world economy is contingent upon overcoming low average productivity in the TBCs and ultimately underdevelopment. The focus of globalization critics on the three horror scenarios above (Strange 1996: 226f) blocks any real discussion of an alternative.

## 11. Alternative paths of development

A simple solution would involve intensifying the opening of markets in TLCs for products of the South. In the case of textiles, clothing, and other labor-intensive products there is no need for discussion. The TLCs should outsource production in these branches to the TBCs in order to accelerate their own transformation to technically more demanding products. A similar proposal for opening up markets to agricultural products of the South was turned down at the 2003 WTO conference in Cancun (Le Monde 14/15-9-2003: 4). The English experience in India where railways were built in order to transport staple food from temporary surplus to temporary deficit regions in the late nineteenth century may serve as an initial warning. The creation of outlets for agricultural surpluses did not create "empowerment" in the deficit regions, but merely increased supply on the world market, with food prices rising in the surplus and deficit regions of India (Connell 1885: 262). With completely free access to the markets of TLCs for basic staple foods, policies for keeping the price levels for food low in TBCs would become impossible and efforts for diversification through devaluation-driven export-led growth would be unsuccessful.

The expansion of modernized agricultural production systems may soon be characterized by high degrees of mechanization and the displacement of farm labor, with the prices for exported food high in relation to imported equipment. But the intensification of agriculture based on increasing labor inputs of non-mechanized labor might not occur, so that a large internal mass market made up of relatively well-to-do agricultural producers and which could serve as the basis for a thriving small and medium-scale industry may not emerge. There is no longer any free territory to be colonized, as was the case during Western Europe's period of transition to capitalism within the framework of the nineteenth-century transatlantic economy. Reserves of not yet intensively cultivated agricultural land exist only in certain TLCs, which would never allow the migration of marginal workers from the TBCs to engage in labor-intensive farming on smaller plots (Krishna 1985: 31).

Given the low levels of transnational migration and the limited transformative capacity of export-led growth, the transition to a worldwide convoy model of globalization is only feasible if marginality is dealt with more directly in marginality-ridden economies. In the wake of the oil-price crisis, there was hope that the enormous amount of financial resources might constitute the basis of development policies that would considerably reduce marginality in the underdeveloped world. This option was rejected politically for two reasons. On the one hand, US oil policy had succeeded in transforming the resource richness of Saudi Arabia and the Golf emirates into an asset allowing development policies with limited social reforms to be imposed on the recipients of oil money, who were to use this money to overcome difficulties in the wake of oil-price rises. Support was often handed out to so-called fundamentalist movements, for whom structural reforms, especially the redistribution of property rights in agriculture and rising mass incomes, were hardly a priority. On the other hand, oil-exporting countries like Algeria that were at least verbally committed to the use of oil rent as "seed money" for the improvement of economic and social conditions for the masses engaged in extremely statist economic policies. They failed to realize the necessity of expanding the internal mass market in order to create markets for private small-scale industry. Where a small scale industry of this type could emerge because of the inefficiency of an over-financed public industrial sector, it was considered a political threat to the power of the ruling state classes (Elsenhans/Kleiner/Dreves 2000: 231).

Marginality was dealt with not by increasing decentralized wage-goods production in agriculture and small and medium-scale enterprises (which could have engaged in local investment-goods production) but by overstaffing large, state-owned enterprises, which were almost totally dependent on imported technology. The impact of this strategy on the absorption of marginal labor was too weak to create full employment and the capacity to improve the productivity of marginal labor by means of locally produced investment goods. The rent was appropriated by more or less centralized "bureaucracies," which I have defined as state classes (Elsenhans 1996e). Because of the absence of competition even idealistically-minded segments of these state classes (Sklar 1967: 8f) encountered problems of overstaffing, described by Ibn Khaldûn (1967: 579–616) for precapitalist state classes, and inefficient investment.

All strategies for dealing with marginality and underdevelopment involve a short-term management of marginality and a long-term strategy of productivity increases in wage-goods production with the aim of raising the marginal product of labor (Elsenhans 1997e). They do this by using demand as a pull factor in order to avoid the inefficient use of rent implied in a necessarily bureaucratic process of selecting, managing and, in particular, monitoring economic projects that are not yet profitable but which can become profitable if the intended objectives are achieved: economic diversification and rising mass incomes (Rosenstein-Rodan 1943). Strategies for launching small-scale industries which entail entry into the production of initially simple investment goods based on a subsidy to marginal labor allow synergetic effects to emerge between fighting poverty and raising the marginal product of labor.

Historically speaking, the simplest configuration of supporting a marginal population and launching economic growth was the English poor laws of the seventeenth to early nineteenth centuries. Parishes were responsible for the upkeep of their poor, who had to work if they were able-bodied (Burden 2005: 78–82). As the marginal product of these laborers was lower than their costs of subsistence, parishes were obliged to farm out their poor to businessmen, often large-scale farmers. Marx's (1890/1972a: 703, 711) argument that this was proof of capitalists not being willing even to pay labor's costs of reproduction is wrong. The parishes had to tax the rich to pay the difference between the wages paid out by employers and the costs of reproduction for the poor. The farm operators paid a part of labor regardless of their readiness to employ them, i.e., in the form of taxes, and part on the basis of their actual use of this labor, in the form of wages. As the marginal product of labor did not decrease and the costs of unsubsidized labor did not increase through these measures, there was no reduction of employment among unsubsidized labor. The surplus of the rich decreased (Elsenhans 1992d). But as markets for food and simple products expanded, the tremendous investment in English agriculture and the resulting growth of small-scale industries provided opportunities for investment spending and hence reinforced profit against rent.

Through agricultural reform in the marginality-ridden economies with a redistribution of land to small farmers, marginal labor is internalized on the farm. Small landowners achieve high levels of production with only a limited amount of labor time, but will also have to use additional labor time which adds only little to production and was therefore not used before land redistribution. They will have to do so as long as their highly productive hours do not provide them with enough food for survival, and as long as there are no alternative employment opportunities (Elsenhans 1979a: 552–562; Janvry 1981: 384–92). Agrarian reform implies low supply prices for off-farm by-employment in rural industries. Farmers offer their labor if the wage rate in these industries is higher than the marginal product of this labor in agriculture. A laborer with no access to land would have to claim a wage that is at least equal to the average product of the farm family calculated per hour of work which, by definition, is higher than the marginal product of this farm family (Dasgupta/Ray 1987: 176–82). After redistribution, the rent previously appropriated by landowners now supports marginal labor and promotes the disappearance of luxury consumption, whereas the increase in mass consumption favors local investment spending and, thus, profit. Wherever agriculture thrives in underdeveloped countries, the so-called informal sector is highly dynamic,[36] as was the case in Europe (Elsenhans 1992f; Crafts 1980; 1985) and in Japan.[37]

NGOs rarely have the instruments at their disposal to restructure an economy (Elsenhans 1995d: 154–57). They channel resources from foreign countries or the local richer strata to the marginal population, which subsequently increases its bargaining power on the labor market.

Agrarian reforms and NGO-led subsidies to the poor are forms of channeling rent into the support of marginalized segments of the population. In this respect, they are no different from devaluation-driven export-led growth or import-substituting industrialization. They offer alternative forms of managing rents, thereby improving the management of these rents. They do this especially by providing an additional element of control. On the one hand they favor an investment orientation in small units through market incentives; on the other hand they increase the political empowerment of the poor, either through employment (agrarian reform) or by raising their potential for political organization (NGOs).

All the strategies mentioned above – import-substituting industrialization, devaluation-driven export-led growth, agrarian reform, and NGO support to the poor – require support from non-market segments of the politico-economic structure, and imply side effects involving decreasing returns. Agrarian reforms create anxieties over the loss of property rights; export-led devaluation-driven industrialization depends on the limited absorptive capacities of OECD markets (Elsenhans 1981c; 1987a; Cline 1982); NGOs often suffer from bureaucratization and clientelistic practices vis-à-vis their

---

[36] Storm 1995: 773; Gray/Singer 1988: 403; Hwa 1988; Dutt 1991.
[37] Nakamura 1966: 159f.; Craig/Fairbank/Reischauer 1973: 147; Yasuba 1986: 224; Grabowski 1994: 180–83.

target groups if staff can no longer be motivated by the ideals and charisma of the initial founders.[38]

A syncretistic approach is therefore advisable, combining in an eclectic and decentralized manner elements from all of these domains. Export-led growth combined with agrarian reforms and NGO activists helping marginal populations to avail themselves of new opportunities, the government concentrating on subsidizing investment-goods production for the sectors that grow via exports and expansion of the internal market – this could serve as a rough description of the kind of eclecticism foreseen.

Overcoming underdevelopment will reduce the marginal populations' dependency on the powerful. Thus, the argument is often heard that elites will reject such policies. With resources around double that of current development assistance, the annual income of about one billion poor could be raised by about $150, which would raise the lowest quintile up to the level of the next quintile, and bring these poorest of the poor out of the marginality trap. It has been estimated that the approximately 70 million families living below the poverty line in India would need about $25 billion (including their current incomes) to accomplish this feat (Nayyar 2000: 3741), which, given India's high share of the world's poor, confirms the relatively modest magnitude of this task.

If no strategy of channeling these resources to marginal populations can prevent the misuse of resources by large communities of development-assistance "experts" (Haas 1992), the new lords of poverty (Hancock 1989), one could easily imagine an alternative strategy of throwing easily identifiable stones that can only be imitated at high costs into remote areas by helicopter (Elsenhans 1991c: 281–83). The donors would announce that they will exchange these stones for their own convertible currency, at rates where the daily gatherings of a worker correspond to the daily subsistence costs of this worker and his family. The family will migrate to an area where these stones are dropped. As physical labor is required to gather these stones, especially if difficult terrain is chosen where the stones are to be dropped, the laborer cannot be deprived of his income, because he cannot survive otherwise and will not be available for this type of work. At appropriate rates for these gatherings, only marginal laborers will engage in this artificially productive work. They will sell the stones at markets, probably to truck drivers,

---

[38] Gordon 1997: 60; Westergaard 1996: 50–51; Avina 1993; Hashemi 1990: 51.

and buy food and simple industrial products with their income. Farmers will see their markets grow, and some of them will invest in improving their land to increase their yields. Small industrial shops will expand, as observed already in the agriculturally rich regions. Farmers and small industrialists in the informal sector will choose the most appropriate, i.e., efficient, technology available on the market, initially labor-intensive technologies, since they will most likely not consider their own and their family's labor time as costs to be reduced by labor-saving devices. Moral hazard is limited to the personnel in the exchange offices and the helicopter pilots. The strategy is sustainable not because the stones themselves create any direct productivity increases, but because investments increase the yields of a multitude of small and large-scale farmers as demand for their products expands. The lower the learning costs, the more they will invest, so that Western donor agencies will discover a new field of activity: offering appropriate technology, a field they have long claimed to understand.

I do not see why elites in aid-dependent countries would reject such a strategy, since they, too, would receive convertible currency, and, moreover, would have no opportunity to divert resources. There is no local inflationary danger, as the stones are paid for in convertible currency, so that a deficit in wage goods can be temporarily bridged by imports, which, at an appropriate exchange rate, are soon replaced by local production, at least in the industrial sector. German reunification has demonstrated that the suggested flow of resources of about double the present disbursements of overseas development assistance, an amount equal to the flows from West to East Germany over the past decade, would not involve inflationary dangers.

## 12. Concluding Remarks

The proposed strategy of alternative development will lead to technical capacities all over the world. The production of appropriate technology is triggered off by demand-led growth (based on exports and expansion of the internal market of TBCs). This technology will initially be of a simple character. Even if it takes time to improve skills, the basic mechanism of capitalist growth will still be transferred to the marginality-ridden world. The transformation of marginality-ridden countries into truly welfare-state capitalist countries where neoclassical mechanisms apply would transform the current pattern of globalization into a convoy model.

In the convoy model of globalization the challenges created by the globalization of financial markets, which have not been extensively dealt with here, are easily met. The most serious challenge is not the outflow of financial resources but the inflow. Switzerland had to deal with this problem of an overvalued exchange rate and the subsequent lack of competitiveness of its productive activities for long periods during the second half of the twentieth century. It even introduced taxes on finance capital held by foreigners. These foreigners had to pay a sort of negative interest rate on these financial assets.

Capital outflows are a sanction for the holders of financial assets against monetary policies aimed at relaunching economic activity through "cheap money" or fiscal deficits. Both are expected to ultimately lead to inflation. Initial doubts have been expressed concerning the relevance of this danger. The erstwhile effect, however, is a decrease of the exchange rate and a subsequent increase in competitiveness.

The problem inherent to the globalization of financial markets is the emergence of a new rentier class (Elsenhans 2000a). These financial markets act like a money-printing machine that is out of control. In Keynesian theory, money creation was justified during a slump with the goal of relaunching the economy. Additional production in the boom phase would later justify the creation of this initially worthless scriptural money. With full convertibility, no government will risk raising interest rates if this will negatively affect the increase in stock prices, as shifts in the portfolio of international "investors" (speculators, since nearly none of them have performed the noble role of a Schumpeterian innovative investor) will drive down the exchange rate. Despite the general experience that a low exchange rate favors labor because it increases the demand for its services, there exists the widespread illusion that a high exchange rate is necessary to maintain the wealth of individual households. Most Europeans did not feel the decline in parity of the euro in their own pockets in the late 1990s, but, nonetheless, majorities in Western Europe believe that the decline of the euro vs. the dollar is bad. The rise of the euro against the dollar in late 2003 has been rightly perceived by nearly all mainstream economists as a danger for economic growth in the euro zone.

The consequences may be quite different for TBCs, however, and this for two reasons. Devaluation implies a rise in the price of international liabilities in relation to the earnings devaluating TBCs can fetch from increased exports. In addition, technical dependency on imported investment goods may make devaluation difficult.

The proposed deepening of globalization through the expansion of the internal mass market may help make catch-up TBCs less dependent on technology imports. The possibility of creating a local investment-goods industry, initially for the manufacture of technically simple export products, and an expanding internal mass market characterized by a relative homogeneity of demand due to a relatively egalitarian distribution of income has been largely dealt with in the literature.[39] Even mainstream economists with close connections to the World Bank now accept the link between equality and development (Li/Squire/Zon 1998; Squire 1999; Adelman 1984: 938).

This eases the problem of the internationalization of financial markets. An economy with a diversified productive apparatus does not have to fear the outflow but, rather, the inflow of capital. With an outflow of capital, the exchange rate depreciates and the economy becomes more competitive. Devaluation presents a problem only if the productive apparatus cannot react flexibly to the increasing internal demand for products previously imported. Food and technology are the basic bottlenecks. The necessary capacity to produce an agricultural surplus in order to be able to benefit from globalization has been dealt with above.

The problem of finance capital outflows is thus a problem of technical dependency. Taiwan had a high level of local investment-goods production dominated by small and medium-scale industries (Yi 1988; Fujita/James 1990; Cheng 1990: 150). It fared much better during the Asian crisis than the Chaebol-dominated economy of South Korea with its high degree of technical dependence on Japan. Reorienting the world economy from its current pattern of globalization to a convoy model will not only make its component national economies resistant to the sanction of international finance capital; it will also make international finance capital less relevant.

Financial markets are fed by financial resources that cannot be profitably invested in the goods-and-services-producing real economy. Their growth is associated with expansionary monetary policies which governments resort to in order to launch their economies via the demand for investment goods,

---

[39] Among many others: Strassmann 1956; Furtado 1970; Oshima 1971, 1977: 563, 1984: 104; Stewart/Streeten 1971: 146f; Figueroa 1972; Lafaiete Lopes 1972; Sideri 1972: 14; Sunman 1974: 64–73; Hinkelhammert 1975: 299; Amsden 1977: 229f; Bequele/Freedman 1979: 320; Kuzmin 1979: 175; Santos 1979: 20; Alamgir 1980: 426f; Benachenhou 1980: 18; Pashardes 1980; Pack 1974: 402; Faroque/Butterfield 1987; Quadir 1987: 63; Nowak 1988: 14; Murphy/Schleifer/Vishny 1989: 189; Leightner 1992.

neglecting the necessary parallel expansion of mass demand. Rising values of financial assets because of the continual supply of fresh money will lead to expectations about returns completely delinked from the profit rate in the goods-and-service-producing economy. Speculators will opt for credit and other liquidity-raising substitutes in order to benefit from the rising value of assets. With full convertibility, governments may be hesitant to raise interest rates if this has a negative effect on the increase in stock prices, as speculators can migrate from one currency area to another when they expect either a decline in the values of stocks or a decline in the exchange rate. An increasing volatility of financial markets is always a sign of insufficient increases in the real economy. Speculators receive monetary assets with no counterpart in the production of real goods. Monetary resources drawn from speculation have social consequences similar to those of only sectorally increasing productivity in TBCs, which does not lead to rising mass incomes because of its too limited effect on the labor market. They reinforce rent as a special form of surplus which keeps the holders of financial assets from investing in productive capacity – the basis for employing factors of production which earn incomes that contribute to rising mass demand. The underconsumptionist pattern of globalization is therefore closely linked to various mechanisms leading to an increase in the importance of rent.

With a convoy model of globalization, demand-led expansion of investment in plant and equipment worldwide reduces the flow of financial resources to financial markets and raises profit rates in the goods-and-services-producing real economy. The difference in the relative importance of rent and profit means that implementing the convoy model will impinge on the interpretation of economic growth and hence on the hegemonic discourse in economics. When devaluation is no longer considered a threat to prosperity, because it easily launches new exports and new import-substituting productive activities, curbing the expansion of credit going to financial markets will not be considered an unpleasant option anymore. The relevance of the goods-and-services-producing economy as opposed to pure monetary bubbles will be re-established.

The illusion about certain economic processes is the biggest obstacle to efficiently dealing with globalization. There is a widespread conviction that globalization destroys the capacity of the nation-state to steer its economy. Although it certainly involves a number of changes for the state, the only sanction available to international capital is flight. Capital flight triggers off a decline in the exchange rate, hence better conditions for capital accumulation for any fairly diversified economy. This fact is not taken into account in the analyses of mainstream neoclassical authors and orthodox Marxists who depict a doomsday scenario of the state being short-circuited. Both theoretical schools consider capital to be something you can touch, like banknotes. In reality, capital is a social relation whereby an enterprise can, by means of credit expansion, mobilize surplus labor for producing new investment goods. This basically occurs locally, as most studies about the non-internationalized character of capital formation have shown (Feldstein/Horioka 1980: 328; Feldstein 1994: 684).

This contribution demonstrates that a pattern of globalization made socially acceptable by the inclusion of economic development in the marginality-ridden world is possible if internal mass markets expand. With expanding internal mass markets, the possibilities as well as the necessity of employment creation on the basis of devaluation become more limited. Moreover, the dangers of devaluation are reduced as the "elasticity" of the productive apparatus increases. Thus, the perspectives of international speculators also change, as devaluation is limited and leads to rapid growth.

Launching the marginality-ridden economies on the transition path to capitalism is certainly not a panacea. There are many other measures which deserve discussion. I would, however, claim that a strategy of overcoming underdevelopment that does not entail the transition of the marginality-ridden world to capitalism is neither possible nor desirable. It is not possible because the alternative is a deep and generalized underconsumptionist crisis in which the tendencies to rent appropriation are strengthened worldwide. It is not a question of more or less globalization but of the alternative between the globalization of rent and the globalization of profit. The embeddedness of globalization in the transition to capitalism is desirable because, in contrast to the opinions of orthodox Marxists and bankers, capitalism does not result in the deterioration of mass incomes, but is in fact dependent upon rising mass incomes (Elsenhans 1983a; 1983c). The Marxist ideal of a society "appropriating itself," i.e., of consciously and democratically controlling its own destiny, is at the basis of this transition to capitalism. It does not lie somewhere in the distant future, attainable only after a revolutionary big bang.

The generation of 1968 lost politically because it was unable to transform its utopian project into a relevant strategy of practical reform. My greatest fear is that the same will occur in the struggle over globalization.

# References

Abramovitz, Moses: Thinking About Growth and Other Essays on Economic Growth and Welfare (Cambridge: Cambridge University Press, 1989).

Abuaf, Niso; Jorion, Philippe: Purchasing Power Parity in the Long Run, in: Journal of Finance, 45, 1 (March 1990); pp. 157–175.

Acharya, Rohini: The Emergence and Growth of Biotechnology. Experiences in Industrialised and Developing Countries (Cheltenham: Elgar, 1999).

Adam, Markus: Die Entstehung des Governance-Konzepts bei Weltbank und UN: Die EZ wird politischer, in: Entwicklung und Zusammenarbeit, 41, 10 (October 2000); pp. 272–274.

Adelman, Irma: Beyond Export-led Growth, in: World Development, 12, 9 (September 1984); pp. 937–949.

Agarwal, Jamuna P.: Zur Struktur der westdeutschen Direktinvestitionen in Entwicklungsländern – Einfluß von Außenhandelsverflechtung und relativen Lohnkosten, in: Weltwirtschaft, 2 (1978); pp. 114–132.

Akamatsu, Kaname: A Theory of Unbalanced Growth in the World Economy, in: Weltwirtschaftliches Archiv, 86, 2 (1961); pp. 196–217.

Akamatsu, Kaname: A Historical Pattern of Economic Growth in Developing Countries, in: Developing Economies, 1, 1 (March-August 1962); pp. 3–25.

Akyüz, Yilmaz; Gore Charles: The Investment-Profits Nexus in East Asian Industrialization. Discussion Paper 91 (Geneva: UNCTAD, 1994).

Alam, M.Shahid: Convergence in Developed Countries: An Empirical Investigation, in: Weltwirtschaftliches Archiv, 128, 2 (1992); pp. 189–201.

Albert, Matthias; Brock, Lothar: Debordering the World of States. New Spaces in International Relations. Working Paper 2 (Darmstadt, Frankfurt am Main: World Society Research Group, 1995).

Albert, Michel: Capitalisme contre capitalisme (Paris: Editions du Seuil, 1991).

Albo, Gregory: Competitive Austerity and the Impasse of Capitalist Employment Policy, in: Socialist Register, 31 (1994); pp. 144–170.

Aldcroft, Derek H.: The Entrepreneur and the British Economy, 1870–1914, in: Economic History Review, 17, 1 (1964); pp. 113–134.

Alderson, Arthur S.: Globalization and Deindustrialization: Direct Investment and the Decline of Manufacturing Employment in 17 OECD Nations, in: Journal of World-Systems Research, 3, 1 (1997); pp. 1–34.

Alila, Patrick O.: Informal Credit and Rural Small Enterprises Growth. A Local Level Perspective on Sustainable Development in Vinija, Western Kenya, in: Journal of Asian and African Studies (Leiden), 33, 2 (May 1998); pp. 158–182.

Allais, Maurice: Fondements théoriques, perspectives et conditions d'un marché commun effectif. Vol. 68: Le Marché Commmun et ses problèmes, in: Revue d'économie politique (1958); pp. 56–99.

Allen, Robert C.: The Peculiar Productivity of American Blast Furnaces 1840–1913, in: Journal of Economic History, 37, 3 (September 1977); pp. 605–633.

Allen, Robert C.: Collective Invention, in: Journal of Economic Behaviour and Organization, 4, 1 (1983); pp. 1–24.

Allub, Leopoldo: Heterogeneidad estructural, disigualdad social y privación relativa en regiones petroleras, in: Revista Mexicana de Sociología, 45, 1 (January-March 1983); pp. 169–190.

# References

Altmann, Franz Lothar: Wirtschaftsentwicklung und Strukturpolitik in der Tschechoslowakei nach 1968 (Munich: Olzog, 1987).

Amacher, Ryan C.; Conger, Darius J.: Structural Disequilibrium and Growth Retardation in the Soviet Union, in: Weltwirtschaftliches Archiv, 113, 2 (1977); pp. 308–321.

Amendola, Giovanni; Dosi, Giovanni; Papagni, Erasmo: The Dynamics of International Competitiveness, in: Weltwirtschaftliches Archiv, 129, 3 (1993); pp. 452–471.

Amsden, Alice H.: Asia's Next Giant (New York; Oxford: Oxford University Press, 1989).

Anderson, Robert T.: Rotating Credit Associations in India, in: Economic Development and Cultural Change, 15, 3 (1966); pp. 334–339.

Ansari, Mohammed: The Dutch Disease: The Canadian Evidence, in: Weltwirtschaftliches Archiv, 125, 4 (1989); pp. 804–813.

Anthony, Vivian Stanley: Britain's Overseas Trade: The Recent History of British Trade, 1868 – 1968 (London: Heinemann, 1969).

Aoki, Masahiko; Murdock, Kevin; Okuno-Fujiwara, Masahiro: Beyond the East Asian Miracle. Introducing the Market Enhancing View. CEPR Publication 442 (Stanford, Calif.: CEPR, 1995).

Aoudia, Jacques Ould: Les enjeux économiques de la nouvelle politique méditérranéenne de l'Europe, in: Maghreb-Machrek/Monde Arabe, 153 (July-September 1996); pp. 24–60.

Ark, Bart van: International Comparisons of Output and Productivity. Manufacturing Productivity Performance of Ten Countries from 1950 – 1990 (Groningen: Groningen Growth and Development Centre, 1993).

Ark, Bart van: The Manufacturing Sector in East Germany. A Reassessment of Comparative Productivity Performance 1950–1988, in: Jahrbuch für Wirtschaftsgeschichte, 36, 2 (1995); pp. 75–89.

Armstrong, Philip; Glyn, Andrew: The Law of the Falling Rate of Profit and Oligopoly: A Comment on Shaikh, in: Cambridge Journal of Economics, 4, 1 (March 1980); pp. 67–70.

Arrow, Kenneth J.: The Economic Implications of Learning by Doing, in: Review of Economic Studies, 29, 80 (June 1962); pp. 155–173.

Assunçào, Pedro: Portugal und Afrika: Die neokolonialistische Unmöglichkeit, in: Verfassung und Recht in Übersee, 20, 3 (July-September 1987); pp. 343–356.

Audretsch, David B.; Yamawaki, Hideki: Research and Development Rivalry, Industrial Policy and U.S.-Japanese Trade, in: Review of Economics and Statistics, 70, 3 (August 1988); pp. 438–447.

Aukrust, Odd: Factors of Economic Development: A Review of Recent Research, in: Weltwirtschaftliches Archiv, 93, 1 (1964); pp. 23–43.

Auty, Richard M.: Industrial Policy Reform in Six Large Newly Industrializing Countries: The Resource Curse Thesis, in: World Development, 22, 1 (January 1994); pp. 11–26.

Avina, Jeffrey: The Evolutionary Life Cycles of Non-governmental Development Organisations, in: Public Administration and Development, 13, 5 (December 1993); pp. 453–474.

Baar, Lothar; Müller, Uwe; Zschaler, Frank: Strukturveränderungen und Wachstumsschwankungen. Investitionen und Budget in der DDR 1949 bis 1989, in: Jahrbuch für Wirtschaftsgeschichte, 36, 2 (1995); pp. 47–74.

Baer, Werner; Figueroa, Adolfo: State Enterprise and the Distribution of Income: Brazil and Peru, in: Bruneau, Thomas C.; Faucher, Philippe (eds.): Authoritarian Capitalism: Brazil's

Contemporary Economic and Political Development (Boulder, Colo.: Westview Press, 1982); pp. 59–84.
Baer, Werner; Miles, William R.; Moran, Alan B.: The End of the Asian Myth: Why Were the Experts Fooled, in: World Development, 27, 10 (October 1999); pp. 1735–1747.
Bagchi, Amiya Kumar: Private Investment in India 1900–1938 (Cambridge: Cambridge University Press, 1972).
Bai, Moo-Ki: The Turning Point in the Korean Economy, in: Developing Economies, 20, 1 (March 1982); pp. 117–140.
Bairoch, Paul: Globalization, Myths and Realities: One Century of External Trade and Foreign Investment, in: Boyer, Robert; Drache, Daniel (eds.): States Against Markets. The Limits of Globalization (London: Routledge, 1996); pp. 173–192.
Bajt, Alexander: Investment Cycles in European Socialist Economies: A Review Article, in: Journal of Economic Literature, 9, 1 (1971); pp. 53–63.
Balassa, Bela: Tariffs and Trade Policy in the Andean Common Market, in: Journal of Common Market Studies, 12, 1 (January 1974); pp. 176–195.
Balassa, Bela: The Economic Consequences of Social Policies in the Industrial Countries, in: Weltwirtschaftliches Archiv, 120, 2 (1984); pp. 213–227.
Balliano, Piera; Bartone, Giovanni; Mosini, Filippo: Studio sull'evoluzione della concentrazione nell'industria cotoniera italiana (Brussels: Soris, s.p.a. Commissione delle comunità Europee, 1975).
Bandopadhyay, Manohar: Story of Public Steel (New Delhi: Publications Division, Ministry of Information and Broadcasting, Government of I, 1987).
Baran, Paul A.; Sweezy, Paul M.: Monopoly Capital. An Essay on the American Economic and Social Order (New York: Monthly Review Press, 1967).
Barchiesi, Franco: The Social Construction of Labour in the Struggle for Democracy: The Case of Post-Independence Nigeria, in: Review of African Political Economy, 24, 69 (1996); pp. 349–369.
Bardhan, Pranab Kumar: The Political Economy of Development in India (Oxford et al.: Basil Blackwell, 1984).
Barro, Robert J.: Human Capital and Economic Growth, in: Auerbach, Alan J. (ed.): Policies for Long-Run Economic Growth. Symposium Sponsored by The Federal Reserve Bank of Kansas City, 27.–29.8.1992 (Kansas City, Mo.: Federal Reserve Bank, 1992); pp. 199–216.
Barro, Robert J.; Sala-i-Martin, Xavier: Convergence across States and Regions, in: Brookings Papers on Economic Activity, 1 (1991); pp. 107–158.
Barro, Robert J.; Sala-i-Martin, Xavier: Convergence, in: Journal of Political Economy, 100, 2 (1992); pp. 223–251.
Barry, Françoise: La prise de décisions en URSS, in: Economies et Sociétés, 10, 2 (February 1976); pp. 365–387.
Barth, Ernst: Entwicklungslinien der deutschen Maschinenbauindustrie von 1870–1914 (Berlin: Akademie-Verlag, 1973).
Barthel, Wilfried; Karbstein, Werner: Zur Diskussion über einige neue Aspekte in der Beurteilung der Wachstumsrelationen zwischen gesellschaftlichem Gesamtprodukt und Nationaleinkommen sowie zwischen Abteilungen I und II, in: Wirtschaftswissenschaft, 15, 2 (February 1967); pp. 198–222.

Bartl, Wilhelm; Luck, Herbert: Zu den Beziehungen zwischen den Investitionen und dem Wachstum des gesellschaftlichen Gesamtprodukts sowie des Nationaleinkommens, in: Wirtschaftswissenschaft, 9, 6 (June 1961); pp. 1477–1501.

Basant, Rakesh: Corporate Response to Economic Reforms, in: Economic and Political Weekly, 35, 10 (March 2000); pp. 813–822.

Bastian, Dietmar: Institutional Change in Rent-Seeking Environments: The Efforts of Eastern European and Central Asian Governments to Coordinate Transnational Networks of Economic Assistance. Analysed on the Basis of a Comparison of Six Eastern European Countries and an In-depth study into the Case of Ukraine (Leipzig: Dissertation, 2001).

Bauer, Peter Tamás: The Vicious Circle of Poverty, in: Weltwirtschaftliches Archiv, 95, 1 (1965); pp. 4–19.

Becker, Gary S.: Human Capital. A Theoretical and Empirical Analysis with Special References to Education (New York; London: Columbia University Press, 1964).

Bell, Spurgeon: Productivity, Wages and National Income (Washington: Brookings Institution, 1940).

Bello, Walden; Rosenfeld, Stephanie: Dragons in Distress: Asia's Miracle Economies in Crisis (San Francisco: Institute for Food and Development Policy, 1990).

Benissad, Mohamed El-Hocine: Economie du développement en Algérie. Sous-développement et socialisme (Algiers: OPU, 1979).

Berend, Ivan T.: The Historical Background of the Recent Economic Reforms in East Europe. The Hungarian Experiences, in: East European Quarterly, 2, 1 (March 1968); pp. 75–90.

Bergeijk, Peter A. G. van; Mensink, Nico W.: Measuring Globalization, in: Journal of World Trade, 31, 3 (June 1997); pp. 159–168.

Bergson, Abram: Development under Two Systems: Comparative Productivity Growth Since 1950, in: World Politics, 23, 4 (July 1971); pp. 579–617.

Bergson, Abram: Toward New Growth Problems, in: Problems of Communism, 22, 2 (March–April 1973); pp. 1–10.

Bergson, Abram: Communist Efficiency Revisited, in: American Economic Review, 82, 2 (May 1992); pp. 26–30.

Bernanke, Ben S.; Carey, Kevin: Nominal Wage Stickiness and Aggregate Supply in the Great Depression, in: Quarterly Journal of Economics, 111, 3 (August 1996); pp. 853–883.

Bernard, Mitchell; Ravenhill, John: Beyond Product Cycles and Flying Geese: Regionalization, Hierarchy and the Industrialization of East Asia, in: World Politics, 47, 2 (January 1995); pp. 171–209.

Berry, Sara S.: Economic Development with Surplus Labour: Further Complications Suggested by Contemporary African Experience, in: Oxford Economic Papers, 22, 2 (July 1970); pp. 275–287.

Bettelheim, Charles: The Specifity of Soviet Capitalism, in: Monthly Review, 37, 4 (September 1985); pp. 43–61.

Bhagwati, Jagdish N.: Immizering Growth: A Geometrical Note, in: Review of Economic Studies, 25, 68 (1958); pp. 201–204.

Bhagwati, Jagdish N.: Why Are Services Cheaper in Poor Countries, in: Economic Journal, 94, 374 (June 1984); pp. 279–286.

Bhagwati, Jagdish N.: Poverty and Public Policy, in: World Development, 16, 5 (May 1988); pp. 539–555.
Bhagwati, Jagdish: Is Free Trade Passé After All?, in: Weltwirtschaftliches Archiv, 125, 1 (1989); pp. 17–44.
Bicanic, Rudolf: The Threshold of Economic Growth, in: Kyklos, 15, 1 (1962); pp. 7–28.
Bidard, Christian: The Falling Rate of Profit and Joint Production, in: Cambridge Journal of Economics, 12, 3 (September 1988); pp. 355–360.
Binswanger, Hans P.; Deininger, Klaus; Feder, Gershon: Agricultural Land Relations in the Developing World, in: American Journal of Agricultural Economics, 75, 5 (December 1993); pp. 1242–1248.
Bitar, Sergio; Moyano, Eduardo: Redistribución del consumo y transición al socialismo, in: Garretón, Manuel Antonio (ed.): Economia politica en la Unidad Popular. Materiales de los Cuadernos de la Realidad Nacional (1970–1973) (Barcelona: Editorial Fontanella, 1975); pp. 223–252.
Blainey, Geoffrey: A Theory of Mineral Discovery. Australia in the Nineteenth- Century, in: Economic History Review, 23, 2 (1970); pp. 298–319.
Boatler, Robert W.: Trade Theory Predictions and the Growth of Mexico's Manufactured Exports, in: Economic Development and Cultural Change, 23, 4 (July 1975); pp. 491–506.
Boatler, Robert W.: Comparative Advantage; A Division among Developing Countries, in: Interamerican Economic Affairs, 32, 2 (Autumn 1978); pp. 59–66.
Boeck, Klaus: Integrationspolitische Konsequenzen für die regionale Entwicklung in der Europäischen Gemeinschaft, in: Köhler, Klaus; Scharrer, Hans-Eckart (eds.): Die Europäische Gemeinschaft in der Krise (Hamburg: Weltarchiv, 1974); pp. 101–114.
Boltho, Andrea: The Assessment: International Competitiveness, in: Oxford Review of Economic Policy, 12, 3 (Autumn 1996); pp. 1–16.
Bomsel, Olivier: The Future of the Mining Countries in the Third World (Budapest: UNDP, 1987).
Borjas, George J.; Ramey, Valerie A.: Rising Wage Inequality in the United States: Causes and Consequences, in: American Economic Review, 84, 2 (May 1994); pp. 10–16.
Borsay, Peter: The English Urban Renaissance. Culture and Society in the Provincial Town 1660–1770 (Oxford: Clarendon, 1989).
Bortkiewicz, Ladislaus von: Wertrechnung und Preisrechnung im Marxschen System, 3. Teil, in: Archiv für Sozialwissenschaft und Sozialpolitik, 25, 2 (1907); pp. 445–489.
Börzel, Tanja A.: Europäisches Regieren, in: Zeitschrift für Internationale Beziehungen, 11, 2 (2004); pp. 347–355.
Boss, Alfred; Döpke, Klaus et al.: Zögerliche Erholung der Konjunktur, in: Die Weltwirtschaft, 1 (1994); pp. 28–53.
Bouman, F.J.A.: Rotating and Accumulating Savings and Credit Associations: A Development Perspectives, in: World Development, 23, 3 (March 1995); pp. 371–384.
Bourdieu, Pierre: Etude sociologique, in: Darbel, Alain; Rivet, Jean-Paul; Seibel, Claude (eds.): Travail et Travailleurs en Algérie (Paris/Den Haag: Mouton, 1963); pp. 253–566.
Bovenberg, A. Lans; Gordon, Roger H.: Why Is Capital so Immobile Internationally? Possible Explanations and Implications for Capital Income Taxation, in: American Economic Review, 86, 5 (December 1996); pp. 1057–1076.

Bowles, Samuel: Technical Change and the Profit Rate: A Simple Proof of the Okishio Theorem, in: Cambridge Journal of Economics, 5, 2 (1981); pp. 183–186.
Brady, Dorothy: Relative Prices in the Nineteenth Century, in: Journal of Economic History, 24, 2 (June 1964); pp. 145–203.
Brady, Robert A.: Rationalization Movement in German Industry: A Study in the Evolution of Economic Planning (Cambridge: Cambridge University Press; California University Press, 1933).
Brasch, Hans: Der heutige Stand des amerikanischen Werkzeugmaschinenbaus für Massen- und Sonderleistungen, in: Maschinenbau, 3, 25 (October 1924); pp. 931–947.
Braun, Dietmar: Grenzen politischer Regulierung. Der Weg in die Massenarbeitslosigkeit am Beispiel der Niederlande (Wiesbaden: Deutscher Universitäts Verlag, 1989).
Braun, Hans-Gert: Die Industrialisierung der Entwicklungsländer – Konkurrenz für die Industrieländer – und die deutsche Wirtschaft, in: IFO-Schnelldienst, 32, 17/18 (June 1979); pp. 59–63.
Brenner, Robert: The Civil War Politics of London's Merchant Community, in: Past and Present, 58 (February 1973); pp. 53–107.
Brink, Rogier van den/Chavas, Jean-Paul: The Microeconomics of an Indigenous African Institution: The Rotating Savings and Credit Association, in: Economic Development and Cultural Change, 45, 4 (July 1997); pp. 745–773.
Broad, Dave: Global Economic Restructuring and the (Re)Casualization of Work in the Center, in: Review, 14, 4 (Autumn 1991); pp. 555–592.
Broad, Dave: Globalization versus Labour, in: Monthly Review, 47, 7 (December 1995); pp. 20–31.
Broadberry, Stephen N.: Comparative Productivity in British and American Manufacturing During the Nineteenth Century, in: Explorations in Economic History, 31, 4 (October 1994a); pp. 521–548.
Broadberry, Stephen N.: Technological Leadership and Productivity Leadership in Manufacturing Since the Industrial Revolution: Implications for the Convergence Debate, in: Economic Journal, 104, 423 (May 1994b); pp. 291–302.
Broadberry, Stephen N.: The Productivity Race: British Manufacturing in International Perspective, 1850–1990 (Cambridge et al.: Cambridge University Press, 1997).
Broadberry, Stephen N.: How Did the United States and Germany Overtake Britain? A Sectoral Analysis of Comparative Productivity Levels, 1870–1990, in: Journal of Economic History, 58, 2 (June 1998); pp. 375–407.
Brown, John Christopher: The Condition of England and the Standard of Living: Cotton Textiles in the Northwest, 1806–1850, in: Journal of Economic History, 50, 3 (September 1990); pp. 591–614.
Brown, John Christopher: Imperfect Competition and Anglo-German Trade Rivalry: Markets for Cotton Textiles before 1914, in: Journal of Economic History, 55, 3 (September 1995); pp. 494–528.
Brown, Nathan J.: Who Abolished Corvee Labour in Egypt and Why?, in: Past and Present, 144 (August 1994); pp. 116–137.
Brubaker, Earl R.: Embodied Technology, the Asymptotic Behavior of Capital's Age and Soviet Growth, in: Review of Economics and Statistics, 50, 3 (August 1968); pp. 304–311.

Bruton, Henry J.: Import Substitution and Productivity Growth, in: Journal of Development Studies, 4, 3 (April 1968); pp. 306–326.
Buffie, Edward F.: Devaluation, Investment and Growth in LDCs, in: Journal of Development Economics, 20, 2 (March 1986); pp. 361–379.
Burckhardt, Helmuth: Der Energiemarkt in Europa. Energiewirtschaftliche und energiepolitische Beiträge zur Diskussion der Gegenwart (Basle; Tübingen: Kyklos J.C.B. Mohr, 1963).
Burden, Tom: The British Welfare State: Development and Challenges, in: Vivekanandan, Bhagavathi Panicker; Kurian, Nimmi (eds.): Welfare States and the Future (Basingstoke: Palgrave Macmillan, 2005); pp. 78–96.
Burns, Arthur Frank: Production Trends in the United States Since 1870 (New York: National Bureau for Economic Research, 1934).
Busch, Klaus: Die Krise der Europäischen Gemeinschaft (Cologne: Europäische Verlagsanstalt, 1978).
Buxbaum, Bertold: Der englische Werkzeugmaschinen- und Werkzeugbau im 18. und 19. Jahrhundert, in: Beiträge zur Geschichte der Technik und der Industrie, 11 (1921); pp. 117–142.
Caballé, Jordi; Santos, Manuel S.: On Endogenous Growth with Physical and Human Capital, in: Journal of Political Economy, 101, 6 (December 1993); pp. 1042–1067.
Caesar, Rolf: Demonstrationseffekte in der Lohnpolitik. Der direkte internationale Lohnzusammenhang, in: Hamburger Jahrbücher für Wirtschafts- und Gesellschaftspolitik, 20 (1975); pp. 196–218.
Cairncross, Alec Kirkland: Home and Foreign Investment 1870–1913. Studies in Capital Accumulation (Cambridge: Cambridge University Press, 1953).
Cameron, Rondo: Geschichte der Weltwirtschaft (1): Vom Paläothikum bis zur Industrialisierung (Stuttgart: Klett-Cotta, 1991).
Cantwell, John: The Globalisation of Technology: What Remains of the Product Cycle Model, in: Cambridge Journal of Economics, 19, 1 (February 1995); pp. 155–179.
Carlier, Omar: Von der islamischen Reform zur islamischen Militanz: Die politisch-religiöse Therapie der Islamischen Heilsfront, in: Comparativ. Leipziger Beiträge zur Universalgeschichte und vergleichenden Gesellschaftsforschung, 4, 6 (1994); pp. 21–57.
Cecchini, Paolo et al.: The European Challenge, 1992. The Benefit of a Single Market (Aldershot: Wildwood House, 1988).
Cerny, Philip G.: Paradoxes of the Competition State. The Dynamics of Political Globalization, in: Government and Opposition, 32, 2 (1997); pp. 251–274.
Cerny, Philip G.: Globalization and the Erosion of Democracy, in: European Journal of Political Research, 36, 1 (August 1999); pp. 1–26.
Chakravarty, Sukhamoy: Aspects of India's Development Strategy for 1980s, in: Economic and Political Weekly, 19, 20/21 (May 1984); pp. 845–852.
Chambre, Henri: Les freinages de la croissance en URSS, in: Tiers Monde, 8, 30 (April-June 1967); pp. 265–302.
Chandra, N. K.: The Law of Priority Development of Producers Goods, in: Artha Vijnana, 10, 3/4 (September-December 1968); pp. 522–538.
Chao, Kang: Man and Land in Chinese History (Stanford, Cal.: Stanford University Press, 1986).

Chaussinand-Nogaret, Guy: Aux origines de la révolution: noblesse et bourgeoisie, in: Annales E.S.C., 30, 2/3 (1975); pp. 265–299.
Chen, Haichun; Gordon, M.J.; Zhiming, Yan: The Real Income and Consumption of an Urban Chinese Family, in: Journal of Development Studies, 31, 1 (October 1994); pp. 201–213.
Cheng, Tu-Jen: Political Regimes and Developmental Strategies: South Korea and Taiwan, in: Gereffi, Gary; Wyman, Donald L. (eds.): Manufacturing Miracles. Paths of Industrialization in Latin America and East Asia (Princeton, NJ: Princeton University Press, 1990); pp. 139–179.
Chiswick, Barry R.: Earnings Inequality and Economic Development, in: Quarterly Journal of Economics, 85, 1 (February 1971); pp. 21–40.
Clague, Christopher K.: An International Comparison of Industrial Efficiency: Peru and the United States, in: Review of Economics and Statistics, 49, 4 (November 1967); pp. 487–493.
Clague, Christopher K.: Capital-Labour Substitution in Manufacturing in Underdeveloped Countries, in: Econometrica, 37, 3 (July 1969); pp. 528–537.
Clague, Christopher K.: Relative Efficiency, Self-Containment and Comparative Costs of Less Developed Countries, in: Economic Development and Cultural Change, 39, 2 (April 1991); pp. 506–530.
Clark, Colin: The Fundamental Problems of Economic Growth, in: Weltwirtschaftliches Archiv, 94, 1 (1965); pp. 1–9.
Clark, Gregory; Huberman, Michael; Lindert, Peter H.: A British Food Puzzle, 1770–1850, in: Economic History Review, 48, 2 (May 1995); pp. 215–237.
Clark, Victor Selden: History of Manufactures in the United States (Washington: Carnegie Institution of Washington, 1929).
Cline, William: Can the East Asian Model of Development Be Generalized?, in: World Development, 10, 2 (February 1982); pp. 81–90.
Clough, Shepard Bancroft; Marburg, Theodore F.: The Economic Basis of American Civilization (New York: Thomas Y. Crowell, 1968).
Cohen, Paul T.: Problems of Tenancy and Landlessness in Northern Thailand, in: Developing Economies, 21, 3 (September 1983); pp. 244–267.
Collins, Susan M.; Bosworth, Barry P.: Economic Growth in East Asia: Accumulation versus Assimilation, in: Brookings Papers on Economic Activity, 2 (Summer 1996); pp. 135–203.
Colm, Gerhard: Deutschland und die Weltkrise, in: Colm, Gerhard (ed.): Deutschland und die Weltkrise (Munich; Leipzig: Duncker und Humblot, 1932); pp. 36–51.
Commandeur, Peter: The Japanese Government's Role in Biotechnology R&D, in: Biotechnology and Development Monitor, 23, 22 (March 1995); pp. 3–4/16.
Connell, Arthur Knatchbull: Indian Railways and Indian Wheat, in: Journal of the Royal Statistical Society, 68, 5 (June 1885); pp. 236–267.
Corden, W. Max; Neary, J. Peter: Booming Sector and De-Industrialisation in a Small Open Economy, in: Economic Journal, 92, 368 (December 1982); pp. 825–848.
Costello, Donna M.: A Cross-Country, Cross-Industry Comparison of Productivity Growth, in: Journal of Political Economy, 101, 2 (February 1993); pp. 207–222.
Cox, Robert W.: Labor and Transnational Relations, in: International Organization, 25, 3 (Summer 1971); pp. 554–584.

Crafts, Nicholas F.R.: National Income Estimates and the British Standard of Living Debate: A Re-appraisal of 1801–1831, in: Explorations in Economic History, 17, 2 (April 1980); pp. 176–188.
Crafts, Nicholas F.R.: English Workers' Real Wages During the Industrial Revolution: Some Remaining Problems, in: Journal of Economic History, 45, 1 (June 1985); pp. 139–144.
Crafts, Nicholas F.R.: British Industrialization in an International Context, in: Journal of Interdisciplinary History, 19, 3 (Winter 1989); pp. 415–428.
Craig, Albert M.; Fairbank, John K.; Reischauer, Edwin O.: East Asia. Tradition and Transformation (Boston, Mass.: Houghton Mifflin, 1973).
Czempiel, Ernst-Otto: Das deutsche Dreyfus-Geheimnis: Eine Studie über den Einfluß des monarchischen Regierungssystems auf die Frankreichpolitik des Wilhelminischen Reiches (Munich; Bern; Vienna: Scherz, 1966).
Dandekar, V.M.: Economic Theory and Agrarian Reform, in: Oxford Economic Papers, 14, 1 (February 1962); pp. 69–80.
Daniel, Jean: La guerre d'Algérie, in: Le Nouvel Observateur, 2060 (April 29, 2004).
Dasgupta, Partha; Ray, Debraj: Inequality as a Determinant of Malnutrition and Unemployment, in: Economic Journal, 97, 385 (March 1987); pp. 176–188.
Davis, Graham A.: Learning to Love Dutch Disease: Evidence from the Mineral Economies, in: World Development, 23, 10 (October 1995); pp. 1765–1779.
Deane, Phyllis; Cole, W.A.: British Economic Growth 1688–1959. Trends and Structures (Cambridge: Cambridge University Press, 1967).
Decressin, Jörg W.: Internal Migration in West Germany and Implications for East-West Salary Convergence, in: Weltwirtschaftliches Archiv, 130, 2 (1994); pp. 231–257.
Delattre, Lucas: La représentation syndicale diminue partout dans le monde, in: Le Monde (le 6 November 1997); p. 3.
Demarco, Domenico; Dhondt, Jan; Fauvel-Rouif, Denise: Étude Comparée: Mouvements Ouvriers et dépression économique de 1929 à 1939, in: Fauvel-Rouif, Denise (ed.): Mouvements ouvriers et dépression économique de 1929 à 1939 (Assen: Van Gorcum, 1966); pp. 3–33.
Denison, Edward F.: Why Growth Rates Differ: Postwar Experience in Nine Western Countries. (Washington D.C.: Brookings Institution, 1967).
Der Stellenmarkt ist leergefegt, in: Handelsblatt (26. August 1998); p. 21.
Deutsche Bundesbank: Entwicklung und Bestimmungsfaktoren des Außenwertes der D-Mark, in: Monatsberichte der Deutschen Bundesbank, 45, 11 (November 1993); pp. 41–60.
Deutsches Institut für Wirtschaftsforschung: Gefährdet die Lohnkostenentwicklung die Wettbewerbsfähigkeit der Bundesrepublik Deutschland, in: DIW-Wochenbericht, 59, 11 (March 1992); pp. 121–125.
Diaz-Alejandro, Carlos F.: Industrialization and Labour Productivity Differentials, in: Review of Economics and Statistics, 47, 2 (May 1965); pp. 207–213.
Dicke, Hugo; Glismann, Hans H.; Horn, Ernst-Jürgen: Beschäftigungswirkungen einer verstärkten Arbeitsteilung zwischen der Bundesrepublik und den Entwicklungsländern (Tübingen: J.C.B. Mohr, 1976).
Diebold Institute: A Growing Role for Business in the Developing Countries, in: Economic Impact, 6 (1973); pp. 13–20.

Dijk, Meine Pieter van: Informal Finance Structures for Small Enterprises (West African and Indian Experiences), in: Molenaar, N.; El-Namaki, M.S.S.; Dijk, Pieter Meine van (eds.): Small-Scale Industry Promotion in Developing Countries (Delft: Research Institute for Management Science, 1983); pp. 151–167.

DN: The End of Catch-Up Industrialization: Notes on South-East and East Asian Crisis, in: Economic and Political Weekly, 33, 20 (May 1998); pp. 1161–1163.

Dobb, Maurice Herbert: Wages (Cambridge: Cambridge University Press, 1960).

Dolata, Ulrich: Innovationsnetzwerke in der Biotechnologie?, in: WSI-Mitteilungen, 52, 2 (1999); pp. 132–141.

Dollar, David; Wolff, Edward N.: Convergence of Industry Labour Productivity among Advanced Economies 1963–1982, in: Review of Economics and Statistics, 70, 4 (November 1988); pp. 549–558.

Domar, Evsey D.: The Capital-Output Ratio in the United States: Its Variation and Stability, in: Lutz, F.A.; Hague, D.C. (eds.): The Theory of Capital. Proceedings of a Conference Held by the International Economic Association (New York; London: Macmillan; St.Martins Press, 1961); pp. 95–117.

Dormois, Jean-Pierre; Bardini, Carlo: La productivité du travail dans l'industrie de divers pays d'Europe avant 1914, in: Economies et Sociétés, 29, 12 (December 1995); pp. 77–103.

Dosi, Giovanni; Pavitt, Keith; Soete, Luc: The Economics of Technical Change and International Trade (New York et al.: Wheatsheaf, 1990).

Dunning, John H.: Studies in International Investment (London: Allen & Unwin, 1970).

Dutt, Amitava Krishna: Stagnation, Income Distribution and the Agrarian Constraint: A Note, in: Cambridge Journal of Economics, 15, 3 (September 1991); pp. 343–351.

Easterly, William; Fischer, Stanley: The Soviet Economic Decline, in: World Bank Economic Review, 9, 3 (September 1995); pp. 341–371.

Edwards, Sebastian: Coffee, Money and Inflation in Colombia, in: World Development, 12, 11–12 (November-December 1984); pp. 1107–1117.

Eliasberg, George: Der Ruhrkrieg von 1920 (Bonn-Bad Godesberg: Neue Gesellschaft, 1974).

Elliott, William: The Political Economy of American Foreign Policy. Its Concepts, Strategy and Limits. Report of a Study Group Sponsored by the Woodrow Wilson Foundation and the National Planning Association (New York: Henry Holt, 1955).

Ellison, Thomas: The Cotton Trade of Great Britain. Including a History of the Liverpool Cotton Market and the Liverpool Cotton Brokers' Association (London: E. Wilson, 1886).

Elsenhans, Hartmut: Die Überwindung von Unterentwicklung, in: DGFK-Informationen, SH 2 (1974a); pp. 18–32.

Elsenhans, Hartmut: Geschichte und Struktur des internationalen Systems, analysiert unter besonderer Berücksichtigung der Entwicklung des Faktors Arbeitskraft und seiner politischen Konfliktmanifestationen. Projektantrag der Sektion Internationale Politik der Deutschen Vereinigung für Politische Wissenschaft (Berlin, 1974b).

Elsenhans, Hartmut: Der algerische Weg der Überwindung von Unterentwicklung, in: Leggewie, Klaus; Nikolinakos, Marios (eds.): Europäische Peripherie. Zur Frage der Abhängigkeit des Mittelmeerraumes von Westeuropa. Tendenzen und Entwicklungsperspektiven (Meisenheim am Glan: Anton Hain, 1975a); pp. 169–232.

Elsenhans, Hartmut: Overcoming Underdevelopment. A Research Paradigm, in: Journal of Peace Research, 12, 4 (December 1975b); pp. 293–313.

Elsenhans, Hartmut: Die Neue Internationale Wirtschaftsordnung – Chancen für die Überwindung von Unterentwicklung oder die letzte Karte im Kampf der Industrieländer um die Aufrechterhaltung der ungleichen Spezialisierung? Das Beispiel des Integrierten Rohstoffprogramms und der exportorientierten Industrialisierung, in: Internationale Entwicklung, 2 (1976a); pp. 13–27.

Elsenhans, Hartmut: Geschichte und Ökonomie der europäischen Welteroberung. Vom Zeitalter der Entdeckungen zum 1. Weltkrieg (Berlin: Habilitationsschrift, 1976b).

Elsenhans, Hartmut: Lohnerhöhungen: Wachstumschance für den Kapitalismus. Eine Kritik am Gesetz vom tendenziellen Fall der Profitrate, in: Forum DS. Zeitschrift für Theorie und Praxis des demokratischen Sozialismus, 1, 2 (1976c); pp. 78–133.

Elsenhans, Hartmut: Ökonomie der Rohstoffproduktion am Beispiel Tee und Kaffee: Welche Preissteigerungen erlaubt ihr Markt in der BRD, in: Leviathan, 4, 1 (1976d); pp. 122–129.

Elsenhans, Hartmut: Zur Rolle der Staatsklasse bei der Überwindung von Unterentwicklung, in: Schmidt, Alfred (ed.): Strategien gegen Unterentwicklung. Zwischen Weltmarkt und Eigenständigkeit (Frankfort on the Main; New York: Campus, 1976); pp. 250–265.

Elsenhans, Hartmut: La République Fédérale d'Allemagne et une nouvelle politique européenne en Méditerranée, in: Revue d'intégration européenne (January 1978); pp. 191–219.

Elsenhans, Hartmut: Agrarverfassung, Akkumulationsprozeß, Demokratisierung, in: Elsenhans, Hartmut (ed.): Agrarreform in der Dritten Welt (Frankfort on the Main; New York: Campus, 1979a); pp. 505–652.

Elsenhans, Hartmut: Entwicklungsstrategien für die Dritte Welt, in: Kiersch, Gerhard; Seidelmann, Raimund (eds.): Eurosozialismus. Die demokratische Alternative (Cologne; Frankfort on the Main: Europäische Verlagsanstalt, 1979b); pp. 112–122.

Elsenhans, Hartmut: Für eine sozialreformerische Ausgestaltung der NIWO, in: Entwicklung und Zusammenarbeit, 19, 5 (May 1979c); pp. 19–23.

Elsenhans, Hartmut: Grundlagen der Entwicklung der kapitalistischen Weltwirtschaft, in: Senghaas, Dieter (ed.): Kapitalistische Weltökonomie. Kontroversen über ihren Ursprung und ihre Entwicklungsdynamik (Frankfort on the Main: Suhrkamp, 1979d); pp. 101–148.

Elsenhans, Hartmut: Englisches Poor Law und egalitäre Agrarreform in der Dritten Welt. Einige Aspekte der Theorie, daß Wachstum historisch die Erweiterung des Massenmarktes erforderte und heute die Erweiterung des Massenmarktes erfordert, in: Verfassung und Recht in Übersee, 13, 4 (1980a); pp. 283–318. English translation: Elsenhans 1992d.

Elsenhans, Hartmut: Gesellschaftliche Reformen in der Dritten Welt gegen Konzessionen in der Weltwirtschaftsordnung, in: Wirtschaftsdienst, 60, 10 (October 1980b); pp. 482–485.

Elsenhans, Hartmut: Abhängiger Kapitalismus oder bürokratische Entwicklungsgesellschaft. Versuch über den Staat in der Dritten Welt (Frankfort on the Main; New York: Campus, 1981a).

Elsenhans, Hartmut: Egalitarisme social et critique des modes de production dans la périphérie au lieu d'antiimpérialisme et critique des rapports économiques entre le Centre et la Périphérie, in: EADI Working Group Multinationales et développement (ed.): Transfert de technologie et développement: Un débat. Symposium de Paris du 10 octobre 1980 (Paris, 1981b); pp. 1–71.

Elsenhans, Hartmut: Social Consequences of the NIEO. No Change for Continued Reformist Strategies in the Centre Without Structural Change in the Periphery, in: Jahn, Egbert; Sakamoto, Yoshikazu (eds.): Elements of World Instability: Armaments, Communication, Food, International Division of Labour. Proceedings of the Eighth International Peace Research Association Conference (Frankfort on the Main; New York: Campus, 1981c); pp. 86–95.

Elsenhans, Hartmut: Égalité et développement. L'expérience européenne et le monde sous-développé d'aujourd'hui, in: Cultures et développement, 15, 2 (1983a); pp. 187–216.

Elsenhans, Hartmut: Handlungsspielräume für reformistische Entwicklungsstrategien, in: Evers, Hans-Dieter; Senghaas, Dieter; Wienholtz, Huberta (eds.): Auf dem Weg zu einer Neuen Weltwirtschaftsordnung (Baden-Baden: Nomos, 1983b); pp. 141–157.

Elsenhans, Hartmut: Rising Mass Incomes as a Condition of Capitalist Growth: Implications for the World Economy, in: International Organization, 37, 1 (Winter 1983c); pp. 1–38.

Elsenhans, Hartmut: Le développement autocentré contradictoire, in: Cahiers du CREAD, 3 (July-September 1984); pp. 4–47.

Elsenhans, Hartmut: Chesamschekae Konguphwaoui Shilpaewa Oetche, in: Jung, Jun Hueng (ed.): Chesa mschekaewa Oetche Wiki (Seoul: Tshangchakwa Bipyungh, 1985a); pp. 131–149.

Elsenhans, Hartmut: Kukka pumun-ui yoek-hal, in: University Sung-Kyun-Kwan, Institute for Social Science (ed.): Che sam segye-ui cheong-chi-wa kyong-che (Seoul: Seong-kyunkuan, 1985b); pp. 207–238.

Elsenhans, Hartmut: Der Mythos der Kapitalintensität und die notwendig falsche Technologiewahl der Entwicklungsländer, in: Kohler-Koch, Beate (ed.): Technik und internationale Politik (Baden-Baden: Nomos, 1986); pp. 267–290.

Elsenhans, Hartmut: Absorbing Global Surplus Labor, in: Annals of the American Academy of Political and Social Science, 492 (July 1987a); pp. 124–135.

Elsenhans, Hartmut: Dependencia, Underdevelopment and the Third World State, in: Law and State, 36 (1987b); pp. 65–94.

Elsenhans, Hartmut: Economie sous-développée et société civile: surcharge du système politique et possibilités de pluralisme politique, in: CERES (ed.): Actes du Colloque: Pluralisme social, pluralisme politique et démocratie. Cahier du CERES, Série Sociologie No. 19 (Tunis, 1991a); pp. 23–52.

Elsenhans, Hartmut: Global Change and Implications for India. A Talk Given on Tuesday, 18th December 1990 at Claridge's Hotel, New Delhi (New Delhi: Radiant, 1991b).

Elsenhans, Hartmut: Problems Central to Economic Policy Deregulation in Bangladesh, in: Internationales Asienforum, 22, 3/4 (November 1991c); pp. 259–286.

Elsenhans, Hartmut: Reforming the Economic System of Bangladesh: Main Fields of Action, in: Sautter, Hermann (ed.): Wirtschaftspolitische Reformen in Entwicklungsländern. Schriften des Vereins für Socialpolitik 209 (Berlin: Duncker und Humblot, 1991d); pp. 109–133.

Elsenhans, Hartmut: The Great Depression of the 1930s and the Third World, in: International Studies, 28, 3 (1991e); pp. 273–290.

Elsenhans, Hartmut: Die Logik des Profits und die Logik der Rente – Gefährdungen beim Übergang zu einem neuen internationalen System, in: Forndran, Erhard (ed.): Politik nach dem Ost-West-Konflikt (Baden-Baden: Nomos, 1992a); pp. 41–78.

Elsenhans, Hartmut: Die Rente und der Übergang zum Kapitalismus. Grundfragen der politischen Ökonomie von Unterentwicklung, in: Journal für Entwicklungspolitik, 8, 2 (1992b); pp. 111–134.

Elsenhans, Hartmut: Ein neues internationales System, in: Kohler-Koch, Beate (ed.): Staat und Demokratie in Europa. 18. Wissenschaftlicher Kongreß der Deutschen Vereinigung für Politische Wissenschaft (Opladen: Leske und Budrich, 1992c); pp. 244–268.

Elsenhans, Hartmut: English Poor Law and Egalitarian Agrarian Reform in the Third World, in: Elsenhans, Hartmut: Equality and Development (Dhaka: Center for Social Studies, 1992d); pp. 130–162.

Elsenhans, Hartmut: Equality and Development (Dhaka: Center for Social Studies, 1992e).

Elsenhans, Hartmut: Foundation of Development of the Capitalist World Economy, in: Elsenhans, Hartmut: Equality and Development (Dhaka: Center for Social Studies, 1992f); pp. 21–79.

Elsenhans, Hartmut: Global Change and Implications for India (New Delhi: Lancer Books, 1992g).

Elsenhans, Hartmut: La transition à l'économie de marché à partir d'économies sous-développées, in: Naqd – Revue d'études et de critique sociale (June-November 1992h); pp. 23–34.

Elsenhans, Hartmut: State and the Market in Economic Development, in: Weiland, Heribert; Braham, Matthew (eds.): Towards a New South African Economy: Comparative Perspectives. Freiburger Beiträge zu Entwicklung und Politik 10 (Freiburg: Arnold-Bergstraesser-Institut, 1992i); pp. 3–34.

Elsenhans, Hartmut: The Crisis of the Development State and the New International System. Coleção Documentos. Série: assuntos internacionais – 25 (São Paulo: Universidade de São Paulo. Instituto de Estudos Avançados, 1992j).

Elsenhans, Hartmut: The Logic of Profit and the Logic of Rent, in: Voice of Peace and Integration, 1, 1 (October 1992k); pp. 4–48.

Elsenhans, Hartmut: Underdevelopment, Nationalism, and the Free Market Economy, in: Journal of Social Studies, 58 (October 1992m); pp. 113–133.

Elsenhans, Hartmut: European Union, an Expanding Political Process: Defining its Limits, in: Lall, K.B.; Chopra, H.S.; Meyer, Thomas (eds.): EC-92, United Germany, and the Changing World Order (New Delhi: Radiant, 1993a); pp. 16–33.

Elsenhans, Hartmut: State, Economy and Power and the Future of the International System, in: Europe – India: New Perspectives in Changing Power Structures in the International System (New Delhi: Friedrich-Ebert-Stiftung, India Office, 1993b); pp. 15–39.

Elsenhans, Hartmut: Bedingungen für eine freie Weltwirtschaft: Marktsteuerung reicht allein nicht für die Integration Osteuropas und des Südens in die Weltwirtschaft, in: IWVWW Forschungsberichte, 4, 27 (October 1994a); pp. 30–49.

Elsenhans, Hartmut: Crisis of the Development State and the New International System, in: Foreign Trade Review, 29, 1 (April-June 1994b); pp. 50–83.

Elsenhans, Hartmut: Decolonisation: From the Failure of the Colonial Export Economies to the Decline of Westernised State Classes, in: The Maghreb Review, 19, 1/2 (1994c); pp. 95–122.

Elsenhans, Hartmut: Rent, State and the Market: The Political Economy of the Transition to Self-sustained Capitalism, in: Pakistan Development Review, 33, 4 (December 1994d); pp. 393–428.

# References

Elsenhans, Hartmut: State, Economy, Power and the Future of the International System, in: Strategic Digest, 24, 4 (April 1994e); pp. 551–563.

Elsenhans, Hartmut: Die ‚holländische Krankheit' – oder: Warum es nicht immer gesund ist, den Gürtel enger zu schnallen, in: Comparativ. Leipziger Beiträge zur Universalgeschichte und vergleichenden Gesellschaftsforschung, 5, 1 (1995a); pp. 133–146.

Elsenhans, Hartmut: Die Rolle internationaler Entwicklungszusammenarbeit unter veränderten wirtschaftlichen und gesellschaftsstrukturellen Rahmenbedingungen, in: Barsch, Dietrich; Karrasch, Heinz (eds.): Die Dritte Welt im Rahmen weltpolitischer und weltwirtschaftlicher Neuordnung (Stuttgart: Franz Steiner, 1995b); pp. 140–157.

Elsenhans, Hartmut: Durch Standortsicherung zur Weltwirtschaftskrise, in: Zeitschrift für sozialistische Politik und Wirtschaft, 2, 82 (March-April 1995c); pp. 22–27.

Elsenhans, Hartmut: Marginality, Rent and Non-Governmental Organizations, in: Indian Journal of Public Administration, 41, 2 (April-June 1995d); pp. 139–159.

Elsenhans, Hartmut: The Internal Structure of the European Unification Process and its Projection to the Outer World with Special Reference to the Third World, in: Shen, Cen-chu; Song, Yann-huei (eds.): EC Integration and EC-ROC Relation (Taipei, Taiwan: Academia Sinica, 1995e); pp. 135–160.

Elsenhans, Hartmut: Third World Development State in Crisis and the Crisis of Mainstream Development Theory, in: Journal of Social Studies, 70 (October 1995f); pp. 1–41.

Elsenhans, Hartmut: Überwindung von Marginalität als Gegenstand der Armutsbekämpfung, in: Schäfer, Hans Bernd (ed.): Bevölkerungsdynamik und Grundbedürfnisse in Entwicklungsländern. Schriften des Vereins für Socialpolitik 246 (Berlin: Duncker und Humblot, 1995g); pp. 193–221.

Elsenhans, Hartmut: A Welfare Capitalist World System or the Feudalisation of the Global System, in: Babu, B. Ramesh (ed.): Changing Global Political/Ideological Context and Afro-Asia Strategies for Development (New Delhi: South Asian Books, 1996a); pp. 57–130.

Elsenhans, Hartmut: Eléments pour une théorie de l'importance de la demanade dans la croissance capitaliste. Texte de recherche 33 (Paris: Institut d'Etude du Développement Economique et Social, 1996b).

Elsenhans, Hartmut: Gegen das Gespenst der Globalisierung, in: Fricke, Werner (ed.): Jahrbuch Arbeit und Technik 1996: Zukunft der Industriegesellschaft (Bonn: Dietz, 1996c); pp. 25–36.

Elsenhans, Hartmut: Kein Ende der großen Theorie, in: Asien-Afrika-Lateinamerika, 24, 2 (1996d); pp. 111–146.

Elsenhans, Hartmut: State, Class and Development (New Delhi; London; Columbia, Mo.: Radiant; Sangam; South Asia Books, 1996e).

Elsenhans, Hartmut: Eklektizismus zur Erreichung von Kohärenz. Die Theorie der Rente und ihre Implikationen für das Zusammenwirken ökonomischen, politischen und sozialen Engineering in der Entwicklungspolitik, in: Kappel, Robert (ed.): Weltwirtschaft und Armut (Hamburg: Deutsches Übersee-Institut, 1997a); pp. 1–46.

Elsenhans, Hartmut: Globalisation: Myths and Real Challenges, in: Journal of the Third World Spectrum, 4, 2 (Autumn 1997b); pp. 1–22.

Elsenhans, Hartmut: Rent and the Transition to Capitalism, in: Asien-Afrika-Lateinamerika, 25, 6 (1997c); pp. 651–686.

Elsenhans, Hartmut: Staatsklassen, in: Schulz, Manfred (ed.): Entwicklung, die Perspektive der Entwicklungssoziologie (Cologne; Opladen: Westdeutscher Verlag, 1997d); pp. 161–185.

Elsenhans, Hartmut: The Relevance of the Principles of Keynesian Economics for the Transition to Capitalism in Today's Underdeveloped World, in: Davidson, Paul; Kregel, Jan A. (eds.): Improving the Global Economy. Keynesianism and the Growth in Output and Employment (Cheltenham: Edward Elgar, 1997e); pp. 283–303.

Elsenhans, Hartmut: Über Bedingungen und Chancen zu einer sozial verträglichen und dann auch vertieften Globalisierung der Weltwirtschaft, in: Fricke, Werner (ed.): Jahrbuch Arbeit und Technik 1997: Globalisierung und institutionelle Reform (Bonn: Dietz, 1997f); pp. 147–158.

Elsenhans, Hartmut: Europäische Einigung unter dem Druck der Globalisierung, in: IWVWW Forschungsberichte, 8, 66 (January 1998); pp. 11–34.

Elsenhans, Hartmut: Autonomy of Civil Society, Empowerment of Labour, and the Transition to Capitalism, in: Jain, Randhir B.; Khator, Renu (eds.): Bureaucracy – Citizen Interface: Conflict and Consensus (New Delhi: B.R., 1999a); pp. 15–60.

Elsenhans, Hartmut: Globalization or Dutch Disease: Its Political and Social Consequences, in: Singer, Hans Wolfgang; Hatti, Neelambar; Tandon, Rameshwar (eds.): Technological Diffusion in Third World. New World Order Series, Volume 16 (Part-I) (New Delhi: B.R. Publishing Corporation, 1999b); pp. 425–469.

Elsenhans, Hartmut: La Mondialisation: Mythes et véritables défis, in: Naqd – Revue d'études et de critique sociale, 12 (Summer-Autumn 1999c); pp. 105–123.

Elsenhans, Hartmut: Rent and Technology Distortion: The Two Cul-de-Sac of State Correction and Market Orientation in IAC and IBC, in: Journal of the Third World Spectrum, 6, 1 (Autumn 1999d); pp. 33–56.

Elsenhans, Hartmut: Wirtschaftswachstum und institutionelle Entwicklung. Korreferat zum Beitrag von Rainer Klump, in: Schubert, Renate (ed.): Neue Wachstums- und Außenhandelstheorie – Implikationen für die Entwicklungstheorie und -politik. Schriften des Vereins für Socialpolitik, Band 269 (Berlin: Duncker und Humblot, 1999e); pp. 115–128.

Elsenhans, Hartmut: Die Globalisierung der Finanzmärkte und die Entstehung einer neuen Rentenklasse, in: Menzel, Ulrich (Hrsg.) (ed.): Vom Ewigen Frieden und vom Wohlstand der Nationen. Dieter Senghaas zum 60. Geburtstag (Frankfort on the Main: Suhrkamp, 2000a); pp. 518–542.

Elsenhans, Hartmut: Globalisation in a Labourist Keynesian Approach, in: Journal of Social Studies, 89 (July-September 2000b); pp. 1–66.

Elsenhans, Hartmut: La guerre d'Algérie 1954–1962. La transition d'une France à une autre. Le passage de la IV à la Ve République (Paris: Publisud, 2000c).

Elsenhans, Hartmut: Political Economy or Economic Politics? The Prospects of Civil Society in an Era of Globalization, in: Indian Journal of Public Administration, 46, 4 (October-December 2000d); pp. 567–600.

Elsenhans, Hartmut: The Rise and Fall of Really Existing Socialism, in: Journal of Social Studies, 87 (January-March 2000e); pp. 1–16.

Elsenhans, Hartmut: Intensifying Globalisation to Make it Socially Acceptable, in: India Quarterly, 57, 1 (January-March 2001a); pp. 51–74.

Elsenhans, Hartmut: The Political Economy of Good Governance, in: Journal of the Developing Societies, 17, 2 (2001b); pp. 33–56.
Elsenhans, Hartmut: Productivity, Wages, Profits, and Exchange Rates in an Era of Globalization, in: Brazilian Journal of Political Economy, 22, 1 (January-March 2002); pp. 53–78.
Elsenhans, Hartmut: Globalization, "New" Trade Theory, and a Keynesian Reformist Project, in: Tétreault, Mary Ann; Denemark, Robert A.; Thomas, Kenneth P.; Burch, Kurt (eds.): Rethinking International Political Economy: Emerging Issues, Unfolding Odysseys (London; New York: Routledge, 2003); pp. 165–194.
Elsenhans, Hartmut: A Convoy Model vs. an Underconsumptionist Model of Globalisation, in: Convergence Asia, 2, 2 (April-June 2004a); pp. 15–33.
Elsenhans, Hartmut: On the Development of World-System Studies, in: Review (Fernand Braudel Center), 27, 1 (2004b); pp. 1–35.
Elsenhans, Hartmut: A Benign Globalization vs. a Doomsday Scenario: How to Make Globalization in a Capital and Welfare Perspective, in: Review of Global Politics, 10 (April 2005a); pp. 1–66.
Elsenhans, Hartmut: Globalisierung von Profit oder Globalisierung von Rente, in: Jahrbuch für Wirtschaftswissenschaften, 3 (2005b); pp. 263–289.
Elsenhans, Hartmut; Kleiner, Elmar; Dreves, Reinhart Joachim: Développement, équité et extension du marché des masses. Une autre alternative. Le cas algérien. L'enjeu des PME industrielles (Paris: Publisud, 2000).
Elsenhans, Hartmut; Kleiner, Elmar; Dreves, Reinhart Joachim: Gleichheit, Markt, Profit, Wachstum. Kleinindustrie und Expansion des Massenmarkts mit einer Untersuchung aus Algerien (Hamburg: Deutsches Übersee-Institut, 2001).
Elsenhans, Hartmut; Olschewski, Margit: Der Fall Kaffee. Rohstoffpreissteigerung oder Fortsetzung der Armut durch UNCTAD, in: Dritte-Welt-Magazin, 14, 1 (January-February 1976); pp. 8–17.
Emmanuel, Arghiri: L'échange inégal. Essai sur les antagonismes dans les rapports économiques internationaux (Paris: Maspéro, 1969).
Enders, Klaus; Herberg, Horst: The Dutch Disease: Causes, Consequences, Cures and Calmatives, in: Weltwirtschaftliches Archiv, 119, 3 (1983); pp. 473–495.
Engel, Ernst: Die Lebenskosten belgischer Arbeiter-Familien früher und jetzt (Dresden: Heinrich, 1895).
Epstein, Gerald; Gintis, Herbert: International Capital Markets and National Economic Policy, in: Review of International Political Economy, 2, 4 (Autumn 1995); pp. 693–718.
Epstein, Gerald: International Capital Mobility and the Scope for National Economic Management, in: Boyer, Robert; Drache, Daniel (eds.): States Against Markets. The Limits of Globalization (London: Routledge, 1996); pp. 211–224.
Ezeala-Harrison, Fidel: Structural Re-Adjustment in Nigeria: Diagnosis of a Severe Dutch Disease Syndrome, in: American Journal of Economics and Sociology, 52, 2 (April 1993); pp. 193–208.
Fabricant, Solomon: The Output of Manufacturing Industries 1899–1937 (New York: NBER, 1940).
Fagerberg, Jan: Technological Progress, Structural Change and Productivity Growth: A Comparative Study, in: Structural Change and Economic Dynamics, 11, 4 (December 2000); pp. 393–411.

Fajnzylber, Fernando; Martínez Tarragó, Trinidad: Las empresas transnacionales. Expansión a nivel mundial y proyección en la industria mexicana (Mexico: Fundo de Cultura Económica, 1976).

Faulkner, Harold Underwood: American Economic History (New York: Harper & Brothers, 1949).

Faxen, Karl-Olof: Disembodied Technical Progress: Does Employee Participation in Decision Making Contribute to Change and Growth?, in: American Economic Review, 68, 2 (May 1978); pp. 131–134.

Feddema, Raymond: South Korea Plans its Biotechnology Future, in: Biotechnology and Development Monitor, 31, 50 (March 2003); pp. 8–13.

Feder, Ernest: The Latifundia Puzzle of Professor Schultz; Comment, in: Journal of Farm Economics, 49, 2 (May 1967); pp. 507–511.

Fei, Hsiao-tung: Peasant Life in China. A Field Study of Country Life in the Yangtze Valley (London: Routledge & Kegan Paul, 1939).

Fei, John C.H.; Ranis, Gustav: Development of a Labor Surplus Economy. Theory and Policy (Homewood, Ill.: Irwin, 1964).

Feinstein, Charles Hilliard; Pollard, Sidney: Studies in Capital Formation in the United Kingdom 1750–1920 (Oxford: Clarendon Press, 1988).

Feis, Herbert: Europe: the World's Banker, 1870–1914. An Account of European Foreign Investment and the Connection of World Finance With Diplomacy Before the War (New Haven, Conn.: Yale University Press, 1930).

Feiwel, George R.: Poland's Industrialization Policy: A Current Analysis. Sources of Economic Growth and Retrogression (New York: Praeger, 1971).

Feiwel, George R.: Industrialization in Post-War Bulgaria, in: Osteuropa-Wirtschaft, 23, 1 (March 1978); pp. 1–17.

Feld, Lars P.: Sozialstandards und Welthandelsordnung, in: Außenwirtschaft, 51, 1 (1996); pp. 51–73.

Feldstein, Martin: Tax Policy and International Capital Flows, in: Weltwirtschaftliches Archiv, 130, 4 (1994); pp. 676–697.

Feldstein, Martin; Horioka, Charles: Domestic Saving and International Capital Flows, in: Economic Journal, 90, 358 (June 1980); pp. 314–329.

Felix, David: Industrial Development in East Asia: What are the Lessons for Latin America. Discussion Paper 84 (Geneva: UNCTAD, 1994).

Fellner, William: Appraisal of the Labour-Saving and Capital Saving Character of Innovations, in: Lutz, F.A.; Hague, D.C. (eds.): The Theory of Capital. Proceedings of a Conference Held by the International Economic Association (London; New York: Macmillan; St.Martins Press, 1961); pp. 58–74.

Fels, Gerhard: Zum Konzept der internationalen Wettbewerbsfähigkeit, in: Jahrbuch für Sozialwissenschaft, 39 (1988); pp. 135–144.

Fields, Gary S.: Changing Labor Market Conditions and Economic Development in Hong Kong, the Republic of Korea, Singapore and Taiwan China, in: World Bank Economic Review, 8, 3 (September 1994); pp. 395–414.

Fink, Philipp: Purchased Development: The Irish Republic's Export-oriented Development Strategy. With a Preface by Hartmut Elsenhans (Münster: LIT Verlag, 2004).

Fisher, Douglas: The Industrial Revolution. A Macroeconomic Interpretation (New York: St. Martin's Press, 1992).

Flaherty, Mark; Jengjalern, Anchalu: Differences in Assessments of Forest Adequacy among Women in Northern Thailand, in: Journal of Developing Areas, 29, 1 (January 1995); pp. 237–254.

Flassbeck, Heiner: Die Standortqualität der Bundesrepublik Deutschland, in: Konjunkturpolitik, 34, 5/6 (1988); pp. 255–267.

Flassbeck, Heiner: Theoretische Aspekte der Messung von Wettbewerbsfähigkeit, in: Vierteljahreshefte zur Wirtschaftsforschung, 61, 1/2 (1992); pp. 5–26.

Flassbeck, Heiner: Standort Deutschland in Gefahr, in: Vorwärts, 11 (1995); pp. 18–19.

Flux, A.W.: Industrial Productivity in Great Britain and the United States, in: Quarterly Journal of Economics, 47, 1 (November 1933); pp. 1–38.

Fogarty, Michael P.: The White Collar Pay Structure in Britain, in: Economic Journal, 69, 273 (March 1959); pp. 55–65.

Foreman-Peck, James: A Political Economy of International Migration, 1815–1914, in: Manchester School of Economic and Social Studies, 60, 4 (December 1992); pp. 359–376.

Forschungsgruppe Weltgesellschaft: Weltgesellschaft: Identifizierung eines 'Phantoms', in: Politische Vierteljahresschrift, 37, 1 (March 1996); pp. 5–26.

Fortune, J. Neill: Expected Purchasing Power Parity, in: Weltwirtschaftliches Archiv, 121, 1 (1985); pp. 97–104.

Fralon, J.A.: Le dossier de Lomé II (Brussels: Agence Européenne d'Informations, 1978).

Frank, André Gunder: ReOrient. Global Economy in the Asian Age (Berkeley, Cal. et al.: University of California Press, 1998).

Frankel, Marvin: Anglo-American Productivity Differences: Their Magnitude and Some Causes, in: American Economic Review, 45, 2 (May 1955); pp. 94–111.

Franz, Wolfgang: Strukturelle und friktionelle Arbeitslosigkeit in der Bundesrepublik Deutschland: Eine theoretische und empirische Analyse der Beveridge-Kurve, in: Bombach, Gottfried et al. (ed.): Arbeitsmärkte und Beschäftigung – Fakten, Analysen, Perspektiven (Tübingen: Mohr, 1987); pp. 301–324.

Franzmeyer, Fritz; Seidel, Bernhard: Wirtschaftspolitische Prioritätsunterschiede in der EG als Hindernis für die Errichtung der Wirtschafts- und Währungsunion und Instrumente zur Überwindung. DIW Sonderheft 96 (Berlin: Duncker und Humblot, 1973).

Freeman, Chris: The National System of Innovation in Historical Perspective, in: Cambridge Journal of Economics, 19, 1 (January 1995); pp. 5–24.

Fremdling, Rainer: Productivity Comparisons between Great Britain and Germany, 1855–1913, in: Scandinavian Economic History Review, 39, 1 (1991); pp. 28–42.

Frenkel, Jakob A.: International Interdependence and the Constraints on Macroeconomic Policies, in: Weltwirtschaftliches Archiv, 122, 2 (1986); pp. 615–647.

Freyberg, Thomas von: Industrielle Rationalisierung in der Weimarer Republik (Frankfort on the Main; New York: Campus, 1989).

Fröbel, Volker; Heinrichs, Jürgen; Kreye, Otto: Die Neue Internationale Arbeitsteilung. Strukturelle Arbeitslosigkeit in den Industrieländern und die Industrialisierung der Entwicklungsländer (Reinbeck b. Hamburg: Rowohlt, 1977).

Fry, Maxwell J.: Turkey's First Five-Year Development Plan: An Assessment, in: Economic Journal, 81, 322 (June 1971); pp. 306–326.
Fujita, Natsuki; James, William E.: Export Oriented Growth of Output and Employment in Taiwan and Korea, 1973/74–1983/84, in: Weltwirtschaftliches Archiv, 126, 4 (1990); pp. 737–753.
Funke, Michael: Technikwahl und Profitrate. Ein kritischer Überblick über die augenblickliche Diskussion zum Gesetz des tendenziellen Falls der Profitrate, in: Zeitschrift für Wirtschafts- und Sozialwissenschaften, 104, 3 (1984); pp. 307–325.
Furedi, Frank: Creating a Breathing Space: The Political Management of Colonial Emergencies, in: Journal of Imperial and Commonwealth History, 21, 3 (September 1993); pp. 89–106.
Furness, James Wilson; Leith, Charles Kenneth; Lewis, Cleona: World Minerals and World Peace (Washington: Brookings Institution, 1943).
Furnivall, John S.: Netherlands India. A Study of Plural Economy (Cambridge: Cambridge University Press, 1937).
Furtwängler, Franz Josef: Die weltwirtschaftliche Konkurrenz des indischen Industriearbeiters (Leipzig: Deutsche Wissenschaftliche Buchhandlung, 1929).
Gallissot, René: Libérez l'histoire de la guerre d'indépendance algérienne, des allégeances nationales, in: L'Annuaire de l'Afrique du Nord (2005); forthcoming
Geertz, Clifford: The Rotating Credit Association, in: Economic Development and Cultural Change, 10, 3 (April 1962); pp. 241–263.
Gentil, Dominique: Les avatars du modèle Grameen Bank, in: Tiers Monde, 37, 145 (January-March 1996); pp. 115–133.
Georgescu-Roegen, Nicholas: Economic Theory and Agrarian Economics, in: Oxford Economic Papers, 12, 1 (February 1960); pp. 1–40.
Gerschenkron, Alexander: Economic Backwardness in Historical Perspective (Cambridge, Mass.: The Belknap Press of Harvard University Press, 1962).
Ghosh, Atish R.: International Capital Mobility Amongst the Major Industrialized Countries: Too Little Or Too Much, in: Economic Journal, 105, 428 (January 1995); pp. 107–128.
Gillman, Joseph M.: Das Gesetz des tendenziellen Falls der Profitrate (Frankfort on the Main: Europäische Verlagsanstalt, 1969).
Gilpin, Robert: U.S. Power and the Multinational Corporation: The Political Economy of Foreign Direct Investment (New York; London: Basic Books, 1975).
Goldman, Marshall I.: More Heat in the Soviet Hothouse. It Will Take More Than Massive Transplants of Western Technology to Make Soviet Industry Competitive, in: Harvard Business Review, 49, 4 (July-August 1971); pp. 4–15.
Golub, Stephen S.: Comparative Advantage, Exchange Rates, and Sectoral Trade Balances of Major Industrial Countries, in: IMF Staff Papers, 41, 2 (June 1994); pp. 286–313.
Gonzalez-Vigil, Fernando: New Technologies, Industrial Restructuring and Changing Patterns of Metal Consumption, in: Raw Materials Report, 3, 3 (1985); pp. 10–31.
Gordon R., Sara: La cultura política de las organizaciones no gubernamentales en México, in: Revista Mexicana de Sociología, 59, 1 (January-March 1997); pp. 53–67.
Gordon, Robert J.: $ 45 Billion of US Private Investment Has Been Mislaid, in: American Economic Review, 59, 1 (March 1969); pp. 221–237.

Gordon, Robert J.: Has the "New Economy" Rendered the Productivity Slowdown Obsolete? (Evanston, Ill.: MS, 1999a).
Gordon, Robert J.: US Economic Growth Since 1870: One Big Wave?, in: American Economic Review, 89, 2 (May 1999b); pp. 123–128.
Görzig, Bernd; Schintke, Joachim; Schmidt, Manfred: Produktion und Faktoreinsatz nach Branchen des verarbeitenden Gewerbes Westdeutschlands. Berechnungen für 31 Branchen in europäischer Klassifikation. Statistische Kennziffern 1980 bis 1996 (Berlin: Deutsches Institut für Wirtschaftsforschung, December 1997).
Grabowski, Richard: Peasant Agriculture and the Distribution of Power in Prewar East Asia, in: Canadian Journal of Development Studies, 15, 2 (1994); pp. 171–191.
Grauwe, Peter de; Kennes, Walter; Peeters, Theo: Trade Expansion with the Less Developed Countries and Employment, in: Weltwirtschaftliches Archiv, 115, 1 (1979); pp. 98–113.
Gray, Patricia; Singer, Hans Wolfgang: Trade Policy and Growth of Developing Countries: Some New Data, in: World Development, 16, 3 (March 1988); pp. 395–403.
Griffin, Keith; James, Jeffrey: Problems of Transition to Egalitarian Development, in: Manchester School of Economic and Social Studies, 47, 3 (September 1979); pp. 248–269.
Grigg, David B.: The Agricultural Revolution in Western Europe, in: Bayliss-Smith, Tim P.; Wanmali, Sudhir (eds.): Understanding Green Revolutions. Agrarian Change and Development Planning in South Asia (Cambridge: Cambridge University Press, 1984); pp. 1–17.
Grossman, Gene M.: Strategic Export Promotion: A Critique, in: Krugman, Paul R. (ed.): Strategic Trade Policy and the New International Economics (Cambridge, Mass.: MIT Press, 1992); pp. 47–68.
Grossman, Gene M.; Helpman, Elhanan: Trade, Innovation and Growth, in: American Economic Review, 80, 2 (1990); pp. 86–91.
Grossman, Gene M.; Helpman, Elhanan: Endogenous Innovation in the Theory of Growth, in: Journal of Economic Perspectives, 8, 1 (Winter 1994); pp. 23–44.
Grossman, Gene M.; Richardson, J. David: Strategic Trade Policy: A Survey of Issues and Early Analysis. Special Papers in International Economics 15. International Finance Section, Department of Economics (Princeton, N.J.: Princeton University Press, 1985).
Guérin, Daniel: La lutte de classes sous la Première République: 1793–1797. vol. 1 (Paris: Gallimard, 1968).
Guha, Ashok S.: The Political Economy of Liberalization, in: Guha, Ashok S. (ed.): Economic Liberalization, Industrial Structure and Growth in India (New Delhi et al.: Oxford University Press, 1990); pp. 38–50.
Guillaumont, Patrick; Guillaumont-Jeanneney, Sylviane; Brun, Jean-Francois: How Instability Lowers African Growth, in: Journal of African Economies, 8, 1 (1999); pp. 87–107.
Guillaumont-Jeanneney, Sylviane; Hua, Ping: Politique du change et développement des exportations manufacturées en Chine, in: Revue économique, 47, 3 (May 1996); pp. 851–860.
Gulhati, Ravi et al.: Exchange Rate Policies in Africa. How Valid is the Scepticism?, in: Development and Change, 17, 3 (July 1986); pp. 399–423.
Haas, Peter M.: Conclusion: Epistemic Communities, World Order, and the Creation of a Reflective Research Programme, in: International Organization, 46, 1 (Winter 1992); pp. 367–390.

Habakkuk, Hrothgar John: American and British Technology in the Nineteenth Century. The Search for Labour-Saving Inventions (Cambridge: Cambridge University Press, 1962).
Habakkuk, Hrothgar John: Fluctuations and Growth in the 19th Century, in: Robertson, H. M.; Kooy, M. (eds.): Studies in Economics and Economic History (London: Macmillan, 1972); pp. 259–279.
Haggard, Stephan Mark: Pathways from the Periphery: The Newly Industrializing Countries in the International System (Berkeley, Cal.: Dissertation, 1983).
Hakkio, Craig S.: A Re-examination of Purchasing Power Parity: A Multicountry Multiperiod Study, in: Journal of International Economics, 17, 3 (1984); pp. 265–277.
Halbach, Axel J.: Produktionsverlagerungen in Entwicklungsländer. Zum Ergebnis einer IFO-Umfrage, in: IFO-Schnelldienst, 29, 35 (December 1976); pp. 16–25.
Han, Tai-Sun: The Inefficient Problems of the Korean Bureacracy. A Journey Searching for a Problem and Answer. Kurze Fassung von Han, Tai-Sun (1998) (o. O.: Forschungsplan, 2000).
Hancock, Graham: Lords of Poverty. The Free-Wheeling Lifestyles, Power, Prestige and Corruption of the Multi-Billion Dollar Aid Business (London: Macmillan, 1989).
Hanes, Christopher: The Development of Nominal Wage Rigidity in the Late 19th Century, in: American Economic Review, 83, 4 (September 1993); pp. 732–746.
Hanes, Christopher: Changes in the Cyclical Behaviour Real Wage Rates, in: Journal of Economic History, 56, 4 (December 1996); pp. 837–861.
Hankel, Wilhelm: Capital Markets and Financial Institutions in the Development Process, in: Economics, 44 (1991); pp. 32–65.
Hankel, Willhelm: Die USA und die Schweiz weisen den Weg aus der Rentenmisere, in: Handelsblatt (August 30, 1999); p. 2.
Hanson, James: Inflation and Imported Input Prices in Some Inflationary Latin American Economies, in: Journal of Development Economics, 18, 2/3 (August 1985); pp. 395–410.
Harada, Katsumara: Technological Independence and Progress of Standardization of Japanese Railways, in: Developing Economies, 18, 3 (September 1980); pp. 313–332.
Hardin, Einar; Strassmann, W. Paul: La productividad industrial y la intensidad de capital de México y los Estados Unidos, in: Trimestre Económico, 35, 137 (1968); pp. 51–61.
Harrod, Roy Forbes: Economic Essays (London: Macmillan, 1952).
Harvey, Charles; Press, Jon: Overseas Investment and the Professional Advance of British Mining Engineers, 1851–1914, in: Economic History Review, 42, 1 (1989); pp. 64–89.
Harvey, Charles; Press, Jon: The City and International Mining, 1870–1914, in: Business History, 32, 3 (July 1990); pp. 98–119.
Hashemi, Syed M.: NGOs in Bangladesh: Development Alternative or Alternative Rhetoric (Manchester: University of Manchester, 1990).
Hayek, Friedrich A. von: The Pure Theory of Capital (Chicago, Ill.: University of Chicago Press, 1941).
Hayek, Friedrich A. von: Monetary Theory and the Trade Cycle (New York: Augustus M. Kelley, 1966).
Heckscher, Eli F.: The Aspects of Economic History, in: o\.A\. (ed.): Economic Essays in Honour of Gustav Cassel (London: Allen & Unwin, 1933); pp. 705–719.

Heckscher, Eli F.: The Effect of Foreign Trade on the Income, in: Ellis, Howard S. (ed.): Readings in the Theory of International Trade (Philadelphia, Penn.: Blakiston, 1949); pp. 272–301.
Helleiner, Eric: State and the Reemergence of Global Finance. From Bretton Woods to the 1990s (Ithaca, N.Y. et al.: Cornell University Press, 1994).
Helleiner, Eric: Explaining the Globalization of Financial Markets: Bringing States Back in, in: Review of International Political Economy, 2, 2 (1995); pp. 315–342.
Helmstädter, Ernst: Der Kapitalkoeffizient. Eine kapitaltheoretische Untersuchung (Stuttgart: Gustav Fischer, 1969).
Helpman, E.: International Trade in the Presence of Product Differentiation, Economies of Scale and Monopolistic Competition. A Chamberlain- Heckscher- Ohlin Approach, in: Journal of International Economics, 11 (August 1981); pp. 306–340.
Hemmer, Hans-Rimbert: Die endogene Wachstumstheorie als Reaktion auf die Erklärungsdefizite der traditionellen neoklassischen Wachstumstheorie, in: Schubert, Renate (ed.): Neue Wachstums- und Außenhandelstheorie – Implikationen für die Entwicklungstheorie und -politik. Schriften des Vereins für Socialpolitik, Band 269 (Berlin: Duncker und Humblot, 1999); pp. 11–44.
Hensley, Roy; Schwartz, Eli: The Terms of Trade and Balance of Payment and Development Problems, in: Weltwirtschaftliches Archiv, 100, 1 (1968); pp. 87–112.
Heo, Uk: The Political Economy of Financial Crisis in South Korea: From Economic Miracle to Financial Crisis, in: Journal of East Asian Affairs, 14, 1 (Spring/Summer 2000); pp. 37–59.
Hicks, John: Money, Interest and Wages. Collected Essays on Economic Theory (Oxford: Basil Blackwell, 1982).
Hilferding, Rudolf: Das Finanzkapital. Eine Studie über die jüngste Entwicklung des Kapitalismus (Frankfort on the Main: Europäische Verlagsanstalt, 1968).
Hillman, John: The Emergence of the Tin Industry in Bolivia, in: Journal of Latin American Studies, 16, 2 (November 1984); pp. 403–437.
Hirsch, Joachim: Nation-state, International Regulation and the Question of Democracy, in: Review of International Political Economy, 2, 2 (Summer 1995); pp. 267–284.
Hobsbawm, Eric J.: The British Standard of Living, 1790–1850, in: Economic History Review, 10, 1 (1957); pp. 46–68.
Hofmann, Bert; Koop, Michael J.: Die 'Neue Wachstumstheorie' und ihre Bedeutung für die Wirtschaftspolitik, in: Weltwirtschaft, 2 (1991); pp. 86–94.
Holtgrave, Wilfried: Industrialisierung in Singapur. Chancen und Risiken industrieorientierter Spezialisierung (Frankfort on the Main; New York: Campus, 1987).
Homburg, Stefan: Humankapital und endogenes Wachstum, in: Zeitschrift für Wirtschafts- und Sozialwissenschaften, 115, 3 (1995); pp. 339–366.
Honyden, Yosio: Der Durchbruch des Kapitalismus in Japan, in: Weltwirtschaftliches Archiv, 46, 1 (1937); pp. 28–44.
Horrell, Sara: Home Demand and British Industrialisation, in: Journal of Economic History, 56, 3 (September 1996); pp. 561–597.
Horrel, Sara; Humphries, Jane: Old Questions, New Data, and Alternative Living Standards in the Industrial Revolution, in: Journal of Economic History, 52, 4 (December 1992); pp. 849–880.

Hounshell, David A.: From the American System to Mass Production 1800–1932. The Development of Manufacturing Technology in the United States (Baltimore, Md.; London: Johns Hopkins University Press, 1984).

Howard, Earl Dean: The Cause and Extent of the Recent Industrial Progress of Germany (Cambridge, Mass.: Houghton Mifflin, 1907).

Hsieh, Chang-Tai: Measuring the Effects of Trade Expansion on Employment. A Review of Some Research, in: International Labour Review, 107, 1 (January 1973); pp. 1–29.

Hughes, J.R.T.: Measuring British Economic Growth, in: Journal of Economic History, 24, 1 (March 1964); pp. 60–83.

Hundt, Dieter: Interview, in: Leipziger Volkszeitung (October 9, 1996); p. 17.

Hunt, Ian: An Obituary or a New Life for the Tendency of the Rate of Profit to Fall, in: Review of Radical Political Economics, 15, 1 (Spring 1983); pp. 131–148.

Huntington, Samuel P.: The Clash of Civilizations?, in: Foreign Affairs, 72, 3 (Summer 1993); pp. 22–49.

Hutchison, Michael M.: Manufacturing Sector Resiliency to Energy Booms: Empirical Evidence from Norway, the Netherlands and the United Kingdom, in: Oxford Economic Papers, 46, 2 (April 1994); pp. 311–329.

Hwa, Erh-Cheng: The Contribution of Agriculture to Economic Growth: Some Empirical Evidence, in: World Development, 16, 11 (November 1988); pp. 1329–1339.

Ibn Khaldûn, Abd-al-Rahman: Discours sur l'Histoire universelle. Al-Muqaddima. Traduction nouvelle, préface et notes par Vincent Monteil (Paris: Sindbad, 1967).

Institut für Wirtschaftsforschung (ifo): Umfang und Bestimmungsgründe ein- und ausfließender Direktinvestitionen, in: IFO-Schnelldienst, 49, 22 (August 1996); pp. 3–6.

Ikonicoff, Moïses: Concentration du revenu – Grandes firmes multinationales et modèle de développement en Argentine, in: Tiers Monde, 15, 58 (April-June 1974); pp. 327–340.

Imlah, Albert H.: The Terms of Trade of the United Kingdom 1798–1913, in: Journal of Economic History, 10, 2 (November 1950); pp. 170–194.

Imlah, Albert H.: Economic Elements in the Pax Britannica: Studies in British Foreign Trade in the 19th Century (Cambridge, Mass.: Harvard University Press, 1958).

Irwan, Alexander: Business Patronage, Class Struggle and the Manufacturing Sector in South Korea, Indonesia and Thailand, in: Journal of Contemporary Asia, 19, 4 (1989); pp. 398–434.

Irwin, Douglas A.: The United States in a New Global Economy? A Century's Perspective, in: American Economic Review, 86, 2 (March 1996); pp. 41–46.

Irwin, Douglas A.; Klenow, Peter J.: High Tech R&D Subsidies. Estimating the Effects of SEMATECH, in: Journal of International Economics, 40, 3/4 (May 1996); pp. 323–344.

Iwami, Toru: Japan's Experiences under the Bretton Woods System: Capital Controls and the Fixed Exchange Rate, in: Banca Nazionale del Lavoro Quarterly Review, 183 (December 1992); pp. 431–462.

Jacoby, Henry: Die Bürokratisierung der Welt (Frankfort on the Main; New York: Campus, 1984).

Jaffrelot, Christophe: The Hindu Nationalist Movement and Indian Politics 1925 to the 1990s. Strategies of Identity-Building, Implantation and Mobilisation (with Special Reference to Central India) (London: Hurst, 1996).

Janvry, Alain de: The Role of Land Reform in Economic Development: Policies and Politics, in: American Journal of Agricultural Economics, 63, 2 (May 1981); pp. 384 –392.
Jenks, Leland Hamilton: The Migration of British Capital to 1875 (New York: Alfred A. Knopf, 1927).
Joly, Pierre-Benoît; Looze, Marie-Angèle de: An Analysis of Innovation Strategies and Industrial Differentiation Through Patent Applications: The Case of Plant Biotechnology, in: Research Policy, 25, 7 (1996); pp. 1027–1047.
Jomo, Kwame Sundaram: Lessons from Growth and Structural Change in the Second-tier South East Asian Newly Industrializing Countries. East Asian Development: Lessons for a New Global Environment 4 (Kuala Lumpur: UNCTAD, 1996).
Jung, Woo S.; Lee, Gyn: The Effectiveness of Export Promotion Policies: The Case of Korea, in: Weltwirtschaftliches Archiv, 122, 2 (1986); pp. 340–358.
Junge, Georg: Trends and Random Walks of Real Exchange Rates, in: Weltwirtschaftliches Archiv, 121, 3 (1985); pp. 427–437.
Kaiwar, Vasant: The Colonial State, Capital and the Peasantry in Bombay Presidency, in: Modern Asian Studies, 28, 4 (1994); pp. 793–832.
Kaldor, Nicholas: Dual Exchange Rates and Economic Development, in: Economic Bulletin for Latin America, 9, 2 (November 1964); pp. 215–222.
Kaldor, Nicholas: The Role of Increasing Returns, Technical Progress and Cumulative Causation in the Theory of International Trade and Economic Growth, in: Economie appliquée, 34, 4 (October-December 1981); pp. 593–617.
Kalecki, Michal: Selected Essays on the Dynamics of the Capitalist Economy 1933–1970 (Cambridge: Cambridge University Press, 1971).
Kamas, Linda: Dutch Disease Economics and the Colombian Export Boom, in: World Development, 14, 9 (September 1986); pp. 1177–1198.
Kantzenbach, Erhard: Deutschland im internationalen Wettbewerb. Vortrag auf dem Karl-Schiller-Symposium (Hamburg: HWWA-Institut für Wirtschaftsforschung, 1995).
Kaplan, Norman M.: Retardation in Soviet Growth, in: Review of Economics and Statistics, 50, 3 (August 1968); pp. 293–303.
Kasper, Wolfgang E.; Stahl, Heinz Michael: Integration through Monetary Union. A Sceptical View, in: Giersch, Herbert (ed.): Integration durch Währungsunion (Tübingen: J.C.B. Mohr, 1970); pp. 149–169.
Kato, Yuzuru: Factors Contributing to the Recent Increase of Productivity in Japanese Agriculture, in: Journal of Development Studies, 2, 1 (October 1965); pp. 38–58.
Katseli, Louka T.: Devaluation: A Critical Appraisal of the IMF's Policy Prescriptions, in: American Economic Review, 73, 2 (May 1983); pp. 359–363.
Keesing, Donald B.: Income Distribution from Outward Looking Development Policies. Research Memorandum No. 59 (Williamstown, Mass.: Center for Development Economics. Williams College, 1974).
Kehr, Eckart: Schlachtflottenbau und Parteipolitik 1894–1901. Versuch eines Querschnitts durch die innenpolitischen, sozialen und ideologischen Voraussetzungen des deutschen Imperialismus (Berlin: Dr. Emil Ebering, 1930).

Keller, Dietmar: Should Europe Provide Selective Assistance for Key Industries, in: Intereconomics, 27, 3 (May-June 1992); pp. 110–117.
Keller, Edmond J.: The State in Contemporary Africa: A Critical Assessment of Theory and Practice, in: Rustow, Dankwart A.; Erickson, Kenneth Paul (eds.): Comparative Political Dynamics. Global Research Perspectives (New York: Harper Collins, 1991); pp. 134–160.
Kendrick, John W.: Productivity Trends in the United States: A Study by the National Bureau of Economic Research (Princeton, N.J.: Princeton University Press, 1961).
Kendrick, John W.; Sato, Ryuzo: Factor Prices, Productivity and Growth, in: American Economic Review, 53, 5 (December 1963); pp. 974–1003.
Kenwood, Albert George; Lougheed, Alan L.: The Growth of the International Economy: 1820 – 1960. An Introductory Text (London: Allen & Unwin, 1971).
Kenwood, Albert George; Lougheed, Alan L.: The Growth of the International Economy, 1820–1960. An Introductory Text (London; New York: Routledge, 1972).
Keynes, John Maynard: Relative Movements of Real Wages and Output, in: Economic Journal, 49, 193 (March 1939); pp. 34–57.
Keynes, John Maynard: The General Theory of Employment, Interest and Money. The Collected Writings of John Maynard Keynes (Cambridge University Press: Macmillan, 1973).
Khan, Mohammad Irshad: A Note on Consumption Patterns in the Rural Areas of East Pakistan, in: Pakistan Development Review, 3, 3 (Autumn 1963); pp. 399–413.
Khan, Mushtaq H.; Jomo, Kwame Sundaram: Introduction, in: Khan, Mushtaq H.; Jomo, Kwame Sundaram (eds.): Rents, Rent-Seeking and Economic Development. Theory and Evidence in Asia (Cambridge et al.: Cambridge University Press, 2000a); pp. 1–20.
Khanna, Sushil: Market Sharing Under Multifiber Arrangement: Consequences of Non-Tariff-Barriers in the Textile Trades, in: Journal of World Trade, 24, 1 (February 1990); pp. 71–104.
Kim, Eui-Young: The Business Interest Association and the Political Economy of Development in South Korea (Seoul: International Political Science Association, 1997).
Kim, Hong Joo: Kanalisierung von Renten und Transitionsproblematik – am Beispiel der Republik Korea, in: Zinecker, Heidrun (ed.): Unvollendete Demokratisierung in Nichtmarktökonomien. Die Blackbox zwischen Staat und Wirtschaft in den Transitionsländern des Südens und Ostens (Amsterdam: G+B Verlag Fakultas, 1999); pp. 57–70.
Kim, Hong Joo: Demokratisierung der öffentlichen Verwaltung in der Republik Korea: Übergang zu Marktwirtschaft und marktfreundlicher Ordnungspolitik im Kampf um den demokratischen Rechtsstaat (Leipzig: Dissertation, 2005).
Kim, Sun-Hyuk: Civil Society in South Korea: From Grand Democracy Movements to Petty Interest Groups, in: Journal of Northeast Asian Studies, 15, 2 (Summer 1996); pp. 81–97.
Kim, Sun-Hyuk: The Politics of Democratization in Korea. The Role of Civil Society (Pittsburgh, Penn.: University of Pittsburgh Press, 2000).
Kindleberger, Charles P.: The Terms of Trade: A European Case Study (New York; London: Technology Press of M.I.T.; John Wiley; Chapman & Hall, 1956).
Kindleberger, Charles P.: Germany's Overtaking of England 1806–1914 (2), in: Weltwirtschaftliches Archiv, 111, 3 (1975); pp. 477–504.

Kiyosi, Yabuuti: The Pre-History of Modern Science in Japan. The Importation of Western Science During the Tokugawa Period, in: Cahiers d'histoire mondiale, 9, 2 (1965); pp. 208–232.
Klaus, Joachim; Stahmer, Carsten: Die Profitrate als Bestandteil gesamtwirtschaftlicher Zielkonzeptionen, in: Jahrbücher für Nationalökonomie und Statistik, 184, 2 (1970); pp. 97–113.
Klein, Michael W.; Rosengreen, Eric: The Real Exchange Rate and Foreign Direct Investment in the United States. Relative Wealth vs. Relative Wage Effects, in: Journal of International Economics, 36, 3/4 (May 1994); pp. 373–389.
Kliman, Andrew J.: The Okishio Theorem: An Obituary, in: Review of Radical Political Economics, 29, 3 (Autumn 1997); pp. 42–50.
Klodt, Henning: Wirtschaftsförderung in den neuen Bundesländer: Qualifizierungsgutscheine als Alternative, in: Weltwirtschaft, 1 (1991); pp. 91–103.
Klundert, Theo van; Meijdam, Lex: Endogenous Growth and Income Distribution, in: Journal of Economics, 58, 1 (1993); pp. 53–75.
Knowles, Lilian Charlotte Anne: The Industrial and Commercial Revolution in Great Britain During the Nineteenth Century (London; New York: Routledge E.P. Dutton, 1926).
Köhler, Gernot; Tausch, Arno: Global Keynesianism – Unequal Exchange and Global Exploitation (New York: New Science Publishers, 2002).
Korpi, Walter: Eurosclerosis and the Sclerosis of Objectivity: On the Role of Values Among Economic Policy Experts, in: Economic Journal, 106, 439 (November 1996); pp. 1727–1746.
Kosta, Jiri: Abriß der sozialökonomischen Entwicklung der Tschechoslowakei 1945–1977 (Frankfort on the Main: Suhrkamp, 1978).
Krämer, Gudrun: Die Attraktion des politischen Islam: Fallbeispiel Ägypten, in: Comparativ. Leipziger Beiträge zur Universalgeschichte und vergleichenden Gesellschaftsforschung, 4, 6 (1994); pp. 58–77.
Kravis, Irving B.: The U.S. Trade Position and the Common Market, in: Balassa, Bela (ed.): Changing Patterns in Foreign Trade and Payments (New York: W.W. Norton, 1970); pp. 12–26.
Kregel, Jan A.: Rate of Profit, Distribution and Growth. Two Views (London: Macmillan, 1971).
Kregel, Jan A.: Capital Flows: Globalization of Production and Financing Development, in: UNCTAD Review (1994); pp. 23–38.
Kremb, Jürgen: Reportagen aus China: Einblicke in die Volksrepublik, Taiwan, Hongkong und Tibet (Hamburg: Junius, 1987).
Krishna, Raj: The Inequity of the International Economic Order. Some Explanations and Policy Implications (New Delhi: Research & Information System of the Non-aligned and Other Developing Countries, 1985).
Krol, Gerd-Jan: Die Wirtschaftsreform in der DDR und ihre Ursachen (Tübingen: J.C.B. Mohr, 1972).
Krugman, Paul R.: Increasing Returns, Monopolistic Competition, and International Trade, in: Journal of International Economics, 9, 4 (November 1979); pp. 469–479.
Krugman, Paul R.: Trade, Accumulation, and Uneven Development, in: Journal of Development Economics, 8, 2 (April 1981); pp. 149–161.

Krugman, Paul R.: Is Free Trade Passé?, in: Journal of Economic Perspectives, 1, 2 (Autumn 1987); pp. 131–144.
Krugman, Paul R.: Increasing Returns and Economic Geography, in: Journal of Political Economy, 99, 3 (June 1991); pp. 483–499.
Krugman, Paul R.: The Narrow and Broad Arguments for Free Trade, in: American Economic Review, 83, 2 (May 1993); pp. 362–366.
Krugman, Paul R.: The Myth of Asia's Miracle, in: Foreign Affairs, 73, 6 (November-December 1994); pp. 62–78.
Kuznets, Simon: Economic Growth of Nations. Total Output and Production Structure (Cambridge, Mass.: The Belknap Press of Harvard University Press, 1971).
Kwak, Jin-Young: Democratization of Political Parties in Korea: Becoming Cartel Parties? (Quebec: International Political Science Association, August 2000).
Kwon, Jene K.: The East Asian Model: An Exploration of Rapid Economic Growth in the Republic of Korea and Taiwan Province of China. Discussion Paper 135 (Geneva: UNCTAD, 1998).
Lafaiete Lopes, Francisco: Disugaldade e crescimento: um modelo de programmação com aplicação ao Brasil, in: Pesquisa e planejamento econômico, 2, 2 (December 1972); pp. 189–226.
Lafay, Gérard: La compétitivité européenne face au durcissement de la concurrence internationale, in: Revue économique, 46, 3 (May 1995); pp. 679–689.
Lafay, Gérard: Les origines internationales du chômage européen, in: Revue d'économie politique, 106, 6 (November-December 1996); pp. 943–963.
Lal, Deepak: Trade Blocs and Multilateral Free Trade, in: Journal of Common Market Studies, 31, 3 (September 1993); pp. 349–359.
Lall, Sanjaya: Technical Effort and Disembodied Technology Exports: An Econometric Analysis of Inter-Industry Variations in India, in: World Development, 11, 6 (1983); pp. 527–535.
Lall, Sanjaya: Industrial Policy: The Role of Government in Promoting Industrial and Technological Development, in: UNCTAD Review (1994); pp. 65–90.
Langille, Brian A.: Eight Ways to Think About International Labour Standards, in: Journal of World Trade, 31, 4 (August 1997); pp. 27–54.
Latham, Earl: The Communist Controversy in Washington. From the New Deal to Mc Carthy (Cambridge, Mass.: Harvard University Press, 1966).
Le Pors, Annicet: La contrainte extérieure – parlons en, in: Economie et politique, 302 (September 1979); pp. 36–44.
Lee, Su-Hoon: Transitional Politics of Korea, 1987–1992: Activation of Civil Society, in: Pacific Affairs, 66, 3 (Autumn 1993); pp. 351–367.
Lefebvre, Georges: The Great Fear of 1789. Rural Panic in Revolutionary France (London: NLB, 1973).
Leff, Nathaniel H.: Optimal Investment Choice for Developing Countries. Rational Theory and Rational Decision-Making, in: Journal of Development Economics, 18, 2/3 (August 1985); pp. 335–360.
Lehmann, Jean-Pierre: Corporate Governance in East Asia and Western Europe. Competition, Confrontation and Co-operation. Paper presented at the Second International Forum on Asian Perspectives: Investing in Asia. Paris, 3 and 4 June 1996 (Paris: OECD, 1996).

# References

Lenel, Hans Otto: Zu den Megafusionen in den letzten Jahren, in: Ordo, 51 (2000); pp. 1–32.
Lenin, Vladimir Ilyich: A Characterisation of Economic Romanticism (Moscow: Progress Publishers, 1951).
Lenin, Vladimir Ilyich: The Development of Capitalism in Russia (Moscow: Progress Publishers, 1956).
Lenin, Vladimir Ilyich: Imperialism. The Highest Stage of Capitalism. A Popular Outline (Moscow: Progress Publishers, 1964).
Lenin, Wladimir Iljitsch: Der Imperialismus als höchstes Stadium des Kapitalismus. Gemeinverständlicher Abriß. Lenin Werke 22 (Berlin: Dietz, 1977).
Leontief, Wassily: Domestic Production and Foreign Trade: The American Capital Position Re-Examined, in: Economia Internazionale, 7, 1 (1954); pp. 9–38.
Leontief, Wassily: Factor Proportions and the Structure of American Trade: Further Theoretical and Empirical Analysis, in: Review of Economics and Statistics, 38, 4 (November 1956); pp. 386–407.
Leptin, Gert: Langfristige Wandlungen im Wirtschaftswachstum und in der Wachstumspolitik der Sowjetunion, in: Thalheim, Karl Christian (ed.): Wachstumsprobleme in den osteuropäischen Volkswirtschaften. Schriften des Vereins für Socialpolitik 50/1 (Berlin: Duncker und Humblot, 1968); pp. 45–88.
Lerner, Abba P.: Saving Equals Investment, in: Quarterly Journal of Economics, 52, 2 (February 1938); pp. 297–309.
Lettieri, Antonio: Die Illusionen des Reformismus, in: Rossanda, Rossana et al. (ed.): Der lange Marsch durch die Krise (Frankfort on the Main: Suhrkamp, 1976); pp. 93–114.
Levcik, Friedrich; Skolka, Jiri: East-West Technology Transfer. Study of Czechoslovakia (Paris: Organisation for Economic Cooperation and Development, 1984).
Levenson, Alec R.; Bastey, Timothy: The Anatomy of an Informal Financial Market: ROSCA Participation in Taiwan, in: Journal of Development Economics, 51, 1 (October 1996); pp. 45–68.
Levi, Mario: Colloque franco-allemand sur l'énergie, Rouen, in: Politique étrangère, 38, 3 (Autumn 1973); pp. 343–364.
Levin, Jonathan V.: The Export Economies. Their Pattern of Development in Historical Perspective (Cambridge, Mass.: Harvard University Press, 1960).
Levine, Aaron Lawrence: Industrial Retardation in Britain 1880–1914 (Letchworth: Weidenfeld & Nicolson, 1967).
Lew, Seok-Jin; Lee, Nae-Young: Democratization and Changing Industrial Policy Making. A Case of the Southern Korean Automobile Industry (Seoul: International Political Science Association, 1997).
Lewin, Günter: Die staatliche Leitung und Kontrolle von Manufakturen und handwerklicher Produktion im China der frühen Song Zeit, in: Jahrbuch für Wirtschaftsgeschichte, 3 (1974); pp. 179–199.
Lewis, Peter: From Prebendalism to Predation: The Political Economy of Decline in Nigeria, in: Journal of Modern African Studies, 34, 1 (1996); pp. 79–103.
Lewis, William Arthur: Economic Development with Unlimited Supply of Labour, in: Manchester School of Economic and Social Studies, 22, 4 (May 1954); pp. 139–191.

Lewis, William Arthur: The Evolution of the International Economic Order (Princeton, N.J.: Princeton University Press, 1978b).
Li, Hongyi; Squire, Lyn; Zon, Heng-fu: Explaining International and Intertemporal Variations in Income Inequality, in: Economic Journal, 108, 446 (January 1998); pp. 26–43.
Liberman, Evsey G.: Economic Methods and the Effectiveness of Production (Garden City, N.Y.: Doubleday, 1977).
Lipietz, Alain: The Post-Fordist World: Labour Relations, International Hierarchy and Global Ecology, in: Review of International Political Economy, 4, 1 (1997); pp. 1–41.
Lokanathan, P.S.: Industrial Organization in India (London: Allen & Unwin, 1935).
Lombard, Marc: A Re-examination of the Reasons for the Failure of Keynesian Expansionary Politics in France, 1981–1983, in: Cambridge Journal of Economics, 19, 3 (April 1995); pp. 359–372.
Looney, Robert E.: Oil Revenues and Dutch Disease in Saudi Arabia: Differential Impacts on Sectoral Growth, in: Canadian Journal of Development Studies, 11, 1 (1990); pp. 119–133.
Lorenz, Richard: Sozialgeschichte der Sowjetunion, I. 1917–1945 (Frankfort on the Main: Suhrkamp, 1976).
Lorenzi, Jean-Hervé; Pastré, Olivier; Toledano, Joelle: La crise du XXe siècle (Paris: Economica, 1980).
Lucas, Robert E.: On the Mechanics of Economic Development, in: Journal of Monetary Economics, 22, 1 (March 1988); pp. 3–42.
Luh, Yir-Hueih; Stefanou, Spiro E.: Productivity Growth in U.S. Agriculture Under Dynamic Adjustment, in: American Journal of Agricultural Economics, 73, 4 (November 1991); pp. 1116–1123.
Lukács, Georg: Geschichte und Klassenbewusstsein (Amsterdam: Verlag de Munter, 1923/1967).
Luxemburg, Rosa: Die Akkumulation des Kapitals. Ein Beitrag zur ökonomischen Erklärung des Imperialismus (Berlin: Vereinigung internationaler Verlagsanstalten, 1923).
Lydall, Harold F.: Employment Effects of Trade Expansion, in: International Labour Review, 111, 3 (March 1975); pp. 219–234.
MacCloskey, Donald N.: Productivity Change in British Pig Iron, 1870–1939, in: Quarterly Journal of Economics, 82, 2 (May 1968); pp. 281–296.
MacCoy, Jennifer L.; Smith, William C.: Democratic Disequilibrium in Venezuela, in: Journal of Interamerican Studies and World Affairs, 37, 2 (Summer 1995); pp. 113–179.
MacKinley, Terry; Alarcón González, Diana: The Prevalence of Rural Poverty in Mexico, in: World Development, 23, 9 (September 1995); pp. 1575–1585.
MacMillan, James; Harris, Bernard: The American Take-over of Britain (London: Leslie Frewin, 1968).
Maddison, Angus: Economic Growth in the West. A Comparative Experience in Europe and North America (New York; London: Twentieth Century Fund; Allen & Unwin, 1964).
Mahalanobis, P.C.: Some Observations on the Process of Growth of National Income, in: Sankhya, 12, 4 (1953); pp. 307–312.
Mahon, James E.: Was Latin America Too Rich to Prosper? Structural and Political Obstacles to Export-Led Industrial Growth, in: Journal of Development Studies, 28, 2 (January 1992); pp. 241–263.

Maizels, Alfred: Import Trends in the Industrial Countries, in: New Directions of World Trade. Proceedings of a Chatham House Conference Bellagio, 16–24 September 1963. Issued under the Auspices of the Royal Institute of International Affairs (London et al.: Oxford University Press, 1964); pp. 23–50.
Malthus, Thomas Robert: An Essay on Population, Vol.II (London: Dent & Sons, 1958).
Mankiw, N. Gregory: The Growth of Nations, in: Brookings Papers on Economic Activity, 26, 1 (1995); pp. 275–326.
Manning, Brian: The Levellers, in: Ives, Eric W. (ed.): The English Revolution (1600–1660) (New York: Barnes & Noble, 1969); pp. 144–158.
Manning, Chris: Approaching the Turning Point? Labor Market Change under Indonesia's New Order, in: Developing Economies, 33, 1 (March 1995); pp. 52–81.
Marglin, Stephen A.: Growth, Distribution and Inflation: A Centennial Synthesis, in: Cambridge Journal of Economics, 8, 2 (June 1984); pp. 115–144.
Marx, Karl: Das Kapital (1): Kritik der politischen Ökonomie: Der Produktionsprozeß des Kapitals. MEW 23 (Berlin: Dietz, 1890/1972a).
Marx, Karl: Das Kapital (2): Der Zirkulationsprozeß des Kapitals. MEW 24 (Berlin: Dietz, 1893/1972b).
Marx, Karl: Das Kapital (3): Der Gesamtprozeß der kapitalistischen Akkumulation. MEW 25 (Berlin: Dietz, 1894/1972c).
Marx, Karl: Zur Kritik der politischen Ökonomie. Erstes Heft (Berlin: Dietz, 1859/1963).
Marx, Karl; Engels, Friedrich: Die deutsche Ideologie. Kritik der neuesten deutschen Philosophie in ihren Repräsentanten Feuerbach, B. Bauers und Stirner, und des deutschen Sozialismus in seinen verschiedenen Propheten. MEW3 (Berlin: Dietz, 1845–46/1969).
Masujima, Ken: "Good Governance" and the Development Assistance Committee (DAC) – Ideas and Organisational Constraints, in: Boas, Morten; MacNeill, Desmond (eds.): Framing the World? The Role of Ideas in Multilateral Institutions (London; New York: Routledge, 2003); pp. 110–121.
Matthews, Robert C.O.; Feinstein, Charles H.; Odling-Smee, John O.: British Economic Growth: 1856 – 1973 (Oxford: Clarendon Press, 1982).
Mauer, Kuno: Die Samurai. Ihre Geschichte und ihr Einfluß auf das moderne Japan (Düsseldorf; Vienna: Econ Verlag, 1981).
Mayer, Jörg: The Fallacy of Composition: A Review of the Literature. Discussion Papers 166 (Geneva: UNCTAD, February 2003).
Mayor, Thomas: The Decline of the United States Capital-Output Ratio, in: Economic Development and Cultural Change, 16, 4 (July 1968); pp. 495–516.
Meade, James E.: The Rate of Profit in a Growing Economy, in: Economic Journal, 73, 292 (December 1963); pp. 665–674.
Meynier, Gilbert: Préface in: Elsenhans, Hartmut: La guerre d'Algérie 1954–1962. La transition d'une France à une autre. Le passage de la IV à la Ve République (Paris: Publisud, 2000.); pp. 7–60.
Michalet, Charles-Albert: Les placements des épargnants français de 1815 à nos jours (Paris: Presses Universitaires de France, 1968).

Michie, Jonathan; Pitelis, Christos: Demand and Supply-Side Approaches to Economic Policy, in: Work, Unemployment and Need: Theory, Evidence, Policies. 1996 Conference Papers (Antwerpen: European Association for Evolutionary Political Economy, 1996); pp. 1–15.

Mieczkowski, Bogdan: Estimates of Changes in Real Wages in Poland During the 1960s, in: Slavic Review, 31, 3 (September 1972); pp. 651–656.

Minami, Ryoshin: A Model of Economic Development from Classical to Neoclassical Stages, in: Weltwirtschaftliches Archiv, 97, 2 (1966); pp. 345–355.

Minami, Ryoshin: Economic Development of Japan: Factors, Consequences, Implications, in: Journal of Economic Development, 17, 2 (December 1992); pp. 7–35.

Mitchell, Brian R.; Deane, Phyllis: Abstracts of British Historical Statistics (Cambridge: Cambridge University Press, 1962).

Möckel, Carola: Technologietransfers in der ersten Phase der industriellen Revolution. Die Cockerills in Preußen, in: Jahrbuch für Wirtschaftsgeschichte, 3 (1987); pp. 9–27.

Mokyr, Joel: Is there Still Life in the Pessimist Case? Consumption During the Industrial Revolution, 1790–1850, in: Journal of Economic History, 48, 1 (March 1988); pp. 69–92.

Mommertz, Karl Heinz: Vom Bohren, Drehen und Fräsen. Zur Kulturgeschichte von Werkzeugmaschinen (Munich: Deutsches Museum, 1979).

Mommsen, Ernst-Wolf: Strukturwandlungen in der Rohstoffversorgung der europäischen Eisen- und Stahlindustrie, in: Kyklos, 15, 4 (1962); pp. 758–776.

Mommsen, Hans: Arbeiterbewegung und nationale Frage. Ausgewählte Aufsätze (Göttingen: Vandenhoeck & Ruprecht, 1979).

Montgomery, Arthur: How Sweden Overcame the Depression (Stockholm: Alb. Bonniers Boktryckeri, 1938).

Moon, Chung-In: Changing Patterns of Business – Government Relations in South Korea, in: Choi, Sang-Yong (ed.): Democracy in Korea. Its Ideals and its Realities (Seoul: Seoul Press, 1997); pp. 447–472.

Moon, Chung-In; Mo, Jongryn: Economic Crisis and Structural Reforms in South Korea: Assessments and Implications (Washington, DC: Economic Strategy Institute, 2000).

Morimotu, Kokichi: The Standard of Living in Japan. John Hopkins University Studies in Historical and Political Studies (Baltimore, Md.: Johns Hopkins University Press, 1918).

Morishima, Michio: Marx's Economics. A Dual Theory of Value and Growth (Cambridge: Cambridge University Press, 1973).

Morkre, Morris E.: Rent-Seeking and Hongkong's Textile Quota System, in: Developing Economies, 17, 1 (March 1979); pp. 110–118.

Morkre, Morris E.: Rent Seeking and Hong Kong's Textile Quota System: Reply, in: Developing Economies, 19, 3 (September 1981); pp. 276–277.

Mouly, Jean: Wages Policy in Sweden, in: International Labour Review, 95, 3 (March 1967); pp. 166–201.

Mukherjee, Santosh: Restructuring of Industrial Economies and Trade with Developing Countries (Geneva: International Labour Office, 1978).

Mulé, Rosa: Does Democracy Promote Equality, in: Democratization, 5, 1 (Spring 1998); pp. 1–22.

Müller, Wolfgang; Neusüß, Christel: Die Sozialstaatsillusion und der Widerspruch von Lohnarbeit und Kapital, in: Sozialistische Politik, 2, 6/7 (June 1970); pp. 4–67.

Mundorf, Hans: Wechselkurse spielen bei internationalen Lohnvergleichen eine entscheidende Rolle. Auch Zahlen sind nur Schall und Rauch, in: Handelsblatt, 94 (August 11, 1994); p. 2.
Mundorf, Hans: Die realen Nettolöhne sind nicht zu hoch, in: Handelsblatt (August 29, 1995); p. 2.
Mundorf, Hans: Der technische Fortschritt läßt sich durch Lohnsenkungen nicht aufhalten, in: Handelsblatt (July 19–20, 1996).
Mundorf, Hans: Amtliche Wechselkurse dienen oft der Verfälschung der Wirklichkeit, in: Handelsblatt (August 28/29, 1998); p. 2.
Mürle, Holger: Entwicklungstheorie nach dem Scheitern der „großen Theorie" (Duisburg: Institut für Entwicklung und Frieden, 1997).
Murphy, Kevin M.; Shleifer, Andrei; Vishny, Robert: Income Distribution, Market Size and Industrialization, in: Quarterly Journal of Economics, 104, 3 (August 1989); pp. 537–564.
Mussler, Werner: Die Senkung der Arbeitskosten erfordert einen langen Atem: Deutschland dürfte auf absehbare Zeit Spitzenreiter bleiben – Lohnsteigerungen dieses Jahres wirken kontraproduktiv, in: Handelsblatt (July 14, 1999); p. 2.
Musson, A. E.: Joseph Whitworth and the Growth of Mass-Production Engineering, in: Business History, 17, 2 (July 1975); pp. 109–149.
Myant, Martin: The Czechoslovak Economy 1948–1988. The Battle for Economic Reform. Soviet and Eastern European Studies (Cambridge: Cambridge University Press, 1989).
Mytelka, Lynn Krieger: The Transfer of Technology: Myth or Reality? (Brugge: Manuskript, 1985).
Mytelka, Lynn Krieger: The Transfer of Technology: Myth or Reality?, in: Cosgrove, Carol; Jamar, J. (eds.): The European Community's Development Policy: The Strategies Ahead. Conference organised at the College of Europe, Bruges, 4–6 July 1985 (Brugge: De Tempel, 1986); pp. 243–281.
Nakamura, James I.: Agricultural Production and the Economic Development of Japan 1873–1922 (Princeton, N.J.: Princeton University Press, 1966).
Narrassiguin, Philippe: Croissance tirée par les exportations et politique de change: Le cas de l'île Maurice, in: Revue d'économie politique, 105, 2 (March 1995); pp. 315–331.
Nayyar, Depak: Globalisation: The Past is our Present, in: Indian Economic Journal, 43, 3 (January-March 1996); pp. 1–18.
Nayyar, Dhiraj: Alleviating Poverty: Role of Good Governance and Institutional Reform, in: Economic and Political Weekly, 35, 42 (October 2000); pp. 3739–3742.
Nef, Arthur; Dean, Edwin: Comparative Changes in Labour Productivity and Unit Labour Costs by Manufacturing Industry: United States and Western Europe (Washington: American Enterprise Institute, 1984).
Nef, John U.: Cultural Foundations of Industrial Civilization (Cambridge: Cambridge University Press, 1958).
Nelson, Richard R.: National Innovation Systems: A Comparative Analysis (Oxford: Oxford University Press, 1993).
Neumeister, Werner: Die natürlichen Grundlagen für die Eisenindustrie in Deutschland und in den Vereinigten Staaten (Leipzig: Duncker und Humblot, 1910).
Neuthinger, Egon: Germany's Enduring Current Account Surplus, in: Intereconomics, 24, 3 (May-June 1989); pp. 138–148.

Nitzan, Jonathan: Mergers, Stagflation, and the Logic of Globalization, in: Tétreault, Mary Ann; Denemark, Robert A.; Thomas, Kenneth P.; Burch, Kurt (eds.): Rethinking Global Political Economy: Emerging Issues, Unfolding Odysseys (London; New York: Routledge, 2003); pp. 109–146.
North, Robert C.; Holsti, Ole R.; Zaninovich, M. George: Content Analysis. A Handbook with Applications for the Study of International Crisis (Evanston, Ill.: Northwestern University Press, 1963).
Nun, José: Superpoblación relativa, ejército industrial de reserva y masa marginal, in: Revista Latinoamericana de Sociología, 5, 2 (July 1969); pp. 178–236.
Nunnenkamp, Peter; Gundlach, Erich; Agarwal, Jamuna P.: Globalisation of Production and Markets (Tübingen: Mohr, 1994).
Nuti, Domenico Mario: Capitalism, Socialism and Steady Growth, in: Economic Journal, 80, 317 (March 1970); pp. 32–57.
O'Brien, Patrick Karl; Keyder, Çaglar: Economic Growth in Britain and France 1780–1914. Two Paths to the Twentieth Century (London: Allen & Unwin, 1978).
O'Brien, Philip: A Critique of Latin American Theory of Dependency, in: Oxaal, Ivar; Barnett, Tony; Booth, David (eds.): Beyond the Sociology of Development: Economy and Society in Latin America and Africa. (London; Boston, Mass.: Routledge & Kegan Paul, 1975); pp. 7–25.
O'Rourke, Kevin H.; Williamson, Jeffrey Gale: Late Nineteenth-Century Anglo-American Factor-Price Convergence: Were Heckscher and Ohlin Right?, in: Journal of Economic History, 54, 4 (December 1994); pp. 892–917.
Obser, Andreas: Communicative Structuration and Governance of the Global Environment Through Policy Networks of International Aid Organizations. The Global Environmental Facility (GEF) and the Tropical Forestry Action Programme (TFAP), Including the Current Policy Dialog of the Intergovernmental Panel on Forests (IPF). Dissertation (Leipzig: Dissertation, 1997).
Obst, Werner: Unrentabel bis zum jüngsten Tag, in: Managers Magazine, 3 (March 1979); pp. 141–148.
Obst, Werner: Reiz der Idee – Pleite der Praxis. Ein deutsch-deutscher Wirtschaftsvergleich (Zurich: Interform, 1983).
Ohlin, Bertil: Ist eine Modernisierung der Außenhandelstheorie erforderlich?, in: Weltwirtschaftliches Archiv, 26, 1 (1927); pp. 97–115.
Okishio, Nobuo: Technical Changes and the Rate of Profit, in: Kobe University Economic Review, 7 (1961); pp. 85–90.
Olsen, Gorm Rye: North-South Relations in the Process of Change: The Significance of International Civil Society, in: European Journal of Development Research, 7, 2 (December 1995); pp. 233–256.
Olson, Mancur: The Devolution of the Nordic Teutonic Economies, in: American Economic Review, 85, 3 (May 1995); pp. 22–27.
Oman, Charles: Policy Competition for Foreign Direct Investment: A Study of Competition among Governments to Attract FDI. Development Centre Studies (Paris: OECD, 2000).
Oshima, Harry T.: Consumer Asset Formation and the Future of Capitalism, in: Economic Journal, 71, 281 (March 1961); pp. 20–35.

Oshima, Harry T.: 'Labour-Force Explosion' and the Labour Intensive Sector in Asian Growth, in: Economic Development and Cultural Change, 19, 2 (January 1971); pp. 161–183.

Oshima, Harry T.: Towards a Model of Monsoon Asian Economic Growth, in: Singapore Economic Review, 29, 2 (1984); pp. 93–110.

Ozaga, S.A.: The Propensity to Save, the Capital Output Ratio and the Equilibrium Rate of Growth, in: Economica, 31, 124 (November 1964); pp. 363–371.

Pack, Howard: Endogeneous Growth Theory: Intellectual Appeal and Empirical Shortcoming, in: Journal of Economic Perspectives, 8, 1 (Winter 1994); pp. 55–72.

Page, John et al.: The East Asian Miracle. Economic Growth and Public Policy (Washington: World Bank, 1993).

Palma, Gabriel: Dependency: A Formal Theory of Underdevelopment or a Methodology for the Analysis of Concrete Situations of Underdevelopment, in: World Development, 6, 7/8 (July-August 1978); pp. 881–924.

Paqué, Karl Heinz: Technologie, Wissen und Wirtschaftspolitik – Zur Rolle des Staates in Theorien des endogenen Wachstums, in: Die Weltwirtschaft, 3 (1995); pp. 237–253.

Parijs, Philippe van: The Falling-Rate-of-Profit Theory of Crisis: A Rational Reconstruction by Way of Obituary, in: Review of Radical Political Economics, 12, 1 (Spring 1980); pp. 1–16.

Parvin, Manoucher; Dezhbakhsh, Hashem: Trade, Technology Transfer, and Hyper-Dutch Disease in OPEC: Theory and Evidence, in: International Journal of Middle East Studies, 20, 4 (November 1988); pp. 469–477.

Patel, Parimal; Pavitt, Keith: The Continuing, Widespread (and Neglected) Importance of Improvements in Mechanical Technologies, in: Research Policy, 23 (1994); pp. 533–545.

Patel, Surendra J.: Economic Transition in Africa, in: Journal of Modern African Studies, 2, 3 (1964); pp. 329–349.

Payne, P.L.: The Emergence of Large-Scale Company in Great Britain, 1870- 1914, in: Economic History Review, 20, 3 (1967); pp. 519–542.

Peet, Richard: Industrial Devolution, Underconsumption and Third World Debt Crisis, in: World Development, 15, 6 (June 1987); pp. 777–788.

Perroux, François: Les industries motrices et la croissance d'une économie nationale, in: Economie appliquée, 16, 2 (April-June 1963); pp. 151–196.

Pervillé, Guy: La guerre d'Algérie 1954–1962. La transition d'une France à une autre. Le passage de la IVème à la Vème République., in: Maghreb Review, 28, 1 (2003); pp. 75–79.

Peterson, Florence: Die amerikanischen Gewerkschaften. Ihr Wesen und Wirken (Munich: Freitag, 1945).

Petzina, Dietmar: Die deutsche Wirtschaft in der Zwischenkriegszeit (Wiesbaden: Franz Steiner, 1977).

Petzina, Dietmar; Abelshauser, Werner; Faust, Anselm: Sozialgeschichtliches Arbeitsbuch III. Materialien zur Statistik des Deutschen Reiches 1914–1945 (Munich: C. H. Beck, 1978).

Pfeifer, Albrecht: Probleme der internationalen Nahrungssicherung. Vortrag gehalten an der Universität Leipzig am 18.06.96 (Leipzig, 1996).

Phelps Brown, E. H.; Weber, B.: Accumulation, Productivity and Distribution in the British Economy 1870–1938, in: Economic Journal, 63, 250 (June 1953); pp. 263–288.

Phelps, Edmund S.: Second Essay on the Golden Rule of Accumulation, in: American Economic Review, 55, 4 (September 1965); pp. 793–814.
Pickett, James; Robson, R.: A Note on Operating Conditions and Technology in African Textile Production, in: World Development, 5, 9/10 (September-October 1977); pp. 879–882.
Piehl, Ernst: Multinationale Konzerne und internationale Gewerkschaftsbewegung: ein Beitrag zur Analyse und zur Strategie der Arbeiterbewegung im international organisierten Kapitalismus insbesondere in Westeuropa (Frankfort on the Main: Europäische Verlagsanstalt, 1974).
Pietsch, Anne-Jutta: Der Arbeitsplatzwechsel als Konfliktmanifestation in der Sowjetunion, in: Elsenhans, Hartmut (ed.): Migration und Wirtschaftsentwicklung (Frankfort on the Main; New York: Campus, 1978); pp. 257–282.
Pietsch, Anne-Jutta: Das Reduktionsproblem und die Kategorien produktive und unproduktive Arbeit. Ein Beitrag zur politischen Ökonomie des Ausbildungssektors (Frankfort on the Main; New York: Campus, 1979).
Pilat, Dirk: Comparative Productivity of Korean Manufacturing, 1967–1987, in: Journal of Development Economics, 46, 1 (February 1995); pp. 123–144.
Pilat, Dirk; Rao, D. S. Prasada: Multilateral Comparisons of Output, Productivity, and Purchasing Parities in Manufacturing, in: Review of Income and Wealth, 42, 2 (June 1996); pp. 113–130.
Pirker, Theo: Zum Verhalten der Organisationen der deutschen Arbeiterbewegung in der Endphase der Weimarer Republik, in: Erdmann, Karl Dietrich; Schulze, Hagen (eds.): Weimar: Selbstpreisgabe einer Demokratie. Eine Bilanz heute. Kölner Kolloquium der Fritz Thyssen Stiftung, Juni 1979 (Düsseldorf: Droste, 1980); pp. 323–332.
Platt, Desmond Christopher M.: Latin America and British Trade 1808–1914 (London: Adam & Charles Black, 1972).
Poirine, Bernard: Le développement par la rente dans les petites economies insulaires, in: Revue économique, 44, 6 (November 1993); pp. 1169–1200.
Polanyi, Michael: Towards a Theory of Conspicuous Production, in: Soviet Survey, 34 (October-December 1960); pp. 90–99.
Pontusson, Jonas: Explaining the Decline of European Social Democracy. The Role of Structural Economic Change, in: World Politics, 47, 4 (July 1995); pp. 495–533.
Porter, Michael E.: The Competitive Advantage of Nations (London: Macmillan, 1990).
Porzecanski, Arturo C.: The Inflationary Impact of Repetitive Devaluation, in: Journal of Development Studies, 11, 4 (July 1975); pp. 337–365.
Posner, M.V.: International Trade and Technical Change, in: Oxford Economic Papers, 13, 3 (October 1961); pp. 323–342.
Powell, Raymond P.: The Soviet Capital Stock from Census to Census, 1960–1973, in: Soviet Studies, 31, 1 (January 1979); pp. 56–75.
Prebisch, Raúl: The Economic Development of Latin America and its Principal Problems, in: Economic Bulletin for Latin America, 7, 1 (February 1962); pp. 1–22.
Preobrazenskij, Evgenij: Die neue Ökonomik. Übersetzung der zweiten erweiterten Ausgabe (Berlin: Verlag Neuer Kurs, 1971).
Pye, Lucian W.: Asian Power and Politics. The Cultural Dimensions of Authority (Cambridge, Mass. et al.: Belknap, 1985).

Quijano Obregón, Aníbal E.: Imperialismo y "marginalidad" en América Latina (Lima: Mosca Azul, 1977).
Raffer, Kunibert: Raw Material Supply of Western and Eastern Countries: The Case of African Minerals, in: Dobozi, István; Mándi, Péter (eds.): Emerging Development Patterns: European Contributions. Selected Papers of the 3rd General Conference of EADI, Nov. 11–14, Budapest, Hungary (Budapest: European Association of Development Training and Research Institutes, 1983); pp. 489–508.
Ramos, Joseph: A Heterodoxical Interpretation of the Employment Problem in Latin America, in: World Development, 2, 7 (July 1974); pp. 47–58.
Ranis, Gustav: Science, Technology, and Development: A Retrospective View, in: Beranek, William jr.; Ranis, Gustav (eds.): Science, Technology and Economic Development. A Historical and Comparative Study (New York: Praeger, 1978); pp. 1–30.
Rao, S. K.; Sanyal, Amal: On Promoting Employment Through Labour-Intensity of Technique, in: Economic and Political Weekly, 13, 6/7 (February 1978); pp. 287–290.
Ray, John: The Battle of Britain: Dowding and the First Victory 1940 (London: Cassell, 2000).
Rayback, Joseph G.: A History of American Labor (New York; London: The Free Press; Collier Macmillan, 1966).
Reichenberg, Rudolf: Zur Diskussion über das Gesetz der vorrangigen Entwicklung der Produktionsmittelproduktion im Sozialismus, in: Wirtschaftswissenschaft, 15, 11 (November 1967); pp. 1775–1786.
Reischauer, Edwin O.; Fairbank, John K.: East Asia. The Great Tradition (Boston, Mass.: Houghton Mifflin, 1960).
Renten, Geert: Accumulation of Capital and the Foundation of the Tendency of the Rate of Profit to Fall, in: Cambridge Journal of Economics, 15, 1 (March 1991); pp. 79–93.
Reynolds, Lloyd George; Taft, Cynthia H.: The Evolution of Wage Structure (New Haven, Conn.: Yale University Press, 1958).
Rhee, Jong-Chan: The State and the Industry in South Korea. The Limits of the Authoritarian State (London: Routledge, 1994).
Rhee, Jong-Chan: The Political Management of Corporate Restructuring in the Korean Crisis: The Dilemma between Weak Market Capabilities and Weak State Capacities (Quebec: International Political Science Association, August 2000).
Ricardo, David: On the Principles of Political Economy and Taxation. The Works and Correspondence of David Ricardo (1) (Cambridge et al.: Cambridge University Press, 1951).
Richardson, Henry: Real Wage Movements, in: Economic Journal, 49, 195 (September 1939); pp. 425–441.
Rimmer, Douglas: The Overvalued Currency and Over-Administered Economy of Nigeria, in: African Affairs, 84, 336 (July 1987); pp. 435–446.
Ritschl, Albrecht O.: Aufstieg und Niedergang der Wirtschaft der DDR: Ein Zahlenbild 1945–1989, in: Jahrbuch für Wirtschaftsgeschichte, 36, 2 (1995); pp. 11–46.
Ritschl, Albrecht O.: An Exercise in Futility: East German Economic Growth and Decline, 1945–89, in: Crafts, Nicholas F. R.; Toniolo, G. (eds.): Economic Growth in Europe since 1945 (Cambridge et al.: Cambridge University Press, 1996); pp. 498–540.
Ritter, Gerhard Albert; Kocka, Jürgen: Deutsche Sozialgeschichte 1870–1914: Dokumente und Skizzen (Munich: C. H. Beck, 1974).

Robinson, Joan Violet: An Essay on Marxian Economics (London: Macmillan, 1949).
Robinson, Joan Violet: Collected Economic Papers (Oxford: Basil Blackwell, 1951).
Rodbertus-Jagetzow, Carl: Das Kapital. Vierter sozialer Brief an von Kirchmann (Berlin: Puttkammer & Mühlbrecht, 1913).
Roemer, John E.: Continuing Controversy on the Falling Rate of Profit: Fixed Capital and Other Issues, in: Cambridge Journal of Economics, 3, 4 (December 1979); pp. 379 –398.
Romer, Paul M.: Increasing Returns and Long-Term Growth, in: Journal of Political Economy, 94, 2 (September-October 1986); pp. 1002–1037.
Romer, Paul M.: Growth Based on Increasing Returns Due to Specialization, in: American Economic Review, 77 (1987); pp. 56–62.
Romer, Paul M.: Endogenous Technological Change, in: Journal of Political Economy, 98, 5 (1990); pp. 71–102.
Romer, Paul M.: The Origins of Endogenous Growth, in: Journal of Economic Perspectives, 8, 1 (1994); pp. 3–22.
Romer, Paul M.: Why Indeed in America? Theory, History, and the Origins of Modern Economic Growth, in: American Economic Review, 86, 2 (May 1996); pp. 202–206.
Röpke, Wilhelm: Crises and Cycles (London; Edinburgh; Glasgow: William Hodge, 1936).
Rosenberg, Arthur: Geschichte der Weimarer Republik (Frankfort on the Main: Europäische Verlagsanstalt, 1961).
Rosenberg, Hans: Die Weltwirtschaftskrise von 1857–1859 (Stuttgart; Berlin: Kohlhammer, 1934).
Rosenberg, Nathan: Innovative Responses to Materials Shortages, in: American Economic Review, 63, 2 (May 1973); pp. 111–118.
Rosenberg, Nathan: Perspectives on Technology (Cambridge: Cambridge University Press, 1976).
Rosenbloom, Joshua L.: Anglo-American Technological Differences in Small Arms Manufacturing, in: Journal of Interdisciplinary History, 23, 4 (Spring 1993); pp. 683–698.
Rosenstein-Rodan, P.N.: Problems of Industrialization of Eastern and South Eastern Europe, in: Economic Journal, 53, 210 (June-September 1943); pp. 202–211.
Ross, Robert; Trachte, Kent: Global Cities and Global Classes: The Peripheralization of Labor in New York City, in: Review, 6, 3 (Winter 1983); pp. 393–431.
Rostas, László: Comparative Productivity in British and American Manufacturing (Cambridge: Cambridge University Press, 1948).
Rostow, Walt Whitman: Investment and the Great Depression, in: Economic History Review, 8, 2 (May 1938); pp. 136–158.
Rostow, Walt Whitman: The World Economy. History and Prospect (London: Macmillan, 1978).
Rowthorn, Robert: East Asian Development: The Flying Geese Paradigm Reconsidered. East Asian Development: Lessons for a New Global Environment 8 (Kualalumpur: UNCTAD, 1996).
Royal Institute of International Affairs: The Problem of International Investment (Oxford, 1937).

Rozelle, Scott Douglas; Taylor, J. Edward; DeBrauw, Alan: Migration, Remittances, and Agricultural Productivity in China, in: American Economic Review, 89, 2 (Summer 1999); pp. 287–291.
Rubinson, Richard: Political Tranformation in Germany and the United States, in: Kaplan, Barbara Hockey (ed.): Social Change in the Capitalist World Economy. Political Economy of the World-System Annuals. Political Economy of the World-System Annuals, Vol.1 (Series Editor: Immanuel Wallerstein) (Beverly Hills, Cal.; London: Sage, 1978); pp. 39–74.
Ruffert, Christina: Staatsinterventionismus und wirtschaftliche Entwicklung in Ostasien – Der Fall Malaysia (Constance: Universität Konstanz, Diplomarbeit, 1996).
Sachs, Jeffrey D.; Larrain, Felipe B.: Macroeconomics in the Global Economy (New York, et al.: Harvester Wheatsheaf, 1993).
Saito, Masaru: Introduction of Foreign Technology in the Industrializing Process. Japanese Experience since the Meiji Restoration (1868), in: Developing Economies, 12, 2 (June 1975); pp. 168–186.
Salvadori, Neri: Falling Rate of Profit With a Constant Real Wage – An Example, in: Cambridge Journal of Economics, 5, 1 (May 1981); pp. 57–66.
Samuelson, Paul A.: International Trade and the Equalization of Factor Prices, in: Economic Journal, 58, 230 (June 1948); pp. 163–184.
Santos, Milton: The Shared Space. The Two Circuits of the Urban Economy in Underdeveloped Countries (London; New York: Methuen, 1979).
Sarkar, Parbirjit; Singer, Hans Wolfgang: Manufactured Exports of Developing Countries and their Terms of Trade Since 1965, in: World Development, 19, 4 (April 1991); pp. 333–340.
Sarkar, Prabirjit; Singer, Hans W.: Manufacture – Manufacture Terms of Trade Deterioration. A Reply, in: World Development, 21, 10 (October 1993); pp. 1617–1620.
Sato, Kazuo: International Variations in the Incremental Capital Output Ratios, in: Economic Development and Cultural Change, 19, 4 (July 1971); pp. 621–640.
Saul, Samuel Berrick: Technological Change: The United States and Britain in the Nineteenth Century (London: Methuen, 1970).
Sawyer, Malcolm: Some Aspects of the Analysis of an Endogenous Money System (o.O.: Ms., August 2001).
Saxonhouse, Gary R.: A Tale of Japanese Technological Diffusion in the Meiji Period, in: Journal of Economic History, 34, 1 (March 1974); pp. 149–165.
Say, Jean-Baptiste: Traité d'économie politique (Paris: Calmann-Lévy, 1803/1972).
Schäfer, Hans-Bernd: Landwirtschaftliche Akkumulationslasten und industrielle Entwicklung: Analyse und Beschreibung entwicklungspolitischer Optionen in dualistischen Wirtschaften (Berlin et al.: Springer, 1983).
Schäfer, Wolf: Globlisierung: Entmonopolisierung des Nationalen?, in: Berg, Hartmut; Berthold, Norbert (eds.): Globalisierung der Wirtschaft: Ursachen-Formen-Konsequenzen. Schriften des Vereins für Socialpolitik 263 (Berlin: Duncker und Humblot, 1999); pp. 9–22.
Scherr, Sara J.: Agriculture in an Export Boom Economy: A Comparative Analysis of Policy and Performance in Indonesia, Mexico and Nigeria, in: World Development, 17, 4 (April 1989); pp. 543–560.

Schilfert, Gerhard: Bürgerliche Revolution und Reform in England (1640–1832), in: Kossok, Manfred (ed.): Studien zur vergleichenden Revolutionsgeschichte, 1500- 1917 (Berlin: Akademie-Verlag, 1974); pp. 53–73.

Schlesinger, Georg: Die amerikanischen Werkzeugmaschinenausstellungen in New Haven und Boston, in: Werkstattgeschichte, 19, 1 (January 1925); pp. 1–48.

Schmidt, Reinhard H.: Credit Supply, Self-Help, and the Survival of Financial Institutions in Developing Countries, in: Jahrbuch für Neue Politische Ökonomie, 5 (1986); pp. 262–277.

Schmitt, Bernadotte Everly: England and Germany 1740–1914 (New York: Howard Fertig, 1967).

Schmitt-Rink, Gerhard: Funktionelle Verteilung, personelle Verteilung und Multiplikatoreffekt, in: Jahrbücher für Nationalökonomie und Statistik, 183, 5 (1970); pp. 361–377.

Schmitz, Christopher: The Rise of Big Business in the World Copper Industry 1870- 1930, in: Economic History Review, 39, 3 (1986); pp. 392–410.

Schmookler, Jacob: Invention and Economic Growth (Cambridge, Mass.: Harvard University Press, 1966).

Schömmel, Markus: Entwicklungszusammenarbeit als spezifisches Instrument der Außenwirtschaftspolitik (Leipzig: Dissertation, 2005).

Schorske, Carl E.: German Social Democracy, 1905–1917. The Great Schism (Cambridge, Mass.: Harvard University Press, 1965).

Schultz, Thedore W.: Perspectivas económicas de los productos primarios, in: Ellis, Howard S.; Wallich, Henry C. (eds.): El desarrollo económico y América Latina (Buenos Aires; Mexico: Fondo de Cultura Económica, 1960); pp. 363–390.

Schumacher, Dieter: Beschäftigungswirkungen von Importen aus Entwicklungsländern nicht dramatisieren, in: DIW-Wochenbericht, 45, 1 (November 1978); pp. 6–11.

Schumacher, Dieter: Lohnerhöhungen, internationale Wettbewerbsfähigkeit und Aufholprozeß in Ostdeutschland, in: Konjunkturpolitik, 39, 3 (1993); pp. 121–147.

Schutz, Erich: Non-Produced Inputs, Differential Profit Rates and the Okishio Theorem, in: Review of Radical Political Economics, 19, 2 (Summer 1987); pp. 43–61.

Scott, C.V.: International Capital and the Oil-Producing States in Africa. An Analysis of Angola, Nigeria and Algeria, in: Journal of Developing Societies, 8, 2 (1992); pp. 179–193.

Seers, Dudley: The Mechanism of an Open Petroleum Economy, in: Social and Economic Studies, 13, 2 (June 1964); pp. 233–242.

Segerstrom, Paul S.: Innovation, Imitation and Economic Growth, in: Journal of Political Economy, 99, 4 (December 1991); pp. 807–827.

Selucky, Radoslav: Economic Reforms in Eastern Europe. Political Background and Economic Significance (New York: Praeger, 1972).

Sen, Amartya Kumar: Peasants and Dualism with or without Surplus Labour, in: Journal of Political Economy, 74, 5 (October 1966); pp. 427–450.

Sen, Amartya Kumar: Poverty and Famines. An Essay on Entitlement and Deprivation (Oxford: Clarendon, 1981).

Sen, Asim: Followers' Strategy for Technological Development, in: Developing Economies, 17, 4 (December 1979); pp. 505–529.

Shammas, Carole: Food Expenditures and Economic Well-Being in Early Modern England, in: Journal of Economic History, 43, 1 (March 1983); pp. 89–100.
Shammas, Carole: The Pre-industrial Consumer in England and America (Oxford: Clarendon, 1990).
Shanmugan, Bala: Socio-Economic Development through the Informal Credit Market, in: Modern Asian Studies, 25, 2 (May 1991); pp. 209–225.
Shih, Chien-Sheng: Economic Development in Taiwan After the Second World War, in: Weltwirtschaftliches Archiv, 100, 1 (1968); pp. 112–134.
Shin, Roy W.: The Role of Industrial Policy Agents: A Study of a Korean Intermediate Organization as a Policy Network, in: Revue internationale des sciences administratives, 59, 1 (March 1993); pp. 115–130.
Sid Ahmed, Abdelkader: Development and Resource-Based Industry. The Case of the Petroleum Economies. A Brief Survey of Recent Studies (Vienna: OPEC Fund for International Development, 1990).
Siebert, Horst: Wirtschaftliche Zwänge für offene Volkswirtschaften, in: Weltwirtschaftliches Archiv, 121, 4 (1985); pp. 609–627.
Sik, Ota: Czechoslovakia. The Bureaucratic Economy (White Plains, N.Y.: International Arts and Sciences Press, 1972).
Singer, Hans Wolfgang: Obstacles to Economic Development, in: Social Research, 20, 1 (Spring 1953); pp. 19–31.
Singer, Hans Wolfgang: U.S. Foreign Investment in Underdeveloped Areas. The Distribution of Gains between Investing and Borrowing Countries, in: American Economic Review, 40, 2 (May 1950); pp. 473–485.
Sinn, Hans Werner: Das Marx'sche Gesetz des tendenziellen Falls der Profitrate, in: Zeitschrift für die gesamte Staatswissenschaft/Journal of Institutional and Theoretical Economics, 131, 4 (1975); pp. 647–696.
Skinner, G. William: Chinese Peasants and the Closed Community: An Open and Shut Case, in: Comparative Studies in Society and History, 13, 3 (July 1971); pp. 270–281.
Sklar, Richard L.: Political Science and National Integration – A Radical Approach, in: Journal of Modern African Studies, 5, 1 (1967); pp. 1–11.
Smith, Adam: An Inquiry into the Nature and Causes of the Wealth of Nations Vol. 1, 2 (Chicago, Ill.: University of Chicago Press, 1976).
Sombart, Werner: Krieg und Kapitalismus (Munich; Berlin: Duncker und Humblot, 1913).
Sombart, Werner: Der moderne Kapitalismus: Die vorkapitalistische Wirtschaft. Vol. 1 (Munich: Duncker und Humblot, 1921a).
Sombart, Werner: Der moderne Kapitalismus: Das europäische Wirtschaftsleben im Frühkapitalismus. Vol. 2 (Munich: Duncker und Humblot, 1921b).
Sombart, Werner: Der moderne Kapitalismus: Das Wirtschaftsleben des Hochkapitalismus. Vol. 3 (Munich: Duncker und Humblot, 1921c).
Sparks, Christopher; Greiner, Mary: U.S. and Foreign Productivity and Unit Labour Costs, in: Monthly Labour Review, 120, 2 (February 1997); pp. 26–35.
Squire, Lyn: Einkommensverteilung und Wirtschaftswachstum, in: Schubert, Renate (ed.): Neue Wachstums- und Außenhandelstheorie – Implikationen für die Entwicklungstheorie

und -politik. Schriften des Vereins für Socialpolitik, Band 269 (Berlin: Duncker und Humblot, 1999); pp. 156–176.
Stahl, Heinz-Michael: Regionalpolitische Implikationen einer EWG-Währungsunion (Tübingen: J.C.B. Mohr, 1974).
Staley, Aloah Eugene: War and the Private Investor. A Study in the Relations of International Politics and International Private Investment (Garden City, N.Y.: Doubleday & Doran, 1935).
Stannard, David E.: American Holocaust: The Conquest of the New World (New York; Oxford: Oxford University Press, 1992).
Statistics Bureau: Japan Statistical Yearbook 1994. (Tokyo: Management and Coordination Agency, 1994).
Sternberg, Marvin J.: Agrarian Reform and Employment, with Special Reference to Latin America, in: International Labour Review, 95, 1/2 (January-February 1967); pp. 1–26.
Storm, Servaas: On the Role of Agriculture in India's Longer-Term Development Strategy, in: Cambridge Journal of Economics, 19, 6 (December 1995); pp. 761–788.
Strack, D.; Helmscholdt, H.; Schönherr, S.: Internationale Einkommensvergleiche auf der Basis von Kaufkraftparitäten: Das Gefälle zwischen Industrie- und Entwicklungsländern verringert sich, in: IFO-Schnelldienst, 50, 10 (April 1997); pp. 8–14.
Strange, Susan: The Retreat of the State. The Diffusion of Power in the World Economy (Cambridge: Cambridge University Press, 1996).
Strassmann, W. Paul: Economic Growth and Income Distribution, in: Quarterly Journal of Economics, 70, 3 (August 1956); pp. 425–440.
Strikwerda, Carl: Tides of Migration, Currents of History: The State, Economy, and the Transatlantic Movement of Labor in the Nineteenth and Twentieth Centuries, in: International Review of Social History, 44, 3 (December 1999); pp. 367–394.
Stürmer, Wilhelmine: Die Entwicklungskomponenten des Kapitalkoeffizienten. Dargestellt am Beispiel des Maschinenbaus und der chemischen Industrie der Bundesrepublik, in: Mitteilungen des Rheinisch-Westfälischen Instituts für Wirtschaftsforschung, 19, 1 (1968); pp. 13–28.
Suh, Suk Tai: The Theory of Unequal Exchange and the Developing Countries, in: Kim, Kyong Dong (ed.): Dependency Issues in Korean Development. Comparative Perspectives (Seoul: Seoul National University Press, 1987); pp. 110–131.
Suntum, Ulrich van: Internationale Wettbewerbsfähigkeit einer Volkswirtschaft. Ein sinnvolles wirtschaftspolitisches Ziel, in: Zeitschrift für Wirtschafts- und Sozialwissenschaften, 106, 4 (1986); pp. 495–507.
Suntum, Ulrich van: Die Wechselkurse sind keine Entschuldigung für die Lohnpolitik, in: Handelsblatt (July 4, 1996); p. 2.
Svennilson, Ingvar: Growth and Stagnation in the European Economy (Geneva: United Nations Economic Commission for Europe, 1954).
Swann, G.M. Peter; Prevezer, Martha: Introduction, in: Swann, G. M. Peter (ed.): The Dynamics of Industrial Clustering: International Comparisons in Computing and Biotechnology. (Oxford: Oxfort University Press, 1998); pp. 1–12.
Szelenyi, Ivan: Social Inequalities in State Socialist Redistributive Economies. Dilemmas for Social Policy in Contemporary Socialist Societies of Eastern Europe, in: International Journal of Comparative Sociology, 19 (1978); pp. 61–87.

Takacs, Wendy E.: Economic Aspects of Quota Licensing Auctions, in: Journal of World Trade, 22, 5 (October 1988); pp. 39–51.

Takahashi, H. Kohachiro: The Transition from Feudalism to Capitalism. A Contribution to the Sweezy-Dobb Controversy, in: Science and Society, 16, 4 (Autumn 1952); pp. 313–345.

Tarr, S.Byron: Undermining the Political Logic of African Governments' Poor Economic Policies, in: Genève-Afrique, 30, 1 (1992); pp. 29–34.

Tatur, Melanie: Taylorismus in der Sowjetunion. Die Rationalisierungspolitik der UdSSR in den siebziger Jahren (Frankfort on the Main; New York: Campus, 1983).

Taylor, George V.: Noncapitalist Wealth and the Origins of the French Revolution, in: American Historical Review, 72, 2 (January 1967); pp. 469–496.

Taylor, Ian: Hegemony, Neo-Liberal "Good-Governance" and the International Monetary Fund: A Gramscian Perspective, in: Boas, Morten; MacNeill, Desmond (eds.): Framing the World? The Role of Ideas in Multilateral Institutions (London; New York: Routledge, 2003); pp. 85–96.

Taylor, Lance: The Revival of the Liberal Creed – The IMF and the World Bank in a Globalized Economy, in: World Development, 25, 2 (February 1997); pp. 145–152.

Theurl, Theresia: Globalisierung als Selektionsprozeß ordnungspolitischer Paradigmen, in: Berg, Hartmut; Berthold, Norbert (eds.): Globalisierung der Wirtschaft: Ursachen-Formen-Konsequenzen. Schriften des Vereins für Socialpolitik 263 (Berlin: Duncker und Humblot, 1999); pp. 23–50.

Thoborn, John: Multinationals, Mining and Development: A Study of the Tin Industry (Gower: Farnborough, 1981).

Thompson, Grahame: The American Industrial Policy Debate: Lessons for the U.K, in: Economy and Society, 16, 1 (February 1987); pp. 1–74.

Thomson, Ross: The Eco-Technic Process and the Development of the Sewing Machine, in: Research in Economic History, SH 3 (1984); pp. 243–269.

Tilly, Charles: Food Supply and Public Order in Modern Europe, in: Tilly, Charles (ed.): The Formation of National States in Western Europe (Princeton, N.J.: Princeton University Press, 1975); pp. 380–455.

Tilly, Charles: Globalization Threatens Labor's Rights, in: International Labor and Working Class History, 47 (Spring 1995); pp. 1–23.

Tönnies, Ferdinand: Gemeinschaft und Gesellschaft: Grundbegriffe der reinen Soziologie (Berlin: Curtius, 1935).

Trébouil, Guy: Agriculture pionnière, révolution verte et dégradation de l'environnement en Thailande: Le cinquième dragon ne sera pas vert, in: Tiers Monde, 34, 134 (April-June 1993); pp. 365–384.

Tucker, Rufus S.: Real Wages of Artisans in London, 1729–1935, in: Journal of the American Statistical Association, 31, 1 (1936); pp. 73–84.

Tuge, Hideomi: Historical Development of Science and Technology in Japan (Tokyo: Kokusai Bunka Shinkokai, 1961).

Tzannatos, P. Zafiris: International Competitiveness in East Asian Manufacturing: Unit Labor Cost Analysis for Selected Countries (Washington: World Bank, 1997).

U.S. Department of Commerce: Statistical Abstract of the United States: 1996 (Washington, DC, 1996).

Ufer, Horst: Wachstums- und Strukturprobleme der Energiewirtschaften der RGW-Länder, in: Wirtschaftswissenschaft, 23, 8 (August 1975); pp. 1121–1138.

UNCTAD: New and Emerging Technologies: Some Economic, Commercial and Developmental Aspects (Geneva: UNCTAD, 1984).

UNCTAD: Commodity Survey 1980–85 (Geneva: UNCTAD, 1985).

UNCTAD: Impact of Technological Change on Patterns of International Trade (Geneva: UNCTAD, May 1989).

UNCTAD: World Investment Report 1994. Transnational Corporations, Employment and the Workplace. An Executive Summary (New York: United Nations, 1994).

Ungerer, Horst: A Concise History of European Monetary Integration. From EPU to EMU. (New York: Quorum, 1997).

Usher, Dan: The Dynastic Cycle and the Stationary State, in: American Economic Review, 79, 4 (December 1989); pp. 1031–1044.

Valenzuela, Luis: Challenges to the British Copper Smelting Industry in the World Market 1840–1860, in: Journal of European Economic History, 19, 3 (Winter 1990); pp. 657–686.

Verdier, Daniel: Domestic Responses to Capital Market Internationalization under the Gold Standard, in: International Organization, 52, 1 (Winter 1998); pp. 1–34.

Vernon, Raymond: International Investment and International Trade in the Product Cycle, in: Quarterly Journal of Economics, 80, 2 (May 1966); pp. 190–207.

Vickrey, William: We Need a Bigger "Deficit". Working Paper 2 (Kansas City: Center for Full Employment and Price Stablity, 2000).

Wade, Robert Hunter: Globalization and its Limits: Reports of the Death of the National Economy are Greatly Exaggerated., in: Higgott, Richard; Payne, Anthony (eds.): The New Political Economy of Globalisation. Volume 1 (Ithaca, N.Y. et al.: Cornell University Press, 1996); pp. 60–88.

Wade, Robert Hunter: From 'Miracle' to 'Cronyism': Explaining the Great Asian Slump, in: Cambridge Journal of Economics, 22, 6 (November 1998); pp. 693–706.

Waer, Paul: Social Clauses in International Trade – The Debate in the European Union, in: Journal of World Trade, 30, 4 (August 1996); pp. 25–42.

Wakeman, Frederic: Rebellion and Revolution: The Study of Popular Movements in Chinese History, in: Journal of Asian Studies, 36, 2 (February 1977); pp. 201–237.

Wälde, Thomas: Third World Mineral Development: Current Issues, in: Columbia Journal of World Business, 19, 1 (Spring 1984); pp. 27–34.

Waller, Peter P.: Aid and Conditionality: The Case of Germany. Workshop Berlin, 13–15 September 1993; Aid and Conditionality (Oslo: Norwegian Institute of International Affairs (NUPI), 1993).

Wallerstein, Immanuel Maurice: The Modern World-System. Capitalist Agriculture and the Origins of the European World-Economy in the Sixteenth Century (New York; Orlando, Fla.: Academic Press, 1974).

Warren, Bill: Imperialism and Capitalist Industrialisation, in: New Left Review, 81 (September-October 1973); pp. 3–44.

Warren, Bill: Imperialism: Pioneer of Capitalism (London: NLB, 1980).

Warren, James G.H.: A Century of Locomotive Building by Robert Stephenson & Co 1823–1923 (London: Andrew Reid, 1923).

Wasserfallen, Walter; Kyburz, Hans: The Behaviour of Flexible Exchange Rates in the Short Run. A Systematic Investigation, in: Weltwirtschaftliches Archiv, 121, 4 (1985); pp. 646–659.

Watanabe, Susumu: The Japanese Quality Control Circle: Why it Works, in: International Labour Review, 130, 1 (January-February 1991); pp. 56–80.

Weiss, Thomas G.: Governance, Good Governance and Global Governance: Conceptual and Actual Challenges, in: Third World Quarterly, 21, 5 (October 2000); pp. 795–814.

Weitzman, Martin L.: Soviet Postwar Economic Growth and Capital Labor Substitution, in: American Economic Review, 60, 4 (September 1970); pp. 676–686.

Weizsäcker, Carl C. von; Samuelson, Paul A.: A New Labor Theory of Value for Rational Planning through Use of Bourgeois Profit Rate, in: Proceedings of the National Academy of Sciences, USA, 68, 6 (June 1971); pp. 1192–1194.

Weliwita, Ananda: Cointegration Tests and the Long-Run Purchasing Power Parity: Examination of Six Currencies in Asia, in: Journal of Economic Development, 23, 1 (June 1998); pp. 103–113.

Welzmüller, Rudolf: Zu den Folgen der Globalisierung für die nationalen Güter-, Finanz- und Arbeitsmärkte, in: Aus Politik und Zeitgeschichte, 33–34 (August 1997); pp. 20–28.

Westergaard, Kirsten: People's Empowerment in Bangladesh – NGO Strategies, in: Journal of Social Studies, 72 (April 1996); pp. 27–57.

Westphal, Larry E.; Kim, Linsu; Dahlman, Carl J.: Reflections on the Republic of Korea's Acquistion of Technological Capability, in: Rosenberg, Nathan (ed.): International Technology Transfer. Concepts, Measures and Comparisons (New York: Praeger, 1985); pp. 167–221.

White, Harry Dexter: The French International Accounts 1880–1913 (Cambridge, Mass.: Harvard University Press, 1933).

Wiesenthal, Helmut: Dimensionen und Folgen der Globalisierung. Einige Koordinaten auf unbekanntem Terrain, in: Petschow, Ulrich (ed.) (ed.): Globalisierung und Nachhaltigkeit. Zu den Chancen einer wirkungsvollen Umweltpolitik unter den Bedingungen Globalisierter Wirtschaftsbeziehungen (Berlin: Friedrich-Ebert-Stiftung, Forum Berlin, 1998); pp. 17–24.

Wijnbergen, Sweder van: The 'Dutch Disease', in: Economic Journal, 94, 373 (March 1984); pp. 41–55.

Williamson, Jeffrey G.: Globalization, Convergence and History, in: Journal of Economic History, 56, 2 (June 1996); pp. 277–306.

Wilson, T.: Effective Devaluation and Inflation, in: Oxford Economic Papers, 28, 1 (March 1976); pp. 1–24.

Winkler, Heinrich August: Die Sozialdemokratie und die Revolution von 1918/19. Ein Rückblick nach sechzig Jahren (Berlin; Bonn: Dietz, 1979).

Wolff, Edward N.: Capital Formation and Productivity Convergence Over the Long Term, in: American Economic Review, 81, 3 (June 1991); pp. 565–579.

Wolfstetter, E.: Surplus Labour, Synchronised Labour Costs and Marx's Theory of Value, in: Economic Journal, 83, 331 (September 1973); pp. 787–809.

Wolman, Leo: Ebb and Flow in Trade Unionism (New York: NBER, 1936).

Woodruff, William: The Impact of Western Man. A Study of Europe's Role in World Economy 1750–1960 (New York; London, 1966).

Woodruff, William: America's Impact on the World. A Study of the Role of the United States in the World Economy, 1750–1970 (London: Macmillan, 1975).
World Bank: World Development Report 1987 (New York, et al.: Oxford University Press, 1987).
World Bank: World Development Report 1997: The State in a Changing World (Washington: World Bank, 1997).
World Bank: World Development Report 2000/2001: Attacking Poverty (Washington: World Bank, 2000).
Woroniak, Alexander: Technological Transfer in Eastern Europe: Receiving Countries, in: Wasowski, Stanislas (ed.): East-West Trade and the Technology Gap. A Political and Economic Appraisal (New York: Praeger, 1970); pp. 85–136.
Woytinsky, Wladimir: Drei Ursachen der Arbeitslosigkeit (Geneva: International Labour Office, 1935).
Woytinsky, Wladimir: Les conséquences sociales de la crise (Geneva: International Labour Office, 1936).
Xu, Yingfeng: China's Exchange Rate Policy, in: China Economic Review, 11, 3 (January 2000); pp. 262–277.
Yamada, Hideo: The Origins of British Colonization of Malaya with Special References to its Tin, in: Developing Economies, 9, 3 (September 1971); pp. 225–245.
Yasuba, Yasukichi: Standard of Living in Japan Before Industrialisation: From What Level Did Japan Begin? A Comment, in: Journal of Economic History, 46, 1 (March 1986); pp. 217–224.
Yi, Guk-Yueng: Staat und Kapitalakkumulation in ostasiatischen Ländern: Ein Vergleich zwischen Korea und Taiwan (Saarbrücken: Breitenbach, 1988).
Yoon, Young-Kwan: Globalization and Institutional Reform: The Case of Korean Economic Crisis in the Late 1990s (Quebec: International Political Science Association, August 2000).
Yotopoulos, Pan A.: Exchange Rate Parity for Trade and Development: Theory, Tests, and Case Studies (Cambridge et al.: Cambridge University Press, 1996).
Yotopoulos, Pan A.; Lin, Jenu-Yih: Purchasing Power Parities for Taiwan: The Basic Data for 1985 and International Comparisons, in: Journal of Economic Development, 18, 1 (June 1993); pp. 7–52.
Young, Allyn A.: Increasing Returns and Economic Progress, in: Economic Journal, 38, 152 (December 1928); pp. 528–542.
Young, Alwyn: Learning by Doing and the External Effects of International Trade, in: Quarterly Journal of Economics, 106, 2 (May 1991); pp. 369–405.
Younger, Stephen D.: Aid and the Dutch Disease: Macroeconomic Management When Everybody Loves You, in: World Development, 20, 11 (November 1992); pp. 1587–1597.
Yukizawa, Kenzo: Changes in Japanese-United States Productivity Differentials and the Yen-Dollar Problem, in: Japanese Economic Studies, 1, 4 (Summer 1973); pp. 33–47.
Zagorin, Perez: The English Revolution 1640–1660 (2), in: Cahiers d'histoire mondiale (1955); pp. 894–914.
Zauberman, Alfred: Industrial Progress in Poland, Czechoslovakia, and East Germany 1937–1962 (London: Oxford University Press, 1964).

# References

Ziebura, Gilbert: Die deutsche Frage in der öffentlichen Meinung Frankreichs von 1911–1914. Studien zur europ. Geschichte (1) (Berlin: Colloquium, 1955).

Ziebura, Gilbert; Ansprenger, Franz; Kiersch, Gerhard: Bestimmungsfaktoren der Außenpolitik in der zweiten Hälfte des 20.Jahrhunderts. Forschungsstrategie und -programm eines Sonderforschungsbereichs (Berlin: Fachbereich Politische Wissenschaft, 1974).

Zielinski, Janusz G.: Economic Reforms in Polish Industry (London; New York; Toronto: Oxford University Press, 1973).

Zimmermann, Louis Jacques: Sparquote und Kapitalkoeffizient als Elemente des wirtschaftlichen Wachstums in Entwicklungsländern (Tübingen: J.C.B. Mohr, 1971).

Zysman, John: The Myth of 'Global Economy': Enduring National Foundations and Emerging Regional Realities, in: New Political Economy, 1, 2 (1996); pp. 157–184.